Short Fourth Edition

Practical Argument

Laurie G. Kirszner

University of the Sciences, Emeritus

Stephen R. Mandell

Drexel University

bedford/st.martin's

Macmillan Learning

Boston | New York

For Bedford/St. Martin's

Vice President, Editorial, Macmillan Learning Humanities: Edwin Hill
Executive Program Director for English: Leasa Burton
Senior Program Manager: John E. Sullivan III
Executive Marketing Manager: Joy Fisher Williams
Director of Content Development, Humanities: Jane Knetzger
Senior Developmental Editor: Jesse Hassenger
Associate Content Project Manager: Matt Glazer
Senior Workflow Project Manager: Jennifer Wetzel
Production Coordinator: Brianna Lester
Media Project Manager: D. Rand Thomas
Media Editor: Julia Domenicucci
Assistant Editor: Cari Goldfine
Editorial Services: Lumina Datamatics, Inc.
Composition: Lumina Datamatics, Inc.
Text Permissions Manager: Kalina Ingham
Rights Platform Permissions Project Manager: Mark Schaefer, Lumina Datamatics, Inc.
Photo Permissions Editor: Angela Boehler
Photo Researcher: Krystyna Borgen, Lumina Datamatics, Inc.
Director of Design, Content Management: Diana Blume
Text Design: Jerilyn Bockorick
Cover Design: William Boardman
Cover Image: ViewStock/Getty Images
Printing and Binding: LSC Communications

Manufactured in the United States of America.

1 2 3 4 5 6   24 23 22 21 20 19

For information, write: Bedford/St. Martin's, 75 Arlington Street, Boston, MA 02116

ISBN 978-1-319-20721-2

Acknowledgments
Text acknowledgments and copyrights appear at the back of the book on pages C-1–C-2, which constitute an extension of the copyright page. Art acknowledgments and copyrights appear on the same page as the art selections they cover.

In recent years, many college composition programs have integrated argumentation into their first-year writing sequence, and there are good reasons for this. Argumentation is central to both academic and public discourse, so students who are skilled at argumentation are able to participate in the dynamic, ongoing discussions that take place in their classrooms and in their communities. Argumentation teaches the critical-thinking skills that are valuable in an often contentious, sometimes divided sociopolitical landscape—and particularly necessary for academic success.

What has surprised and troubled us as teachers, however, is that many college argument texts are simply too difficult, with excessively technical terminology and unnecessarily abstract discussions. We want students to feel that they are part of a discourse community within which they can use the principles of argumentation with confidence and skill. With this in mind, we drew on our years of classroom experience to create *Practical Argument*. In this short fourth edition, *Practical Argument* remains a straightforward and accessible introduction to argumentative writing that explains concepts in understandable language and illustrates them with examples that actually mean something to students, covering contemporary issues that affect their lives as well as the kinds of visual arguments they see every day. *Practical Argument* is an ideal alternative for instructors who see currently available argument texts as too big, too complicated, and too intimidating for their students.

In short, our goal in this text is to demystify the study of argument. To this end, we focus on the things that students actually need to know. *Practical Argument* works because its approach is *practical*: It helps students make connections between what they learn in the classroom and what they experience outside of it. As they do so, they become comfortable with the rhetorical skills that are central to effective argumentation. We (and our many users) believe that there's no other book like it.

Organization

Practical Argument includes everything students and instructors need for an argument course in a single book.

- **Part 1, Understanding Argument,** discusses the role of argument in everyday life and the value of studying argument, offers definitions of what argument is and is not, explains the means of persuasion (appeals to *logos*, *pathos*, and *ethos*), and defines and illustrates the basic elements of argument (thesis, evidence, refutation, and concluding statement).

■ **Part 2, Reading and Responding to Arguments,** explains and illustrates critical thinking and reading; visual argument; writing a rhetorical analysis; logic and logical fallacies; and Rogerian argument, Toulmin logic, and oral arguments.

■ **Part 3, Writing an Argumentative Essay,** traces and illustrates the process of planning, drafting, and revising an argumentative essay.

■ **Part 4, Using Sources to Support Your Argument,** covers locating and evaluating print and online sources; summarizing, paraphrasing, quoting, and synthesizing sources; documenting sources in MLA style; and using sources responsibly.

■ **Appendixes.** Appendix A provides instruction on writing literary arguments, and Appendix B covers APA documentation style.

Key Features

Accessible in a Thoughtful Way

Practical Argument covers everything students need to know about argument but doesn't overwhelm them. It limits technical vocabulary to what students and instructors actually need to understand and discuss key concepts in argument and argumentative writing. In short, *Practical Argument* is argument made accessible.

Argument Step by Step, Supported by Helpful Apparatus

Practical Argument takes students through a step-by-step process of reading and responding to others' arguments and writing, revising, and editing their own arguments. The book uses a classroom-tested, exercise-driven approach that encourages students to participate actively in their own learning process. Chapters progress in a clear, easy-to-understand sequence: students are asked to read arguments, identify their key elements, and develop a response to an issue in the form of a complete, documented argumentative essay based on in-book focused research.

Exercises and writing assignments for each selection provide guidance for students as they work toward creating a finished piece of writing. Throughout the text, checklists, grammar-in-context and summary boxes, and source and gloss notes provide support. In addition, templates for paragraph-length arguments, located with the end-of-chapter exercises, provide structures that students can use for guidance. Sentence templates also frequently appear in the questions that follow the readings, providing an opportunity for students to work up to arguments at the paragraph level.

A Thematically Focused Approach with Compelling Chapter Topics

Students learn best when they care about and are engaged in an issue. For this reason, *Practical Argument* uses readings and assignments to help students learn argumentation in the context of one high-interest contemporary issue per chapter. Chapter topics include environmental solutions, free speech, technology and privacy, and gender bias in STEM fields—issues that have real meaning in students' lives.

Readings on Relevant and Interesting Issues

Practical Argument, Short Fourth Edition, includes over 40 accessible and thought-provoking professional readings on issues that students will want to read about and debate including selections from journals and blogs. The book also uses a variety of new visual argument selections, and seventeen sample student essays, more than in any other argument book, provide realistic models. Each student essay, including complete MLA and APA research papers, is annotated to further assist students through their own writing process.

To help students better understand the context of the sources included in *Practical Argument*, each is marked with an icon that shows how it was originally presented.

Magazine or journal

National newspaper

Poem

Professional essay

Report

Speech

Student essay

Student newspaper

Visual Argument

Website

An Open and Inviting Full-Color Design

The fresh, contemporary look of *Practical Argument* will engage students. This open, colorful design eliminates the sea of dense type that is typical of many other argument books. Plenty of photographs and other visuals—such as advertisements, cartoons, charts and graphs, and web pages—provide appealing and instructive real-world examples. The use of open space and numerous images reinforces the currency of the book's themes and also creates an inviting and visually stimulating format.

New to This Edition

Essays, Topics, and Images

The short fourth edition includes over twenty-five engaging new essays, covering such timely topics as campus environmental programs, online privacy, free speech, and gender discrimination. These essays have been carefully selected for their high-interest subject matter as well as for their effectiveness as sources and as teaching models for student writing.

Visual Arguments

Coverage of visual arguments has been expanded in this edition, with additional visual "texts" added to many chapters and accompanied by questions designed to focus students' attention on how to "read" a visual and understand its persuasive elements. These images include photos, advertisements, public-service announcements, cartoons, and more, adding an extra dimension and additional perspective to the process of analyzing arguments.

Bedford/St. Martin's puts you first

From day one, our goal has been simple: to provide inspiring resources that are grounded in best practices for teaching reading and writing. For more than 35 years, Bedford/St. Martin's has partnered with the field, listening to teachers, scholars, and students about the support writers need. We are committed to helping every writing instructor make the most of our resources.

How can we help you?

- Our editors can align our resources to your outcomes through correlation and transition guides for your syllabus. Just ask us.

- Our sales representatives specialize in helping you find the right materials to support your course goals.

- Our *Bits* blog on the Bedford/St. Martin's English Community (**community.macmillan.com**) publishes fresh teaching ideas weekly. You'll also find easily downloadable professional resources and links to author webinars on our community site.

Contact your Bedford/St. Martin's sales representative or visit **macmillan learning.com** to learn more.

Print and Digital Options for Practical Argument

Choose the format that works best for your course, and ask about our packaging options that offer savings for students.

Print

- *Full edition.* For instructors who want expanded coverage of argumentative strategies and a reader comprising dates and casebooks on additional current topics, we offer a full fourth edition of *Practical Argument.* To order the full-size version, use ISBN 978-1-319-19445-1.

- *Loose-leaf edition.* This format does not have a traditional binding; its pages are loose and hole punched to provide flexibility and a lower price to students. It can be packaged with our digital space for additional savings.

Digital

- *Innovative digital learning space.* Bedford/St. Martin's suite of digital tools makes it easy to get everyone on the same page by putting student writers at the center. For details, visit **macmillanlearning.com /englishdigital.**

- *Popular e-book formats.* For details about our e-book partners, visit **macmillanlearning.com/ebooks.**

- *Inclusive Access.* Enable every student to receive their course materials through your LMS on the first day of class. Macmillan Learning's Inclusive Access program is the easiest, most affordable way to ensure all students have access to quality educational resources. Find out more at **macmillanlearning.com/inclusiveaccess.**

Your Course, Your Way

No two writing programs or classrooms are exactly alike. Our Curriculum Solutions team works with you to design custom options that provide the resources your students need. (Options below require enrollment minimums.)

- *ForeWords for English.* Customize any print resource to fit the focus of your course or program by choosing from a range of prepared topics, such as Sentence Guides for Academic Writers.

- *Macmillan Author Program (MAP).* Add excerpts or package acclaimed works from Macmillan's trade imprints to connect students with prominent authors and public conversations. A list of popular examples or academic themes is available upon request.

- *Bedford Select.* Build your own print handbook or anthology from a database of more than 900 selections, and add your own materials to create your ideal text. Package with any Bedford/St. Martin's text for additional savings. Visit **macmillanlearning.com/bedfordselect.**

Instructor Resources

You have a lot to do in your course. We want to make it easy for you to find the support you need—and to get it quickly.

Resources for Teaching Practical Argument is available as a PDF that can be downloaded from **macmillanlearning.com**. In addition to chapter overviews and teaching tips, the instructor's manual includes sample syllabi, sample answers to questions from the book, and suggested classroom activities.

Acknowledgments

The following reviewers gave us valuable feedback as we prepared the short fourth edition of *Practical Argument*: Yaw Adu-Gyamfi, Liberty University; Emily Andrews, Volunteer State Community College; Kathryn Baker, Santa Fe College; Carol Bledsoe, Florida Gulf Coast University; Molly Brown, Clinton Community College; Jennifer Coenen, University of Florida; Emily Cosper, Delgado Community College; Joseph Couch, Montgomery College; Jason DePolo, North Carolina A&T State University; Andrea D. Green, Motlow State Community College; Lindsey Jungman, University of Minnesota Duluth; Jill Kronstadt, Montgomery College; Leslie LaChance, Volunteer State Community College; Felicia M. Maisey, LaSalle University; Danizete Martinez, University of New Mexico-Valencia; Carola Mattord, Kennesaw State University; James Mense, St. Louis Community College at Florissant Valley; Amanda Palleschi, University of the District of Columbia Community College; Barbara B. Parsons, Tacoma Community College; Christina Rothenbeck, Louisiana State University; David Seelow, Maria College; Wayne Sneath, Davenport University; Roger Swafford, Des Moines Area Community College—Ankeny Campus; David M. Taylor, St. Louis Community College—Meramec; Marlea Trevino, Grayson College; Ashley Whitmore, University of Michigan-Dearborn; Alex Wulff, Maryville University.

We thank Jeff Ousborne, Deja Ruddick, Elizabeth Rice, and Michelle McSweeney for their valuable contributions to this text.

At Bedford/St. Martin's, Joan Feinberg, Denise Wydra, Karen Henry, Steve Scipione, Leasa Burton, and John Sullivan were involved and supportive from the start of the project. John, in particular, helped us to shape this book and continues to provide valuable advice and support. In this short fourth edition, we have had the pleasure of working with Jesse Hassenger, our knowledgeable, professional, and creative editor. His addition to our team has helped to make *Practical Argument* a better book. Coeditor Lexi DeConti and assistant editor Cari Goldfine devoted many hours to locating images and helping with manuscript prep where needed. Once again, Matt Glazer patiently and efficiently shepherded the book through the production process. Others on our team included project manager Nagalakshmi Karunanithi; Joy Fisher Williams who was instrumental in marketing the book; Krystyna Borgen and Angela Boehler, who obtained image permissions; Kalina Ingham and Mark Schaefer, who handled text permissions; and Diana Blume, who developed our design. We are grateful to everyone on our team for their help.

Finally, we would like to thank each other for lunches past—and lunches to come.

Laurie G. Kirszner

Stephen R. Mandell

How *Practical Argument* Supports WPA Outcomes for First-Year Composition

The following chart provides information on how *Practical Argument* helps students build proficiency and achieve the learning outcomes set by the Council of Writing Program Administrators, which writing programs across the country use to assess their students' work.

Rhetorical Knowledge	
Learn and use key rhetorical concepts through analyzing and composing a variety of texts.	**An Introduction to Argument** features a detailed section on determining the rhetorical situation, considering the writer, purpose, audience, and context, and more. **Part 2: Reading and Responding to Arguments** takes students through a scaffolded process of reading, analyzing, and responding to texts.
Gain experience reading and composing in several genres to understand how genre conventions shape and are shaped by readers' and writers' practices and purposes.	*Practical Argument* features **over 100 readings** from a variety of genres, sources, and authors, including sample student work throughout the book.
Develop facility in responding to a variety of situations and contexts calling for purposeful shifts in voice, tone, level of formality, design, medium, and/or structure.	**All chapters include multiple exercises,** building students up to writing responses to various types of arguments.
Understand and use a variety of technologies to address a range of audiences.	*Practical Argument* covers **both written and oral arguments**, and discusses **a variety of technologies** particularly in the location and evaluation of sources.
Match the capacities of different environments (e.g., print and electronic) to varying rhetorical situations.	In addition to coverage noted above that helps students understand rhetorical situations, specific guidance on different environments includes the use of images of arguments (**Chapter 3**) and composing/delivering oral arguments (**Chapter 6**).
Critical Thinking, Reading, and Composing	
Use composing and reading for inquiry, learning, critical thinking, and communicating in various rhetorical contexts.	**Chapter 2** guides students through active reading, critical thinking, and composing critical responses based on those skills.

Read a diverse range of texts, attending especially to relationships between assertion and evidence, to patterns of organization, to the interplay between verbal and nonverbal elements, and to how these features function for different audiences and situations.	Dozens of readings are new to this edition of *Practical Argument*, with an emphasis on **diverse authors and sources**, and more visuals for analysis than ever before.
Locate and evaluate (for credibility, sufficiency, accuracy, timeliness, bias, and so on) primary and secondary research materials, including journal articles and essays, books, scholarly and professionally established and maintained databases or archives, and informal electronic networks and Internet sources.	**Part 4: Using Sources to Support Your Argument** includes two full chapters of material on locating and evaluating research materials: **Chapter 8** and **Chapter 9**.
Use strategies—such as interpretation, synthesis, response, critique, and design/redesign—to compose texts that integrate the writer's ideas with those from appropriate sources.	As mentioned above, **Chapter 9** gives students a complete picture of how to quote, summarize, paraphrase, synthesize, and otherwise integrate sourced material.
Processes	
Develop a writing project through multiple drafts.	**Chapter 7** covers drafting, revising, and polishing essays.
Develop flexible strategies for reading, drafting, reviewing, collaborating, revising, rewriting, rereading, and editing.	**Chapter 2** covers reading strategies including previewing, close reading, and looking for comprehension clues, while the above-mentioned **Chapter 7** includes drafting, reviewing, collaborating, revising, rewriting, and editing.
Use composing processes and tools as a means to discover and reconsider ideas.	**Chapter 4** gives the framework of composing as a means of students considering and analyzing ideas about arguments.
Experience the collaborative and social aspects of writing processes.	**Chapter 7** includes guidelines for peer review.
Learn to give and to act on productive feedback to works in progress.	**Chapter 7** also includes a section about getting feedback.

Adapt composing processes for a variety of technologies and modalities.	**Chapter 6** covers oral arguments, while **Part 4** includes digital-based sources.
Reflect on the development of composing practices and how those practices influence their work.	**Checklists throughout the book** invite students to reflect on their reading and writing processes, and scaffolded exercises throughout provide opportunities for active reflection.
Knowledge of Conventions	
Develop knowledge of linguistic structures, including grammar, punctuation, and spelling, through practice in composing and revising.	**Grammar in Context** boxes throughout the text offer practical tips that can be applied to the processes of composing, revising, and editing.
Understand why genre conventions for structure, paragraphing, tone, and mechanics vary.	In addition to the book's grammar coverage, the "Understanding Your Purpose and Audience" section in **Chapter 7** helps students examine how an author's methods differ in relation to their purpose and audience.
Gain experience negotiating variations in genre conventions.	The **exercises and assignments throughout the book** offer a variety of writing assignments in different formats, including Rogerian, Toulmin, definition, cause-and-effect, ethical, evaluation, and proposal arguments.
Learn common formats and/or design features for different kinds of texts.	**Chapter 3** includes examination of design elements and visually augmented texts.
Explore the concepts of intellectual property (such as fair use and copyright) that motivate documentation conventions.	**Chapter 11** goes into detail about the responsibilities of using intellectual property in an academic context.
Practice applying citation conventions systematically in their own work.	**Chapter 10** offers all the essentials of MLA documentation.

BRIEF CONTENTS

CONTENTS

CHAPTER 4   # Writing a Rhetorical Analysis   103

PART

3   Writing an Argumentative Essay   249

PART
4   Using Sources to Support Your Argument   283

CHAPTER 11   Using Sources Responsibly   353

APPENDIX **A**
Writing Literary Arguments   A-1

APPENDIX **B**
Documenting Sources: APA   A-13

DISCIPLINARY CONTENTS

Environmental Science

History

Law/Criminal Justice

Political Science

Sociology

Understanding Argument

Ron Chapple/The Image Bank/Getty Images

An Introduction to Argument

Recognizing Arguments

Arguments are everywhere. Whenever you turn on the television, read a newspaper or magazine, talk to friends and family, enter an online discussion, or engage in a debate in one of your classes, you encounter arguments. In fact, it is fair to say that much of the interaction that takes place in society involves argument. Consider, for example, a lawyer who tries to persuade a jury that a defendant is innocent, a doctor who wants to convince a patient to undergo a specific form of treatment, a lawmaker who wants to propose a piece of legislation, an executive who wants to institute a particular policy, an activist who wants to pursue a particular social agenda, a parent who wants to convince a child to study harder, a worker who wants to propose a more efficient way of performing a task, an employee who thinks that he or she deserves a raise, or a spokesperson in an infomercial whose goal is to sell something: all these people are engaging in argument.

In college, you encounter arguments on a daily basis; in fact, both class discussions and academic writing often take the form of argument. Consider, for example, the following questions that might be debated (and written about) in a first-year writing class:

- Do the benefits of fossil fuels outweigh their risks?
- How free should free speech be?
- How far should schools go to keep students safe?
- Is organic food worth the cost?
- Do bystanders have an ethical responsibility to help in a crisis?

What these questions have in common is that they all call for argumentation. To answer these questions, students would be expected to state their opinions and support them.

3

Wake Up, America! (1917) James Montgomery Flagg. Published by the Hegeman Print, New York/ Library of Congress Prints and Photographs Division [LC-USZC4-3802].

World War I propaganda poster (1917)

Defining Argument

Now for the obvious question: exactly what is an argument? Perhaps the best way to begin is by explaining what argument is *not*. An argument (at least an academic argument) is not a **quarrel** or an angry exchange. The object of argument is not to attack someone who disagrees with you or to beat an opponent into submission. For this reason, the shouting matches that you routinely see on television or hear on talk radio are not really arguments. Argument is also not **spin**—the positive or biased slant that politicians routinely put on facts—or **propaganda**—information (or misinformation) that is spread to support a particular viewpoint. Finally, argument is not just a contradiction or denial of someone else's position. Even if you establish that an opponent's position is unwarranted or misguided, you still have to establish that your own position has merit by presenting evidence to support it.

There is a basic difference between **formal arguments**—those that you develop in academic discussion and writing—and **informal arguments**—those that occur in daily life, where people often get into arguments about politics, sports, social issues, and personal relationships. These everyday disputes are often just verbal fights in which one person tries to outshout another. Although they sometimes include facts, they tend to rely primarily on emotion and unsupported opinions.

Moreover, such everyday arguments do not have the formal structure of academic arguments: they do not establish a logical link between a particular viewpoint and reliable supporting evidence. There is also no real effort to address opposing arguments. In general, these arguments tend to be disorganized, emotional disputes that have more to do with criticizing an opponent than with advancing and supporting a position on an issue. Although such informal arguments can serve as starting points for helping you think about issues, they do not have the structure or the intellectual rigor of formal arguments.

So exactly what is an argument—or, more precisely, what is an academic argument? An **academic argument** is a type of formal argument that takes a stand, presents evidence, includes documentation, and uses logic to convince an audience to accept (or at least consider) the writer's position. Of course, academic arguments can get heated, but at their core they are civil exchanges. Writers of academic arguments strive to be fair and to show respect for others—especially for those who present opposing arguments.

Keep in mind that arguments take positions with which reasonable people may disagree. For this reason, an argument never actually proves anything. (If it did, there would be no argument.) The best that an argument can do is to convince other people to accept (or at least acknowledge) the validity of its position.

An angry exchange is not an academic argument.

Jim Watson/AFP/Getty Images

WHAT KINDS OF STATEMENTS ARE NOT DEBATABLE?

To be suitable for argument, a statement must be **debatable**: in other words, there must be conflicting opinions or conflicting facts that call the validity of the statement into question. For this reason, the following types of statements are generally *not* suitable for argument:

- **Statements of fact:** A statement of fact can be verified, so it is not debatable. For example, there is no point in arguing that your school makes instructors' lectures available as podcasts. This is a question of fact that can easily be checked. You can, however, argue that making instructors' lectures available as podcasts would (or would not) enhance education at your school. This is a debatable statement that can be supported by facts and examples.

- **Statements of personal preference or taste:** Expressions of personal preference or taste are not suitable for argument. For example, if you say that you don't like the taste of a particular soft drink, no one can legitimately argue that you are wrong. This statement is beyond dispute because it is a matter of personal taste. You could, however, argue that soft drinks should not be sold in school cafeterias because they contribute to obesity. To support this position, you would supply evidence—facts, statistics, and expert opinion.

> **NOTE**
>
> Although personal expressions of religious belief are difficult to debate, the interpretation of religious doctrine is a suitable subject for argument—and so are the political, social, philosophical, and theological effects of religion on society.

It is a mistake to think that all arguments have just two sides—one right side and one wrong side. In fact, many arguments that you encounter in college focus on issues that are quite complex. For example, if you were considering the question of whether the United States should ban torture of enemy combatants, you could answer this question with a yes or a no, but this would be an oversimplification. To examine the issue thoroughly, you would have to consider it from a number of angles:

- Should torture be banned in all situations?

- Should torture be used as a last resort to elicit information that could prevent an imminent attack?

- What actually constitutes torture? For example, is sleep deprivation torture? What about a slap on the face? Loud music? A cold cell? Are "enhanced interrogation techniques"—such as waterboarding—torture?

- Who should have the legal right to approve interrogation techniques?

If you were going to write an argument about this issue, you would have to take a position that adequately conveyed its complex nature—for example, "Although torture may be cruel and even inhuman, it is sometimes necessary." To do otherwise might be to commit the **either/or fallacy** (see p. 155)—to offer only two choices when there are actually many others.

Arguments in Real Life

In blogs, social media posts, work-related proposals, letters to the editor, emails to businesses, letters of complaint, and other types of communication, you formulate arguments that are calculated to influence readers. Many everyday situations call for argument:

- A proposal to the manager of the UPS store where you work to suggest a more efficient way of sorting packages

- A letter to your local newspaper in which you argue that creating a walking trail would be good use of your community's tax dollars

- An email to your child's principal asking her to extend after-school hours

- A letter to a credit card company in which you request an adjustment to your bill

- A blog post in which you argue that the federal government could do more to relieve the student loan burden

Because argument is so prevalent, the better your arguing skills, the better able you will be to function—not just in school but also in the wider world. When you have a clear thesis, convincing support, and effective refutation of opposing arguments, you establish your credibility and go a long way toward convincing readers that you are someone worth listening to.

Presenting a good argument does not guarantee that readers will accept your ideas. It does, however, help you to define an issue and to express your position clearly and logically. If you present yourself as a well-informed, reasonable person who is attuned to the needs of your readers—even those who disagree with you—you increase your chances of convincing your audience that your position is worth considering.

Arguments are also central to our democratic form of government. Whether the issue is taxation, health care, border control, the environment, abortion, gun ownership, energy prices, gay marriage, terrorism, or cyber-bullying, political candidates, media pundits, teachers, friends, and family members all try to influence the way we think. So in a real sense, argument is the way that all of us participate in the national (or even global) conversation about ideas that matter. The better you understand the methods of argumentation, the better able you will be to recognize, analyze, and respond to the arguments that you hear. By mastering the techniques of argument, you will become a clearer thinker, a more informed citizen, and a person who is better able to influence those around you.

Voting rights protest

Chip Somodevilla/Getty Images News/Getty Images

Winning and Losing Arguments

People often talk of "winning" and "losing" arguments, and of course, the aim of many arguments is to defeat an opponent. In televised political debates, candidates try to convince viewers that they should be elected. In a courtroom, a defense attorney tries to establish a client's innocence. In a job interview, a potential employee tries to convince an employer that he or she is the best-qualified applicant. However, the goal of an argument is not always to determine a winner and a loser. Sometimes the goal of an argument is to identify a problem and suggest solutions that could satisfy those who hold a number of different positions on an issue.

If, for example, you would like your college bookstore to lower the price of items (such as sweatshirts, coffee mugs, and backpacks) with a school logo, you could simply state your position and then support it with evidence. A more effective way of approaching this problem, however, might be to consider all points of view and find some middle ground. For example, how would lowering these prices affect the bookstore? A short conversation with the manager of the bookstore might reveal that the revenue generated by these products enables the bookstore to discount other items—such as art supplies and computers—as well as to hire student help. Therefore, decreasing the price of products with college logos would negatively affect some students. Even so, the high prices also make it difficult for some students to buy these items.

To address this problem, you could offer a compromise solution: the price of items with college logos could be lowered, but the price of other items—such as magazines and snacks—could be raised to make up the difference.

The Rhetorical Situation

In everyday use, the term *rhetoric* has distinctly negative connotations. When a speech is described as being nothing but *rhetoric*, the meaning is clear: the speech consists of empty words and phrases calculated to confuse and manipulate listeners. When writing instructors use the term *rhetoric*, however, it means something quite different: it refers to the choices someone makes to structure a message—written, oral, or visual.

The **rhetorical situation** refers to the factors that influence the creation of any type of communication—especially its words, images, and structure. Applied to argument, the rhetorical situation refers to five factors you should consider when planning an effective argument. Before you begin to write, you should analyze the rhetorical situation and consider the choices you will have to make to construct an effective argument.

Although every rhetorical situation is different, all rhetorical situations involve the following five elements: the *writer*, the *purpose*, the *audience*, the *question*, and the *context*. The following diagram shows the relationship of these elements to one another.

Rhetorical situation

Considering the Writer

Every argument begins with a writer, the person who creates the text. For this reason, it is important to understand how your biases or preconceptions could affect what you produce. For example, if you were home schooled, you might have very definite ideas about education. Likewise, a former Navy Seal might have preconceptions concerning the war in Syria. Strongly held beliefs like these can, and often do, color arguments. The following factors can affect the tone and content of your argument:

age

education

gender

ethnicity

cultural experiences

political affiliation

religion

sexuality

social standing

Before you plan an argument, ask yourself what preconceived ideas you may have about a particular topic. Do your beliefs prevent you from considering all sides of an issue, reaching a logical and fair conclusion, or acknowledging the validity of opposing arguments? It is important that you present yourself as a fair and open-minded person, one whom readers can trust. For this reason, you should maintain a reasonable tone and avoid the use of words or phrases that indicate bias.

Considering the Purpose

A writer's **purpose** is his or her reason for writing. The purpose of an argument is to present a position and to change (or at least influence) people's ideas about an issue. In addition to this general purpose, a writer may have more specific goals. For example, you might want to criticize the actions of others or call into question a particular public policy. You may also want to take a stand on a controversial topic or convince readers that certain arguments are weak. Finally, you may want to propose a solution to a problem or convince readers to adopt a certain course of action.

When you write an argument, you may want to state your purpose directly—usually in your introduction. (Key words in your thesis statement can indicate the direction the argument will take as well as the points that you will discuss.) At other times, especially if you think readers will not readily accept your ideas, you may want to indicate your purpose later in your essay or simply imply it.

Considering the Audience

When you write argumentative essays, you don't write in a vacuum; you write for real people who may or may not agree with you. As you are writing, it is easy to forget this fact and address a general group of readers. However, this would be a mistake. Defining your audience and keeping this audience in mind as you write is important because it helps you decide what material to include and how to present it.

One way to define an audience is by its **traits**—the age, gender, interests, values, knowledge, preconceptions, and level of education of audience members. Each of these traits influences how audience members will react to your ideas, and understanding them helps you determine how to construct your argument. For instance, suppose you were going to write an essay with the following thesis:

> Although college is expensive, its high cost is justified.

How you approach this subject would depend on the audience you were addressing. For example, college students, parents, and college administrators would have different ideas about the subject, different perspectives, different preconceptions, and different levels of knowledge. Therefore, the argument you write for each of these audiences would be different from the others in terms of content, organization, and type of appeal.

- **College students** have a local and personal perspective. They know the school and have definite ideas about the value of the education they are getting. Most likely, they come from different backgrounds and have varying financial needs. Depending on their majors, they have different expectations about employment (and salary) when they graduate. Even with these differences, however, these students share certain concerns. Many probably have jobs to help cover their expenses. Many also have student loans that they will need to start paying after graduation.

  An argumentative essay addressing this audience could focus on statistics and expert opinions that establish the worth of a college degree in terms of future employment, job satisfaction, and lifetime earnings.

- **Parents** probably have limited knowledge of the school and the specific classes their children are taking. They have expectations—both realistic and unrealistic—about the value of a college degree. Some parents may be able to help their children financially, and others may be unable to do so. Their own life experiences and backgrounds probably color their ideas about the value of a college education. For example, parents who have gone to college may have different ideas about the value of a degree from those who haven't.

  An argumentative essay addressing this audience could focus on the experience of other parents of college students. It could also include statistics that address students' future economic independence and economic security.

- **College administrators** have detailed knowledge about college and the economic value of a degree. They are responsible for attracting students, scheduling classes, maintaining educational standards, and providing support services. They are familiar with budget requirements, and they understand the financial pressures involved in running a school. They also know how tuition dollars are spent and how much state and federal aid the school needs to stay afloat. Although they are sympathetic to the plight of both students and parents, they have to work with limited resources.

   An argumentative essay addressing this audience could focus on the need to make tuition more affordable by cutting costs and providing more student aid.

Another way to define an audience is to determine whether it is *friendly, hostile,* or *neutral.*

- A **friendly audience** is sympathetic to your argument. This audience might already agree with you or have an emotional or intellectual attachment to you or to your position. In this situation, you should emphasize points of agreement and reinforce the emotional bond that exists between you and the audience. Don't assume, however, that because this audience is receptive to your ideas, you do not have to address their concerns or provide support for your points. If readers suspect that you are avoiding important issues or that your evidence is weak, they will be less likely to take your argument seriously—even though they agree with you.

- A **hostile audience** disagrees with your position and does not accept the underlying assumptions of your argument. For this reason, you have to work hard to overcome their preconceived opinions, presenting your points clearly and logically and including a wide range of evidence. To show that you are a reasonable person, you should treat these readers with respect even though they happen to disagree with you. In addition, you should show that you have taken the time to consider their objections and that you value their concerns. Even with all these efforts, however, the best you may be able to do is get them to admit that you have made some good points in support of your position.

- A **neutral audience** has few or no preconceived opinions about the issue you are going to discuss. (When you are writing an argument for a college class, you should assume that you are writing for a neutral audience.) For this reason, you need to provide background information about the issue and about the controversy surrounding it. You should also summarize opposing points of view, present them logically, and refute them effectively. This type of audience may not know much about an issue, but it is not necessarily composed of unsophisticated or unintelligent people. Moreover, even though such readers are neutral, you should assume that they are **skeptical**—that is, that they will question your assumptions and require supporting evidence before they accept your conclusions.

> **NOTE**
>
> Some audiences are so diverse that they are difficult to categorize. In this case, it is best to define the audience yourself—for example, *concerned parents, prudent consumers,* or *serious students*—and then address them accordingly.

Keep in mind that identifying a specific audience is not something that you do at the last minute. Because your audience determines the kind of argument you present, you should take the time to make this determination before you begin to write.

Considering the Question

All arguments begin with a question that you are going to answer. To be suitable for argument, this question must have more than one possible answer. If it does not, there is no basis for the argument. For example, there is no point trying to write an argumentative essay on the question of whether head injuries represent a danger for football players. The answer to this question is so obvious that no thoughtful person would argue that they are not. The question of whether the National Football League (NFL) is doing enough to protect players from head injuries, however, is one on which reasonable people can (and do) disagree. Consider the following information:

- In recent years, the NFL has done much to reduce the number of serious head injuries.

- New protocols for the treatment of players who show signs of head trauma, stricter rules against helmet-to-helmet tackles, and the use of safer helmets have reduced the number of concussions.

- Even with these precautions, professional football players experience a high number of head injuries, with one in three players reporting negative effects—some quite serious—from repeated concussions.

Because there are solid arguments on both sides of this issue, you could write an effective argument in which you address this question.

Considering the Context

An argument takes place in a specific **context** — the set of circumstances that surrounds the issue. As you plan your argument, consider the social, political, historical, and cultural events that define the debate.

Assume that you were going to argue that the public school students in your hometown should be required to purchase iPads. Before you begin your argument, you should give readers the background—the context—they will need to understand the issue. For example, they should know that school officials have been debating the issue for over a year. School administrators say that given the advances in distance learning as well as the high quality of online resources, iPads will enhance the educational experience of students. They also say that it is time to bring the schools' instructional methods into the twenty-first century. Even so, some parents say that requiring the purchase of iPads will put an undue financial burden on them. In addition, teachers point out that a good deal of new material will have to be developed to take advantage of this method of instruction. Finally, not all students will have access at home to the high-speed internet capacity necessary for this type of instruction.

If it is not too complicated, you can discuss the context of your argument in your introduction; if it requires more explanation, you can discuss it in your first body paragraph. If you do not establish this context early in your essay, however, readers will have a difficult time understanding the issue you are going to discuss and the points you are going to make.

Logos, Pathos, and Ethos

To be effective, your argument has to be persuasive. **Persuasion** is a general term that refers to how a speaker or writer influences an audience to adopt a particular belief or to follow a specific course of action.

In the fifth century B.C.E., the philosopher Aristotle considered the issue of persuasion. Ancient Greece was primarily an oral culture (as opposed to a written or print culture), so persuasive techniques were most often used in speeches. Public officials had to speak before a citizens' assembly, and people had to make their cases in front of various judicial bodies. The more persuasive the presentation, the better the speaker's chance of success. In *The Art of Rhetoric*, Aristotle examines the three different means of persuasion that a speaker can use to persuade listeners (or writers):

- The appeal to reason (*logos*)
- The appeal to the emotions (*pathos*)
- The appeal to authority (*ethos*)

The Appeal to Reason (Logos)

According to Aristotle, argument is the appeal to reason or logic (**logos**). He assumed that, at their core, human beings are logical and therefore would respond to a well-constructed argument. For Aristotle, appeals to reason focus primarily on the way that an argument is organized, and this organization is determined by formal logic, which uses deductive and inductive reasoning to reach valid conclusions. Aristotle believed that appeals to reason convince an audience that a conclusion is both valid and true (see Chapter 5 for a discussion of deductive and inductive reasoning and logic). Although Aristotle believed that ideally, all arguments should appeal to reason, he knew that given the realities of human nature, reason alone was not always enough. Therefore, when he discusses persuasion, he also discusses the appeals to *ethos* and *pathos*.

Logos *in Action*

Notice how the ad below for the Tesla Model 3, an all-electric automobile, appeals primarily to reason. It uses facts as well as a logical explanation of the car's advantages to appeal to reason.

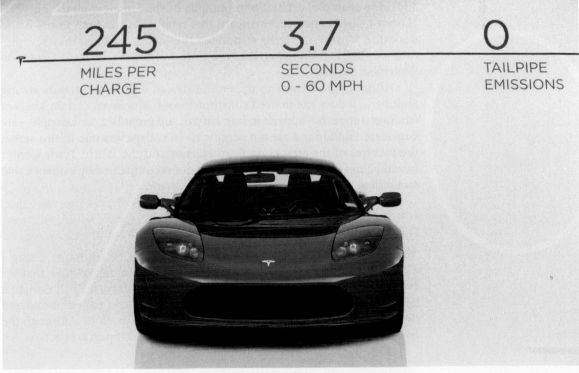

245	3.7	0
MILES PER CHARGE	SECONDS 0 - 60 MPH	TAILPIPE EMISSIONS

Andy Cross/Denver Post/Getty Images

You can assess the effectiveness of *logos* (the appeal to reason) in an argument by asking the following questions:

- Does the argument have a clear thesis? In other words, can you identify the main point the writer is trying to make?

- Does the argument include the facts, examples, and expert opinion needed to support the thesis?

- Is the argument well organized? Are the points the argument makes presented in logical order?

- Can you detect any errors in logic (**fallacies**) that undermine the argument's reasoning?

The Appeal to the Emotions (Pathos)

Aristotle knew that an appeal to the emotions (*pathos*) could be very persuasive because it adds a human dimension to an argument. By appealing to an audience's sympathies and by helping them to identify with the subject being discussed, emotional appeals can turn abstract concepts into concrete examples that can compel people to take action. After December 7, 1941, for example, explicit photographs of the Japanese attack on Pearl Harbor helped convince Americans that retaliation was both justified and desirable. Many Americans responded the same way when they saw pictures of planes crashing into the twin towers of the World Trade Center on September 11, 2001.

Although an appeal to the emotions can add to an already strong argument, it does not in itself constitute proof. Moreover, certain kinds of emotional appeals—appeals to fear, hatred, and prejudice, for example—are considered unfair and are not acceptable in college writing. In this sense, the pictures of the attacks on Pearl Harbor and the World Trade Center would be unfair arguments if they were not accompanied by evidence that established that retaliation was indeed necessary.

Pathos *in Action*

The following ad makes good use of the appeal to the emotions. Using a picture of children's shoes, the ad includes a tag that tells people that for every pair of children's shoes they buy, the manufacturer will donate a new pair of shoes to a needy child. The small shoes and their embroidered designs suggest the children who the shoes will be given to. Although the ad contains little supporting evidence, its emotional appeal is effective.

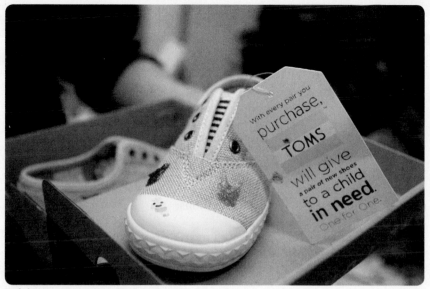

Rachel Murray/Getty Images Entertainment/Getty Images

You can assess the effectiveness of *pathos* (the appeal to the emotions) in an argument by asking the following questions:

- Does the argument include words or images designed to move readers?

- Does the argument use emotionally loaded language?

- Does the argument include vivid descriptions or striking examples calculated to appeal to readers' emotions?

- Are the values and beliefs of the writer apparent in the argument?

- Does the tone seem emotional?

The Appeal to Authority (Ethos)

Finally, Aristotle knew that the character and authority of a speaker or writer (*ethos*) could contribute to the persuasiveness of an argument. If the person making the argument is known to be honorable, truthful, knowledgeable, and trustworthy, audiences will likely accept what he or she is saying. If, on the other hand, the person is known to be deceitful, ignorant, dishonest, uninformed, or dishonorable, audiences will probably dismiss his or her argument—no matter how persuasive it might seem. Whenever you analyze an argument, you should try to determine whether the writer is worth listening to—in other words, whether the writer has **credibility**.

(For a discussion of how to establish credibility and demonstrate fairness in your own writing, see Chapter 7.)

Ethos *in Action*

The following ad uses an appeal to authority. It shows record producer and entrepreneur Dr. Dre and professional basketball player LeBron James wearing Beats headphones. The idea behind celebrity endorsements is simple. People like certain celebrities, so if they endorse a product, people will probably buy that product. (Recent studies seem to support this theory.)

You can assess the effectiveness of *ethos* (the appeal to authority) in an argument by asking the following questions:

- Does the person making the argument demonstrate knowledge of the subject?

- What steps does the person making the argument take to present its position as reasonable?

- Does the argument seem fair?

- If the argument includes sources, do they seem both reliable and credible? Does the argument include proper documentation?

- Does the person making the argument demonstrate respect for opposing viewpoints?

Dr. Dre and LeBron James in an ad promoting Beats headphones

Anthony J. Causi/Icon SMI 942/Newscom

The Rhetorical Triangle

The relationship among the three kinds of appeals in an argument is traditionally represented by a triangle.

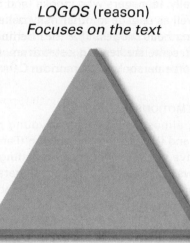

LOGOS (reason)
Focuses on the text

ETHOS (authority)
Focuses on the writer

PATHOS (emotions)
Focuses on the audience

In the diagram above—called the **rhetorical triangle**—all sides of the triangle are equal, implying that the three appeals occur in an argument in equal measure. In reality, however, this is seldom true. Depending on the audience, purpose, and situation, an argument may include all three appeals or just one or two. Moreover, one argument might emphasize reason, another might stress the writer's authority (or credibility), and still another might appeal mainly to the emotions. (In each of these cases, one side of the rhetorical triangle would be longer than the others.) In academic writing, for example, the appeal to reason is used most often, and the appeal to the emotions is less common. As Aristotle recognized, however, the three appeals often work together (to varying degrees) to create an effective argument.

Each of the following paragraphs makes an argument against smoking, illustrating how the appeals are used in an argument. Although each paragraph includes all three of the appeals, one appeal outweighs the others. (Keep in mind that each paragraph is aimed at a different audience.)

APPEAL TO REASON (*LOGOS*)

Among young people, the dangers of smoking are clear. According to the World Health Organization, smoking can cause a variety of problems in young people—for example, lung problems and shortness of breath. Smoking also contributes to heart attacks, strokes, and coronary artery disease (72). In addition, teenage smokers have an increased risk of developing lung cancer as they get older (CDC). According to one study, teenage smokers see doctors or other health professionals at higher rates than those who do not smoke (Ardly 112). Finally, teenagers who smoke tend to abuse alcohol and marijuana as well as engage in other risky behaviors (CDC). Clearly, tobacco is a dangerous drug that has serious health risks for teenage smokers. In fact, some studies suggest that smoking takes thirteen to fourteen years off a person's life (American Cancer Society).

APPEAL TO THE EMOTIONS (*PATHOS*)

Every day, almost four thousand young people begin smoking cigarettes, and this number is growing (Family First Aid). Sadly, most of you have no idea what you are getting into. For one thing, smoking yellows your teeth, stains your fingers, and gives you bad breath. The smoke also gets into your hair and clothes and makes you smell. Also, smoking is addictive; once you start, it's hard to stop. After you've been smoking for a few years, you are hooked, and as television commercials for the nicotine patch show, you can have a hard time breaking the habit. Finally, smoking is dangerous. In the United States, one out of every five deaths can be attributed to smoking (Teen Health). If you have ever seen anyone dying of lung cancer, you understand how bad long-term smoking can be. Just look at the pictures on the internet of diseased, blackened lungs, and it becomes clear that smoking does not make you look cool or sophisticated, no matter what cigarette advertising suggests.

APPEAL TO AUTHORITY (*ETHOS*)

My advice to those who are starting to smoke is to reconsider — before it's too late. I began using tobacco over ten years ago when I was in high school. At first, I started using snuff because I was on the baseball team and wanted to imitate the players in the major leagues. It wasn't long before I had graduated to cigarettes — first a few and then at least a pack a day. I heard the warnings from teachers and the counselors from the D.A.R.E. program, but they didn't do any good. I spent almost all my extra money on cigarettes. Occasionally, I would stop — sometimes for a few days, sometimes for a few weeks — but I always started again. Later, after I graduated, the health plan at my job covered smoking cessation treatment, so I tried everything — the patch, Chantix, therapy, and even hypnosis. Again, nothing worked. At last, after I had been married for four years, my wife sat me down and begged me to quit. Later that night, I threw away my cigarettes and haven't smoked since. Although I've gained some weight, I now breathe easier, and I am able to concentrate better than I could before. Had I known how difficult quitting was going to be, I never would have started in the first place.

When you write an argumentative essay, keep in mind that each type of appeal has its own particular strengths. Your purpose and audience as well as other elements of the rhetorical situation help you determine what strategy to use. Remember, however, that even though most effective arguments use a combination of appeals, one appeal predominates. For example, even though academic arguments may employ appeals to the emotions, they do so sparingly. Most often, they appeal primarily to reason by using facts and statistics—not emotions—to support their points.

AP Images/Butch Dill

1

The Four Pillars of Argument

Is a College Education Worth the Money?

In recent years, more and more high school graduates have been heading to college, convinced that higher education will enhance their future earning power. At the same time, the cost of a college education has been rising, and so has the amount of student-loan debt carried by college graduates. (During 2017–18, average tuition and fees at nonprofit private four-year colleges rose 1.9 percent, to $34,740, while tuition for in-state students at four-year public schools went up 1.3 percent to $9,970. On average, 2017 graduates with student-loan debt owed nearly $40,000.) This situation has led some observers to wonder if the high cost of college actually pays off—not only in dollars but also in future job satisfaction. Will a college degree protect workers who are threatened by high unemployment, the rise of technology, the declining power of labor unions, and the trend toward outsourcing? Given the high financial cost of college, do the rewards of a college education—emotional and intellectual as well as financial—balance the sacrifices that students make in time and money? These and other questions have no easy answers.

Later in this chapter, you will be introduced to readings that explore the pros and cons of investing in a college education, and you will be asked to write an argumentative essay in which you take a position on this controversial topic.

In a sense, you already know a lot more than you think you do about how to construct an argumentative essay. After all, an argumentative essay is a variation of the thesis-and-support essays that you have been writing in your college classes: you state a position on a topic, and then you support that position. However, with argumentative essays, some special concerns in terms of structure, style, and purpose come into play. Throughout this book, we introduce you to the unique features of argument. In this chapter, we focus on structure.

The Elements of Argument

An argumentative essay includes the same three sections—*introduction, body,* and *conclusion*—as any other essay. In an argumentative essay, however, the introduction includes an argumentative **thesis statement**, the body includes both the supporting **evidence** and the **refutation** of opposing arguments, and the conclusion includes a strong, convincing **concluding statement** that reinforces the position stated in the thesis.

The following diagram illustrates one way to organize an argumentative essay.

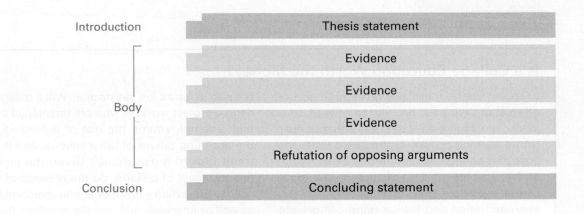

Introduction — Thesis statement

Body — Evidence / Evidence / Evidence / Refutation of opposing arguments

Conclusion — Concluding statement

The elements of an argumentative essay are like the pillars of an ancient Greek temple. Together, the four elements—thesis statement, evidence, refutation of opposing arguments, and concluding statement—help you build a strong argument.

Ancient Greek temple

AP Images/Alessandro Fucarini

Thesis Statement

A **thesis statement** is a single sentence that states your position on an issue. An argumentative essay must have an **argumentative thesis**—one that takes a firm stand. For example, on the issue of whether colleges should require all students to study a language other than English, your thesis statement could be any of the following (and other positions are also possible):

- Colleges should require all students to study a foreign language.

- Colleges should require all liberal arts majors to study a foreign language.

- Colleges should require all students to study Spanish, Chinese, or Farsi.

- Colleges should not require any students to study a foreign language.

An argumentative thesis must be **debatable**—that is, it must have at least two sides, stating a position with which some reasonable people might disagree. To confirm that your thesis is debatable, you should see if you can formulate an **antithesis**, or opposing argument. For example, the statement, "Our school has a foreign-language requirement" has no antithesis because it is simply a statement of fact; you could not take the opposite position because the facts would not support it. However, the following thesis statement takes a position that *is* debatable (and therefore suitable for an argumentative thesis):

THESIS   Our school should institute a foreign-language requirement.

ANTITHESIS Our school should not institute a foreign-language requirement.

(For more on thesis statements, see Chapter 7.)

Evidence

Evidence is the material—facts, observations, expert opinion, examples, statistics, and so on—that supports your thesis statement. For example, you could support your position that foreign-language study should be required for all college students by arguing that this requirement will make them more employable, and you could cite employment statistics to support this point. Alternatively, you could use the opinion of an expert on the topic—for example, an experienced college language instructor—to support the opposite position, arguing that students without an interest in language study are wasting their time in such courses.

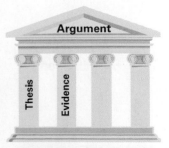

You will use both *facts* and *opinions* to support the points you make in your arguments. A **fact** is a statement that can be verified (proven to be true). An **opinion** is always open to debate because it is simply a personal judgment. Of course, the more knowledgeable the writer is, the more credible his or her opinion is. Thus, the opinion of a respected expert on language study will carry more weight than the opinion of a student with no particular expertise on the issue. However, if the student's opinion is supported by facts, it will be much more convincing than an unsupported opinion.

FACTS

- Some community colleges have no foreign-language requirements.

- Some selective liberal arts colleges require all students to have two years or more of foreign-language study.

- At some universities, undergraduates must take as many as fourteen foreign-language credits.

- Some schools grant credit for high school language classes, allowing these courses to fulfill the college foreign-language requirement.

UNSUPPORTED OPINIONS

- Foreign-language courses are not as important as math and science courses.

- Foreign-language study should be a top priority on university campuses.

- Engineering majors should not have to take a foreign-language course.

- It is not fair to force all students to study a foreign language.

SUPPORTED OPINIONS

- The university requires all students to take a full year of foreign-language study, but it is not doing enough to support those who need help. For example, it does not provide enough student tutors, and the language labs have no evening hours.

- According to Ruth Fuentes, chair of the Spanish department, nursing and criminal justice majors who take at least two years of Spanish have an easier time finding employment after graduation than students in those majors who do not study Spanish.

Refutation

Because every argument has more than one side, you should not assume that your readers will agree with you. On the contrary, readers usually need to be convinced that your position on an issue has merit. This means that you need to do more than just provide sufficient evidence in support of your position; you also need to **refute** (disprove or call into question) arguments that challenge your position, possibly conceding the strengths of those opposing arguments and then pointing out their shortcomings.

For example, if you take a position in favor of requiring foreign-language study for all college students, some readers might argue that college students already have to take too many required courses. After acknowledging the validity of this argument, you could refute it by pointing out that a required foreign-language course would not necessarily be a burden for students because it could replace another, less important required course.

Other readers might point out that in today's competitive job market, which is increasingly dependent on technology, it makes more sense to study coding than to study a foreign language. In this case, you would concede the strength of the position, acknowledging the importance of proficiency in computer languages. You could then go on to refute the argument by explaining that foreign-language study expands students' ability to engage with people from other cultures, thereby becoming more competitive in a global economy. (You could also argue, of course, that students could benefit by studying *both* coding and foreign languages.) (For more on refutation, see Chapter 7.)

Concluding Statement

After you have provided convincing support for your position and refuted opposing arguments, you should end your essay with a strong **concluding statement** that reinforces your position. (The position that you want readers to remember is the one stated in your thesis, not the opposing arguments that you have refuted.) For example, you might conclude an essay in support of a foreign-language requirement by making a specific recommendation or by predicting the possible negative outcome of *not* implementing this requirement.

CHECKLIST

Does Your Argument Stand Up?

When you write an argumentative essay, check to make sure it includes all four of the elements you need to build a strong argument.

☐ Does your essay have an argumentative **thesis**?

☐ Does your essay include solid, convincing **evidence** to support your thesis?

☐ Does your essay include a **refutation** of the most compelling arguments against your position?

☐ Does your essay include a strong **concluding statement**?

⊙ The following student essay includes all four of the elements that are needed to build a convincing argument.

WHY FOREIGN-LANGUAGE STUDY SHOULD BE REQUIRED

NIA TUCKSON

Introduction

"What do you call someone who speaks three languages? Trilingual. 1 What do you call someone who speaks two languages? Bilingual. What do you call someone who speaks only one language? American." As this old joke illustrates, many Americans are unable to communicate in a language other than English. Given our global economy and American companies' need to conduct business with other countries, this problem

Thesis statement

needs to be addressed. A good first step is to require all college students to study a foreign language.

First body paragraph: Evidence

After graduation, many students will work in fields in which 2 speaking (or reading) another language will be useful or even necessary. For example, health-care professionals will often be called on to communicate with patients who do not speak English; in fact, a patient's life may depend on their ability to do so. Those who work in business and finance may need to speak Mandarin or Japanese; those who have positions in the military or in the foreign service may need to speak Persian or Arabic. A working knowledge of one of these languages can help students succeed in their future careers, and it can also make them more employable.

Second body paragraph: Evidence

In addition to strengthening a résumé, foreign-language study can 3 also give students an understanding of another culture's history, art, and literature. Although such knowledge may never be "useful" in a student's career, it can certainly enrich the student's life. Too narrow a focus on career can turn college into a place that trains students rather than educates them. In contrast, expanding students' horizons to include subjects beyond those needed for their careers can better equip them to be lifelong learners.

Third body paragraph: Evidence

When they travel abroad, Americans who can speak a language 4 other than English will find that they are better able to understand people from other countries. As informal ambassadors for the United States, tourists have a responsibility to try to understand other languages and cultures. Too many Americans assume that their own country's language and culture are superior to all others. This shortsighted attitude is not likely to strengthen relationships between the United States and other nations. Understanding a country's language can help students to build bridges between themselves and others.

Some students say that learning a language is not easy and that it takes a great deal of time. College students are already overloaded with coursework, jobs, and family responsibilities, and a new academic requirement is certain to create problems. In fact, students may find that adding just six credits of language study will limit their opportunities to take advanced courses in their majors or to enroll in electives that interest them. However, this burden can be eased if other, less important course requirements—such as physical education—are eliminated to make room for the new requirement.

5 Fourth body paragraph: Refutation of opposing argument

Some students may also argue that they, not their school, should be able to decide what courses are most important to them. After all, a student who struggled in high school French and plans to major in computer science might understandably resist a foreign-language requirement. However, challenging college language courses might actually be more rewarding than high school courses were, and the student who struggled in high school French might actually enjoy a college-level French course (or study a different language). Finally, a student who initially plans to major in computer science may actually wind up majoring in something completely different—or taking a job in a country in which English is not spoken.

6 Fifth body paragraph: Refutation of opposing argument

Entering college students sometimes find it hard to envision their personal or professional futures or to imagine where their lives may take them. Still, a well-rounded education, including foreign-language study, can prepare them for many of the challenges that they will face. Colleges can help students keep their options open by requiring at least a year (and preferably two years) of foreign-language study. Instead of focusing narrowly on what interests them today, American college students should take the extra step to become bilingual—or even trilingual—in the future.

7 Conclusion

Concluding statement

➲ EXERCISE 1.1 IDENTIFYING THE ELEMENTS OF ARGUMENT

The following essay, "Learn a Language, but Not a Human One," by Andy Kessler, includes all four of the basic elements of argument discussed so far. Read the essay, and then answer the questions that follow it, consulting the diagram on page 24 if necessary.

This commentary appeared on July 17, 2017, in the *Wall Street Journal*.

LEARN A LANGUAGE, BUT NOT A HUMAN ONE

ANDY KESSLER

Donald Trump, whose wife speaks five languages, just wrapped up a pair 1 of trips to Europe during which he spoke only English. Good for him. If Mr. Trump studied a language in college or high school, as most of us were required to, it was a complete waste of his time. I took five years of French and can't even talk to a French poodle.

Maybe there's a better way for students to spend their time. Last month 2 Apple CEO Tim Cook urged the president: "Coding should be a requirement in every public school." I propose we do a swap.

Why do American schools still require foreign languages? Translating at 3 the United Nations is not a growth industry. In the 1960s and '70s everyone suggested studying German, as most scientific papers were in that language. Or at least that's what they told me. In the '80s it was Japanese, since they ruled manufacturing and would soon rule computers. In the '90s a fountain of wealth was supposed to spout from post-Communist Moscow, so we all needed to learn Russian. Now parents elbow each other getting their children into immersive Mandarin programs starting in kindergarten.

Don't they know that the Tower of Babel has been torn down? On your 4 average smartphone, apps like Google Translate can do real-time voice translation. No one ever has to say worthless phrases like *la plume de ma tante* anymore. The app Waygo lets you point your phone at signs in Chinese, Japanese, or Korean and get translations in English. Sometime in the next few years you'll be able to buy a Bluetooth-based universal translator for your ear.

Yet students still need to take at least two years of foreign-language classes 5 in high school to attend most four-year colleges. Three if they want to impress the admissions officer. Four if they're masochists. Then they need to show language competency to graduate most liberal-arts programs. We tried to get my son out of a college language requirement. He pointed to his computer skills and argued that the internet is in English. (It's true. As of March, 51.6 percent of websites were in English. Just 2 percent were Chinese.) We lost the argument. He took Japanese and has fun ordering sushi.

It's not as if learning another language comes with a big payday. In 2002 6 the Federal Reserve and Harvard put out a study showing those who speak a foreign language earn 2 percent more than those who don't.

High schools tend to follow colleges' lead, but maybe that's beginning to change. 7 I read through all 50 states' language requirements and only one requires either two years of a foreign language or two years of "computer technology approved for college admission requirements." Wow. Is that California? No. New York? No. Would you believe Oklahoma? South Dakota and Maryland also have flexible language skill laws. Foolishly, the Common Core State Standards are silent on coding.

The U.S. is falling behind. In 2014 England made computing a part of its national 8 primary curriculum. Estonia had already started coding in its schools as early as first grade. The Netherlands, Belgium, and Finland also have national programs.

Maybe the U.S. can start the ball rolling by requiring colleges and high 9 schools to allow computer languages to count as foreign languages. A handful of high schools already teach the Java computer language using a free tool called Blue J. Nonprofit Code.org exposes students to a visual programming language called Blockly. To compete in this dog-eat-dog world, America should offer Python and Ruby on Rails instead of French and Spanish.

Knowledge is good. Great literature reshuffles the mind. Tough trigonom- 10 etry problems provide puzzles for the brain. Yet there is no better challenge than writing code that teaches a machine to do exactly what you want. Some will respond, "So you want us to do vocational education?" As if computer programming is akin to auto shop and plumbing. Sorry, that's a *faux* argument. Even I remember the French word for bogus.

Let's face it, the world is headed toward one language anyway. The 11 American-based Germanic-named Uber was *originato* at the Le Web conference in Paris. In Shanghai, I've seen ads on trains and storefronts signs that read "Learn Wall Street English."

Mr. Cook is right to want more coders, though a tad self-serving as Apple 12 basically sells software wrapped in glass and metal. Same with Code.org, supported by Google and Microsoft. But every company requires coders. Even the formerly blue-collar job of operating machine tools now requires expertise in programming to control them. This will be increasingly true in workerless retail, doctorless medicine, and even teacherless education. Time to modernize the dated curriculum—*pronto*.

Identifying the Elements of Argument

1. What is this essay's thesis? Restate it in your own words.

2. List the arguments Kessler presents as evidence to support his thesis.

3. Summarize the main opposing argument the essay identifies. Then, summarize Kessler's refutation of this argument.

4. Restate the essay's concluding statement in your own words.

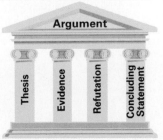

Is a College Education Worth the Money?

AP Images/Butch Dill

Reread the At Issue box on page 23, which summarizes questions raised on both sides of this issue. As the following sources illustrate, reasonable people may disagree about this controversial topic.

As you review the sources, you will be asked to answer some questions and to complete some simple activities. This work will help you understand both the content and the structure of the sources. When you have finished, you will be ready to write an essay in which you take a position on the topic "Is a College Education Worth the Money?"

SOURCES

This essay appeared in the *New York Times* on May 16, 2018.

COLLEGE MAY NOT BE WORTH IT ANYMORE

ELLEN RUPPEL SHELL

Last year, New York became the first state to offer all but its wealthiest residents tuition-free access to its public community colleges and four-year institutions. Though this Excelsior Scholarship didn't make college completely free, it highlights the power of the pro-college movement in the United States. 1

Recent decades have brought agreement that higher education is, if not a cure, then at least a protection against underemployment and the inequality it engenders. In 2012, President Barack Obama called a college degree an "economic imperative that every family in America has to be able to afford." 2

Americans strove to rise to that challenge: A third of them ages 25 to 29 now hold at least a bachelor's degree, and many paid heavily for the privilege. By last summer, Americans owed more than $1.3 trillion in student loans, more than two and a half times what they owed a decade earlier. 3

Young people and their families go into debt because they believe that college will help them in the job market. And on average it does. But this raises a question: Does higher education itself offer that benefit, or are the people who earn bachelor's degrees already positioned to get higher-paying jobs? 4

If future income was determined mainly by how much education people received, then you would assume that some higher education would be better than none. But this is often not the case. 5

People who have dropped out of college—about 40 percent of all who attend—earn only a bit more than do people with only a high school education: $38,376 a year versus $35,256. For many, that advantage is barely enough to cover their student loan debt. 6

And not all have even that advantage: African-American college dropouts on average earn less than do white Americans with only a high school degree. Meanwhile, low-income students of all races are far more likely to drop out of college than are wealthier students. Even with scholarships or free tuition, these students struggle with hefty fees and living costs, and they pay the opportunity cost of taking courses rather than getting a job. 7

The value of a college degree also varies depending on the institution bestowing it. The tiny minority of students who attend elite colleges do far better on average than those who attend nonselective ones. Disturbingly, black and Hispanic students are significantly less likely than are white and Asian students to attend elite colleges, even when family income is controlled for. That is, students from wealthy black and Hispanic families have a lower chance of attending an elite college than do students from middle-class white families. 8

It's a cruel irony that a college degree is worth less to people who most 9 need a boost: those born poor. This revelation was made by the economists Tim Bartik and Brad Hershbein. Using a body of data, the Panel Study of Income Dynamics, which includes 50 years of interviews with 18,000 Americans, they were able to follow the lives of children born into poor, middle-class, and wealthy families.

They found that for Americans born into middle-class families, a college 10 degree does appear to be a wise investment. Those in this group who received one earned 162 percent more over their careers than those who didn't.

But for those born into poverty, the results were far less impressive. College 11 graduates born poor earned on average only slightly more than did high school graduates born middle class. And over time, even this small "degree bonus" ebbed away, at least for men: By middle age, male college graduates raised in poverty were earning less than nondegree holders born into the middle class. The scholars conclude, "Individuals from poorer backgrounds may be encountering a glass ceiling that even a bachelor's degree does not break."

The authors don't speculate as to why this is the case, but it seems that 12 students from poor backgrounds have less access to very high-income jobs in technology, finance and other fields. Class and race surely play a role.

We appear to be approaching a time when, even for middle-class students, 13 the economic benefit of a college degree will begin to dim. Since 2000, the growth in the wage gap between high school and college graduates has slowed to a halt; 25 percent of college graduates now earn no more than does the average high school graduate.

Part of the reason is oversupply. Technology increased the demand for 14 educated workers, but that demand has been consistently outpaced by the number of people—urged on by everyone from teachers to presidents—prepared to meet it.

No other nation punishes the "uneducated" as harshly as the United 15 States. Nearly 30 percent of Americans without a high school diploma live in poverty, compared to 5 percent with a college degree, and we infer that this comes from a lack of education. But in 28 other wealthy developed countries, a lack of a high school diploma increases the probability of poverty by less than 5 percent. In these nations, a dearth of education does not predestine citizens for poverty.

It shouldn't here, either: According to the Bureau of Labor Statistics, fewer 16 than 20 percent of American jobs actually require a bachelor's degree. By 2026, the bureau estimates that this proportion will rise, but only to 25 percent.

Why do employers demand a degree for jobs that don't require them? 17 Because they can.

What all this suggests is that the college-degree premium may really be 18 a no-college-degree penalty. It's not necessarily college that gives people the leverage to build a better working life, it's that not having a degree decreases whatever leverage they might otherwise have.

This distinction is more than semantic. It is key to understanding the growing chasm between educational attainment and life prospects. For most of us, it's not our education that determines our employment trajectory but rather where that education positions us in relation to others.

> "No other nation punishes the 'uneducated' as harshly as the United States."

19

None of this is to suggest that higher education is not desirable: I've encouraged my own children to take that path. But while we celebrate the most recent crop of college graduates, we should also acknowledge the many more Americans who will never don a cap and gown. They, too, deserve the chance to prove themselves worthy of good work, and a good life. 20

⊘ AT ISSUE: SOURCES FOR STRUCTURING AN ARGUMENT

1. Shell opens her essay by pointing to New York State's offer of free college tuition to most residents. Is this an appropriate introduction for the discussion that follows? Why or why not?

2. Paraphrase this essay's thesis statement by filling in the following template:

   Although college may be worth the cost for many students, _____ _____.

3. Does Shell introduce arguments against her position? If so, where? If not, should she have done so, or is her essay convincing without mention of these counterarguments?

4. In paragraph 9, Shell refers to a study by two economists. How does this study support her position? What other kinds of supporting evidence does she include? Does she need to supply more?

5. In paragraph 18, Shell contrasts the "college-degree premium" with the "no-college-degree penalty." What is the difference? Why, according to Shell, is this distinction so important?

6. In her conclusion, Shell refers to her own children. Why? Do you think this is a good way for her to end her essay, or do you think she should have ended on a less personal note? Explain.

This undated essay is from MartyNemko.com.

WE SEND TOO MANY STUDENTS TO COLLEGE

MARTY NEMKO

Among my saddest moments as a career counselor is when I hear a story like 1 this: "I wasn't a good student in high school, but I wanted to prove to myself that I can get a college diploma—I'd be the first one in my family to do it. But it's been six years and I still have 45 units to go."

I have a hard time telling such people the killer statistic: According to the 2 U.S. Department of Education, if you graduated in the bottom 40 percent of your high school class and went to college, 76 of 100 won't earn a diploma, even if given 8½ years. Yet colleges admit and take the money from hundreds of thousands of such students each year!

Even worse, most of those college dropouts leave college having learned 3 little of practical value (see below) and with devastated self-esteem and a mountain of debt. Perhaps worst of all, those people rarely leave with a career path likely to lead to more than McWages. So it's not surprising that when you hop into a cab or walk into a restaurant, you're likely to meet workers who spent years and their family's life savings on college, only to end up with a job they could have done as a high school dropout.

Perhaps yet more surprising, even the high school students who are fully 4 qualified to attend college are increasingly unlikely to derive enough benefit to justify the often six-figure cost and four to eight years it takes to graduate— and only 40 percent of freshmen graduate in four years; 45 percent never graduate at all. Colleges love to trumpet the statistic that, over their lifetimes, college graduates earn more than nongraduates. But that's terribly misleading because you could lock the college-bound in a closet for four years and they'd earn more than the pool of non-college-bound—they're brighter, more motivated, and have better family connections. Too, the past advantage of college graduates in the job market is eroding: ever more students are going to college at the same time as ever more employers are offshoring ever more professional jobs. So college graduates are forced to take some very nonprofessional jobs. For example, Jill Plesnarski holds a bachelor's degree in biology from the private ($160,000 published total cost for four years) Moravian College. She had hoped to land a job as a medical research lab tech, but those positions paid so little that she opted for a job at a New Jersey sewage treatment plant. Today, although she's since been promoted, she must still occasionally wash down the tower that holds raw sewage.

Or take Brian Morris. After completing his bachelor's degree in lib- 5 eral arts from the University of California, Berkeley, he was unable to find a decent-paying job, so he went yet deeper into debt to get a master's degree from the private Mills College. Despite those degrees, the best job he could land was teaching a three-month-long course for $3,000. At that point, Brian was married and had a baby, so to support them, he reluctantly took a job as a truck driver. Now Brian says, "I just *have* to get out of trucking."

Colleges are quick to argue that a college education is more about enlight- 6
enment than employment. That may be the biggest deception of all. There is a Grand Canyon of difference between what the colleges tout in their brochures and websites and the reality.

Colleges are businesses, and students are a cost item while research is a profit center. So colleges tend to educate students in the cheapest way

> "Colleges are businesses, and 7
> students are a cost item."

possible: large lecture classes, with small classes staffed by rock-bottom-cost graduate students and, in some cases, even by undergraduate students. Professors who bring in big research dollars are almost always rewarded, while even a fine teacher who doesn't bring in the research bucks is often fired or relegated to the lowest rung: lecturer.

So, no surprise, in the definitive *Your First College Year* nationwide survey 8
conducted by UCLA researchers (data collected in 2005, reported in 2007), only 16.4 percent of students were very satisfied with the overall quality of instruction they received and 28.2 percent were neutral, dissatisfied, or very dissatisfied. A follow-up survey of seniors found that 37 percent reported being "frequently bored in class," up from 27.5 percent as freshmen.

College students may be dissatisfied with instruction, but despite that, 9
do they learn? A 2006 study funded by the Pew Charitable Trusts found that 50 percent of college *seniors* failed a test that required them to do such basic tasks as interpret a table about exercise and blood pressure, understand the arguments of newspaper editorials, or compare credit card offers. Almost 20 percent of seniors had only basic quantitative skills. For example, the students could not estimate if their car had enough gas to get to the gas station.

What to do? Colleges, which receive billions of tax dollars with minimum 10
oversight, should be held at least as accountable as companies are. For example, when some Firestone tires were defective, the government nearly forced it out of business. Yet year after year, colleges turn out millions of defective products: students who drop out or graduate with far too little benefit for the time and money spent. Yet not only do the colleges escape punishment; they're rewarded with ever greater taxpayer-funded student grants and loans, which allow colleges to raise their tuitions yet higher.

What should parents and guardians do? 11

1. If your student's high school grades and SAT or ACT are in the bottom 12
   half of his high school class, resist colleges' attempts to woo him. Their marketing to your child does *not* indicate that the colleges believe he will succeed there. Colleges make money whether or not a student learns, whether or not she graduates, and whether or not he finds good employ-ment. If a physician recommended a treatment that cost a fortune and

required years of effort without disclosing the poor chances of it working, she'd be sued and lose in any court in the land. But colleges—one of America's most sacred cows—somehow seem immune.

So let the buyer beware. Consider nondegree options: 13

- Apprenticeship programs (a great portal to apprenticeship websites: www.khake.com/page58.html)
- Short career-preparation programs at community colleges
- The military
- On-the-job training, especially at the elbow of a successful small business owner

2. Let's say your student *is* in the top half of his high school class and is moti- 14 vated to attend college by more than the parties, being able to say she went to college, and the piece of paper. Then have her apply to perhaps a dozen colleges. Colleges vary less than you might think, yet financial aid awards can vary wildly. It's often wise to choose the college that requires you to pay the least cash and take on the smallest loan. College is among the few products where you don't get what you pay for—price does not indicate quality.

3. If your child is one of the rare breed who, on graduating high school, 15 knows what he wants to do and isn't unduly attracted to college academics or the *Animal House* environment that college dorms often are, then take solace in the fact that in deciding to forgo college, he is preceded by scores of others who have successfully taken that noncollege road less traveled. Examples: the three most successful entrepreneurs in the computer industry, Bill Gates, Michael Dell, and Apple cofounder Steve Wozniak, all do not have a college degree. Here are some others: Malcolm X, Rush Limbaugh, Barbra Streisand, PBS *NewsHour*'s Nina Totenberg, Tom Hanks, Maya Angelou, Ted Turner, Ellen DeGeneres, former governor Jesse Ventura, IBM founder Thomas Watson, architect Frank Lloyd Wright, former Israeli president David Ben-Gurion, Woody Allen, Warren Beatty, Domino's pizza chain founder Tom Monaghan, folksinger Joan Baez, director Quentin Tarantino, ABC-TV's Peter Jennings, Wendy's founder Dave Thomas, Thomas Edison, Blockbuster Video founder and owner of the Miami Dolphins Wayne Huizenga, William Faulkner, Jane Austen, McDonald's founder Ray Kroc, Oracle founder Larry Ellison, Henry Ford, cosmetics magnate Helena Rubinstein, Benjamin Franklin, Alexander Graham Bell, Coco Chanel, Walter Cronkite, Walt Disney, Bob Dylan, Leonardo DiCaprio, cookie maker Debbi Fields, Sally Field, Jane Fonda, Buckminster Fuller, DreamWorks cofounder David Geffen, *Roots* author Alex Haley, Ernest Hemingway, Dustin Hoffman, famed anthropologist Richard Leakey, airplane inventors Wilbur and Orville Wright, Madonna, satirist H. L. Mencken, Martina Navratilova, Rosie O'Donnell, Nathan Pritikin (Pritikin diet), chef Wolfgang Puck, Robert Redford, oil billionaire John D. Rockefeller, Eleanor Roosevelt, NBC mogul David Sarnoff, and seven U.S. presidents from Washington to Truman.

4. College is like a chain saw. Only in certain situations is it the right tool. 16 Encourage your child to choose the right tool for her post–high school experience.

⊘ AT ISSUE: SOURCES FOR STRUCTURING AN ARGUMENT

1. Which of the following statements best summarizes Nemko's position? Why?

   ■ "We Send Too Many Students to College" (title)

   ■ "There is a Grand Canyon of difference between what the colleges tout in their brochures and websites and the reality" (para. 6).

   ■ "Colleges, which receive billions of tax dollars with minimum oversight, should be held at least as accountable as companies are" (10).

   ■ "College is like a chain saw. Only in certain situations is it the right tool" (16).

2. Where does Nemko support his thesis with appeals to logic? Where does he appeal to the emotions? Where does he use an appeal to authority? (Refer to the discussions of *logos*, *pathos*, and *ethos* on pages 14–18 if necessary.) Which of these three kinds of appeals do you find the most convincing? Why?

3. List the arguments Nemko uses to support his thesis in paragraphs 2–4.

4. In paragraph 4, Nemko says, "Colleges love to trumpet the statistic that, over their lifetimes, college graduates earn more than nongraduates." In paragraph 6, he says, "Colleges are quick to argue that a college education is more about enlightenment than employment." How does he refute these two opposing arguments?

5. Nemko draws an **analogy** between colleges and businesses, identifying students as a "cost item" (7). Does this analogy—including his characterization of weak students as "defective products" (10)—work for you? Why or why not?

6. What specific solutions does Nemko propose for the problem he identifies? To whom does he address these suggestions—and, in fact, his entire argument?

7. Reread paragraph 15. Do you think the list of successful people who do not hold college degrees is convincing support for Nemko's position? What kind of appeal does this paragraph make? How might you refute its argument?

This personal essay is from talk,onevietnam.org, where it appeared on May 9, 2011.

WHAT DOES IT MEAN TO BE A COLLEGE GRAD?

JENNIE LE

After May 14th, I will be a college graduate. By fall, there will be no more a cappella rehearsals, no more papers or exams, no more sleepless nights, no more weekday drinking, no more 1 a.m. milk tea runs, no more San Francisco Bay Area exploring. I won't be with the people I now see daily. I won't have the same job with the same awesome boss. I won't be singing under Sproul every Monday. I won't be booked with weekly gigs that take me all over California. I won't be lighting another VSA Culture Show.

I will also have new commitments: weekly dinner dates with my mom, brother/sister time with my other two brothers, job hunting and career building, car purchasing and maintenance. In essence, my life will be—or at least feel—completely different. From what college alumni have told me, I will soon miss my college days after they are gone.

But in the bigger picture, outside of the daily tasks, what does it mean to hold a college degree? My fellow graduating coworker and I discussed the importance (or lack thereof) of our college degrees: while I considered hanging up my two diplomas, she believed that having a bachelor's was so standard and insubstantial, only a professional degree is worth hanging up and showing off.

> "Nowadays, holding a college degree (or two) seems like the norm."

Nowadays, holding a college degree (or two) seems like the norm; it's not a very outstanding feat.

However, I'd like to defend the power of earning a college degree. Although holding a degree isn't as powerful as it was in previous decades, stats still show that those who earn bachelor's degrees are likely to earn twice as much as those who don't. Also, only 27 percent of Americans can say they have a bachelor's degree or higher. Realistically, having a college degree will likely mean a comfortable living and the opportunity to move up at work and in life.

Personally, my degrees validate my mother's choice to leave Vietnam. She moved here for opportunity. She wasn't able to attend college here or in Vietnam or choose her occupation. But her hard work has allowed her children to become the first generation of Americans in the family to earn college degrees: she gave us the ability to make choices she wasn't privileged to make. Being the fourth and final kid to earn my degree in my family, my mom can now boast about having educated children who are making a name for themselves (a son who is a computer-superstar, a second son and future dentist studying at UCSF, another son who is earning his MBA and manages at Mattel, and a daughter who is thankful to have three brothers to mooch off of).

For me, this degree symbolizes my family being able to make and take the 6 opportunities that we've been given in America, despite growing up with gang members down my street and a drug dealer across from my house. This degree will also mean that my children will have more opportunities because of my education, insight, knowledge, and support.

Even though a college degree isn't worth as much as it was in the past, 7 it still shows that I—along with my fellow graduates and the 27 percent of Americans with a bachelor's or higher—will have opportunities unheard of a generation before us, showing everyone how important education is for our lives and our futures.

◯ AT ISSUE: SOURCES FOR STRUCTURING AN ARGUMENT

1. What purpose do the first two paragraphs of this essay serve? Do you think they are necessary? Do you think they are interesting? How else might Le have opened her essay?

2. Where does Le state her thesis? Do you think she should have stated it more forcefully? Can you suggest a more effectively worded thesis statement for this essay?

3. In paragraph 3, Le summarizes an opposing argument. What is this argument? How does she refute it? Can you think of other arguments against her position that she should have addressed?

4. In paragraphs 5–6, Le includes an appeal to the emotions. Does she offer any other kind of supporting evidence? If so, where? What other kinds of evidence do you think she should include? Why?

5. Echoing a point she made in paragraph 4, Le begins her conclusion with "Even though a college degree isn't worth as much as it was in the past, . . ." Does this concession undercut her argument, or is the information presented in paragraph 4 enough to address this potential problem?

This essay appeared in the January/February 2018 issue of *The Atlantic*.

THE WORLD MIGHT BE BETTER OFF WITHOUT COLLEGE FOR EVERYONE

BRYAN CAPLAN

I have been in school for more than 40 years. First preschool, kindergarten, 1 elementary school, junior high, and high school. Then a bachelor's degree at UC Berkeley, followed by a doctoral program at Princeton. The next step was what you could call my first "real" job—as an economics professor at George Mason University.

Thanks to tenure, I have a dream job for life. Personally, I have no reason 2 to lash out at our system of higher education. Yet a lifetime of experience, plus a quarter century of reading and reflection, has convinced me that it is a big waste of time and money. When politicians vow to send more Americans to college, I can't help gasping, "Why? You want us to waste even more?"

How, you may ask, can anyone call higher education wasteful in an age 3 when its financial payoff is greater than ever? The earnings premium for college graduates has rocketed to 73 percent—that is, those with a bachelor's degree earn, on average, 73 percent more than those who have only a high school diploma, up from about 50 percent in the late 1970s. The key issue, however, isn't whether college pays, but why. The simple, popular answer is that schools teach students useful job skills. But this dodges puzzling questions.

First and foremost: From kindergarten on, students spend thousands 4 of hours studying subjects irrelevant to the modern labor market. Why do English classes focus on literature and poetry instead of business and technical writing? Why do advanced-math classes bother with proofs almost no student can follow? When will the typical student use history? Trigonometry? Art? Music? Physics? Latin? The class clown who snarks "What does this have to do with real life?" is onto something.

The disconnect between college curricula and the job market has a banal 5 explanation: Educators teach what they know—and most have as little first-hand knowledge of the modern workplace as I do. Yet this merely complicates the puzzle. If schools aim to boost students' future income by teaching job skills, why do they entrust students' education to people so detached from the real world? Because, despite the chasm between what students learn and what workers do, academic success is a strong signal of worker productivity.

Suppose your law firm wants a summer associate. A law student with a 6 doctorate in philosophy from Stanford applies. What do you infer? The applicant is probably brilliant, diligent, and willing to tolerate serious boredom. If you're looking for that kind of worker—and what employer isn't?—you'll make an offer, knowing full well that nothing the philosopher learned at Stanford will be relevant to this job.

The labor market doesn't pay you for the useless subjects you master; it 7
pays you for the preexisting traits you signal by mastering them. This is not
a fringe idea. Michael Spence, Kenneth Arrow, and Joseph Stiglitz—all Nobel
laureates in economics—made seminal contributions to the theory of educational signaling. Every college student who does the least work required to get
good grades silently endorses the theory. But signaling plays almost no role in
public discourse or policy making. As a society, we continue to push ever larger
numbers of students into ever higher levels of education. The main effect is not
better jobs or greater skill levels, but a credentialist arms race.

Lest I be misinterpreted, I emphatically affirm that education confers some 8
marketable skills, namely literacy and numeracy. Nonetheless, I believe that signaling accounts for at least half of college's financial reward, and probably more.

Most of the salary payoff for college comes from crossing the graduation 9
finish line. Suppose you drop out after a year. You'll receive a salary bump compared with someone who's attended no college, but it won't be anywhere near
25 percent of the salary premium you'd get for a four-year degree. Similarly, the
premium for sophomore year is nowhere near 50 percent of the return on a bachelor's degree, and the premium for junior year is nowhere near 75 percent of that
return. Indeed, in the average study, senior year of college brings more than twice
the pay increase of freshman, sophomore, and junior years combined. Unless colleges delay job training until the very end, signaling is practically the only explanation. This in turn implies a mountain of wasted resources—time and money
that would be better spent preparing students for the jobs they're likely to do.

The conventional view—that education pays because students learn— 10
assumes that the typical student acquires, and retains, a lot of knowledge. She
doesn't. Teachers often lament summer learning loss: Students know less at
the end of summer than they did at the beginning. But summer learning loss
is only a special case of the problem of fade-out: Human beings have trouble retaining knowledge they rarely use. Of course, some college graduates use
what they've learned and thus hold on to it—engineers and other quantitative
types, for example, retain a lot of math. But when we measure what the average
college graduate recalls years later, the results are discouraging, to say the least.

In 2003, the United States Department of Education gave about 18,000 11
Americans the National Assessment of Adult Literacy. The ignorance it revealed
is mind-numbing. Fewer than a third of college graduates received a composite
score of "proficient"—and about a fifth were at the "basic" or "below basic" level.
You could blame the difficulty of the questions—until you read them. Plenty
of college graduates couldn't make sense of a table explaining how an employee's annual health-insurance costs varied with income and family size, or summarize the work-experience requirements in a job ad, or even use a newspaper
schedule to find when a television program ended. Tests of college graduates'
knowledge of history, civics, and science have had similarly dismal results.

Of course, college students aren't supposed to just download facts; they're 12
supposed to learn how to think in real life. How do they fare on this count?
The most focused study of education's effect on applied reasoning, conducted

by Harvard's David Perkins in the mid-1980s, assessed students' oral responses to questions designed to measure informal reasoning, such as "Would a proposed law in Massachusetts requiring a five-cent deposit on bottles and cans significantly reduce litter?" The benefit of college seemed to be zero: Fourth-year students did no better than first-year students.

Other evidence is equally discouraging. One researcher tested Arizona 13 State University students' ability to "apply statistical and methodological concepts to reasoning about everyday-life events." In the researcher's words:

> Of the several hundred students tested, many of whom had taken more than six years of laboratory science . . . and advanced mathematics through calculus, almost none demonstrated even a semblance of acceptable methodological reasoning.

Those who believe that college is about learning how to learn should 14 expect students who study science to absorb the scientific method, then habitually use it to analyze the world. This scarcely occurs.

College students do hone some kinds of reasoning that are specific to their 15 major. One ambitious study at the University of Michigan tested natural-science, humanities, and psychology and other social-science majors on verbal reasoning, statistical reasoning, and conditional reasoning during the first semester of their first year. When the same students were retested the second semester of their fourth year, each group had sharply improved in precisely one area. Psychology and other social-science majors had become much better at statistical reasoning. Natural-science and humanities majors had become much better at conditional reasoning—analyzing "if . . . then" and "if and only if" problems. In the remaining areas, however, gains after three and a half years of college were modest or nonexistent. The takeaway: Psychology students use statistics, so they improve in statistics; chemistry students rarely encounter statistics, so they don't improve in statistics. If all goes well, students learn what they study and practice.

Actually, that's optimistic. Educational psychologists have discovered that 16 much of our knowledge is "inert." Students who excel on exams frequently fail to apply their knowledge to the real world. Take physics. As the Harvard psychologist Howard Gardner writes,

> Students who receive honor grades in college-level physics courses are frequently unable to solve basic problems and questions encountered in a form slightly different from that on which they have been formally instructed and tested.

The same goes for students of biology, mathematics, statistics, and, I'm 17 embarrassed to say, economics. I try to teach my students to connect lectures to the real world and daily life. My exams are designed to measure comprehension, not memorization. Yet in a good class, four test-takers out of 40 demonstrate true economic understanding.

Economists educational bean counting can come off as annoyingly narrow. 18 Noneconomists—also known as normal human beings—lean holistic: We can't measure education's social benefits solely with test scores or salary premiums. Instead we must ask ourselves what kind of society we want to live in—an educated one or an ignorant one?

Normal human beings make a solid point: We can and should investigate 19 education's broad social implications. When humanists consider my calculations of education's returns, they assume I'm being a typical cynical economist, oblivious to the ideals so many educators hold dear. I am an economist and I am a cynic, but I'm not a typical cynical economist. I'm a cynical idealist. I embrace the ideal of transformative education. I believe wholeheartedly in the life of the mind. What I'm cynical about is people.

I'm cynical about students. The vast majority are philistines. I'm cyn- 20 ical about teachers. The vast majority are uninspiring. I'm cynical about "deciders"—the school officials who control what students study. The vast majority think they've done their job as long as students comply.

Those who search their memory will find noble exceptions to these sad 21 rules. I have known plenty of eager students and passionate educators, and a few wise deciders. Still, my 40 years in the education industry leave no doubt that they are hopelessly outnumbered. Meritorious education survives but does not thrive.

Indeed, today's college students are less willing than those of previous 22 generations to do the bare minimum of showing up for class and temporarily learning whatever's on the test. Fifty years ago, college was a full-time job. The typical student spent 40 hours a week in class or studying. Effort has since collapsed across the board. "Full time" college students now average 27 hours of academic work a week—including just 14 hours spent studying.

What are students doing with their extra free time? Having fun. As 23 Richard Arum and Josipa Roksa frostily remark in their 2011 book, *Academically Adrift,*

> If we presume that students are sleeping eight hours a night, which is a generous assumption given their tardiness and at times disheveled appearance in early morning classes, that leaves 85 hours a week for other activities.

Arum and Roksa cite a study finding that students at one typical college spent 24 13 hours a week studying, 12 hours "socializing with friends," 11 hours "using computers for fun," eight hours working for pay, six hours watching TV, six hours exercising, five hours on "hobbies," and three hours on "other forms of entertainment." Grade inflation completes the idyllic package by shielding students from negative feedback. The average GPA is now 3.2.

What does this mean for the individual student? Would I advise an aca- 25 demically well-prepared 18-year-old to skip college because she won't learn much of value? Absolutely not. Studying irrelevancies for the next four years will impress future employers and raise her income potential. If she tried to leap straight into her first white-collar job, insisting, "I have the right stuff to graduate, I just choose not to," employers wouldn't believe her. To unilaterally curtail your education is to relegate yourself to a lower-quality pool of workers. For the individual, college pays.

This does not mean, however, that higher education paves the way to 26 general prosperity or social justice. When we look at countries around the world, a year of education appears to raise an individual's income by 8 to 11 percent. By contrast, increasing education across a country's population by an average of one year per person raises the national income by only 1 to 3 percent. In other words, education enriches individuals much more than it enriches nations.

How is this possible? Credential inflation: As the average level of education 27 rises, you need more education to convince employers you're worthy of any specific job. One research team found that from the early 1970s through the mid-1990s, the average education level within 500 occupational categories rose by 1.2 years. But most of the jobs didn't change much over that span—there's no reason, except credential inflation, why people should have needed more education to do them in 1995 than in 1975. What's more, *all* American workers' education rose by 1.5 years in that same span—which is to say that a great majority of the extra education workers received was deployed not to get *better* jobs, but to get jobs that had recently been held by people with less education.

As credentials proliferate, so do failed efforts to acquire them. Students can 28 and do pay tuition, kill a year, and flunk their finals. Any respectable verdict on the value of education must account for these academic bankruptcies. Failure rates are high, particularly for students with low high school grades and test scores; all told, about 60 percent of full-time college students fail to finish in four years. Simply put, the push for broader college education has steered too many students who aren't cut out for academic success onto the college track.

The college-for-all mentality has fostered neglect of a realistic substitute: 29 vocational education. It takes many guises—classroom training, apprenticeships and other types of on-the-job training, and straight-up work experience—but they have much in common. All vocational education teaches specific job skills, and all vocational education revolves around learning by doing, not learning by listening. Research, though a bit sparse, suggests that vocational education raises pay, reduces unemployment, and increases the rate of high school completion.

> "Ignorance of the future is no reason to prepare students for occupations they almost surely won't have."

Defenders of traditional education often appeal to the obscurity of the 30 future. What's the point of prepping students for the economy of 2018, when they'll be employed in the economy of 2025 or 2050? But ignorance of the future is no reason to prepare students for occupations they almost surely won't have—and if we know anything about the future of work, we know that the demand for authors, historians, political scientists, physicists, and mathematicians will stay low. It's tempting to say that students on the college track can always turn to vocational education as a Plan B, but this ignores the disturbing possibility that after they crash, they'll be too embittered to go back and learn a trade. The vast American underclass shows that this disturbing possibility is already our reality.

Education is so integral to modern life that we take it for granted. Young 31
people have to leap through interminable academic hoops to secure their place
in the adult world. My thesis, in a single sentence: Civilized societies revolve
around education now, but there is a better—indeed, more civilized—way. If
everyone had a college degree, the result would be not great jobs for all, but
runaway credential inflation. Trying to spread success with education spreads
education but not success.

⊙ AT ISSUE: SOURCES FOR STRUCTURING AN ARGUMENT

1. Why does Caplan begin his essay with a summary of his own educational and employment history? Is this introductory strategy an appeal to *logos*, *ethos*, or *pathos*? (See pages 19–21 for an explanation of these terms.)

2. Caplan identifies a number of shortcomings of today's college students—and of our higher education system in general. What problems does he identify? Where does he seem to place the blame for these problems? Does he offer solutions? If so, where?

3. Where does Caplan cite research studies? How does he use these studies to support his conclusions about the value of a college education?

4. Where does Caplan use personal experience as evidence in support of his points? Do you find this kind of evidence convincing here? Why or why not?

5. Do you think Caplan's use of the first-person pronoun *I* throughout strengthens or weakens his argument? Explain you conclusion.

6. In paragraph 7, Caplan says, "The labor market doesn't pay you for the useless subjects you master; it pays you for the preexisting traits you signal by mastering them." What does he mean? Do you think he is correct about the importance of what he calls "signaling" (para. 8)? Why or why not?

7. In paragraphs 4 and 10, Caplan summarizes arguments against his position. How does he refute these counterarguments? Does he include other arguments against his position? If so, where?

8. In paragraphs 23–24, Caplan says, "For the individual, college pays. This does not mean, however, that higher education paves the way to general prosperity or social justice." What point is he making here about the value of a college education?

9. What is "credential inflation" (29)? How is it related to what Caplan calls his "thesis, in a single sentence"? Do you think this "thesis" is actually the essay's main idea? Explain.

This economic letter was originally posted by the Federal Reserve Bank of San Francisco at www.frbsf.org, where it appeared on May 5, 2014.

IS IT STILL WORTH GOING TO COLLEGE?

MARY C. DALY AND LEILA BENGALI

Media accounts documenting the rising cost of a college education and rela- 1 tively bleak job prospects for new college graduates have raised questions about whether a four-year college degree is still the right path for the average American. In this *Economic Letter*, we examine whether going to college remains a worthwhile investment. Using U.S. survey data, we compare annual labor earnings of college graduates with those of individuals with only a high school diploma. The data show college graduates outearn their high school counterparts as much as in past decades. Comparing the earnings benefits of college with the costs of attending a four-year program, we find that college is still worth it. This means that, for the average student, tuition costs for the majority of college education opportunities in the United States can be recouped by age 40, after which college graduates continue to earn a return on their investment in the form of higher lifetime wages.

Earnings Outcomes by Educational Attainment

A common way to track the value of going to college is to estimate a col- 2 lege earnings premium, which is the amount college graduates earn relative to high school graduates. We measure earnings for each year as the annual labor income for the prior year, adjusted for inflation using the consumer price index (CPI-U), reported in 2011 dollars. The earnings premium refers to the difference between average annual labor income for high school and college graduates. We use data on household heads and partners from the Panel Study of Income Dynamics (PSID). The PSID is a longitudinal study that follows individuals living in the United States over a long time span. The survey began in 1968 and now has more than 40 years of data including educational attainment and labor market income. To focus on the value of a college degree relative to less education, we exclude people with more than a four-year degree.

Figure 1 shows the earnings premium relative to high school graduates 3 for individuals with a four-year college degree and for those with some college but no four-year degree. The payoff from a degree is apparent. Although the premium has fluctuated over time, at its lowest in 1980 it was about $15,750, meaning that individuals with a four-year college degree earned about 43 percent more on average than those with only a high school degree. In 2011, the latest data available in our sample, college graduates earned on average about $20,050 (61 percent) more per year than high school graduates. Over the entire sample period the college earnings premium has averaged about $20,300 (57 percent) per year. The premium is much smaller, although not zero, for workers with some college but no four year degree.

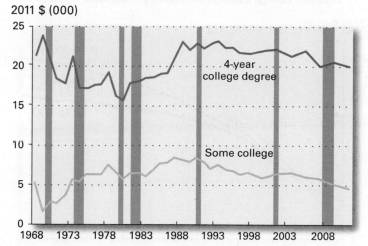

Figure 1: Earnings Premium over High School Education

Data from: PSID and authors' calculations. Premium defined as difference in mean annual labor income. Blue bars denote National Bureau of Economic Research recession dates.

A potential shortcoming of the results in Figure 1 is that they combine the 4 earnings outcomes for all college graduates, regardless of when they earned a degree. This can be misleading if the value from a college education has varied across groups from different graduation decades, called "cohorts." To examine whether the college earnings premium has changed from one generation to the next, we take advantage of the fact that the PSID follows people over a long period of time, which allows us to track college graduation dates and subsequent earnings.

Using these data we compute the college earnings premium for three col- 5 lege graduate cohorts, namely those graduating in the 1950s–60s, the 1970s–80s, and the 1990s–2000s. The premium measures the difference between the average annual earnings of college graduates and high school graduates over their work lives. To account for the fact that high school graduates gain work experience during the four years they are not in college, we compare earnings of college graduates in each year since graduation to earnings of high school graduates in years since graduation plus four. We also adjust the estimates for any large annual fluctuations by using a three-year centered moving average, which plots a specific year as the average of earnings from that year, the year before, and the year after.

Figure 2 shows that the college earnings premium has risen consistently 6 across cohorts. Focusing on the most recent college graduates (1990s–2000s) there is little evidence that the value of a college degree has declined over time, and it has even risen somewhat for graduates five to ten years out of school.

Figure 2: College Earnings Premium by Graduation Decades

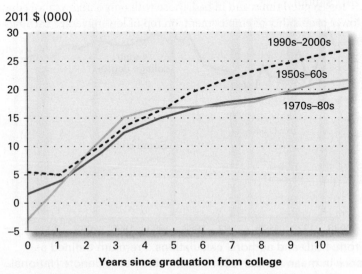

Data from: PSID and authors' calculations. Premium defined as difference in mean annual labor income of college graduates in each year since graduation and earnings of high school graduates in years since graduation plus four. Values are three-year centered moving averages of annual premiums.

The figure also shows that the gap in earnings between college and high 7 school graduates rises over the course of a worker's life. Comparing the earnings gap upon graduation with the earnings gap 10 years out of school illustrates this. For the 1990s–2000s cohort the initial gap was about $5,400, and in 10 years this gap had risen to about $26,800. Other analysis confirms that college graduates start with higher annual earnings, indicated by an initial earnings gap, and experience more rapid growth in earnings than members of their age cohort with only a high school degree. This evidence tells us that the value of a college education rises over a worker's life.

Of course, some of the variation in earnings between those with and 8 without a college degree could reflect other differences. Still, these simple estimates are consistent with a large and rigorous literature documenting the substantial premium earned by college graduates (Barrow and Rouse 2005, Card 2001, Goldin and Katz 2008, and Cunha, Karahan, and Soares 2011). The main message from these and similar calculations is that on average the value of college is high and not declining over time.

Finally, it is worth noting that the benefits of college over high school also 9 depend on employment, where college graduates also have an advantage. High school graduates consistently face unemployment rates about twice as high as those for college graduates, according to Bureau of Labor Statistics data. When the labor market takes a turn for the worse, as during recessions, workers with lower levels of education are especially hard-hit (Hoynes, Miller, and Schaller 2012). Thus, in good times and in bad, those with only a high school education face a lower probability of employment, on top of lower average earnings once employed.

The Cost of College

Although the value of college is apparent, deciding whether it is worthwhile means weighing the value against the costs of attending. Indeed, much of the debate about the value of college stems not from the lack of demonstrated benefit but from the overwhelming cost. A simple way to measure the costs against the benefits is to find the breakeven amount of annual tuition that would make the average student indifferent between going to college versus going directly to the workforce after high school. 10

> "Although the value of college is apparent, deciding whether it is worthwhile means weighing the value against the costs of attending."

To simplify the analysis, we assume that college lasts four years, students 11 enter college directly from high school, annual tuition is the same all four years, and attendees have no earnings while in school. To focus on more recent experiences yet still have enough data to measure earnings since graduation, we use the last two decades of graduates (1990s and 2000s) and again smooth our estimates by using three-year centered moving averages.

We calculate the cost of college as four years of tuition plus the earnings 12 missed from choosing not to enter the workforce. To estimate what students would have received had they worked, we use the average annual earnings of a high school graduate zero, one, two, and three years since graduation.

To determine the benefit of going to college, we use the difference 13 between the average annual earnings of a college graduate with zero, one, two, three, and so on, years of experience and the average annual earnings of a high school graduate with four, five, six, seven, and so on years of experience. Because the costs of college are paid today but the benefits accrue over many future years when a dollar earned will be worth less, we discount future earnings by 6.67 percent, which is the average rate on an AAA bond from 1990 to 2011.

With these pieces in place, we can calculate the breakeven amount of tui- 14 tion for the average college graduate for any number of years; allowing more time to regain the costs will increase our calculated tuition ceiling.

If we assume that accumulated earnings between college graduates 15 and nongraduates will equalize 20 years after graduating from high school (at age 38), the resulting estimate for breakeven annual tuition would be about $21,200. This amount may seem low compared to the astronomical costs for a year at some prestigious institutions; however, about 90 percent of students at public four-year colleges and about 20 percent of students at private nonprofit four-year colleges faced lower annual inflation-adjusted published tuition and fees in 2013–14 (College Board 2013). Although some colleges cost more, there is no definitive evidence that they produce far superior results for all students (Dale and Krueger 2011).

Table 1 shows more examples of maximum tuitions and the correspond- 16 ing percent of students who pay less for different combinations of breakeven years and discount rates. Note that the tuition estimates are those that make the costs and benefits of college equal. So, tuition amounts lower than our estimates make going to college strictly better in terms of earnings than not going to college.

Table 1: Maximum Tuitions by Breakeven Age and Discount Rates

	Breakeven age	
	33 (15 yrs after HS)	38 (20 yrs after HS)
Accumulated earnings with constant annual premium	$880,134	$830,816
Discount rate	Maximum tuition (% students paying less)	
5%	$14,385 (53–62%)	$29,111 (82–85%)
6.67%*	$9,869 (37–53%)	$21,217 (69–73%)
9%	$4,712 (0–6%)	$12,653 (53–62%)

*Average AAA bond rate 1990–2011 (rounded; Moody's).

Data from: PSID, College Board, and authors' calculations. Premia held constant 15 or 20 years after high school (HS) graduation. Percent range gives lower and upper bounds of the percent of full-time undergraduates at four-year institutions who faced lower annual inflation-adjusted published tuition and fees in 2013–14.

Although other individual factors might affect the net value of a col- 17 lege education, earning a degree clearly remains a good investment for most young people. Moreover, once that investment is paid off, the extra income from the college earnings premium continues as a net gain to workers with a college degree. If we conservatively assume that the annual premium stays around $28,650, which is the premium 20 years after high school graduation for graduates in the 1990s–2000s, and accrues until the Social Security normal retirement age of 67, the college graduate would have made about

$830,800 more than the high school graduate. These extra earnings can be spent, saved, or reinvested to pay for the college tuition of the graduate's children.

Conclusion

Although there are stories of people who skipped college and achieved finan- 18
cial success, for most Americans the path to higher future earnings involves a four-year college degree. We show that the value of a college degree remains high, and the average college graduate can recover the costs of attending in less than 20 years. Once the investment is paid for, it continues to pay dividends through the rest of the worker's life, leaving college graduates with substantially higher lifetime earnings than their peers with a high school degree. These findings suggest that redoubling the efforts to make college more accessible would be time and money well spent.

References

Barrow, L., and Rouse, C. E. (2005). "Does college still pay?" *The Economist's Voice* 2(4), pp. 1–8.

Card, D. (2001). "Estimating the return to schooling: progress on some persistent econometric problems." *Econometrica* 69(5), pp. 1127–1160.

College Board. (2013). "Trends in College Pricing 2013."

Cunha, F., Karahan, F., and Soares, I. (2011). "Returns to Skills and the College Premium." *Journal of Money, Credit, and Banking* 43(5), pp. 39–86.

Dale, S., and Krueger, A. (2011). "Estimating the Return to College Selectivity over the Career Using Administrative Earnings Data." *NBER Working Paper* 17159.

Goldin, C., and Katz, L. (2008). *The Race between Education and Technology.* Cambridge and London: The Belknap Press of Harvard University Press.

Hoynes, H., Miller, D., and Schaller, J. (2012). "Who Suffers during Recessions?" *Journal of Economic Perspectives* 26(3), pp. 27–48.

⊖ AT ISSUE: SOURCES FOR STRUCTURING AN ARGUMENT

1. Why does the title of this essay include the word *still*? What does *still* imply in this context?

2. This essay is an "economic letter" from the Federal Reserve Bank of San Francisco, and its language is more technical, and more math- and business-oriented, than that of the other readings in this chapter. In addition, this reading selection *looks* somewhat different from the others. What specific format features set this reading apart from others in the chapter?

3. What kind of supporting evidence do the writers use? Do you think they should have included any other kinds of support—for example, expert opinion? Why or why not?

4. In paragraph 10, the writers make a distinction between the "value of college" and the question of whether a college education is "worthwhile." Explain the distinction they make here.

5. For the most part, this report appeals to *logos* by presenting factual information. Does it also include appeals to *pathos* or *ethos*? If so, where? If not, should it have included these appeals? (See pp. 14–21 for an explanation of these terms.)

TEMPLATE FOR STRUCTURING AN ARGUMENT

Write a one-paragraph argument in which you take a position on the topic of whether a college education is a good investment. Follow the template below, filling in the lines to create your argument.

Whether or not a college education is worth the money is a controversial topic. Some people believe that _____

_____

_____. Others challenge this position, claiming that

_____.

However, _____. Although both

sides of this issue have merit, it seems clear that a college education [is/is not] a worthwhile investment

because _____

_____.

⊙ EXERCISE 1.2 USING INTERVIEW NOTES

Interview two classmates on the topic of whether a college education is a worthwhile investment. Revise the one-paragraph argument that you drafted above so that it includes your classmates' views on the issue.

⊙ EXERCISE 1.3 WRITING AN ESSAY

Write an essay on the topic "Is a College Education Worth the Money?" Cite one or two of the readings on pages 33–48, and be sure to document your sources and to include a works-cited page. (See Chapter 10 for information on documenting sources.)

⊙ EXERCISE 1.4 REVISING YOUR ESSAY

Review the four-point checklist on page 27, and apply each question to your essay. Does your essay include all four elements of an argumentative essay? Add any missing elements. Then, label your essay's thesis statement, evidence, refutation of opposing arguments, and concluding statement.

⊙ EXERCISE 1.5 WRITING A RESPONSE

The following blog post promotes the University of the People, an accredited online university. To whom does this post seem to be addressed? Do you find it convincing? Does it include all four elements of an effective argument? Incorporating what you have learned about the structure and content of an effective argument, write a one-paragraph response to the blog post.

This essay appeared on Businessweek.com in March 2011.

DOES COLLEGE STILL MATTER IN 2018?

AYELET W., UNIVERSITY OF THE PEOPLE

The world seems to be changing faster than ever, doesn't it?   1

So understandably, people everywhere are questioning whether the edu- 2
cational trajectories of our parents' generation are still relevant for today's
fast-moving job market and global society.

We like this type of debate and encourage you to ask questions instead of 3
taking things for granted, so we thought we'd walk our talk and break down
one of the biggest questions facing today's young adults: Does college still matter in 2018?

1) The Financial Investment

College can be expensive. In some cases, crazy expensive. In 2016, Business 4
Insider reported that the University of Cambridge is developing a PhD business program, that's set to cost $332,000.

Yes, that's a PhD program, but bachelor's degrees aren't cheap either. Busi- 5
ness Insider reported that the bachelor's degree of music at Bard College might
be one of the most expensive BAs around, costing $253,520.

If these were the only options, college might be out of reach for many stu- 6
dents, but with degrees available in other top quality universities for as little as
$4,060 for the entire degree, it's something that can be in reach for all. Still, the
question remains—does it still matter in 2018?

2) Finding a Job and Remaining Employed

Let's face it, a college degree holds a higher prestige than a high school diploma, 7
and many people seem to appreciate those who've made the effort and graduated.

According to a 2016 study by Georgetown University, the majority of 8
the jobs still go to bachelor's degree graduates. Reporting on the study, CNN
Money noted that "of the 11.6 million jobs created after the Great Recession,
8.4 million went to those with at least a bachelor's degree." This is a substantial difference in proportional terms: Only 36 percent of Americans earned a
bachelor's degree or higher, compared to 30 percent of Americans holding an
associate degree and 34 percent holding a high school diploma or less.

If you still have doubts on whether a college degree is worth the invest- 9
ment, check out this 2016 report from the United States Bureau of Labor
Statistics about 2015's employment rates by educational attainment:

While the median unemployment rate in the country was 4.3 percent of 10
the population, those with a bachelor's degree were only 2.8 percent of the
unemployed population, and those with only a high school diploma were 5.4
percent of the unemployed population.

In other words, those who graduated from high school but did not go on 11 to college were twice as likely to become unemployed than those with a college degree.

And according to Forbes, the demands for higher education is steadily 12 increasing in the job market.

"86 percent of companies planned to hire recent MBA graduates in 2017 13 compared with 79 percent in 2016, according to the GMAC report . . . 41 percent of employers are now hiring college grads for jobs that high school grads formerly held. . . . Companies are increasingly hiring candidates with master's degrees for jobs that previously required bachelor's degrees," reported Forbes.

3) Meeting People & Networking

Today's fellow students will become tomorrow's colleagues, so making friends 14 in college is an easy way to build your professional network early on. You'll also be able to connect with professors, who might then be able to connect you with their connections in the industry, which could make it easier to find a great first professional job.

4) Developing Skills You Can Use in the Workplace

One of the main arguments of those who are not in favor of going to college is 15 that it doesn't train you to work in the "real world," but according to Entrepreneur, "academic assignments develop skills that are in high demand among top employers," including general communication skills, writing skills, research skills, and collaboration skills.

In the 2016 University of the People Students Satisfaction Survey, many of 16 our students shared that they already use the knowledge and skills they gained in courses in their workplaces.

5) Starting Your Own Business

To be honest, there's more information online now than ever before, not to mention a wealth of books on practically every topic. If you're the kind of person who can study for years on end without any external motivation—then you can become an entrepreneur with no extra costs.

"These success stories 17 happen to the minority of the population—and often seem a lot easier said than done."

However, this is more relevant if you're looking to start your own business 18 rather than getting a traditional job. We've all heard about successful entrepreneurs who never graduated from college—and about teenagers who built successful businesses on YouTube or Instagram from their childhood bedroom before they even graduated from high school.

But keep in mind that these success stories happen to the minority of the 19 population—and often seem a lot easier said than done.

Not to mention that according to Forbes, if you want to start your own busi- 20 ness, you need more than a first degree to become a successful entrepreneur—which is why it might be beneficial to get a masters, too. "Graduate schools actually have a rich tradition of entrepreneurship instruction. Indeed, MBAs have launched nearly a quarter of 'unicorn' startups, defined as those worth $1 billion or more," Forbes reported.

6) Your Potential Salary

If you look at the United States Bureau of Labor Statistics report we men- 21 tioned in the latter, you'll see that a degree significantly impacts your financial prosperity.

The median weekly salary in the general U.S. population is $860. How- 22 ever, those who hold a bachelor's degree can earn up to $1,137 and those with only a high school degree earn a smaller income at $678.

That's $54,576 a year if you have a bachelor's degree, versus $32,544 if you 23 only have a high school diploma.

7) The Return on Your Financial (and Time) Investment When You Get a University Degree

Once you graduate, and assuming you work in the U.S., you're expected to 24 earn $54,576 a year, versus $32,544 if you only have a high school diploma. That's $22,032 more a year, or $110,160 more in the next 5 years, and that's not counting promotions and salary increases, which will be more easily accessible as a university graduate.

As a side note, if you attend an online affordable university, like UoPeople, 25 you can choose your own class hours and study at your own pace, which makes it easier to combine a full-time job and earn more than the average student. Alternatively, because the cost of the degree is so low, you might be able to live off a part-time job and live a more balanced life than the average college student.

● EXERCISE 1.6 CONSIDERING VISUAL ARGUMENTS

Study the image that opens this chapter. What argument about the value of a college education could it support? Could the image itself be considered an argument? Explain your conclusion.

Reading and Responding to Arguments

2

Thinking and Reading Critically

Does Recycling Really Accomplish Anything?

Recycling is woven into our lives; at home, in school, in public spaces, we're used to seeing those separate bins for waste disposal. Given that Americans produce about 254 million tons of trash each year, many probably take the advantages of this practice as a given. The United States now has a recycling rate of about 34 percent, which reduces both the garbage in overflowing landfills and the amount of carbon dioxide released into the atmosphere. There are less obvious benefits, too. In addition to helping the environment, recycling helps create jobs, even as it lowers the amount of energy required to create new products.

But what about the downsides? Critics point out that it is costly, as recycling programs are often prohibitively expensive for small, local communities. Moreover, recycling may be giving us a false sense of "sustainability." In fact, the process still uses a lot of energy, and its overall benefits to the environment are limited because many large industries still do not recycle. In addition, recycling some waste products (such as electronics) is inefficient or even dangerous, and some products made of recycled materials are low quality.

In this chapter and in the chapter that follows, you will be asked to read essays and study images that shed light on the advantages and limitations of recycling. In the process, you will learn critical-thinking and active reading strategies that will help you learn to examine and interpret texts and images.

Now that you understand the structure of an argumentative essay, you can turn your attention to reading arguments more closely. The arguments you encounter may be the subject of class discussion, or they may be source material for the essays you write. In any case, you will need to know how to get the most out of reading them.

Thinking Critically

When you **think critically**, you do not simply accept ideas at face value. Instead, you question the ideas you come across, analyzing them in order to understand them better. You also challenge their underlying assumptions and form your own judgments about them. Throughout this book, discussions and readings encourage you to think critically. The box below shows you where in this text to find material that will help you develop your critical-thinking skills.

USING CRITICAL-THINKING SKILLS

Reading (see Chapter 2): When you read a text, you use critical-thinking skills to help you understand what the text says and what it suggests. You ask questions and look for answers, challenging the ideas you read and probing for information. *Previewing, highlighting,* and *annotating* are active reading strategies that require you to use critical-thinking skills.

Analyzing Visual Texts (see Chapter 3): When you examine an image, you use critical-thinking skills to help you understand what you are seeing, using previewing, highlighting, and annotating to help you analyze the image and interpret its persuasive message.

Writing a Rhetorical Analysis (see Chapter 4): When you write a rhetorical analysis, you use critical-thinking skills to analyze the individual elements of a text and to help you understand how the writer uses various appeals and rhetorical strategies to influence readers. Critical-thinking skills can also help you to understand the argument's context. Finally, you use critical-thinking skills to evaluate the overall effectiveness of the argument.

Analyzing an Argument's Logic (see Chapter 5): When you analyze an argument's logic, you use critical-thinking skills to help you understand the relationships among ideas and the form the argument takes as well as to determine whether its conclusions are both valid and true. You also use critical-thinking skills to identify any **logical fallacies** that may undermine the argument.

Writing an Essay (see Chapter 7): When you plan an essay, you use critical-thinking skills to probe a topic, to consider what you already know and what you need to find out, to identify your essay's main idea, and to decide how to support it—that is, which ideas to include and how to arrange them. As you draft and revise, you use critical-thinking skills to evaluate your supporting evidence, to make sure your arguments are reasonable and fair, and to decide whether ideas are arranged effectively within paragraphs and in the essay as a whole. *Freewriting, brainstorming, clustering,* and *outlining* are activities that require you to use critical-thinking skills.

Refuting Opposing Arguments (see Chapter 7): When you refute opposing arguments, you use critical-thinking skills to identify and evaluate arguments against your position—and to challenge or possibly argue against them.

Evaluating Sources (see Chapter 8): When you evaluate sources, you use critical-thinking skills to assess your sources in terms of their *accuracy, credibility, objectivity,* and *comprehensiveness* and to determine whether a source is trustworthy and appropriate for your purpose and audience.

Summarizing (see Chapter 9): When you summarize a passage, you use critical-thinking skills to identify the writer's main idea.

Paraphrasing (see Chapter 9): When you paraphrase a passage, you use critical-thinking skills to identify the writer's main idea, the most important supporting details and examples, and the ways in which key ideas are related.

Synthesizing (see Chapter 9): When you synthesize material, you use critical-thinking skills to analyze sources and integrate them with your own ideas.

Reading Critically

When you read an argument, you should approach it with a critical eye. Contrary to what you may think, **reading critically** does not mean arguing with every idea you encounter. What it does mean is commenting on, questioning, and evaluating these ideas.

As a critical reader, you do not simply accept that what you are reading is true. Instead, you assess the accuracy of the facts in your sources, and you consider whether opinions are convincingly supported by evidence. You try to judge the appropriateness and reliability of a writer's sources, and you evaluate the scope and depth of the evidence and the relevance of that evidence to the topic. You also consider opposing arguments carefully, weighing them against the arguments developed in your sources. Finally, you watch out for possible **bias** in your sources—and you work hard to keep your own biases in check.

GUIDELINES FOR READING CRITICALLY

As a critical reader, you need to read carefully, keeping the following guidelines in mind:

- Assess the accuracy of a source's information, as well as the authors and publishers of the source itself.

- Be sure opinions are supported convincingly.

- Evaluate the supporting evidence.

- Consider opposing arguments.

- Be on the lookout for bias—in your sources and in yourself.

Becoming an Active Reader

Reading critically means being an active rather than a passive reader. Being an **active reader** means participating in the reading process by taking the time to preview a source and then to read it carefully, highlighting and annotating it. This process will prepare you to discuss the source with others and to respond in writing to what you have read.

Previewing

When you approach an argument for the first time, you **preview** it, skimming the text to help you form a general impression of the writer's position on the issue, the argument's key supporting points, and the context for the writer's remarks.

Begin by looking at the title, the first paragraph (which often contains a thesis statement or overview), and the last paragraph (which often includes a concluding statement or a summary of the writer's key points). Also look at the topic sentences of the essay's body paragraphs. In addition, note any headings, words set in boldface or italic type, and bulleted or numbered lists that appear in the body of the argument. If the argument includes visuals—charts, tables, graphs, photos, and so on—look at them as well. Finally, if an argument includes a headnote or background on the author or on the text, be sure to skim this material. It can help you to understand the context in which the author is writing.

When you have finished previewing the argument, you should have a good general sense of what the writer wants to communicate.

Close Reading

When you finish previewing the argument, you are ready to read through it more carefully. As you read, look for words and phrases that help to shape the structure of the argument and signal the arrangement of the writer's ideas. These words and phrases will help you to understand the flow of ideas as well as the content and emphasis of the argument.

COMPREHENSION CLUES

- Repeated words and phrases

- Phrases that signal emphasis (the *primary* reason, the *most important* problem)

- Words and phrases that signal addition (*also, in addition, furthermore*)

- Words and phrases that signal time sequence (*first, after that, next, then, finally*)

- Words and phrases that identify causes and effects (*because, as a result, for this reason*)

- Words and phrases that introduce examples (*for example, for instance*)

- Words and phrases that signal comparison (*likewise, similarly, in the same way*)

- Words and phrases that signal contrast (*although, in contrast, on the other hand*)

- Words and phrases that signal contradiction (*however, on the contrary*)

- Words and phrases that signal a move from general to specific (*in fact, specifically, in other words*)

- Words and phrases that introduce summaries or conclusions (*all things considered, to sum up, in conclusion*)

➲ EXERCISE 2.1 PREVIEWING AN ESSAY

"The Reign of Recycling" is a *New York Times* opinion essay by John Tierney. In this essay, which begins on the following page, Tierney argues that although recycling remains popular, it may actually not be worth the time and trouble it requires.

In preparation for class discussion and other activities that will be assigned later in this chapter, preview the essay. Then, read it carefully, and answer the questions that follow it.

This article appeared in the *New York Times* on October 3, 2015.

THE REIGN OF RECYCLING

JOHN TIERNEY

If you live in the United States, you probably do some form of recycling. It's 1 likely that you separate paper from plastic and glass and metal. You rinse the bottles and cans, and you might put food scraps in a container destined for a composting facility. As you sort everything into the right bins, you probably assume that recycling is helping your community and protecting the environment. But is it? Are you in fact wasting your time?

In 1996, I wrote a long article for the *New York Times Magazine* argu- 2 ing that the recycling process as we carried it out was wasteful. I presented plenty of evidence that recycling was costly and ineffectual, but its defenders said that it was unfair to rush to judgment. Noting that the modern recycling movement had really just begun just a few years earlier, they predicted it would flourish as the industry matured and the public learned how to recycle properly.

So, what's happened since then? While it's true that the recycling message 3 has reached more people than ever, when it comes to the bottom line, both economically and environmentally, not much has changed at all.

Despite decades of exhortations and mandates, it's still typically more 4 expensive for municipalities to recycle household waste than to send it to a landfill. Prices for recyclable materials have plummeted because of lower oil prices and reduced demand for them overseas. The slump has forced some recycling companies to shut plants and cancel plans for new technologies. The mood is so gloomy that one industry veteran tried to cheer up her colleagues this summer with an article in a trade journal titled, "Recycling Is Not Dead!"

While politicians set higher and higher goals, the national rate of recy- 5 cling has stagnated in recent years. Yes, it's popular in affluent neighborhoods like Park Slope in Brooklyn and in cities like San Francisco, but residents of the Bronx and Houston don't have the same fervor for sorting garbage in their spare time.

The future for recycling looks even worse. As cities move beyond recycling 6 paper and metals, and into glass, food scraps, and assorted plastics, the costs rise sharply while the environmental benefits decline and sometimes vanish. "If you believe recycling is good for the planet and that we need to do more of it, then there's a crisis to confront," says David P. Steiner, the chief executive officer of Waste Management, the largest recycler of household trash in the

United States. "Trying to turn garbage into gold costs a lot more than expected. We need to ask ourselves: What is the goal here?"

Recycling has been relentlessly promoted as a goal in and of itself: an unalloyed public good and private virtue that is indoctrinated in students from kindergarten through college. As a result, otherwise well-informed and educated people have no idea of the relative costs and benefits.

They probably don't know, for instance, that to reduce carbon emissions, you'll accomplish a lot more by sorting paper and aluminum cans than by worrying about yogurt containers and half-eaten slices of pizza. Most people also assume that recycling plastic bottles must be doing lots for the planet. They've been encouraged by the Environmental Protection Agency, which assures the public that recycling plastic results in less carbon being released into the atmosphere.

But how much difference does it make? Here's some perspective: To offset the greenhouse impact of one passenger's round-trip flight between New York and London, you'd have to recycle roughly 40,000 plastic bottles, assuming you fly coach. If you sit in business- or first-class, where each passenger takes up more space, it could be more like 100,000.

Even those statistics might be misleading. New York and other cities instruct people to rinse the bottles before putting them in the recycling bin, but the E.P.A.'s life-cycle calculation doesn't take that water into account. That single omission can make a big difference, according to Chris Goodall, the author of "How to Live a Low-Carbon Life." Mr. Goodall calculates that if you wash plastic in water that was heated by coal-derived, electricity, then the net effect of your recycling could be *more* carbon in the atmosphere.

To many public officials, recycling is a question of morality, not cost-benefit analysis. Mayor Bill de Blasio of New York declared that by 2030 the city would no longer send any garbage to landfills. "This is the way of the future if we're going to save our earth," he explained, while announcing that New York would join San Francisco, Seattle, and other cities in moving toward a "zero waste" policy, which would require an unprecedented level of recycling.

The national rate of recycling rose during the 1990s to 25 percent, meeting the goal set by an E.P.A. official, J. Winston Porter. He advised state officials that no more than about 35 percent of the nation's trash was worth recycling, but some ignored him and set goals of 50 percent and higher. Most of those goals were never met and the national rate has been stuck around 34 percent in recent years.

"It makes sense to recycle commercial cardboard and some paper, as well as selected metals and plastics," he says, "But other materials rarely make sense, including food, waste and other compostables. The zero-waste goal makes no sense at all—it's very expensive with almost no real environmental benefit."

One of the original goals of the recycling movement was to avert a sup- 14
posed crisis because there was no room left in the nation's landfills. But that
media inspired fear was never realistic in a country with so much open space.
In reporting the 1996 article I found that all the trash generated by Americans
for the next 1,000 years would fit on one-tenth of 1 percent of the land available for grazing. And that tiny amount of land wouldn't be lost forever, because
landfills are typically covered with grass and converted to parkland, like the
Freshkills Park being created on Staten Island. The United States Open tennis
tournament is played on the site of an old landfill—and one that never had the
linings and other environmental safeguards required today.

Though most cities shun landfills, they have been welcomed in rural com- 15
munities that reap large economic benefits (and have plenty of greenery to
buffer residents from the sights and smells). Consequently, the great landfill
shortage has not arrived, and neither have the shortages of raw materials that
were supposed to make recycling profitable.

With the economic rationale gone, advocates for recycling have switched 16
to environmental arguments. Researchers have calculated that there are indeed
such benefits to recycling, but not in the way that many people imagine.

Most of these benefits do not come from reducing the need for landfills 17
and incinerators. A modern well-lined landfill in a rural area can have relatively little environmental impact. Decomposing garbage releases methane,
a potent greenhouse gas, but landfill operators have started capturing it and
using it to generate electricity. Modern incinerators, while politically unpopular in the United States, release so few pollutants that they've been widely
accepted in the eco-conscious countries of Northern Europe and Japan for
generating clean energy.

Moreover, recycling operations have their own environmental costs, like 18
extra trucks on the road and pollution from recycling operations. Composting
facilities around the country have inspired complaints about nauseating odors,
swarming rats, and defecating seagulls. After New York City started sending
food waste to be composted in Delaware, the unhappy neighbors of the composting plant successfully campaigned to shut it down last year.

The environmental benefits of recycling come chiefly from reducing the 19
need to manufacture new products—less mining, drilling, and logging. But
that's not so appealing to the workers in those industries and to the communities that have accepted the environmental trade-offs that come with those jobs.

Nearly everyone, though, approves of one potential benefit of recycling: 20
reduced emissions of greenhouse gases. Its advocates often cite an estimate by
the E.P.A. that recycling municipal solid waste in the United States saves the
equivalent of 186 million metric tons of carbon dioxide, comparable to removing the emissions of 39 million cars.

According to the E.P.A.'s estimates, virtually all the greenhouse benefits— 21
more than 90 percent—come from just a few materials: paper, cardboard, and
metals like the aluminum in soda cans. That's because recycling one ton of
metal or paper saves about three tons of carbon dioxide, a much bigger payoff

than the other materials analyzed by the E.P.A. Recycling one ton of plastic saves only slightly more than one ton of carbon dioxide. A ton of food saves a little less than a ton. For glass, you have to recycle three tons in order to get about one ton of greenhouse benefits. Worst of all is yard waste: it takes 20 tons of it to save a single ton of carbon dioxide.

Once you exclude paper products and metals, the total annual savings in 22 the United States from recycling everything else in municipal trash—plastics, glass, food, yard trimmings, textiles, rubber, leather—is only two-tenths of 1 percent of America's carbon footprint.

As a business, recycling is on the wrong side of two long-term global economic trends. For centuries, the real cost of labor has been increasing while the real cost of raw materials has been declining. That's why we can afford to buy so much more stuff than our ancestors could. As a labor-intensive activity, recycling is an increasingly expensive way to produce materials that are less and less valuable.

> "As a business, recycling is on the wrong side of two long-term global economic trends."

Recyclers have tried to improve the economics by automating the sorting 24 process, but they've been frustrated by politicians eager to increase recycling rates by adding new materials of little value. The more types of trash that are recycled, the more difficult it becomes to sort the valuable from the worthless.

In New York City, the net cost of recycling a ton of trash is now $300 more 25 than it would cost to bury the trash instead. That adds up to millions of extra dollars per year—about half the budget of the parks department—that New Yorkers are spending for the privilege of recycling. That money could buy far more valuable benefits, including more significant reductions in greenhouse emissions.

So what is a socially conscious, sensible person to do? 26

It would be much simpler and more effective to impose the equivalent of 27 a carbon tax on garbage, as Thomas C. Kinnaman has proposed after conducting what is probably the most thorough comparison of the social costs of recycling, landfilling and incineration. Dr. Kinnaman, an economist at Bucknell University, considered everything from environmental damage to the pleasure that some people take in recycling (the "warm glow" that makes them willing to pay extra to do it).

He concludes that the social good would be optimized by subsidizing the 28 recycling of some metals, and by imposing a $15 tax on each ton of trash that goes to the landfill. That tax would offset the environmental costs, chiefly the greenhouse impact, and allow each municipality to make a guilt-free choice based on local economics and its citizens' wishes. The result, Dr. Kinnaman predicts, would be a lot less recycling than there is today.

Then why do so many public officials keep vowing to do more of it? 29 Special-interest politics is one reason—pressure from green groups—but it's also because recycling intuitively appeals to many voters: It makes people feel virtuous, especially affluent people who feel guilty about their enormous environmental footprint. It is less an ethical activity than a religious ritual, like the ones performed by Catholics to obtain indulgences for their sins.

Religious rituals don't need any practical justification for the believers 30 who perform them voluntarily. But many recyclers want more than just the freedom to practice their religion. They want to make these rituals mandatory for everyone else, too, with stiff fines for sinners who don't sort properly. Seattle has become so aggressive that the city is being sued by residents who maintain that the inspectors rooting through their trash are violating their constitutional right to privacy.

It would take legions of garbage police to enforce a zero-waste society, but 31 true believers insist that's the future. When Mayor de Blasio promised to eliminate garbage in New York, he said it was "ludicrous" and "outdated" to keep sending garbage to landfills. Recycling, he declared, was the only way for New York to become "a truly sustainable city."

But cities have been burying garbage for thousands of years, and it's still the 32 easiest and cheapest solution for trash. The recycling movement is floundering, and its survival depends on continual subsidies, sermons and policing. How can you build a sustainable city with a strategy that can't even sustain itself?

Identifying the Elements of Argument

1. What is Tierney's thesis? Restate it in your own words.

2. What evidence does Tierney present to support his thesis?

3. What arguments against his position does Tierney identify? How does he refute them?

4. Paraphrase Tierney's concluding statement.

Highlighting

After you read an argument, the next step is to read through it again, this time highlighting as you read. When you **highlight**, you use underlining and symbols to identify the essay's most important points. (Note that the word *highlighting* does not necessarily refer to the underlining done with a yellow highlighter pen.) This active reading strategy will help you to understand the writer's ideas and to see connections among those ideas when you reread.

How do you know what to highlight? As a general rule, you look for the same signals that you looked for when you read the argument the first time—for example, the essay's thesis and topic sentences and the words and phrases that identify the writer's intent and emphasis. This time, however, you physically mark these elements and use various symbols to indicate your reactions to them.

SUGGESTIONS FOR HIGHLIGHTING

- Underline key ideas—for example, ideas stated in topic sentences.

- Box or circle words or phrases you want to remember.

- Place a check mark or a star next to an important idea.

- Place a double check mark or double star next to an especially significant idea.

- Draw lines or arrows to connect related ideas.

- Insert a question mark near an unfamiliar reference or a word you need to look up.

- Number the writer's key supporting points or examples.

🕐 Here is how a student, Neena Thomason, highlighted the *Los Angeles Times* editorial "It's Time to Phase Out All Single-Use Plastic," which appears below. Thomason was preparing to write an essay about the advantages and disadvantages of recycling. She began her highlighting by underlining and starring the thesis statement (para. 4). After boxing the distinctive phrase "unholy tonnage" in the editorial's first line, she went on to underline key pieces of information, starring and placing check marks beside the points she considered the most important. She also circled a word ("pernicious," 4) and a term ("zero sum game," 9) with which she was unfamiliar and added question marks to remind her to look them up. Finally, she underlined and starred the editorial's strong concluding statement.

This essay first appeared in the *Los Angeles Times* on February 20, 2018.

IT'S TIME TO PHASE OUT SINGLE-USE PLASTIC

Faced with an |unholy tonnage| of chip bags, soda bottles, takeout containers, 1 and other disposable plastic items flowing into our landfills and our waters, winding up in wildlife, drinking water, and food, policymakers in California have tried reining in plastic waste bit by bit. For example, more than 100 cities have adopted restrictions on polystyrene takeout containers, and the state has banned single-use plastic grocery bags.

Considering the magnitude of the problem, however, this item-by-item, 2 ✓ city-by-city approach isn't going to cut it.

The state and local rules certainly have raised public awareness about the 3
problem. Denying free plastic bags at checkout or providing plastic straws only
on request sends consumers an important message that there's a bigger cost
to these everyday items than they may have considered. But the actual flow of
trash has been disrupted only modestly.

✓   It's going to take more than a smattering of bans on single items to cure 4
society of its disposable-plastic habit. The sheer volume of plastic trash now
littering Earth has become impossible to ignore. It's time for environmentalists, policymaker, and elected officials to start planning a broader response:
✳   phasing out *all* single-use plastic, not just the most pernicious. 2

That's right, all of it. If that sounds like a pipe dream, consider what's happen- 5
ing across the pond. Last month, British Prime Minister Theresa May outlined
a plan to eliminate plastic waste by 2042. Queen Elizabeth II kicked it off this
month by banning plastic straws and bottles from royal estates, and the Church of
England supported a nascent social media campaign, #plasticlesslent, to encourage
its flock to give up plastic for Lent this year. Simultaneously, the European Union
announced its own plan to significantly reduce plastic waste, including adopting a
possible plastic tax, in a direct response to the news that China, the largest importer
of plastic recyclable material, was no longer accepting "foreign garbage."

We don't expect President Trump or Congress to follow suit, even though 6
it's impossible to pretend that the trash filling up in the ocean is naturally
✓   occurring. That leaves it to states like California to step in.

One strategy is for lawmakers to adopt a reduction goal, as they did for 7
greenhouse-gas emissions and energy derived from fossil fuels, and then to
adopt specific programs to meet that goal. It's a simple but effective approach
to tackling such a formidable environmental threat. Also, it puts makers of disposable plastic on notice, so they can't complain they didn't have time to adapt
or move into other, less harmful product lines.

But even forewarned, the plastic industry isn't likely to take an assault on 8
its bottom line well. Plastic makers spent millions of dollars trying to stop the
state from banning single-use plastic bags. Imagine what they might unleash
if all their disposable plastic products were threatened. As part of that, they
will no doubt argue, as they did in the plastic bag fight, that the efforts to clean
up plastic waste would mean lost jobs. 2

But it's not a zero-sum game. Cutting, jobs on a disposable plastic prod- 9
uct line doesn't automatically translate into fewer people employed. If the door
✓   closes on polystyrene takeout containers, for example, it will open for cardboard and other biodegradable alternatives.

No one expects consumers to give up convenience completely. In fact, the 10
market for bio-plastic alternatives, which are made from cornstarch and other
biodegradable sources, is already growing thanks to public awareness and the
sporadic efforts to curb plastic waste.

✓   Opponents will insist that the answer is just to encourage more recy- 11
cling. Not only is recycling not the answer (see China's diminished appetite
for imported plastic trash), it has only enabled our addiction to convenient,
disposable plastic packaging to deepen for some 60 years.

Yes, it's scary to think about a world where one has to carry around a reus- 12
able bag or worry about a paper drinking straw falling apart mid. . . . Oh, wait.
No, it's not. <u>Knowing that every piece of plastic manufactured on Earth is still
with us and that if we don't cut back now, there will eventually be more plastic
than fish in the ocean—that's the truly frightening thought.</u>   ✳

⊙ EXERCISE 2.2 EVALUATING A STUDENT'S HIGHLIGHTING

Look carefully at Neena Thomason's highlighting of the *Los Angeles Times*
editorial on pages 71–73. How would your own highlighting of this editorial be similar to or different from hers?

⊙ EXERCISE 2.3 HIGHLIGHTING AN ESSAY

Reread "The Reign of Recycling" (pp. 66–70). As you read, highlight the
essay by underlining and starring important points, boxing or circling key
words, writing question marks beside references that need further explanation, and drawing lines and arrows to connect related ideas.

Annotating

As you highlight, you should also annotate what you are reading. **Annotating** means making notes—of your questions, reactions, and ideas for discussion or writing—in the margins or between the lines. Keeping this kind
of informal record of ideas as they occur to you will prepare you for class
discussion and provide a useful source of material when you write.

As you read an argument and think critically about what you are reading, you can use the questions in the following checklist to help you make
useful annotations.

CHECKLIST

Questions for Annotating

☐ What issue is the writer focusing on?

☐ Does the writer take a clear stand on this issue?

☐ What is the writer's thesis?

☐ What is the writer's purpose (his or her reason for writing)?

☐ What kind of audience is the writer addressing?

☐ Does the argument appear in a popular periodical or in a scholarly journal?

☐ Does the writer seem to assume readers will agree with the essay's position?

☐ What evidence does the writer use to support the essay's thesis? Does the writer include enough evidence?

☐ Does the writer consider (and refute) opposing arguments?

☐ Do you understand the writer's vocabulary?

☐ Do you understand the writer's references?

☐ Do you agree with the points the writer makes?

☐ Do the views the writer expresses agree or disagree with the views presented in other essays you have read?

⬇ The following pages, which reproduce Neena Thomason's highlighting of the *Los Angeles Times* editorial on pages 71–73, also include her marginal annotations. In these annotations, Thomason put the editorial's thesis and some of its key points into her own words and recorded questions that she thought she might explore further. She also added definitions of the two items she questioned when she highlighted. Finally, she identified two arguments against the editorial's position and its refutation of those arguments.

This essay first appeared in the *Los Angeles Times* on February 20, 2018.

IT'S TIME TO PHASE OUT SINGLE-USE PLASTIC

THE TIMES EDITORIAL BOARD

Current restrictions

Faced with an unholy tonnage of chip bags, soda bottles, takeout containers, 1 and other disposable plastic items flowing into our landfills and our waters, winding up in wildlife, drinking water, and food, policymakers in California have tried reining in plastic waste bit by bit. For example, more than 100 cities have adopted restrictions on polystyrene takeout containers, and the state has banned single-use plastic grocery bags.

✓ Considering the magnitude of the problem, however, this item-by-item, 2 city-by-city approach isn't going to cut it.

Limitations of current restrictions

The state and local rules certainly have raised public awareness about the 3 problem. Denying free plastic bags at checkout or providing plastic straws only on request sends consumers an important message that there's a bigger cost to these everyday items than they may have considered. But the actual flow of trash has been disrupted only modestly.

Harmful

Thesis: All single-use plastic should be eliminated

Actions in England and EU

It's going to take more than a smattering of bans on single items to cure 4 society of its disposable-plastic habit. The sheer volume of plastic trash now littering Earth has become impossible to ignore. It's time for environmentalists, policymaker, and elected officials to start planning a broader response: ✳ phasing out *all* single-use plastic, not just the most pernicious ?

That's right, all of it. If that sounds like a pipe dream, consider what's happen- 5 ing across the pond. Last month, British Prime Minister Theresa May outlined a plan to eliminate plastic waste by 2042. Queen Elizabeth II kicked it off this month by banning plastic straws and bottles from royal estates, and the Church of England supported a nascent social media campaign, #plasticlesslent, to encourage its flock to give up plastic for Lent this year. Simultaneously, the European Union announced its own plan to significantly reduce plastic waste, including adopting a possible plastic tax, in a direct response to the news that China, the largest importer of plastic recyclable material, was no longer accepting "foreign garbage."

What has been done in other U.S. states?

We don't expect President Trump or Congress to follow suit, even though   6   *Why not?*
it's impossible to pretend that the trash filling up in the ocean is naturally   ✓
occurring. That leaves it to states like California to step in.

One strategy is for lawmakers to adopt a reduction goal, as they did for   7   *Possible action*
greenhouse-gas emissions and energy derived from fossil fuels, and then to
adopt specific programs to meet that goal. It's a simple but effective approach
to tackling such a formidable environmental threat. Also, it puts makers of disposable plastic on notice, so they can't complain they didn't have time to adapt
or move into other, less harmful product lines.

But even forewarned, the plastic industry isn't likely to take an assault on   8   *Problem: Likely industry*
its bottom line well. Plastic makers spent millions of dollars trying to stop the   *response*
state from banning single-use plastic bags. Imagine what they might unleash
if all their disposable plastic products were threatened. As part of that, they   *Opposing argument*
will no doubt argue, as they did in the plastic bag fight, that the efforts to clean
up plastic waste would mean lost jobs. 2

But it's not a zero-sum game. Cutting jobs on a disposable plastic prod-   9   *Situation in which each side's*
uct line doesn't automatically translate into fewer people employed. If the door   *gain or loss is exactly balanced*
closes on polystyrene takeout containers, for example, it will open for card-   *by the other side's.*
board and other biodegradable alternatives.

No one expects consumers to give up convenience completely. In fact, the   10   *Refutation*
market for bio-plastic alternatives, which are made from cornstarch and other
biodegradable sources, is already growing thanks to public awareness and the
sporadic efforts to curb plastic waste.

Opponents will insist that the answer is just to encourage more recy-   11   *Opposing argument*
cling. Not only is recycling not the answer (see China's diminished appetite   ✓ ✓
for imported plastic trash), it has only enabled our addiction to convenient,   *Refutation*
disposable plastic packaging to deepen for some 60 years.

Yes, it's scary to think about a world where one has to carry around a reus-   12
able bag or worry about a paper drinking straw falling apart mid. . . . Oh, wait.
No, it's not. Knowing that every piece of plastic manufactured on Earth is still
with us and that if we don't cut back now, there will eventually be more plastic   ✳   *Prediction for future w/o*
than fish in the ocean—that's the truly frightening thought.   *action*

⊖ EXERCISE 2.4 ANNOTATING AN ESSAY

Reread John Tierney's "The Reign of Recycling" (pp. 66–70). As you read,
refer to the "Questions for Annotating" checklist (p. 73), and use them as
a guide as you write your own reactions and questions in the margins of
Tierney's essay. In your annotations, note where you agree or disagree
with Tierney, and briefly explain why. Quickly summarize any points that
you think are particularly important. Look up any unfamiliar words or references you have identified, and write down brief definitions or explanations. Think about these annotations as you prepare to discuss "The Reign
of Recycling" in class (and, eventually, to write about it).

➔ EXERCISE 2.5 EVALUATING YOUR HIGHLIGHTING

Exchange books with another student, and read his or her highlighting and annotating. How are your written responses similar to the other student's? How are they different? Do your classmate's responses help you to see anything new about Tierney's essay?

➔ EXERCISE 2.6 THINKING CRITICALLY: ANALYZING AN ARGUMENT

The following essay, "Waste Not . . . ?" by Bob Holmes, focuses on how to recycle in an environmentally responsible manner. Read the letter, highlighting and annotating it.

Now, consider how this essay is similar to and different from John Tierney's essay (pp. 66–70). First, identify the writer's thesis, and restate it in your own words. Then, consider his views on recycling and his recommendations for supporting and encouraging the practice.

Where does Holmes identify limitations of recycling? Are the problems he identifies the same ones Tierney discusses? Finally, consider how Holmes's purpose for writing is different from Tierney's.

This essay was published on July 22, 2017, in the journal *New Scientist*.

WASTE NOT . . . ?

BOB HOLMES

Like altruism, The Beatles, and chocolate, recycling is universally acknowl- 1 edged as a good thing. For many of us, it is a way of life. Recycling rates have been rising since the 1970s, and in some places, including Germany, the Netherlands, and California, more than half of all domestic waste is recycled. But now some people are challenging the received wisdom with difficult questions. How do nonrecyclable styrofoam coffee cups compare with paper or ceramic ones, when all the costs of manufacturing are included? Is it worth recycling materials such as glass and plastic that yield only small environmental benefits? Might landfill be a greener option for plastic, much of which is trucked to seaports and shipped to China for recycling? If you've been left wondering whether it's worth it, here's what you need to know to make up your mind.

1. Which materials are worth recycling?

From the most basic environmental point of view, all materials are worth recy- 2 cling, because this reduces the need for energy-intensive mining and smelting of virgin materials. That makes a huge difference for some things—notably aluminum—but even recycling glass leads to a small energy saving and consequent reduction in greenhouse-gas emissions. Recycling can also provide a reliable, nonimported source of scarce resources such as the rare earth metals that are crucial parts of touchscreens and other high-tech devices.

However, the answer gets muddier when we consider economics. The 3 price of recycled material fluctuates wildly, and some often aren't profitable to recycle, especially if the recovered material has to be shipped long distances to a reprocessing plant. Waste managers often have to pay recyclers to take glass off their hands, for example. That can make virgin glass look like a better deal—but only because we often fail to include the environmental costs of mining sand and the carbon emissions from glassmaking furnaces. Similarly, plastics are often reprocessed in China, so proximity to a seaport may dictate whether it is profitable to recycle them.

Other low-value materials such as wood and textiles need to be clean to be 4 recyclable. The extra effort and expense required to separate them from general waste means they often end up in landfill.

2. Can we make landfills greener?

Landfill sites emit methane, a potent greenhouse gas. A growing number cap- 5 ture this and convert it to energy but even in the most efficient systems up to 10 percent escapes. In the U.S. landfill accounts for 18 percent of methane emissions, making it the third-largest source of methane emissions after the fossil-fuel industry and livestock. What's more, most of the methane produced in landfill sites comes from organic waste, which can be disposed of in greener ways. The simplest is composting, but the carbon in organic waste can also be converted to carbon dioxide and carbon monoxide by high-temperature, high-pressure processes. This can then be reconstituted into liquid fuels such as ethanol or methanol, or used as feedstock in other industrial processes. In Edmonton, Canada, for example, one trash-to-methanol process is making headway. According to one calculation, the product has the smallest carbon footprint of any liquid fuel, when methane emissions avoided by not landfilling the waste are included.

3. Why do I have to separate my recyclables?

Keeping recyclables separate from the rest of your rubbish reduces contamina- 6 tion and makes recycling more effective. Recycling companies like it if we also segregate different types of recyclables because then they don't have to incur the extra expense of doing this.

Separate collections of organic waste, recycling, and other rubbish 7 can make waste-handling more efficient, Kitchen waste is dense and self-compacting, so organics can be collected frequently with simple vehicles. With the stinky organics gone, recycling and other rubbish can be collected less often—even once a month or two—which makes more efficient use of expensive compactor trucks.

But the more complex the household sorting task becomes, the more 8 likely householders are to give up and simply pitch something into the rubbish. As a result of this trade-off, local authorities often lump all recycling into a single bin, or just separate paper and cardboard from plastic, metal, and glass.

4. What if my carefully segregated load is contaminated?

Everyone makes mistakes, and recyclers accept a certain amount of contami- 9 nation. But too much of it can downgrade the quality of the batch and reduce the price reprocessors will pay. In practical terms, that means you should take reasonable steps to rinse and sort your recyclables according to your waste-management system's protocol, but don't obsess over every last decision.

Pay particular attention, however, to instructions on how to handle plastic 10 wraps and plastic bags, because these can dog up the shredding and sorting machinery in some systems. If your local authority asks you not to put them in the recycling bin, don't.

5. Does recycling keep plastic from polluting the ocean?

Most of the plastic that ends up in the oceans is "leakage"—the stuff that gets 11 tossed out of car windows, dropped on the street, or otherwise escapes the waste management system. That accounts for 32 percent of global plastic packaging. So, if plastic is recycled—or even sent to landfill or burned—it should stay out of the ocean.

6. Is burning rubbish in incinerators better than dumping it?

Incinerators reduce the volume of waste that might otherwise be dumped into 12 landfill sites, and most also generate heat for electricity or heating homes. Modern waste-to-energy incinerators are very clean, so toxic emissions aren't generally an issue. But then modern landfill sites generally don't leach toxins into their environment either. Incinerators do, however, release a lot of carbon dioxide for every kilowatt-hour of electricity produced—more than many coal-fired power plants, in fact. And as the electricity grid shifts more towards renewables, burning trash to generate electricity is likely to look increasingly less attractive.

Another consideration is that burning waste may reduce levels of recy- 13 cling. Cities that rely too heavily on incineration can find themselves trapped by the system's demands. "These things are hungry," says Thomas Kinnaman, an environmental economist at Bucknell University in Pennsylvania. "They need lots and lots of fuel to stay efficient, and they're increasingly looking at that recycling pile."

7. Is there any point to composting?

Composting is one of the most useful things you can do. Compacted, airless 14 landfill sites are the perfect breeding ground for anaerobic bacteria called methanogens that feed on organic waste. For every kilogram they digest, they produce about 2 kilograms of the powerful greenhouse gas methane. That doesn't happen in a compost bin. Yet households in the UK binned 7.3 million tonnes of food waste in 2015, two-thirds of which could have been composted. Separating kitchen scraps, garden waste, and other organic waste from the rest of the rubbish stream means they can be used to generate high-quality compost to increase soil fertility for crops and gardens. Organic waste contaminated by household chemicals, glass, metal fragment, and the like may only produce compost fit for restoring industrial sites and roadsides.

8. Isn't "recycling" a misnomer?

Some materials, such as glass and aluminum, can be melted and recast into 15
new products that are just as good as those from virgin material. But others can only be "downcycled" into products of lower quality than the original. Each time paper is recycled, for example, its fibers break into shorter lengths so it can be used only for increasingly low-quality papers such as newspaper and toilet paper. Most plastics are downcycled into products that cannot themselves be recycled. In fact, only about 15 percent of recycled plastics end up in products of similar quality. Researchers are working on finding new ways to chemically break down plastics into their component molecules so that they can be rebuilt into high-quality material.

> "Can we create a world without rubbish?"

There is a move to redesign products and packaging to minimize waste. 16
In the meantime, environmentally aware consumers can reduce, reuse, avoid disposable items and repair broken ones instead of throwing them away.

Towards Zero Waste

Can we create a world without rubbish? 17

One of the big impediments to recycling is products made of mixed mate- 18
rials that can't easily be separated—but solutions are on the way. Sachets are a prime example. People living in poorer countries often purchase single-use sachets of things like ketchup and detergent because they cannot afford to buy in bulk. These sachets need to be durable as well as impermeable, so they are often made of layers of different materials. Hundreds of billions are produced annually. Unilever, a major manufacturer of sacheted products, pledged earlier this year to make all of its packaging recyclable by 2025, and is developing new ways to dissolve the polyethylene out of used sachets so that it can be reused. Others are developing ways to separate mixed plastics by shredding them and automatically sorting the millimeter-sized fragments.

Such efforts are part of the "new plastics economy," which recognizes that 19
plastics can have environmental benefits as well as costs, "We don't want to eliminate plastic, we want to eliminate plastic waste," says Joe Iles, a spokesperson for the Ellen MacArthur Foundation, which is leading the initiative. That will require coordination as well as innovation. For example, there's a new generation of biodegradable plastic made from cornstarch that can be used to

make drinking bottles. But we need an easy way to distinguish them from bottles made from polyethylene terephthalate (PET), says Iles, because even a few can contaminate and ruin a batch of recycled PET.

Another way to encourage recycling is to require manufacturers to take back and recycle the products they sell at the end of their useful life. This extended producer responsibility is increasingly being applied to products like electronics and batteries, It encourages manufacturers to think about the disposal of their products, possibly redesigning them to make that easier. Japan, one of the leaders in this approach, adds the price of recycling to new products and has seen an associated 27 percent increase in recycling rates for containers and packaging. 20

Initiatives like these are pushing society towards a "circular" economy, in contrast to today's "take, make, and dispose" economy. We have a long way to go and, even with the most advanced technologies and best intentions, zero waste is an impossible dream. But that shouldn't stop us dreaming. "I sometimes equate it to zero deaths in the emergency room of a hospital," says Jeffrey Morris, a waste consultant at the Sound Resources Management Group in Olympia, Washington. "Any other goal makes no sense." 21

● EXERCISE 2.7 DRAFTING A THESIS STATEMENT

The following magazine article, "We Are So Forked" by Jenny Luna, focuses on the use of plastic utensils. What position does this essay take? Draft a thesis statement that summarizes this position. Then, consider how John Tierney (pp. 66–70) might respond to this thesis—and to Luna's specific recommendations.

This opinion piece appeared in the July/August 2017 issue of *Mother Jones*.

WE ARE SO FORKED

JENNY LUNA

Whether for stabbing salads at our desks or slurping up late-night Thai, plastic cutlery has become a signature side to our growing takeout habit. It's hard to say exactly how many forks, spoons, and knives Americans throw away, but in 2015 we placed nearly 2 billion delivery orders. If at least half those meals involved single-use utensils, that would mean we're tossing out billions of utensils each year. They don't just disappear: A recent study in the San Francisco Bay Area found that food and beverage packaging made up 67 percent of all litter on the streets. 1

Apart from being an eyesore, disposable cutlery endangers wildlife. 2
A survey by four major environmental groups determined that plastic utensils
ranked among the 10 most common trash items found in California—which
contributes to a larger problem: The United Nations estimates that the oceans
contain more than 8 million tons of plastic. As plastic breaks down, it can be
mistaken for food by sea creatures, which can harm them and our seafood
dinners.

A few options have surfaced in recent years. In 2010, a company in India 3
started selling edible spoons and forks made from grains. Closer to home,
California-based SpudWare's forks are made from potato starch. But such
alternatives, which cost about twice as much as plastic, still require a lot of
energy and water to produce, according to Samantha Sommer, who runs a
waste-prevention project for Clean Water Action. What's more, not all major
cities compost. And even if biodegradable or compostable utensils make it
to a facility, there's a chance they'll end up in a landfill, says Robert Reed,
a spokesman for the West Coast recycling and compost plant Recology.
Depending on what they're made of, he says, biodegradable utensils might
not degrade completely; if they don't, they could be plucked out of the pile
and thrown away.

Perhaps diners should take a page
from China, where environmental protesters publicized how the roughly 80
billion pairs of disposable wooden chopsticks produced each year eat up 20 million trees in the process. Greenpeace
China launched a BYOC (Bring Your
Own Chopsticks) campaign and worked

> "Metal spoons have not   4
> yet graced American
> celebrity Instagram
> accounts, but may be
> it's time."

with pop stars to promote reusable chopsticks as a trendy fashion accessory. As
a result, disposable chopsticks were banned from use at many venues hosting
events at Beijing's 2008 Olympics.

Metal spoons have not yet graced American celebrity Instagram 5
accounts, but maybe it's time: Encouraging customers to bring in their own
utensils helps businesses cut down costs and waste. A few years ago, Clean
Water Action ran a test case with restaurant owner Francisco Hernandez
of El Metate in San Francisco. The restaurant staff used to include plastic
utensils with every order. Now, sit-down diners get metal forks, and dis-
posables are in a countertop container for to-go customers who need them.
Hernandez saved money that year—now he buys just one case of disposable forks each week instead of three—and he decreased his restaurant's
waste by more than 3,600 pounds. The change means El Metate has more
to wash, but it's likely that the water used to run his dishwasher (one gallon for every one-minute cycle) is dwarfed by the amount needed to make
those plastic forks.

Still, a sea change might require more research and toothier legislation— 6 something that worked in the fight against plastic bags. A 2013 study found that after San Jose, California, enacted a bag ban, there was nearly 90 percent less plastic in the city's storm drains and almost 60 percent less in its streets than there had been before. Data like that helped California finalize a state-wide ban—over the strenuous lobbying of plastics manufacturers—in 2016. Such legislation appears to be catching on: Chicago, Seattle, and Austin, Texas, have also enacted bag bans, and between 2015 and 2016, lawmakers proposed at least 77 state-level plastic bag bills. Given that success, here's an idea: Charge a small fee for disposable utensils to help nudge consumers to make a habit out of carrying their own forks. Prettier streets, healthier oceans, and cheaper takeout? Sold.

Writing a Critical Response

Sometimes you will be asked to write a **critical response**—a paragraph or more in which you analyze ideas presented in an argument and express your reactions to them.

Before you can respond in writing to an argument, you need to be sure that you understand the writer's position and that you have a sense of how supporting ideas are arranged—and why. You also need to consider how convincingly the writer conveys his or her position.

If you have read the argument carefully, highlighting and annotating it according to the guidelines outlined in this chapter, you should have a good idea what the writer wants to communicate to readers as well as how successfully the argument makes its point.

Before you begin to write a critical response to an argument, you should consider the questions in the checklist on page 83.

Begin your critical response by identifying your source and its author; then, write a clear, concise summary of the writer's position. Next, analyze the argument's supporting points one by one, considering the strength of the evidence that is presented. Also consider whether the writer addresses all significant opposing arguments and whether those arguments are refuted convincingly. Quote, summarize, and paraphrase the writer's key points as you go along, being careful to quote accurately and not to misrepresent the writer's ideas or distort them by quoting out of context. (For information on summarizing, paraphrasing, quoting, and synthesizing sources, see Chapter 9.) As you write, identify arguments you find unconvincing, poorly supported, or irrelevant. At the end of your critical response, sum up your assessment of the argument in a strong concluding statement.

Questions for Critical Reading

☐ What is the writer's general subject?

☐ What purpose does the writer have for presenting this argument?

☐ What is the writer's position?

☐ Does the writer support ideas mainly with facts or with opinion?

☐ What evidence does the writer present to support this position?

☐ Is the evidence convincing? Is there enough evidence?

☐ Does the writer present opposing ideas and refute them effectively?

☐ What kind of audience does the writer seem to be addressing?

☐ Does the writer see the audience as hostile, friendly, or neutral?

☐ Does the writer establish himself or herself as well informed? As a fair and reasonable person?

☐ Does the writer seem to exhibit bias? If so, how does this bias affect the argument?

⬇ Neena Thomason, the student who highlighted and annotated the *Los Angeles Times* editorial on pages 74–75, used those notes to help her develop the following critical response to the editorial.

RESPONSE TO "IT'S TIME TO PHASE OUT ALL SINGLE-USE PLASTIC"

NEENA THOMASON

In "It's Time to Phase Out All Single-Use Plastic," the *Los Angeles Times* editorial board warns of a bleak future unless the "unholy tonnage" (para. 1) of disposable plastic items is controlled. The board's recommendation is a total ban of all single-use plastic items.

1   Article's source and author identified

Although the editorial acknowledges steps that have been taken by state and local government to limit the use of various individual items, such as plastic bags and straws, the writers note that such efforts have not had much effect on the accumulation of trash. They are also not optimistic that the federal government will take significant steps to solve the problem. Therefore, they believe the time has come for the state of California to act.

2   Summary of writer's position

One suggestion they make is the adoption of a "reduction goal" (7). The writers anticipate that industry will object to any such limitations, arguing that they will lead to a loss of jobs. They point out, however,

3   Analysis of supporting evidence

that any lost jobs would be replaced by jobs producing "biodegradable alternatives" (9) to plastic items.

Concluding statement   The editorial writers also expect industry to recommend recycling   4
as a better alternative than banning single-use plastic items. The writers believe, however, that recycling is not the answer—and may, in fact, be part of the problem because it has "enabled our addiction to convenient, disposable plastic packaging" (11).

In short, the writers of the editorial make a convincing case that the   5
only way to avoid a world with "more plastic than fish in the ocean" (12) is to take action now.

Work Cited

Los Angeles Times Editorial Board. "It's Time to Phase Out All Single-Use
    Plastic." *Practical Argument*, 4th ed., edited by Laurie G. Kirszner
    and Stephen R. Mandell. Macmillan, 2020, pp. 71–73.

TEMPLATE FOR WRITING A CRITICAL RESPONSE

Write a one-paragraph critical response to John Tierney's essay on pages 66–70. Use the following template to shape your paragraph.

According to John Tierney, recycling may not be worth the cost or effort required to achieve its goals. He points out, for example, that _____

_____

_____

_____. Tierney also observes that _____

_____

_____.

Tierney makes some convincing points. For example, he says that _____

_____

_____. However, _____

_____

_____. All in

all, _____

_____.

⊙ EXERCISE 2.8 WRITING A CRITICAL RESPONSE

Expand the one-paragraph critical response that you wrote above into a more fully developed critical response to John Tierney's essay on pages 66–70. Refer to the highlighting and annotations that you did for Exercises 2.3 and 2.4. (If you like, you can include references to other readings in this chapter.)

⊙ EXERCISE 2.9 DEVELOPING VISUAL ARGUMENTS

What kind of images would you use to support the argument that recycling is necessary? What kinds of images might support the argument that recycling isn't worth the trouble? Develop two lists of possible visuals, one list for each side of the argument. Then, consider what these images might include and where they might appear.

When recyclable materials are mishandled, such as being dumped near recycling containers rather than placed inside them as in this photo, the process can break down. AP Images/Steve Parsons.

CHAPTER

3

Reading and Responding to Visual Arguments

AT ISSUE

Does Recycling Really Accomplish Anything? (continued)

In Chapter 2, you read essays focusing on the advantages and limitations of recycling. Now, you will be introduced to a variety of visual texts that offer additional insights into this issue. At the same time, you will learn how to use the critical-reading strategies that you practiced in Chapter 2 to help you to interpret visual arguments and to use visuals as springboards for discussion and writing or as sources in your essays.

A **visual argument** can be an advertisement, a chart or graph or table, an infographic, a diagram, a web page, a photograph, a drawing, a cartoon, or a painting. Like an argumentative essay, a visual argument takes a position. Unlike an argumentative essay, however, a visual argument communicates its message (and offers evidence to support that message) largely through images rather than words.

When you approach a visual argument—particularly one that will be the subject of class discussion or writing—you should do so with a critical eye. Your primary goal is to understand the point that the creator of the visual is trying to make, but you also need to understand how the message is conveyed. In addition, you need to evaluate whether the methods used to persuade the audience are both logical and convincing.

VISUALS VERSUS VISUAL ARGUMENTS

Not every visual is an argument; many simply present information. For example, a diagram of a hunting rifle, with its principal parts labeled, tells viewers what the weapon looks like and how it works. However, a photo of two toddlers playing with a hunting rifle could make a powerful argument about the need for gun safety. Conversely, a photo of a family hunting trip featuring a teenager proudly holding up a rifle while his parents look on approvingly might serve as a positive argument for gun ownership.

Reading Visual Arguments

As you learned in Chapter 2, being a critical reader involves responding actively to the text of an argument. The active reading strategies that you practiced in Chapter 2—*previewing, close reading, highlighting,* and *annotating*—can also be applied to visual arguments.

When you approach a visual argument, you should look for clues to its main idea, or message. Some visuals, particularly advertising images, include words (sometimes called *body copy*) as well, and this written text often conveys the main points of the argument. (Such visuals are considered **multimodal** because they combine two methods of communication—in this case, words and images.) Apart from words, however, the images themselves can help you understand the visual's purpose, its intended audience, and the argument that it is making.

COMPREHENSION CLUES

Focusing on the following elements can help you to understand a visual argument:

- The individual images

- The relative distance between images (close together or far apart)

- The relative size of the images

- The relationship between images and background

- The use of empty space

- The use of color and shading (for example, contrast between light and dark)

- If people are pictured, their activities, gestures, facial expressions, positions, body language, dress, and so on

APPEALS: *LOGOS, PATHOS,* AND *ETHOS*

As you study a visual argument, you should consider the appeal (or appeals) that the visual uses to convince its audience:

- An ad produced by Mothers Against Drunk Drivers (MADD) that includes statistics about alcohol-related auto fatalities might appeal to logic (*logos*).

- Another MADD ad could appeal to the emotions (*pathos*) by showing photographs of an accident scene.

- Still another ad could appeal to authority (*ethos*) by featuring a well-known sports figure warning of the dangers of drunk driving.

(For more on these appeals, see pp. 14–21.)

The following photograph presents a strong visual argument, using a powerful image to make an emotional appeal to those concerned about the environment. This photograph appeared on the cover of the June 2018 issue of *National Geographic* magazine.

The visual below highlights one dramatic image: a floating plastic bag shaped like an iceberg. The placement of this image in the center of

the visual emphasizes its importance, and the contrast between the small portion of the image protruding from the water and the large submerged portion makes the visual's message clear: the environmental problems we see today are only "the tip of the iceberg." The clear demarcation of the gray sky and the blue ocean confirms the contrast between the placid surface and the unseen threat that lies beneath it.

The text that accompanies the image is brief and to the point. At the top right, the stark choice that confronts us—"planet or plastic?"—is expressed as a dilemma that seems to have only one reasonable solution. At the bottom left, in smaller type, two succinct sentences spell out the problem, reinforcing the conflict between the natural world (ocean) and the pollution (plastic) that threatens to destroy it.

Because it presents only one image, and because the subject matter is probably familiar to most people, this visual is easy to understand. Its powerful image and text are not difficult to interpret, and the visual's warning is straightforward: if we do not do something about the refuse that is polluting our oceans, we will risk losing them. The visual's accessibility (as well as its obvious emotional appeal) suggests that it is aimed at a wide general audience rather than, for example, environmentalists.

The visual might have been created for any of several purposes. Most obviously, it is intended to raise awareness and, perhaps, to inspire action—for example, to encourage readers to use fewer plastic bags and to dispose of them responsibly. In addition, because it is a magazine cover, it is also intended to encourage people to buy, and to read, this issue of *National Geographic*.

Now, turn your attention to the following bar graph, "U.S. Better at Recycling Some Things Than Others"; it appears in the article "Five Charts That Explain Why Recycling Efforts May Not Result in Zero Waste," published in the online newsletter *Waste Dive*. Unlike the *National Geographic* cover, which appeals to the emotions, this graph appeals to logic by providing evidence to support the article's position: that recycling is not a magic cure.

The graph uses a simple, open design and clearly labels each category it lists, presenting them in a logical order. It provides readily accessible information, in the form of percentages, to show which kinds of waste are most (and least) efficiently disposed of. The main idea, or message, this graph conveys is summarized in its boldfaced title: "U.S. better at recycling some things than others." This in turn supports the thesis of the article in which the graph appeared: that despite Americans' best efforts at recycling, achieving "zero waste" may not be an achievable goal.

This idea might surprise those readers who assume that recycling can lead to the elimination of the waste that pollutes our environment. In a sense, then, this graph can be seen as a **refutation** of a commonly held assumption. Because the graph (like the article in which it appeared) presents information intended to challenge the audience's probable assumptions, its purpose seems to be not just to inform readers but perhaps also to change the way they look at recycling.

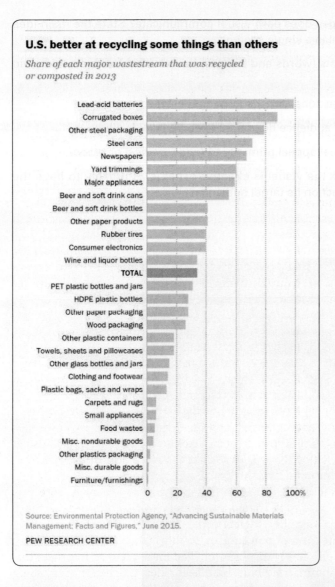

U.S. better at recycling some things than others

Share of each major wastestream that was recycled or composted in 2013

Source: Environmental Protection Agency, "Advancing Sustainable Materials Management: Facts and Figures," June 2015.

PEW RESEARCH CENTER

⊖ EXERCISE 3.1 READING VISUAL ARGUMENTS

Look carefully at each of the visuals on the pages that follow, and then answer the questions on page 99.

Reading Visual Arguments

1. Do you see all of the visuals on pages 92–98 as arguments, created to convey a message or make a point, or do you think any of them were created solely to present information?

2. What main idea does each visual communicate? State the main idea of each visual in a single sentence.

3. What elements (words and images) in each visual support this main idea?

4. What purpose does each visual seem designed to achieve?

5. What kind of audience do you think each visual is aimed at?

6. Does the visual appeal primarily to *logos*, *pathos*, or *ethos*?

7. Do you think the visual is effective? That is, is it likely to have the intended effect on its target audience?

Photo of a bird trapped in a plastic bag.

John Cancalosi/Photolibrary/Getty Images

Cartoon commenting on public's lack of compliance with recycling guidelines.

David Sipress/Conde Nast/The Cartoon Bank

"Waste pie chart" created from items found on a beach in Bali, Indonesia.

Making Oceans Plastic Free

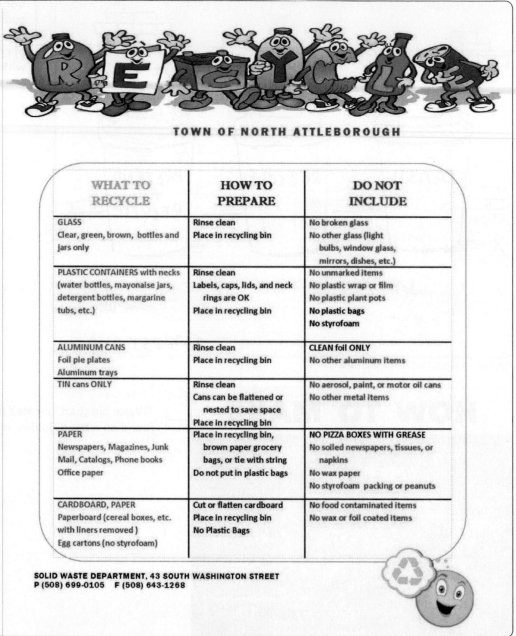

TOWN OF NORTH ATTLEBOROUGH

WHAT TO RECYCLE	HOW TO PREPARE	DO NOT INCLUDE
GLASS Clear, green, brown, bottles and jars only	Rinse clean Place in recycling bin	No broken glass No other glass (light bulbs, window glass, mirrors, dishes, etc.)
PLASTIC CONTAINERS with necks (water bottles, mayonaise jars, detergent bottles, margarine tubs, etc.)	Rinse clean Labels, caps, lids, and neck rings are OK Place in recycling bin	No unmarked items No plastic wrap or film No plastic plant pots **No plastic bags** **No styrofoam**
ALUMINUM CANS Foil pie plates Aluminum trays	Rinse clean Place in recycling bin	**CLEAN foil ONLY** No other aluminum items
TIN cans ONLY	Rinse clean Cans can be flattened or nested to save space Place in recycling bin	No aerosol, paint, or motor oil cans No other metal items
PAPER Newspapers, Magazines, Junk Mail, Catalogs, Phone books Office paper	Place in recycling bin, brown paper grocery bags, or tie with string Do not put in plastic bags	**NO PIZZA BOXES WITH GREASE** No soiled newspapers, tissues, or napkins No wax paper No styrofoam packing or peanuts
CARDBOARD, PAPER Paperboard (cereal boxes, etc. with liners removed) Egg cartons (no styrofoam)	Cut or flatten cardboard Place in recycling bin **No Plastic Bags**	No food contaminated items No wax or foil coated items

SOLID WASTE DEPARTMENT, 43 SOUTH WASHINGTON STREET
P (508) 699-0105   F (508) 643-1268

Town of North Attleborough Massachusetts

Guidelines for town recycling program.

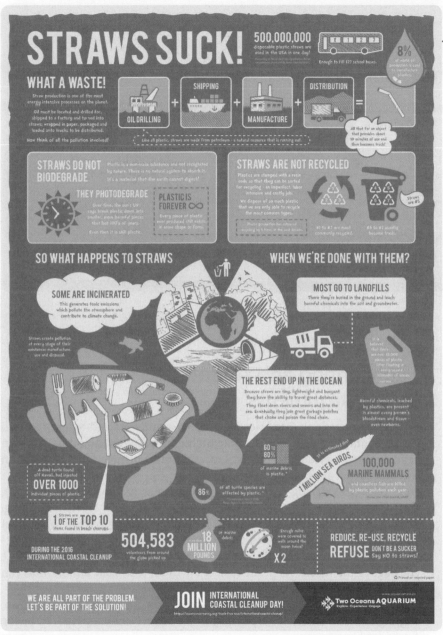

Infographic encouraging consumers not to use nonbiodegradable straws.

Two Oceans Aquarium

Now you know what your empty beverage containers can become.

Mckim Communications Group Ltd

Canadian public service advertisement in support of recycling.

Highlighting and Annotating Visual Arguments

Now, it's time to look more closely at visual arguments and to learn how to *highlight* and *annotate* them. Unlike highlighting and annotating a written text, marking a visual text involves focusing your primary attention not on any words that appear but on the images.

After previewing the visual by looking at its overall appearance, begin highlighting to identify key images—perhaps by starring, boxing, or circling them—and then consider drawing lines or arrows to connect related images. Next, go on to make annotations on the visual, commenting on the effectiveness of its individual images in communicating the message of the whole. As in the case of a written text, your annotations can be in the form of comments or questions.

The visual on the following page shows how a student, Gabriel Dunn, highlighted and annotated a public-service advertisement prepared by the Surfrider Foundation.

When he first looked at this public-service ad, Gabriel Dunn was immediately struck by the way the large blue letters of the central message drew his eye to the blue plastic center of the sushi roll, thus emphasizing its importance. When he highlighted and annotated the ad, he made (and starred) a note about this effective use of color and drew arrows to connect the blue type with the roll's blue center. He then identified the largest (and most important) words and images and boxed the ad's central message, also noting the unexpected presence of plastic and commenting on the partial image of chopsticks. Finally, he underlined and starred a key piece of information in the written text.

Prominent image clearly reveals contamination

Plastic, not fish

Large capitalized words and central position emphasizes ad's message/ warning

Chopsticks suggest roll will be eaten

WHAT GOES IN THE OCEAN GOES IN YOU.

A RECENT STUDY FOUND THAT 35% OF FISH SAMPLED OFF THE WEST COAST HAD INGESTED PLASTIC. FIND OUT HOW YOU CAN HELP. VISIT WWW.SURFRIDER.ORG/RAP MAKE THE PLEDGE. BAN THE BAG.

Blue type here highlights blue centers in rolls above

Use of capital letters makes information stand out

SURFRIDER FOUNDATION

Surfrider

● EXERCISE 3.2 HIGHLIGHTING AND ANNOTATING A VISUAL ARGUMENT

The visual that follows was created as a customizable template to illustrate the benefits of recycling and alternative energy sources. Rather than including text beneath its headings, the visual leaves blank space to be filled in with suitable text. (The images and headlines are designed to stay the same.) Look closely at the visual, and then highlight and annotate it to identify its most important images and their relationship to one another.

seamartini/iStock/Getty Images

Public service advertisement for recycling

Then, think about how the images work together to communicate a central message to the audience. What argument does this visual seem to make? How might that argument change based on the specific text that is supplied? How might it stay the same?

Responding Critically to Visual Arguments

As you learned in Chapter 2, a **critical response** analyzes the ideas in a text and expresses your reactions to them. When you respond in writing to a visual argument, you rely on your highlighting and annotations to help you understand the writer's ideas and see how the words and images work together to convey a particular message.

As you prepare to write a critical response to a visual argument, keep in mind the questions in the following checklist.

When you write a critical response, begin by identifying the source and purpose of the visual. Next, state your reaction to the visual, and then examine its elements one at a time, considering how effective each is and how well the various elements work together to create a convincing visual argument. End with a strong concluding statement that summarizes your reaction.

The critical response that follows was written by the student who highlighted and annotated the visual on page 97.

CHECKLIST

Questions for Responding to Visual Arguments

☐ In what source did the visual appear? What is the target audience for this source?

☐ For what kind of audience was the visual created? Hostile? Friendly? Neutral?

☐ For what purpose was the visual created?

☐ Who (or what organization) created the visual? What do you know (and what can you find out) about the background and goals of this person or group?

☐ What issue is the visual addressing? What position does the visual take on this issue? How does it support this position?

☐ Does the visual include words? If so, are they essential? What purpose do they serve? Does the visual need more—or different—written text?

☐ Does the visual seem to be a *refutation*—that is, an argument against a particular position?

☐ Is the visual interesting? Clear? Attractive? Convincing?

☐ Do you agree with the position the visual takes on the issue? Why or why not?

RESPONSE TO "WHAT GOES IN THE OCEAN GOES IN YOU"

GABRIEL DUNN

The public service advertisement produced by the Surfrider Foundation, an organization whose mission is to protect and enjoy "the world's oceans, waves, and beaches through a powerful activist network," clearly and effectively supports its stated goals.

Both words and images support the ad's message. In the center of the visual, large, capitalized blue letters spell out this message: "What goes in the ocean goes in you." At the top of the visual is a large cross section of a sushi roll. Although the rice remains, the roll is wrapped in plastic rather than seaweed, and it is filled with plastic rather than fish. The blue letters of the ad's central message make the blue of the roll's plastic center more prominent. Off to the side, chopsticks suggest that the roll is ready to be enjoyed. However, as the ad's visual elements show, this usually tasty delicacy is not fit to eat.

1 Identification of visual's source and purpose

Reaction to visual

2 Analysis of visual elements

Analysis, continued   Below the large letters of the central message, information from   3
recent research studies, set in smaller type, reinforces the accuracy and
seriousness of the message, and Surfrider's contact information offers
readers a way to "help turn the tide on plastic pollution."

Concluding statement   Because millennials are probably more likely than other groups to eat   4
sushi, the ad may be primarily directed at them. In any case, the message
the ad conveys to its audience is also a warning: When we pollute our
waters, we contaminate our food—and when we eat contaminated food,
we pollute our bodies.

TEMPLATE FOR RESPONDING TO VISUAL ARGUMENTS

Write a one-paragraph critical response to the visual you highlighted and annotated in
Exercise 3.2 on pages 97–98. Use the following template to shape your paragraph.

The visual created by Surfrider.org shows _____
_____.

The goal of this organization seems to be to _____
_____.

This visual makes a powerful statement about _____.

The central image shows _____
_____.

Other visual elements enhance the central image by _____
_____. The visual includes words as well as images.

These words suggest _____
_____.

The visual [is/is not] effective because _____
_____.

➲ EXERCISE 3.3 DEVELOP YOUR RESPONSE

Consulting the one-paragraph critical response that you wrote in the preceding template, write a more fully developed critical response to the visual on page 97. Refer to the highlighting and annotating that you did for Exercise 3.2.

➲ EXERCISE 3.4 EVALUATING VISUAL ARGUMENTS

Look back at the images in this chapter. Which do you think is the strongest, most convincing visual argument? Why? Write a paragraph in which you explain and support your choice.

Fedor Selivanov/Alamy

CHAPTER 4

Writing a Rhetorical Analysis

AT ISSUE

Is It Ethical to Buy Counterfeit Designer Merchandise?

The demand for counterfeit designer merchandise—handbags, shoes, and jewelry—has always been great. Wishing to avoid the high prices of genuine designer goods, American consumers spend hundreds of millions of dollars per year buying cheap imitations that are made primarily in factories in China (and in other countries as well). According to United States Customs and Border Protection statistics, the counterfeit goods seized in 2013 had a retail value of over $1.7 billion. In 2017, that figure went down to $1.2 billion, but much more counterfeit merchandise gets into the United States than is seized. However hard they try, law enforcement officials cannot seem to stem the tide of counterfeit merchandise that is sold in stores, in flea markets, and by street vendors as well as through the internet. As long as people want these illegal goods, there will be a market for them.

Purchasing counterfeit designer goods is not a victimless crime, however. Buyers are stealing the intellectual property of legitimate businesses that, unlike the manufacturers of fakes, pay their employees fair wages and provide good working conditions. In addition, because counterfeit goods are of low quality, they do not last as long as the genuine articles. This is not a serious problem when people are buying fake watches and handbags, but it can be life threatening when the counterfeit products include pharmaceuticals, tools, baby food, or automobile parts.

Later in this chapter, you will read a rhetorical analysis of an essay that takes a position on this issue, and you will be asked to write a rhetorical analysis of your own about another essay on this topic.

What Is a Rhetorical Analysis?

When you write a **rhetorical analysis**, you systematically examine the strategies a writer employs to achieve his or her purpose. In the process, you explain how these strategies work together to create an effective (or ineffective) argument. To carry out this task, you consider the argument's **rhetorical situation**, the writer's **means of persuasion**, and the **rhetorical strategies** that the writer uses.

OVERVIEW: "LETTER FROM BIRMINGHAM JAIL" BY MARTIN LUTHER KING JR.

Here and throughout the rest of this chapter, we will be analyzing "Letter from Birmingham Jail" by Martin Luther King Jr., which can be found online.

In 1963, civil rights leader Martin Luther King Jr. organized a series of nonviolent demonstrations to protest the climate of racial segregation that existed in Birmingham, Alabama. He and his followers met opposition not only from white moderates but also from some African-American clergymen who thought that King was a troublemaker. During the demonstrations, King was arrested and jailed for eight days. He wrote his "Letter from Birmingham Jail" on April 16, 1963, from the city jail in response to a public statement by eight white Alabama clergymen titled "A Call for Unity." This statement asked for an end to the demonstrations, which the clergymen called "untimely," "unwise," and "extreme." (Their letter was addressed to the "white and Negro" population of Birmingham, not to King, whom they considered an "outsider.")

King knew that the world was watching and that his response to the white clergymen would have both national and international significance. As a result, he used a variety of rhetorical strategies to convince readers that his demands were both valid and understandable and that contrary to the opinions of some, his actions were well within the mainstream of American social and political thought. Today, King's "Letter from Birmingham Jail" stands as a model of clear and highly effective argumentation.

Bettmann/Getty Images

Considering the Rhetorical Situation

Arguments do not take place in isolation. They are written by real people in response to a particular set of circumstances called the **rhetorical situation** (see pp. 9–13). The rhetorical situation consists of the following five elements:

- The writer
- The writer's purpose
- The writer's audience
- The question
- The context

By analyzing the rhetorical situation, you are able to determine why the writer made the choices he or she did and how these choices affect the argument.

ANALYZING THE RHETORICAL SITUATION

To help you analyze the rhetorical situation of an argument, look for information about the essay and its author.

1. **Look at the essay's headnote.** If the essay you are reading has a headnote, it can contain useful information about the writer, the issue being discussed, and the structure of the essay. For this reason, it is a good idea to read headnotes carefully.

2. **Look for clues within the essay.** The writer's use of particular words and phrases can sometimes provide information about his or her preconceptions as well as about the cultural context of the argument. Historical or cultural references can indicate what ideas or information the writer expects readers to have.

3. **Search the web.** Often, just a few minutes online can give you a lot of useful information—such as the background of a particular debate or the biography of the writer. By looking at titles of the other books or essays the writer has written, you may also be able to get an idea of his or her biases or point of view.

The Writer

Begin your analysis of the rhetorical situation by trying to determine whether anything in the writer's background (for example, the writer's education, experience, race, gender, political beliefs, religion, age, and experiences) has influenced the content of the argument. Also consider whether the writer seems to have any preconceptions about the subject. (For a discussion of a writer's biases and preconceptions, see pp. 9–10.)

ANALYZING THE WRITER

- What is the writer's background?

- How does the writer's background affect the content of the argument?

- What preconceptions about the subject does the writer seem to have?

If you were analyzing "Letter from Birmingham Jail," it would help to know that Martin Luther King Jr. was pastor of the Dexter Avenue Baptist Church in Montgomery, Alabama. In 1956, he organized a bus boycott that led to a United States Supreme Court decision that outlawed segregation on Alabama's buses. In addition, King was a leader of the Southern Christian Leadership Conference and strongly believed in nonviolent protest. His books include *Stride towards Freedom* (1958) and *Why We Can't Wait* (1964). His "I Have a Dream" speech, which he delivered on the steps of the Lincoln Memorial on August 28, 1963, is considered by scholars to be one of the most influential speeches of the twentieth century. In 1964, King won the Nobel Prize for peace.

In "Letter from Birmingham Jail," King addresses the injustices that he sees in America—especially in the South—and makes a strong case for civil

"I Have a Dream" speech, Washington, D.C. (August 1963)

© Hulton-Deutsch Collection/CORBIS/Getty Images

rights for all races. Throughout his argument, King includes numerous references to the Bible, to philosophers, and to political and religious thinkers. By doing so, he makes it clear to readers that he is aware of the social, cultural, religious, and political implications of his actions. Because he is a clergyman, King suggests that by battling in-justice, he, like the apostle Paul, is doing God's work. This point is made clear in the following passage (para. 3):

> But more basically, I am in Birmingham because injustice is here. Just as the prophets of the eighth century B.C. left their villages and carried their "thus saith the Lord" far beyond the boundaries of their home towns, and just as the Apostle Paul left his village of Tarsus and carried the gospel of Jesus Christ to the far corners of the Greco-Roman world, so am I compelled to carry the gospel of freedom beyond my own home town. Like Paul, I must constantly respond to the Macedonian call for aid.

The Writer's Purpose

Next, consider what the writer hopes to achieve with his or her argument. In other words, ask yourself if the writer is trying to challenge people's ideas, persuade them to accept new points of view, or influence their behavior. (For a discussion of a writer's purpose, see p. 10.)

ANALYZING THE WRITER'S PURPOSE

- Does the writer state his or her purpose directly, or is the purpose implied?
- Is the writer's purpose simply to convince or to encourage action?
- Does the writer rely primarily on logic or on emotion?
- Does the writer have a hidden agenda?

It is clear that Martin Luther King Jr. wrote "Letter from Birmingham Jail" to convince readers that even though he had been arrested, his actions were both honorable and just. To get readers to understand that, like Henry David Thoreau, he is protesting laws that he considers wrong, he draws a distinction between just and unjust laws. For him, a law is just if it "squares with the moral law or the law of God" (16). A law is unjust if it "is out of harmony with the moral law" (16). As a clergyman and a civil rights leader, King believed that he had an obligation both to point out the immorality of unjust laws and to protest them—even if it meant going to jail.

The Writer's Audience

To analyze the writer's audience, begin by considering whether the writer seems to see readers as friendly, hostile, or neutral. (For a discussion of types of audiences, see pp. 10–13.) Also, determine how much knowledge the writer assumes that readers have. Then, consider how the writer takes into account factors like the audience's race, religion, gender, education, age, and ethnicity. Next, decide what preconceptions the writer thinks readers have about the subject. Finally, see if the writer shares any common ground with readers.

ANALYZING THE WRITER'S AUDIENCE

- Who is the writer's intended audience?

- Does the writer see the audience as informed or uninformed?

- Does the writer see the audience as hostile, friendly, or neutral?

- What values does the writer think the audience holds?

- What does the writer seem to assume about the audience's background?

- On what points do the writer and the audience agree? On what points do they disagree?

In "Letter from Birmingham Jail," King addresses more than one audience. First, he speaks directly to eight clergymen from Birmingham, who are at worst hostile and at best skeptical. They consider King an outsider whose actions are "unwise and untimely" (1). Before addressing their concerns, King tries to establish common ground, referring to his readers as "fellow clergymen" and "my Christian and Jewish brothers." He then goes on to say that he wishes that the clergymen had supported his actions instead of criticizing them. King ends his letter on a conciliatory note by asking his readers to forgive him if he has overstated his case or been unduly harsh.

King also speaks to white moderates, who he assumes are sympathetic to his cause but concerned about his methods. He understands that he has to influence this segment of his audience if he is to gain wide support for his cause. For this reason, King uses a restrained tone and emphasizes the universality of his message, ending his letter with a plea that is calculated to console and inspire those people who need reassurance (50):

> Let us all hope that the dark clouds of racial prejudice will soon pass away and the deep fog of misunderstanding will be lifted from our fear-drenched communities, and in some not too distant tomorrow the radiant stars of love and brotherhood will shine over our great nation with all their scintillating beauty.

Finally, King indirectly addresses the American people. He knows that because of his stature, his letter will be read by a broad, national audience, not just those who live in Birmingham, Alabama. King sees this audience as well meaning but confused about the racial situation in the United States. He realizes that to achieve his ends, he has to win over this audience and motivate them to take action. To do so, he appeals to their innate sense of justice and encourages them to do what's morally right, despite any misgivings.

The Question

Try to determine what question the writer is trying to answer. Is the question suitable for argument? Decide if there are good arguments on both sides of the issue. For example, what issue (or issues) is the writer confronting? Does he or she address them adequately? (For a discussion of the question, see p. 13.)

ANALYZING THE QUESTION

- What is the central question of the argument?

- Are there solid arguments on both sides of the issue?

- Has the writer answered the question fully enough?

The question King attempts to answer in "Letter from Birmingham Jail" is why he has decided to come to Birmingham to lead protests. Because the answer to this question is complicated, King addresses a number of issues. Although his main concern is with racial segregation in Alabama, he also is troubled by the indifference of white moderates who have urged him to call off his protests. In addition, he feels that he needs to explain his actions (for example, engaging in nonviolent protests) and address those who doubt his motives. King answers his critics (as well as his central question) by saying that because the people of the United States are interconnected, the injustices in one state will eventually affect the entire country.

The Context

The **context** is the set of circumstances that creates the need for the argument. As you analyze an argument, try to determine the social, historical, economic, political, and cultural events that set the stage for the argument and the part that these events play in the argument itself. (For a discussion of context, see p. 14.)

ANALYZING THE CONTEXT

- What situation (or situations) set the stage for the argument?

- What social, economic, political, and cultural events triggered the argument?

- What historical references situate this argument in a particular place or time?

The immediate context of "Letter to Birmingham Jail" is well known: Martin Luther King Jr. wrote an open letter to eight white clergymen in which he defended his protests against racial segregation. However, the wider social and political context of the letter is less well known.

In 1896, the U.S. Supreme Court ruled in *Plessy v. Ferguson* that "separate but equal" accommodations on railroad cars gave African Americans the equal protection guaranteed by the Fourteenth Amendment of the U.S. Constitution. Well into the twentieth century, this decision was used to justify separate public facilities—including restrooms, water fountains, and even schools and hospitals—for blacks and whites.

In the mid-1950s, state support for segregation of the races and discrimination against African Americans began to be challenged. For example, Supreme Court decisions in 1954 and 1955 found that segregation in the public schools and other publicly financed locations was unconstitutional. At the same time, whites and blacks alike were calling for an end

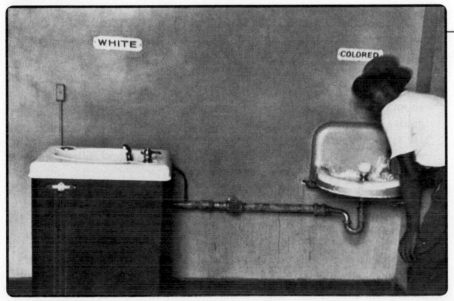

Segregated water fountains in North Carolina (1950)

© Elliott Erwitt/Magnum

to racial discrimination. Their actions took the form of marches, boycotts, and sit-ins (organized nonviolent protests whose participants refused to move from a public area). Many whites, however, particularly in the South, strongly resisted any sudden changes in race relations.

King's demonstrations in Birmingham, Alabama, took place within this larger social and political context. His campaign was a continuation of the push for equal rights that had been gaining momentum in the United States for decades. King, along with the Southern Christian Leadership Conference, had dispatched hundreds of people to Birmingham to engage in nonviolent demonstrations against those who were determined to keep African Americans from gaining their full rights as citizens.

Considering the Means of Persuasion: *Logos, Pathos, Ethos*

In the introduction to this book, you learned how writers of argument use three **means of persuasion**—*logos*, *pathos*, and *ethos*—to appeal to readers. You also saw how the **rhetorical triangle** represents the way these three appeals come into play within an argument. (See p. 19 for more information about the rhetorical triangle.) Of course, the degree to which a writer uses each of these appeals depends on the rhetorical situation. Moreover, a single argument can use more than one appeal—for example, an important research source would involve both the logic of the argument (*logos*) and the credibility of the writer (*ethos*). In "Letter from Birmingham Jail," King uses all three appeals.

The Appeal to Reason (Logos)

In "Letter from Birmingham Jail," King attempts to demonstrate the logic of his position. In paragraph 15, for example, he says that there are two types of laws—just and unjust. He then points out that he has both a legal and a moral responsibility to "disobey unjust laws." In paragraph 16, King supports his position with references to various philosophers and theologians—for example, St. Thomas Aquinas, Martin Buber, and Paul Tillich. He also develops the logical argument that even though all Americans should obey the law, they are responsible to a higher moral authority—God.

The Appeal to the Emotions (Pathos)

Throughout "Letter from Birmingham Jail," King attempts to create sympathy for his cause. In paragraph 14, for example, he catalogs the injustices of life in the United States for African Americans. He makes a particularly emotional appeal by quoting a hypothetical five-year-old boy who might ask, "Daddy, why do white people treat colored people so mean?" In addition, he includes vivid images of racial injustice to provoke anger against those who deny African Americans equal rights. In this way, King creates sympathy (and possibly empathy) in readers.

The Appeal to Authority (Ethos)

To be persuasive, King has to establish his credibility. In paragraph 2, for example, he reminds readers that he is the president of the Southern Christian Leadership Conference, "an organization operating in every southern state." In paragraph 3, he compares himself to the apostle Paul, who carried the gospel "to the far corners of the Greco-Roman world."

In addition, King attempts to show readers that what he is doing is well within the mainstream of American political and social thought. By alluding to Thomas Jefferson, Henry David Thoreau, and the 1954 U.S. Supreme Court decision that outlawed segregation in public schools, he tries to demonstrate that he is not the wild-eyed radical that some believe him to be. Thus, King establishes himself in both secular and religious terms as a leader who has the stature and the authority to present his case.

Finally, King repeatedly uses the words "we" and "us" to establish a connection to his readers. By doing so, he conveys the impression that like him, readers are part of the struggle to achieve social justice for African Americans.

Considering the Writer's Rhetorical Strategies

Writers use various **rhetorical strategies** to present their ideas and opinions. Here are a few of the elements that you should examine when analyzing and evaluating an argument.

Thesis

The **thesis**—the main idea or claim that the argument supports—is of primary importance in every argument. When you analyze an argument, you should always ask, "What is the essay's thesis, and why does the writer state it as he or she does?" You should also consider at what point in the argument the thesis is stated and what the effect of this placement is.

In "Letter from Birmingham Jail," Martin Luther King Jr. begins by telling readers that he is "confined here in the Birmingham city jail" and that he is writing his letter to answer clergymen who have called his demonstrations "unwise and untimely." King clearly (and unapologetically) states his thesis ("But more basically, I am in Birmingham because injustice is here") at the beginning of the third paragraph, right after he explains his purpose, so that readers will have no doubt what his position is as they read the rest of his argument.

Organization

The **organization** of an argument—how a writer arranges ideas—is also important. For example, after stating his thesis, King tells readers why he is in Birmingham and what he hopes to accomplish: he wants unjust laws to be abolished and the 1954 Supreme Court ruling to be enforced. King then **refutes**—disproves or calls into question—the specific charges that were leveled at him by the white clergymen who want him to stop his protests.

The structure of "Letter from Birmingham Jail" enables King to make his points clearly, logically, and convincingly:

- King begins his argument by addressing the charge that his actions are untimely. If anything, says King, his actions are not timely enough: after all, African Americans have waited more than 340 years for their "constitutional and God-given rights" (14).

- He then addresses the issue of his willingness to break laws and makes the distinction between just and unjust laws.

- After chiding white moderates for not supporting his cause, he addresses their claim that he is extreme. According to King, this charge is false: if he had not embraced a philosophy of nonviolent protest, the streets of the South would "be flowing with blood" (29).

- King then makes the point that the contemporary church must recapture the "sacrificial spirit of the early church" (42). He does this by linking his struggle for freedom with the "sacred heritage of our nation and the eternal will of God" (44).

- King ends his argument by asserting both his humility and his unity with the white clergy.

Evidence

To convince an audience, a writer must support the thesis with **evidence**—facts, observations, expert opinion, and so on. King presents a great deal of evidence to support his arguments. For instance, he uses numerous examples (both historical and personal) as well as many references to a wide range of philosophers, political thinkers, and theologians (such as Jesus, St. Paul, St. Augustine, Amos, Martin Luther, Martin Buber, and Abraham Lincoln). According to King, these individuals, who were once considered "extremists," were not afraid of "making waves" when the need arose. Now, however, they are well within the mainstream of social, political, and religious thought. King also presents reasons, facts, and quotations to support his points.

Stylistic Techniques

Writers also use stylistic techniques to make their arguments more memorable and more convincing. For example, in "Letter from Birmingham Jail," King uses figurative devices such as *similes*, *metaphors*, and *allusions* to enhance his argument.

Simile A **simile** is a figure of speech that compares two unlike things using the word *like* or *as*.

> Like a boil that can never be cured so long as it is covered up but must be opened with all its ugliness to the natural medicines of air and light, injustice must be exposed, . . . before it can be cured. (24)

> Isn't this like condemning a robbed man because his possession of money precipitated the evil act of robbery? (25)

Metaphor A **metaphor** is a comparison in which two dissimilar things are compared without the word *like* or *as*. A metaphor suggests that two things that are very different share a quality.

> Frankly, I have yet to engage in a direct-action campaign that was "well timed" in the view of those who have not suffered unduly from the disease of segregation. (13)

> [W]hen you see the vast majority of your twenty million Negro brothers smothering in an airtight cage of poverty . . . (14)

Allusion An **allusion** is a reference within a work to a person, literary or biblical text, or historical event in order to enlarge the context of the situation being written about. The writer expects readers to recognize the allusion and to make the connection to the text they are reading.

> I would agree with St. Augustine that "an unjust law is no law at all." (15)

> Of course, there is nothing new about this kind of civil disobedience. It was evidenced sublimely in the refusal of Shadrach, Meshach, and Abednego to obey the laws of Nebuchadnezzar, on the ground that a higher moral law was at stake. (21) [King expects his audience of clergymen to recognize this reference to the Book of Daniel in the Old Testament.]

In addition to those figurative devices, King uses stylistic techniques such as *parallelism*, *repetition*, and *rhetorical questions* to further his argument.

Parallelism **Parallelism**, the use of similar grammatical structures to emphasize related ideas, makes a passage easier to follow.

In any nonviolent campaign there are four basic steps: collection of the facts to determine whether injustices exist; negotiation; self-purification; and direct action. (6)

Shallow understanding from people of good will is more frustrating than absolute misunderstanding from people of ill will. Lukewarm acceptance is much more bewildering than outright rejection. (23)

I wish you had commended the Negro sit-inners and demonstrators of Birmingham for their sublime courage, their willingness to suffer, and their amazing discipline in the midst of great provocation. (47)

Repetition   Intentional **repetition** involves repeating a word or phrase for emphasis, clarity, or emotional impact.

"Are you able to accept blows without retaliating?" "Are you able to endure the ordeal of jail?" (8)

If I have said anything in this letter that overstates the truth and indicates an unreasonable impatience, I beg you to forgive me. If I have said anything that understates the truth and indicates my having patience that allows me to settle for anything less than brotherhood, I beg God to forgive me. (49)

Rhetorical questions   A **rhetorical question** is a question that is asked to encourage readers to reflect on an issue, not to elicit a reply.

One may well ask: "How can you advocate breaking some laws and obeying others?" (15)

Will we be extremists for hate or for love? (31)

Assessing the Argument

No rhetorical analysis of an argument would be complete without an assessment of its **effectiveness**—whether the rhetorical strategies the writer uses create a clear and persuasive argument or whether they fall short. When you write a rhetorical analysis, you can begin with an assessment of the argument as a whole and go on to support it, or you can begin with a discussion of the various rhetorical strategies that the writer uses and then end with your assessment of the argument.

After analyzing "Letter from Birmingham Jail," you could reasonably conclude that King has written a highly effective argument that is likely to convince his readers that his presence in Birmingham is both justified and necessary. Using *logos*, *pathos*, and *ethos*, he constructs a multifaceted argument that is calculated to appeal to the various segments of his audience—Southern clergymen, white moderates, and a cross section of Americans. In addition, King uses similes, metaphors, and allusions to enrich his argument and to make it more memorable, and he uses parallelism, repetition, and rhetorical questions to emphasize ideas and to reinforce his points. Because it is so clear and powerful, King's argument—in particular, the distinction between just and unjust laws—addresses not only the injustices that were present in 1963 when it was written but also the injustices and inequalities that exist today. In this sense, King has written an argument that has broad significance beyond the audiences for which it was originally intended.

CHECKLIST

Preparing to Write a Rhetorical Analysis

As you read, ask the following questions:

- ☐ Who is the writer? Is there anything in the writer's background that might influence what is (or is not) included in the argument?
- ☐ What is the writer's purpose? What does the writer hope to achieve?
- ☐ What question has the writer decided to address? How broad is the question?
- ☐ What situation created the need for the argument?
- ☐ At what points in the argument does the writer appeal to logic? To the emotions? How does the writer try to establish his or her credibility?

- ☐ What is the argument's thesis? Where is it stated? Why?
- ☐ How does the writer organize the argument? How effective is this arrangement of ideas?
- ☐ What evidence does the writer use to support the argument? Does the writer use enough evidence?
- ☐ Does the writer use similes, metaphors, and allusions?
- ☐ Does the writer use parallelism, repetition, and rhetorical questions?
- ☐ Given your analysis, what is your overall assessment of the argument?

Sample Rhetorical Analysis

In preparation for a research paper, Deniz Bilgutay, a student in a writing class, read the following essay, "Terror's Purse Strings" by Dana Thomas, which makes an argument against buying counterfeit designer goods. Deniz then wrote the rhetorical analysis that appears on pages 119–121. (Deniz Bilgutay's research paper, "The High Cost of Cheap Counterfeit Goods," uses "Terror's Purse Strings" as a source. See Appendix B.)

This essay appeared in the *New York Times* on August 30, 2007.

TERROR'S PURSE STRINGS

DANA THOMAS

Luxury fashion designers are busily putting final touches on the handbags they 1 will present during the spring-summer women's wear shows, which begin next week in New York City's Bryant Park. To understand the importance of the handbag in fashion today consider this: According to consumer surveys conducted by Coach, the average American woman was buying two new handbags a year in 2000; by 2004, it was more than four. And the average luxury bag retails for 10 to 12 times its production cost.

"There is a kind of an obsession with bags," the designer Miuccia Prada 2 told me. "It's so easy to make money."

Counterfeiters agree. As soon as a handbag hits big, counterfeiters around 3 the globe churn out fake versions by the thousands. And they have no trouble selling them. Shoppers descend on Canal Street in New York, Santee Alley in Los Angeles, and flea markets and purse parties around the country to pick up knockoffs for one-tenth the legitimate bag's retail cost, then pass them off as real.

"Judges, prosecutors, defense attorneys shop here," a private investigator 4 told me as we toured the counterfeit section of Santee Alley. "Affluent people from Newport Beach." According to a study by the British law firm Davenport Lyons, two-thirds of British consumers are "proud to tell their family and friends" that they bought fake luxury fashion items.

At least 11 percent of the world's clothing is fake, according to 2000 figures 5 from the Global Anti-Counterfeiting Group in Paris. Fashion is easy to copy: counterfeiters buy the real items, take them apart, scan the pieces to make patterns, and produce almost-perfect fakes.

Most people think that buying an imitation handbag or wallet is harmless, a victimless crime. But the counterfeiting rackets are run by crime syndicates

> "At least 11 percent of the world's clothing is fake." 6

that also deal in narcotics, weapons, child prostitution, human trafficking, and

An international criminal police organization

terrorism. Ronald K. Noble, the secretary general of Interpol,° told the House of Representatives Committee on International Relations that profits from the sale of counterfeit goods have gone to groups associated with Hezbollah, the Shiite terrorist group, paramilitary organizations in Northern Ireland, and FARC, the Revolutionary Armed Forces of Colombia.

Sales of counterfeit T-shirts may have helped finance the 1993 World 7 Trade Center bombing, according to the International AntiCounterfeiting Coalition. "Profits from counterfeiting are one of the three main sources of income supporting international terrorism," said Magnus Ranstorp, a terrorism expert at the University of St. Andrews, in Scotland.

Most fakes today are produced in China, a good many of them by chil- 8 dren. Children are sometimes sold or sent off by their families to work in clandestine factories that produce counterfeit luxury goods. Many in the West consider this an urban myth. But I have seen it myself.

On a warm winter afternoon in Guangzhou, I accompanied Chinese 9 police officers on a factory raid in a decrepit tenement. Inside, we found two dozen children, ages 8 to 13, gluing and sewing together fake luxury-brand handbags. The police confiscated everything, arrested the owner, and sent the children out. Some punched their timecards, hoping to still get paid. (The average Chinese factory worker earns about $120 a month; the counterfeit factory worker earns half that or less.) As we made our way back to the police vans, the children threw bottles and cans at us. They were now jobless and, because the factory owner housed them, homeless. It was *Oliver Twist* in the 21st century.

What can we do to stop this? Much like the war on drugs, the effort to 10 protect luxury brands must go after the source: the counterfeit manufacturers. The company that took me on the Chinese raid is one of the only luxury-goods makers that works directly with Chinese authorities to shut down factories, and it has one of the lowest rates of counterfeiting.

Luxury brands also need to teach consumers that the traffic in fake goods 11 has many victims. But most companies refuse to speak publicly about counterfeiting—some won't even authenticate questionable items for concerned customers—believing, like Victorians,° that acknowledging despicable actions tarnishes their sterling reputations.

So it comes down to us. If we stop knowingly buying fakes, the supply 12 chain will dry up and counterfeiters will go out of business. The crime syndicates will have far less money to finance their illicit activities and their terrorist plots. And the children? They can go home.

The people who lived during the reign of Victoria (1819–1901), queen of Great Britain and Ireland, who are often associated with prudish behavior

A POWERFUL CALL TO ACTION

DENIZ BILGUTAY

In her *New York Times* essay, "Terror's Purse Strings," writer Dana Thomas uses the opening of New York's fashion shows as an opportunity to expose a darker side of fashion—the impact of imitation designer goods. Thomas explains to her readers why buying counterfeit luxury items, like fake handbags, is a serious problem. Her first goal is to raise awareness of the dangerous ties between counterfeiters who sell fake luxury merchandise and international criminal organizations that support terrorism and child labor. Her second goal is to explain how people can be a part of the solution by refusing to buy the counterfeit goods that finance these criminal activities. By establishing her credibility, building

1 Context

Topic

Analysis of writer's purpose

Thesis statement: Assessment of essay

her case slowly, and appealing to both logic and emotions, Thomas succeeds in writing an interesting and informative argument.

Analysis of writer's audience

For Thomas's argument to work, she has to earn her readers' trust.   2
She does so first by anticipating a sympathetic, well-intentioned, educated audience and then by establishing her own credibility. To avoid sounding accusatory, Thomas assumes that her readers are unaware of the problem posed by counterfeit goods. She demonstrates this by presenting basic factual information and by acknowledging what "most people think" or

Writer's use of similes, metaphors, allusions

what "many in the West consider": that buying counterfeit goods is harmless. She also acknowledges her readers' high level of education by drawing comparisons with history and literature—specifically, the Victorians

Writer's use of *ethos*

and *Oliver Twist*. To further earn the audience's trust, she uses her knowledge and position to gain credibility. As the Paris correspondent for *Newsweek* and as the author of a book on luxury goods, Thomas has credibility.

Analysis of the writer

Showing her familiarity with the world of fashion by referring to a conversation with renowned designer Miuccia Prada, she further establishes this credibility. Later in the article, she shares her experience of witnessing the abuse that accompanies the production of fake designer handbags. This anecdote allows her to say, "I've seen it myself," confirming her knowledge not just of the fashion world but also of the world of counterfeiting. Despite her authority, she does not distance herself from readers. In fact, she goes out of her way to identify with them, using informal style and first person, noting "it comes down to us" and asking what "we" can do.

Analysis of essay's organization

In Thomas's argument, both the organization and the use of   3
evidence are effective. Thomas begins her article with statements that

Writer's use of *logos*

are easy to accept, and as she proceeds, she addresses more serious issues. In the first paragraph, she simply asks readers to "understand the importance of the handbag in fashion today." She demonstrates the wide-ranging influence and appeal of counterfeit designer goods, pointing out that "at least 11 percent of the world's clothing is fake." Thomas then makes the point that the act of purchasing these seemingly frivolous goods can actually have serious consequences. For example, crime syndicates and possibly even terrorist organizations actually

Writer's use of evidence

run "the counterfeiting rackets" that produce these popular items. To support this point, she relies on two kinds of evidence—quotations from terrorism experts (specifically, the leader of a respected international police organization as well as a scholar in the field) and her own

personal experience at a Chinese factory. Both kinds of evidence appeal
to our emotions. Discussions of terrorism, especially those that recall
the terrorist attacks on the United States, create fear. Descriptions of
child labor in China encourage readers to feel sympathy.

Writer's use of *pathos*

Thomas waits until the end of her argument to present her thesis   4
because she assumes that her readers know little about the problem she
is discussing. The one flaw in her argument is her failure to provide the
evidence needed to establish connections between some causes and
their effects. For example in paragraph 7, Thomas says that the sale of
counterfeit T-shirts "may have helped finance the 1993 World Trade Center
bombing." By using the word *may*, she qualifies her claim and weakens
her argument. The same is true when Thomas says that profits from the
sale of counterfeit goods "have gone to groups associated with Hezbollah, the Shiite terrorist group." Readers are left to wonder what specific
groups are "associated with Hezbollah" and whether these groups are
in fact terrorist organizations. Without this information, her assertion
remains unsupported. In spite of these shortcomings, Thomas's argument is clear and well organized. More definite links between causes and
effects, however, would have made it more convincing than it is.

Analysis of the essay's
weakness

⊘ EXERCISE 4.1 WRITING A RHETORICAL ANALYSIS

Read the following essay, "Sweatshop Oppression," by Rajeev Ravisankar.
Then, write a one-paragraph rhetorical analysis of the essay. Follow the
template on page 123, filling in the blanks to create your analysis.

This opinion essay was published in the *Lantern*, the student newspaper
of the Ohio State University, on April 19, 2006.

SWEATSHOP OPPRESSION

RAJEEV RAVISANKAR

Being the "poor" college students that we all are, many of us undoubtedly place   1
an emphasis on finding the lowest prices. Some take this to the extreme and
camp out in front of a massive retail store in the wee hours of the morning on
Black Friday,° waiting for the opportunity to buy as much as we can for as little
as possible.

*The Friday after
Thanksgiving, traditionally
the biggest shopping day of
the year*

What often gets lost in this rampant, low-cost driven consumerism is the 2 high human cost it takes to achieve lower and lower prices. Specifically, this means the extensive use of sweatshop labor.

Many of us are familiar with the term sweatshop,° but have difficulty really 3 understanding how abhorrent the hours, wages, and conditions are. Many of these workers are forced to work 70–80 hours per week making pennies per hour. Workers are discouraged or intimidated from forming unions.

A work environment with long hours, low wages, and difficult or dangerous conditions

They must fulfill certain quotas for the day and stay extra hours (with no 4 pay) if these are not fulfilled. Some are forced to sit in front of a machine for hours as they are not permitted to take breaks unless the manager allows them to do so. Unsanitary bathrooms, poor ventilation, and extreme heat, upward of 90 degrees, are also prevalent. Child labor is utilized in some factories as well.

Facing mounting pressure from labor rights activists, trade unions, student 5 protests, and human-rights groups, companies claimed that they would make improvements. Many of the aforementioned conditions, however, persist. In many cases, even a few pennies more could make a substantial difference in the lives of these workers. Of course, multinational corporations are not interested in giving charity; they are interested in doing anything to increase profits. Also, many consumers in the West refuse to pay a little bit more even if it would improve the lives of sweatshop workers.

> "... Corporations are interested in doing anything to increase profits."

Free-market economic fundamentalists have argued that claims made by 6 those who oppose sweatshops actually have a negative impact on the plight of the poor in the developing world. They suggest that by criticizing labor and human-rights conditions, anti-sweatshop activists have forced companies to pull out of some locations, resulting in workers losing their jobs. To shift the blame in this manner is to neglect a simple fact: Companies, not the anti-sweatshop protestors, make the decision to shift to locations where they can find cheaper labor and weaker labor restrictions.

Simply put, the onus should always be on companies such as Nike, Reebok, 7 Adidas, Champion, Gap, Wal-Mart, etc. They are to blame for perpetuating a system of exploitation which seeks to get as much out of each worker for the least possible price.

By continuing to strive for lower wages and lower input costs, they are 8 taking part in a phenomenon which has been described as "the race to the bottom." The continual decline of wages and working conditions will be accompanied by a lower standard of living. This hardly seems like the best way to bring the developing world out of the pits of poverty.

So what can we do about it? Currently, the total disregard for human 9 well-being through sweatshop oppression is being addressed by a number of organizations, including University Students against Sweatshops. USAS seeks to make universities source their apparel in factories that respect workers' rights, especially the right to freely form unions.

According to an article in *The Nation*, universities purchase nearly 10 "$3 billion in T-shirts, sweatshirts, caps, sneakers and sports uniforms adorned with their institutions' names and logos." Because brands do not want to risk losing this money, it puts pressure on them to provide living wages and reasonable conditions for workers. Campaigns such as this are necessary if we are to stop the long race to the bottom.

TEMPLATE FOR WRITING A RHETORICAL ANALYSIS

Ravisankar begins his essay by _____
_____
_____.The problem he identifies is _____
_____
_____. Ravisankar assumes his readers are _____
_____
_____. His purpose in this essay is to _____
_____.

In order to accomplish this purpose, he appeals mainly to _____
_____.
_____. He also appeals to _____
_____.

In his essay, Ravisankar addresses the main argument against his thesis, the idea that _____
_____
_____.

He refutes this argument by saying _____
_____
_____.

Finally, he concludes by making the point that _____
_____

Overall, the argument Ravisankar makes [is/is not] effective because _____
_____
_____
_____

➔ EXERCISE 4.2 WRITING A RHETORICAL ANALYSIS

Read the following essay, "Sweatshops Are Good," by Jerome Sieger, a student at American University. Then, write a rhetorical analysis of Sieger's essay. Be sure to consider the rhetorical situation, the means of persuasion, and the writer's rhetorical strategies. End your rhetorical analysis with an assessment of the strengths and weaknesses of Sieger's argument.

This opinion column was published in *The Eagle*, American University's student newspaper, on February 15, 2017.

SWEATSHOPS ARE GOOD

JEROME SIEGER

If you can, take off one of your shoes. Go ahead; I'll wait. Check to see where 1 it was made. Chances are your shoes, like most clothing we wear, were manufactured in a developing country in Asia or Latin America. Mine, for instance, were made in Vietnam. We all know that our clothes were made in factories commonly referred to as "sweatshops." If you're anything like most people, the thought of buying the products of such sweatshop labor makes you exceedingly guilty. Don't be. When put into their proper context, sweatshops are necessary and beneficial to workers. To quote the renowned Keynesian Jeffrey Sachs, "my concern is not that there are too many sweatshops, but that there are too few."

The ultimate problem for opponents of sweatshops is a failure of imagi- 2 nation. They simply lack empathy—the ability to imagine someone else's perspective. I would not want to work in a sweatshop, and if you have the privilege of attending a university in America, neither would you. But not everyone is a middle-class American. Our country is rich enough to afford such a high minimum wage and strict labor standards. But the truth is, for hundreds of millions of people, sweatshops offer the best hope to escape crippling poverty.

I will present data to back up this point, but just the story of how much 3 effort people put in to work in sweatshops should suffice to prove it. Some 150 million people in China alone have left their homes and moved across the country to get factory jobs. One simply does not uproot their life and leave their home to get a job they don't really want. When factory jobs open up, thousands of people wait in line to apply. The fact that sweatshop workers choose their jobs, and that they put in so much effort to get them, must mean something. Simply put, as bad as sweatshops are, most alternatives are much worse.

And the numbers bear this out. This 2006 study in the *Journal of Labor* 4 *Research* analyzed sweatshops across Asia and Latin America and found that in 90 percent of countries analyzed, working ten-hour days in sweatshops lifts the worker's income above the national average. In half of those countries, income rose to three times the national average. And this 2012 study from researchers at Duke University found that sweatshop workers in El Salvador believed that their factory jobs represented an improvement over their previous jobs in areas such as working conditions, job stability, location, benefits, and schedule.

The research is pretty clear that sweatshops are significantly better than alter- 5
natives, but something is lost when you reduce the difference to numbers alone.
It helps us empathize with sweatshop workers if we imagine the kinds of jobs they
go to when factory work is not an option. Before they work in sweatshops, most
factory workers in developing countries work in subsistence agriculture, which is
one of the three most dangerous industries in the world according to the International Labor Organization—rivaled only by construction and mining. And if
they're not in subsistence agriculture, they might be in commercial agriculture,
often as the slave of a chocolate company, for instance. Furthermore, in the past,
when sweatshops have shut down due to boycotts, many workers have "turned to
street hustling, stone crushing, and prostitution." When people bash sweatshops,
they are unknowingly advocating that poor workers take up these jobs instead.

And sweatshops not only reduce
poverty, but they also provide empow-
erment for women. Research has shown
that work in sweatshops delays marriage

> "Not everyone is a
> middle-class American."

6

and pregnancy for women and girls, and also increases their school enrollment. Poor women in developing countries are among the most vulnerable
people on the planet. Support of sweatshops is a feminist position.

So, what's the endgame here? Surely, even if sweatshop labor is better 7
than its wretched alternatives, we would ultimately want workers in developing countries to move to jobs even better than that. We would want to see an
eventual end to long hours and child labor. These wants are legitimate, and the
path to achieving them is through the arduous process of development. An
economy can't just jump from Bangladesh to Belgium over night, no matter
how much you protest GAP. The truth of the matter is that factory labor is
a necessary step in economic development. The notorious super liberal and
Nobel laureate economist Paul Krugman explains:

> "[T]he growth of manufacturing . . . has a ripple effect throughout the
> economy. The pressure on the land becomes less intense, so rural wages
> rise; the pool of unemployed urban dwellers always anxious for work
> shrinks, so factories start to compete with each other for workers, and
> urban wages also begin to rise."

The past success stories of sweatshops illustrate this principle and provide 8
a model for the rising economies of today. For instance, Hong Kong, South
Korea, Taiwan, and Singapore used sweatshop labor to raise incomes from 10
percent of American levels to 40 percent in just one generation.

Sweatshops are used as a stepping stone to open up new possibilities for 9
workers. Once these new jobs are made available, sweatshop work is no longer
preferable, and conditions inevitably improve. We cannot ascend a ladder by
knocking out the next few rungs.

For all these reasons, boycotting sweatshops is perhaps the worst thing 10
rich, American consumers can do to the world's poor. One more time, look at
your shoe. If you bought it, or anything else, from a sweatshop in a developing
country, pat yourself on the back. You made the world a better place.

Understanding Logic and Recognizing Logical Fallacies

AT ISSUE

How Free Should Free Speech Be?

Ask almost anyone what makes a society free and one of the answers will be free speech. The free expression of ideas is integral to freedom itself, and protecting that freedom is part of a democratic government's job.

But what happens when those ideas are offensive, or even dangerous? If free speech has limits, is it still free? When we consider the question abstractly, it's very easy to say no. After all, there is no shortage of historical evidence linking censorship with tyranny. When we think of limiting free speech, we think of totalitarian regimes, like Nazi Germany. On the other hand, what if the people arguing for the right to be heard are Nazis themselves? In places like Israel and France, where the legacy of Nazi Germany is still all too real, there are some things you simply cannot say. Anti-Semitic language is considered "hate speech," and those who perpetuate it face stiff fines, if not imprisonment. In the United States, speech—even speech that many would consider "hate speech"—is explicitly protected by the First Amendment of the Constitution. Nonetheless, many colleges and universities have sought to combat discrimination and harassment by instituting speech codes that prohibit speech that they deem inappropriate.

On American college campuses, freedom of speech has traditionally been considered fundamental to a liberal education. Indeed, encountering ideas that make you feel uncomfortable is a necessary part of a college education. But the question of free speech is easy to answer when it's theoretical: when the issue is made tangible by racist language or by a discussion of a traumatic experience, it becomes much more difficult to navigate. Should minorities be forced to listen to racists spew hate? Should a rape survivor have to sit through a discussion of rape in American literature? If you penalize a person for saying something hateful, will other subjects soon become off-limits for discussion?

Later in this chapter, you will be asked to think more about this issue. You will be given several sources to consider and asked to write a logical argument that takes a position on how free free speech should be.

The word *logic* comes from the Greek word *logos*, roughly translated as "word," "thought," "principle," or "reason." **Logic** is concerned with the principles of correct reasoning. By studying logic, you learn the rules that determine the validity of arguments. In other words, logic enables you to tell whether a conclusion correctly follows from a set of statements or assumptions.

Why should you study logic? One answer is that logic enables you to make valid points and draw sound conclusions. An understanding of logic also enables you to evaluate the arguments of others. When you understand the basic principles of logic, you know how to tell the difference between a strong argument and a weak argument—between one that is well reasoned and one that is not. This ability can help you cut through the tangle of jumbled thought that characterizes many of the arguments you encounter daily—on television, radio, and the internet; in the press; and from friends. Finally, logic enables you to communicate clearly and forcefully. Understanding the characteristics of good arguments helps you to present your own ideas in a coherent and even compelling way.

Specific rules determine the criteria you use to develop (and to evaluate) arguments logically. For this reason, you should become familiar with the basic principles of *deductive* and *inductive reasoning*—two important ways information is organized in argumentative essays. (Keep in mind that a single argumentative essay might contain both deductive reasoning and inductive reasoning. For the sake of clarity, however, we will discuss them separately.)

Student in a study group making a point

Johner Images/Getty Images

What Is Deductive Reasoning?

Most of us use deductive reasoning every day—at home, in school, on the job, and in our communities—usually without even realizing it.

Deductive reasoning begins with **premises**—statements or assumptions on which an argument is based or from which conclusions are drawn. Deductive reasoning moves from general statements, or premises, to specific conclusions. The process of deduction has traditionally been illustrated with a **syllogism**, which consists of a *major premise*, a *minor premise*, and a *conclusion*:

Thomas Jefferson

© RMN-Grand Palais/Art Resource, NY

MAJOR PREMISE	All Americans are guaranteed freedom of speech by the Constitution.
MINOR PREMISE	Sarah is an American.
CONCLUSION	Therefore, Sarah is guaranteed freedom of speech.

A syllogism begins with a **major premise**—a general statement that relates two terms. It then moves to a **minor premise**—an example of the statement that was made in the major premise. If these two premises are linked correctly, a **conclusion** that is supported by the two premises logically follows. (Notice that the conclusion in the syllogism above contains no terms that do not appear in the major and minor premises.) The strength of deductive reasoning is that if readers accept the major and minor premises, the conclusion must necessarily follow.

Thomas Jefferson used deductive reasoning in the Declaration of Independence (see p. 732). When, in 1776, the Continental Congress asked him to draft this document, Jefferson knew that he had to write a powerful argument that would convince the world that the American colonies were justified in breaking away from England. He knew how compelling a deductive argument could be, and so he organized the Declaration of Independence to reflect the traditional structure of deductive logic. It contains a major premise, a minor premise (supported by evidence), and a conclusion. Expressed as a syllogism, here is the argument that Jefferson used:

MAJOR PREMISE	When a government oppresses people, the people have a right to rebel against that government.
MINOR PREMISE	The government of England oppresses the American people.
CONCLUSION	Therefore, the American people have the right to rebel against the government of England.

In practice, deductive arguments are more complicated than the simple three-part syllogism suggests. Still, it is important to understand the basic structure of a syllogism because a syllogism enables you to map out your argument, to test it, and to see if it makes sense.

Constructing Sound Syllogisms

A syllogism is **valid** when its conclusion follows logically from its premises. A syllogism is **true** when the premises are consistent with the facts. To be **sound**, a syllogism must be *both* valid and true.

Consider the following valid syllogism:

MAJOR PREMISE	All state universities must accommodate disabled students.
MINOR PREMISE	UCLA is a state university.
CONCLUSION	Therefore, UCLA must accommodate disabled students.

In the preceding valid syllogism, both the major premise and the minor premise are factual statements. If both these premises are true, then the conclusion must also be true. Because the syllogism is both valid and true, it is also sound.

However, a syllogism can be valid without being true. For example, look at the following syllogism:

MAJOR PREMISE	All recipients of support services are wealthy.
MINOR PREMISE	Dillon is a recipient of support services.
CONCLUSION	Therefore, Dillon is wealthy.

As illogical as it may seem, this syllogism is valid: its conclusion follows logically from its premises. The major premise states that *recipients of support services*—all such *recipients*—are wealthy. However, this premise is clearly false: some recipients of support services may be wealthy, but more are probably not. For this reason, even though the syllogism is valid, it is not true.

Keep in mind that validity is a test of an argument's structure, not of its soundness. Even if a syllogism's major and minor premises are true, its conclusion may not necessarily be valid.

Consider the following examples of invalid syllogisms.

Syllogism with an Illogical Middle Term

A syllogism with an illogical middle term cannot be valid. The **middle term** of a syllogism is the term that occurs in both the major and minor premises but not in the conclusion. (It links the major term and the minor term together in the syllogism.) A middle term of a valid syllogism must refer to *all* members of the designated class or group—for example, *all* dogs, *all* people, *all* men, or *all* women.

Consider the following invalid syllogism:

MAJOR PREMISE   All dogs are mammals.

MINOR PREMISE   Some mammals are porpoises.

CONCLUSION   Therefore, some porpoises are dogs.

Even though the statements in the major and minor premises are true, the syllogism is not valid. *Mammals* is the middle term because it appears in both the major and minor premises. However, because the middle term *mammal* does not refer to *all mammals*, it cannot logically lead to a valid conclusion.

Cartoonstock.com

In the syllogism that follows, the middle term *does* refer to all members of the designated group, so the syllogism is valid:

MAJOR PREMISE	All dogs are mammals.
MINOR PREMISE	Ralph is a dog.
CONCLUSION	Therefore, Ralph is a mammal.

Syllogism with a Key Term Whose Meaning Shifts

A syllogism that contains a key term whose meaning shifts cannot be valid. For this reason, the meaning of a key term must remain consistent throughout the syllogism.

Consider the following invalid syllogism:

MAJOR PREMISE	Only man is capable of analytical reasoning.
MINOR PREMISE	Anna is not a man.
CONCLUSION	Therefore, Anna is not capable of analytical reasoning.

In the major premise, *man* refers to mankind—that is, to all human beings. In the minor premise, however, *man* refers to males. In the following valid syllogism, the key terms remain consistent:

MAJOR PREMISE	All educated human beings are capable of analytical reasoning.
MINOR PREMISE	Anna is an educated human being.
CONCLUSION	Therefore, Anna is capable of analytical reasoning.

Syllogism with Negative Premise

If *either* premise in a syllogism is negative, then the conclusion must also be negative.

The following syllogism is not valid:

MAJOR PREMISE	Only senators can vote on legislation.
MINOR PREMISE	No students are senators.
CONCLUSION	Therefore, students can vote on legislation.

Because one of the premises of the syllogism above is negative ("No students are senators"), the only possible valid conclusion must also be negative ("Therefore, no students can vote on legislation").

If *both* premises are negative, however, the syllogism cannot have a valid conclusion:

MAJOR PREMISE	Disabled students may not be denied special help.
MINOR PREMISE	Jen is not a disabled student.
CONCLUSION	Therefore, Jen may not be denied special help.

In the preceding syllogism, both premises are negative. For this reason, the syllogism cannot have a valid conclusion. (How can Jen deserve special help if she is not a disabled student?) To have a valid conclusion, this syllogism must have only one negative premise:

MAJOR PREMISE	Disabled students may not be denied special help.
MINOR PREMISE	Jen is a disabled student.
CONCLUSION	Therefore, Jen may not be denied special help.

Recognizing Enthymemes

An **enthymeme** is a syllogism with one or two parts of its argument—usually, the major premise—missing. In everyday life, we often leave out parts of arguments—most of the time because we think they are so obvious (or clearly implied) that they don't need to be stated. We assume that the people hearing or reading the arguments will easily be able to fill in the missing parts.

Many enthymemes are presented as a reason plus a conclusion. Consider the following enthymeme:

Enrique has lied, so he cannot be trusted.

In the preceding statement, the minor premise (the reason) and the conclusion are stated, but the major premise is only implied. Once the missing term has been supplied, the logical structure of the enthymeme becomes clear:

MAJOR PREMISE	People who lie cannot be trusted.
MINOR PREMISE	Enrique has lied.
CONCLUSION	Therefore, Enrique cannot be trusted.

It is important to identify enthymemes in arguments you read because some writers, knowing that readers often accept enthymemes uncritically, use them intentionally to unfairly influence readers.

Consider this enthymeme:

Because Liz receives a tuition grant, she should work.

Although some readers might challenge this statement, others will accept it uncritically. When you supply the missing premise, however, the underlying assumptions of the enthymeme become clear—and open to question:

MAJOR PREMISE   All students who receive tuition grants should work.

MINOR PREMISE   Liz receives a tuition grant.

CONCLUSION   Therefore, Liz should work.

Perhaps some people who receive tuition grants should work, but should everyone? What about those who are ill or who have disabilities? What about those who participate in varsity sports or have unpaid internships? The enthymeme oversimplifies the issue and should not be accepted at face value.

At first glance, the following enthymeme might seem to make sense:

North Korea is ruled by a dictator, so it should be invaded.

However, consider the same enthymeme with the missing term supplied:

MAJOR PREMISE   All countries governed by dictators should be invaded.

MINOR PREMISE   North Korea is a country governed by a dictator.

CONCLUSION   Therefore, North Korea should be invaded.

Once the missing major premise has been supplied, the flaws in the argument become clear. Should *all* nations governed by dictators be invaded? Who should do the invading? Who would make this decision? What would be the consequences of such a policy? As this enthymeme illustrates, if the major premise of a deductive argument is questionable, then the rest of the argument will also be flawed.

BUMPER-STICKER THINKING

Bumper stickers often take the form of enthymemes:

- Self-control beats birth control.
- Peace is patriotic.
- A woman's place is in the House . . . and in the Senate.
- Ban cruel traps.
- Evolution is a theory—kind of like gravity.

- I work and pay taxes so wealthy people don't have to.

- The Bible says it, I believe it, that settles it.

- No one needs a mink coat except a mink.

- Celebrate diversity.

Most often, bumper stickers state just the conclusion of an argument and omit both the major and minor premises. Careful readers, however, will supply the missing premises and thus determine whether the argument is sound.

Bumper stickers on a car. B Christopher/Alamy Stock Photo.

❯ EXERCISE 5.1 CONSTRUCTING A SYLLOGISM

Read the following paragraph. Then, restate its main argument as a syllogism.

Drunk Driving Should Be Legalized

In ordering states to enforce tougher drunk driving standards by making it a crime to drive with a blood-alcohol concentration of .08 percent or higher, government has been permitted to criminalize the content of drivers' blood instead of their actions. The assumption that a driver who has been drinking automatically presents a danger to society even when no harm has been caused is a blatant violation of civil liberties. Government should not be concerned with the probability and propensity of a drinking driver to cause an accident; rather, laws should deal only with actions that damage person or property. Until they actually commit a crime, drunk drivers should be liberated from the force of the law. (From "Legalize Drunk Driving," by Llewellyn H. Rockwell Jr., WorldNetDaily.com)

⊖ EXERCISE 5.2 ANALYZING DEDUCTIVE LOGIC

Read the following paragraphs. Then, answer the questions that follow.

Animals Are Equal to Humans

According to the United Nations, a person may not be killed, exploited, cruelly treated, intimidated, or imprisoned for no good reason. Put another way, people should be able to live in peace, according to their own needs and preferences.

Who should have these rights? Do they apply to people of all races? Children? People who are brain damaged or senile? The declaration makes it clear that basic rights apply to everyone. To make a slave of someone who is intellectually handicapped or of a different race is no more justifiable than to make a slave of anyone else.

The reason why these rights apply to everyone is simple: regardless of our differences, we all experience a life with its mosaic of thoughts and feelings. This applies equally to the princess and the hobo, the brain surgeon and the dunce. Our value as individuals arises from this capacity to experience life, not because of any intelligence or usefulness to others. Every person has an inherent value, and deserves to be treated with respect in order to make the most of their unique life experience. (Excerpted from "Human and Animal Rights," by AnimalLiberation.org)

1. What unstated assumptions about the subject does the writer make? Does the writer expect readers to accept these assumptions? How can you tell?

2. What kind of supporting evidence does the writer provide?

3. What is the major premise of this argument?

4. Express the argument that is presented in these paragraphs as a syllogism.

5. Evaluate the syllogism you constructed. Is it true? Is it valid? Is it sound?

⊖ EXERCISE 5.3 JUDGING THE SOUNDNESS OF A DEDUCTIVE ARGUMENT

Read the following five arguments, and determine whether each is sound. (To help you evaluate the arguments, you may want to try arranging them as syllogisms.)

1. All humans are mortal. Ahmed is human. Therefore, Ahmed is mortal.

2. Perry should order eggs or oatmeal for breakfast. She won't order eggs, so she should order oatmeal.

3. The cafeteria does not serve meat loaf on Friday. Today is not Friday. Therefore, the cafeteria will not serve meat loaf.

4. All reptiles are cold-blooded. Geckos are reptiles. Therefore, geckos are cold-blooded.

5. All triangles have three equal sides. The figure on the board is a triangle. Therefore, it must have three equal sides.

⊙ EXERCISE 5.4 ANALYZING ENTHYMEMES

Read the following ten enthymemes, which come from bumper stickers. Supply the missing premises, and then evaluate the logic of each argument.

1. If you love your pet, don't eat meat.

2. War is terrorism.

3. Real men don't ask for directions.

4. Immigration is the sincerest form of flattery.

5. I eat local because I can.

6. Vote nobody for president 2020.

7. I read banned books.

8. Love is the only solution.

9. It's a child, not a choice.

10. Buy American.

Writing Deductive Arguments

Deductive arguments begin with a general principle and reach a specific conclusion. They develop that principle with logical arguments that are supported by evidence—facts, observations, the opinions of experts, and so on. Keep in mind that no single structure is suitable for all deductive (or inductive) arguments. Different issues and different audiences will determine how you arrange your ideas.

In general, deductive essays can be structured in the following way:

INTRODUCTION	Presents an overview of the issue
	States the thesis
BODY	Presents evidence: point 1 in support of the thesis
	Presents evidence: point 2 in support of the thesis
	Presents evidence: point 3 in support of the thesis
	Refutes the arguments against the thesis
CONCLUSION	Brings argument to a close
	Concluding statement reinforces the thesis

⊙ EXERCISE 5.5 IDENTIFYING THE ELEMENTS OF A DEDUCTIVE ARGUMENT

The following student essay, "College Should Be for Everyone," includes all the elements of a deductive argument. The student who wrote this essay was responding to the question, "Should everyone be encouraged to go to college?" After you read the essay, answer the questions on pages 138–141, consulting the outline above if necessary.

COLLEGE SHOULD BE FOR EVERYONE

CRYSTAL SANCHEZ

Overview of issue

Until the middle of the twentieth century, college was largely for   1
the rich. The G.I. Bill, which paid for the education of veterans returning
from World War II, helped to change this situation. By 1956, nearly half
of those who had served in World War II, almost 7.8 million people, had
taken advantage of this benefit (U.S. Department of Veterans Affairs).
Even today, however, college graduates are still a minority of the
population. According to the U.S. Census Bureau, only 30 percent of
Americans age twenty-five or older have a bachelor's degree. Although
this situation is gradually improving, it is not good for the country.

Thesis statement

Why should college be just for the privileged few? Because a college
education provides important benefits, such as increased wages for
our citizens and a stronger democracy for our nation, every U.S. citizen
should have the opportunity to attend college.

One reason everyone should have the opportunity to go to college   2 Evidence: Point 1
is that a college education gives people a chance to discover what they
are good at. It is hard for people to know if they are interested in statistics or public policy or marketing unless they have the chance to explore
these subjects. College—and only college—can give them this opportunity. Where else can a person be exposed to a large number of courses
taught by experts in a variety of disciplines? Such exposure can open
new areas of interest and lead to a much wider set of career options—
and thus to a better life (Stout). Without college, most people have limited options and never realize their true potential. Although life and work
experiences can teach a person a lot of things, the best education is the
broad kind that college offers.

Another reason everyone should have the opportunity to go to   3 Evidence: Point 2
college is that more and more jobs are being phased out or moved
overseas. Americans should go to college to develop the skills that they
will need to get the best jobs that will remain in the United States. Over
the last few decades, midlevel jobs have been steadily disappearing. If
this trend continues, the American workforce will be divided in two. One
part will consist of low-wage, low-skill service jobs, such as those in food
preparation and retail sales, and the other part will be high-skill, high-wage
jobs, such as those in management and professional fields like business
and engineering. According to a recent report, to compete in the future job
market, Americans will need the skills that colleges teach. Future workers
will need to be problem solvers who can think both critically and creatively
and who can adapt to new situations. They will also need a global awareness, knowledge of many cultures and disciplines, and the ability to communicate in different forms of media. To master these skills, Americans
have to be college educated ("Ten Skills for the Future Workforce").

Perhaps the best reason everyone should have the opportunity to   4 Evidence: Point 3
go to college is that education is an essential component of a democratic society. Those without the ability to understand and analyze news
reports are not capable of contributing to the social, political, and economic growth of the country. Democracy requires informed citizens who
will be able to analyze complicated issues in areas such as finance, education, and public health; weigh competing claims of those running for
public office; and assess the job performance of elected officials.

By providing students with the opportunity to study subjects such as history, philosophy, English, and political science, colleges and universities help them to acquire the critical-thinking skills that they will need to participate fully in American democracy.

Refutation of opposing arguments

Some people oppose the idea that everyone should have the opportunity to attend college. One objection is that educational resources are limited. Some say that if students enter colleges in great numbers they will overwhelm the higher-education system (Stout). This argument exaggerates the problem. As with any other product, if demand rises, supply will rise to meet that demand. In addition, with today's extensive distance-learning options and the availability of open educational resources—free, high-quality, digital materials—it will be possible to educate large numbers of students at a reasonable cost ("Open Educational Resources"). Another objection to encouraging everyone to attend college is that underprepared students will require so much help that they will take time and attention away from better students. This argument is actually a red herring.° Most schools already provide resources, such as tutoring and writing centers, for students who need them. With some additional funding, these schools could expand the services they already provide. This course of action will be expensive, but it is a lot less expensive than leaving millions of young people unprepared for jobs of the future.

An irrelevant side issue used as a diversion

A college education gave the returning veterans of World War II many opportunities and increased their value to the nation. Today, a college education could do the same for many citizens. This country has an obligation to offer all students access to an affordable and useful education. Not only will the students benefit personally but the nation will also. If we do not adequately prepare students for the future, then we will all suffer the consequences.

Concluding statement

5

6

Works Cited

"Open Educational Resources." *Center for American Progress*, 7 Feb. 2012, www.americanprogress.org/issues/labor /news/2012/02/07/11114/open-educational-resources/.

Stout, Chris. "Top Five Reasons Why You Should Choose to Go to College." *Ezine Articles*, 2008, ezinearticles.com/?Top-Five-Reasons -Why-You-Should-Choose-To-Go-To-College&id=384395.

"Ten Skills for the Future Workforce." *The Atlantic,* 22 June 2011, www
.theatlantic.com/education/archive/2011/06/ten-skills-for-future-work
/473484/.

United States Census Bureau. "Highest Educational Levels Reached
by Adults in the U.S. Since 1940." *US Census Bureau Newsroom,*
23 Feb. 2017, www.census.gov/press-releases/2017/cb17-51.html.

---, Department of Veterans Affairs. "Born of Controversy: The GI Bill of
Rights." *GI Bill History*, 20 Oct. 2008, www.va.gov/opa/publications
/celebrate/gi-bill.pdf.

Identifying the Elements of a Deductive Argument

1. Paraphrase this essay's thesis.

2. What arguments does the writer present as evidence to support her thesis? Which do you think is the strongest argument? Which is the weakest?

3. What opposing arguments does the writer address? What other opposing arguments could she have addressed?

4. What points does the conclusion emphasize? Do you think that any other points should be emphasized?

5. Construct a syllogism that expresses the essay's argument. Then, check your syllogism to make sure it is sound.

What Is Inductive Reasoning?

Inductive reasoning begins with specific observations (or evidence) and goes on to draw a general conclusion. You can see how induction works by looking at the following list of observations:

- Nearly 80 percent of ocean pollution comes from runoff.

- Runoff pollution can make ocean water unsafe for fish and people.

- In some areas, runoff pollution has forced beaches to be closed.

- Drinking water can be contaminated by runoff.

- More than one-third of shellfish growing in waters in the United States are contaminated by runoff.

- Each year, millions of dollars are spent to restore polluted areas.

- There is a causal relationship between agricultural runoff and water-borne organisms that damage fish.

After studying these observations, you can use inductive reasoning to reach the conclusion that runoff pollution (rainwater that becomes polluted after it comes in contact with earth-bound pollutants such as fertilizer, pet waste, sewage, and pesticides) is a problem that must be addressed.

Children learn about the world by using inductive reasoning. For example, very young children see that if they push a light switch up, the lights in a room go on. If they repeat this action over and over, they reach the conclusion that every time they push a switch, the lights will go on. Of course, this conclusion does not always follow. For example, the light-bulb may be burned out or the switch may be damaged. Even so, their conclusion usually holds true. Children also use induction to generalize about what is safe and what is dangerous. If every time they meet a dog, the encounter is pleasant, they begin to think that all dogs are friendly. If at some point, however, a dog snaps at them, they question the strength of their conclusion and modify their behavior accordingly.

Scientists also use induction. In 1620, Sir Francis Bacon first proposed the **scientific method**—a way of using induction to find answers to questions. When using the scientific method, a researcher proposes a hypothesis and then makes a series of observations to test this hypothesis. Based on these observations, the researcher arrives at a conclusion that confirms, modifies, or disproves the hypothesis.

Runoff pollution ⊢

Andrew Winning/Reuters

REACHING INDUCTIVE CONCLUSIONS

Here are some of the ways you can use inductive reasoning to reach conclusions:

- **Particular to general:** This form of induction occurs when you reach a general conclusion based on particular pieces of evidence. For example, suppose you walk into a bathroom and see that the mirrors are fogged. You also notice that the bathtub has drops of water on its sides and that the bathroom floor is wet. In addition, you see a damp towel draped over the sink. Putting all these observations together, you conclude that someone has recently taken a bath. (Detectives use induction when gathering clues to solve a crime.)

- **General to general:** This form of induction occurs when you draw a conclusion based on the consistency of your observations. For example, if you determine that Apple Inc. has made good products for a long time, you conclude it will continue to make good products.

- **General to particular:** This form of induction occurs when you draw a conclusion based on what you generally know to be true. For example, if you believe that cars made by the Ford Motor Company are reliable, then you conclude that a Ford Focus will be a reliable car.

- **Particular to particular:** This form of induction occurs when you assume that because something works in one situation, it will also work in another similar situation. For example, if Krazy Glue fixed the broken handle of one cup, then you conclude it will probably fix the broken handle of another cup.

Making Inferences

Unlike deduction, which reaches a conclusion based on information provided by the major and minor premises, induction uses what you know to make a statement about something that you don't know. While deductive arguments can be judged in absolute terms (they are either **valid** or **invalid**), inductive arguments are judged in relative terms (they are either **strong** or **weak**).

You reach an inductive conclusion by making an **inference**—a statement about what is unknown based on what is known. (In other words, you look at the evidence and try to figure out what is going on.) For this reason, there is always a gap between your observations and your conclusion. To bridge this gap, you have to make an **inductive leap**—a stretch of the imagination that enables you to draw an acceptable conclusion. Therefore, inductive conclusions are never certain (as deductive conclusions are) but only probable. The more evidence you provide, the stronger and more probable are your conclusions (and your argument).

Public-opinion polls illustrate how inferences are used to reach inductive conclusions. Politicians and news organizations routinely use public-opinion polls to assess support (or lack of support) for a particular policy, proposal, or political candidate. After surveying a sample population—registered voters, for example—pollsters reach conclusions based on their responses. In other words, by asking questions and studying the responses of a sample group of people, pollsters make inferences about the larger group—for example, which political candidate is ahead and by how much. How solid these inferences are depends to a great extent on the sample populations the pollsters survey. In an election, for example, a poll of randomly chosen individuals will be less accurate than a poll of registered voters or likely voters. In addition, other factors (such as the size of the sample and the way questions are worded) can determine the relative strength of an inductive conclusion.

As with all inferences, a gap exists between a poll's data—the responses to the questions—and the conclusion. The larger and more representative the sample, the smaller the inductive leap necessary to reach a conclusion and the more accurate the poll. If the gap between the data and the conclusion is too big, however, the pollsters will be accused of making a **hasty generalization** (see p. 154). Remember, no matter how much support you present, an inductive conclusion is only probable, never certain. The best you can do is present a convincing case and hope that your audience will accept it.

Constructing Strong Inductive Arguments

When you use inductive reasoning, your conclusion is only as strong as the **evidence**—the facts, details, or examples—that you use to support it. For this reason, you should be on the lookout for the following problems that can occur when you try to reach an inductive conclusion.

Generalization Too Broad

The conclusion you state cannot go beyond the scope of your evidence. Your evidence must support your generalization. For instance, you cannot survey just three international students in your school and conclude that the school does not go far enough to accommodate international students. To reach such a conclusion, you would have to consider a large number of international students.

Atypical Evidence

The evidence on which you base an inductive conclusion must be **representative**, not atypical or biased. For example, you cannot conclude that students are satisfied with the course offerings at your school by sampling just first-year students. To be valid, your conclusion should be based on responses from a cross section of students from all years.

Irrelevant Evidence

Your evidence has to support your conclusion. If it does not, it is **irrelevant**. For example, if you assert that many adjunct faculty members make substantial contributions to your school, your supporting examples must be adjunct faculty, not tenured or junior faculty.

Exceptions to the Rule

There is always a chance that you will overlook an exception that may affect the strength of your conclusion. For example, not everyone who has a disability needs special accommodations, and not everyone who requires special accommodations needs the same services. For this reason, you should avoid using words like *every*, *all*, and *always* and instead use words like *most*, *many*, and *usually*.

⊙ EXERCISE 5.6 IDENTIFYING DEDUCTIVE AND INDUCTIVE ARGUMENTS

Read the following arguments, and decide whether each is a deductive argument or an inductive argument and write *D* or *I* on the lines.

1. Freedom of speech is a central principle of our form of government. For this reason, students should be allowed to wear T-shirts that call for the legalization of marijuana. _____

2. The Chevy Cruze Eco gets twenty-seven miles a gallon in the city and forty-six miles a gallon on the highway. The Honda Accord gets twenty-seven miles a gallon in the city and thirty-six miles a gallon on the highway. Therefore, it makes more sense for me to buy the Chevy Cruze Eco. _____

3. In Edgar Allan Poe's short story "The Cask of Amontillado," Montresor flatters Fortunato. He lures him to his vaults where he stores wine. Montresor then gets Fortunato drunk and chains him to the wall of a crypt. Finally, Montresor uncovers a pile of building material and walls up the entrance to the crypt. Clearly, Montresor has carefully planned to murder Fortunato for a very long time. _____

4. All people should have the right to die with dignity. Garrett is a terminally ill patient, so he should have access to doctor-assisted suicide. _____

5. Last week, we found unacceptably high levels of pollution in the ocean. On Monday, we also found high levels of pollution. Today, we found even higher levels of pollution. We should close the ocean beaches to swimmers until we can find the source of this problem.

_____

➲ EXERCISE 5.7 ANALYZING DEDUCTIVE AND INDUCTIVE ARGUMENTS

Read the following arguments. Then, decide whether they are deductive or inductive. If they are inductive arguments, evaluate their strength. If they are deductive arguments, evaluate their soundness.

1. *The Farmer's Almanac* says that this winter will be very cold. The National Weather Service also predicts that this winter will be very cold. So, this should be a cold winter.

2. Many walled towns in Europe do not let people drive cars into their centers. San Gimignano is a walled town in Europe. It is likely that we will not be able to drive our car into its center.

3. The window at the back of the house is broken. There is a baseball on the floor. A few minutes ago, I saw two boys playing catch in a neighbor's yard. They must have thrown the ball through the window.

4. Every time I go to the beach I get sunburned. I guess I should stop going to the beach.

5. All my instructors have advanced degrees. Richard Bell is one of my instructors. Therefore, Richard Bell has an advanced degree.

6. My last two boyfriends cheated on me. All men are terrible.

7. I read a study published by a pharmaceutical company that said that Accutane was safe. Maybe the government was too quick to pull this drug off the market.

8. Chase is not very good-looking, and he dresses badly. I don't know how he can be a good architect.

9. No fictional character has ever had a fan club. Harry Potter does, but he is the exception.

10. Two weeks ago, my instructor refused to accept a late paper. She did the same thing last week. Yesterday, she also told someone that because his paper was late, she wouldn't accept it. I'd better get my paper in on time.

➲ EXERCISE 5.8 ANALYZING AN INDUCTIVE PARAGRAPH

Read the following inductive paragraph, written by student Pooja Vaidya, and answer the questions that follow it.

When my friend took me to a game between the Philadelphia Eagles and the Dallas Cowboys in Philadelphia, I learned a little bit about American football and a lot about the behavior of football fans. Many of the Philadelphia fans were dressed in green and white football jerseys, each with a player's name and number on the back. One fan had his face painted green and wore a green cape with a large white *E* on it. He ran up and down the aisles in his section and led cheers. When the team was ahead, everyone joined in. When the team fell behind, this fan literally fell on his knees, cried, and begged the people in the stands to support the Eagles. (After the game, several people asked him for his autograph.) A group of six fans sat without shirts. They wore green wigs, and each had one letter of the team's name painted on his bare chest. Even though the temperature was below freezing, none of these fans ever put on his shirt. Before the game, many fans had been drinking at tailgate parties in the parking lot, and as the game progressed, they continued to drink beer in the stadium. By the beginning of the second half, fights were breaking out all over the stadium. Guards grabbed the people who were fighting and escorted them out of the stadium. At one point, a fan wearing a Dallas jersey tried to sit down in the row behind me. Some of the Eagles fans were so threatening that the police had to escort the Dallas fan out of the stands for his own protection. When the game ended in an Eagles victory, the fans sang the team's fight song as they left the stadium. I concluded that for many Eagles fans, a day at the stadium is an opportunity to engage in behavior that in any other context would be unacceptable and even abnormal.

1. Which of the following statements could you *not* conclude from this paragraph?

   a. All Eagles fans act in outrageous ways at games.

   b. At football games, the fans in the stands can be as violent as the players on the field.

   c. The atmosphere at the stadium causes otherwise normal people to act abnormally.

   d. Spectator sports encourage fans to act in abnormal ways.

   e. Some people get so caught up in the excitement of a game that they act in uncharacteristic ways.

2. Paraphrase the writer's conclusion. What evidence is provided to support this conclusion?

3. What additional evidence could the writer have provided? Is this additional evidence necessary, or does the conclusion stand without it?

4. The writer makes an inductive leap to reach the paragraph's conclusion. Do you think this leap is too great?

5. Does this paragraph make a strong inductive argument? Why or why not?

Writing Inductive Arguments

Inductive arguments begin with evidence (specific facts, observations, expert opinion, and so on), draw inferences from the evidence, and reach a conclusion by making an inductive leap. Keep in mind that inductive arguments are only as strong as the link between the evidence and the conclusion, so the stronger this link is, the stronger the argument will be.

Inductive essays frequently have the following structure:

INTRODUCTION	Presents the issue
	States the thesis
BODY	Presents evidence: facts, observations, expert opinion, and so on
	Draws inferences from the evidence
	Refutes the arguments against the thesis
CONCLUSION	Brings argument to a close
	Concluding statement reinforces the thesis

⊘ EXERCISE 5.9 IDENTIFYING THE ELEMENTS OF AN INDUCTIVE ESSAY

The following essay includes all the elements of an inductive argument. After you read the essay, answer the questions on page 151, consulting the preceding outline if necessary.

This essay appeared in *Slate* on September 2, 2006.

PLEASE DO NOT FEED THE HUMANS

WILLIAM SALETAN

Dug

In 1894, Congress established Labor Day to honor those who "from rude 1 nature have delved° and carved all the grandeur we behold." In the century since, the grandeur of human achievement has multiplied. Over the past four decades, global population has doubled, but food output, driven by increases in productivity, has outpaced it. Poverty, infant mortality, and hunger are receding. For the first time in our planet's history, a species no longer lives at the mercy of scarcity. We have learned to feed ourselves.

We've learned so well, in fact, that we're getting fat. Not just the United 2
States or Europe, but the whole world. Egyptian, Mexican, and South African
women are now as fat as Americans. Far more Filipino adults are now overweight than underweight. In China, one in five adults is too heavy, and the
rate of overweight children is 28 times higher than it was two decades ago.
In Thailand, Kuwait, and Tunisia, obesity, diabetes, and heart disease are
soaring.

Hunger is far from conquered. But since 1990, the global rate of malnu- 3
trition has declined an average of 1.7 percent a year. Based on data from the
World Health Organization and the U.N. Food and Agriculture Organization, for every two people who are malnourished, three are now overweight
or obese. Among women, even in most African countries, overweight has
surpassed underweight. The balance of peril is shifting.

Fat is no longer a rich man's disease. For middle- and high-income 4
Americans, the obesity rate is 29 percent. For low-income Americans, it's
35 percent. Among middle- and high-income kids aged 15 to 17, the rate of
overweight is 14 percent. Among low-income kids in the same age bracket,
it's 23 percent. Globally, weight has tended to rise with income. But a study in
Vancouver, Canada, published three months ago, found that preschoolers in
"food-insecure" households were twice as likely as other kids to be overweight
or obese. In Brazilian cities, the poor have become fatter than the rich.

Technologically, this is a triumph. In the early days of our species, even 5
the rich starved. Barry Popkin, a nutritional epidemiologist at the University
of North Carolina, divides history into several epochs. In the hunter-gatherer
era, if we didn't find food, we died. In the agricultural era, if our crops per-
ished, we died. In the industrial era, famine receded, but infectious diseases
killed us. Now we've achieved such control over nature that we're dying not of
starvation or infection, but of abundance. Nature isn't killing us. We're killing
ourselves.

You don't have to go hungry anymore; we can fill you with fats and carbs 6
more cheaply than ever. You don't have to chase your food; we can bring it to
you. You don't have to cook it; we can deliver it ready-to-eat. You don't have
to eat it before it spoils; we can pump it full of preservatives so it lasts forever.
You don't even have to stop when you're full. We've got so much food to sell, we
want you to keep eating.

What happened in America is happening everywhere, only faster. Fewer 7
farmers' markets, more processed food. Fewer whole grains, more refined
ones. More sweeteners, salt, and trans fats. Cheaper meat, more animal fat.
Less cooking, more eating out. Bigger portions, more snacks.

Kentucky Fried Chicken and Pizza Hut are spreading across the planet. 8
Coca-Cola is in more than 200 countries. Half of McDonald's business is
overseas. In China, animal-fat intake has tripled in 20 years. By 2020, meat
consumption in developing countries will grow by 106 million metric tons,
outstripping growth in developed countries by a factor of more than five.
Forty years ago, to afford a high-fat diet, your country needed a gross national

product per capita of nearly $1,500. Now the price is half that. You no longer have to be rich to die a rich man's death.

Soon, it'll be a poor man's death. The rich have Whole Foods, gyms, and 9 personal trainers. The poor have 7-Eleven, Popeyes, and streets unsafe for walking. When money's tight, you feed your kids at Wendy's and stock up on macaroni and cheese. At a lunch buffet, you do what your ancestors did: store all the fat you can.

That's the punch line: Technology has changed everything but us. We 10 evolved to survive scarcity. We crave fat. We're quick to gain weight and slow to lose it. Double what you serve us, and we'll double what we eat. Thanks to technology, the deprivation that made these traits useful is gone. So is the link between flavors and nutrients. The modern food industry can sell you sweetness without fruit, salt without protein, creaminess without milk. We can fatten you and starve you at the same time.

And that's just the diet side of the equation. Before technology, adult men had to expend about 3,000 calories a day. Now they expend about 2,000. **"We evolved to survive scarcity."** 11 Look at the new Segway scooter. The original model relieved you of the need to walk, pedal, or balance. With the new one, you don't even have to turn the handlebars or start it manually. In theory, Segway is replacing the car. In practice, it's replacing the body.

In country after country, service jobs are replacing hard labor. The folks 12 who field your customer service calls in Bangalore are sitting at desks. Nearly everyone in China has a television set. Remember when Chinese rode bikes? In the past six years, the number of cars there has grown from six million to 20 million. More than one in seven Chinese has a motorized vehicle, and households with such vehicles have an obesity rate 80 percent higher than their peers.

The answer to these trends is simple. We have to exercise more and change 13 the food we eat, donate, and subsidize. Next year, for example, the U.S. Women, Infants, and Children program, which subsidizes groceries for impoverished youngsters, will begin to pay for fruits and vegetables. For 32 years, the program has fed toddlers eggs and cheese but not one vegetable. And we wonder why poor kids are fat.

The hard part is changing our mentality. We have a distorted body image. 14 We're so used to not having enough, as a species, that we can't believe the problem is too much. From China to Africa to Latin America, people are trying to fatten their kids. I just got back from a vacation with my Jewish mother and Jewish mother-in-law. They told me I need to eat more.

The other thing blinding us is liberal guilt. We're so caught up in the idea 15 of giving that we can't see the importance of changing behavior rather than filling bellies. We know better than to feed buttered popcorn to zoo animals, yet we send it to a food bank and call ourselves humanitarians. Maybe we should ask what our fellow humans actually need.

Identifying the Elements of an Inductive Argument

1. What is this essay's thesis? Restate it in your own words.

2. Why do you think Saletan places the thesis where he does?

3. What evidence does Saletan use to support his conclusion?

4. What inductive leap does Saletan make to reach his conclusion? Do you think he should have included more evidence?

5. Overall, do you think Saletan's inductive argument is relatively strong or weak? Explain.

Recognizing Logical Fallacies

When you write arguments in college, you follow certain rules that ensure fairness. Not everyone who writes arguments is fair or thorough, however. Sometimes you will encounter arguments in which writers attack the opposition's intelligence or patriotism and base their arguments on questionable (or even false) assumptions. As convincing as these arguments can sometimes seem, they are not valid because they contain **fallacies**—errors in reasoning that undermine the logic of an argument. Familiarizing yourself with the most common logical fallacies can help you to evaluate the arguments of others and to construct better, more effective arguments of your own.

The following pages define and illustrate some logical fallacies that you should learn to recognize and avoid.

Begging the Question

The fallacy of **begging the question** assumes that a statement is self-evident (or obvious) when it actually requires proof. A conclusion based on such assumptions cannot be valid. For example, someone who is very religious could structure an argument the following way:

MAJOR PREMISE	Everything in the Bible is true.
MINOR PREMISE	The Bible says that Noah built an ark.
CONCLUSION	Therefore, Noah's ark really existed.

A person can accept the conclusion of this syllogism only if he or she accepts the major premise as self-evident. Some people might find this line of reasoning convincing, but others would not—even if they were religious.

Begging the question occurs any time someone presents a debatable statement as if it were true. For example, look at the following statement:

You have unfairly limited my right of free speech by refusing to print my editorial in the college newspaper.

This statement begs the question because it assumes what it should be proving—that refusing to print an editorial somehow violates a person's right to free speech.

Circular Reasoning

Closely related to begging the question, **circular reasoning** occurs when someone supports a statement by restating it in different terms. Consider the following statement:

> Stealing is wrong because it is illegal.

The conclusion of the preceding statement is essentially the same as its beginning: stealing (which is illegal) is against the law. In other words, the argument goes in a circle.

Here are some other examples of circular reasoning:

- Lincoln was a great president because he is the best president we ever had.

- I am for equal rights for women because I am a feminist.

- Only someone who is deranged would carry out a school shooting, so he must be mentally ill.

All of the preceding statements have one thing in common: they attempt to support a statement by simply repeating the statement in different words.

Weak Analogy

An **analogy** is a comparison between two items (or concepts)—one familiar and one unfamiliar. When you make an analogy, you explain the unfamiliar item by comparing it to the familiar item.

Waterfall, by M. C. Escher. The artwork creates the illusion of water flowing uphill and in a circle. Circular reasoning occurs when the conclusion of an argument is the same as one of the premises.

Although analogies can be effective in arguments, they have limitations. For example, a senator who opposed a government bailout of the financial industry in 2008 made the following argument:

> This bailout is doomed from the start. It's like pouring milk into a leaking bucket. As long as you keep pouring milk, the bucket stays full. But when you stop, the milk runs out the hole in the bottom of the bucket. What we're doing is throwing money into a big bucket and not fixing the hole. We have to find the underlying problems that have caused this part of our economy to get in trouble and pass legislation to solve them.

The problem with using analogies such as this one is that analogies are never perfect. There is always a difference between the two things being compared. The larger this difference, the weaker the analogy—and the weaker the argument that it supports. For example, someone could point out to the senator that the financial industry—and by extension, the whole economy—is much more complex and multifaceted than a leaking bucket.

This weakness highlights another limitation of an argument by analogy. Even though it can be very convincing, an analogy alone is no substitute for evidence. In other words, to analyze the economy, the senator would have to expand his discussion beyond a single analogy (which cannot carry the weight of the entire argument) and provide convincing evidence that the bailout was a mistake form the start.

Ad Hominem *Fallacy (Personal Attack)*

The ***ad hominem* fallacy** occurs when someone attacks the character or the motives of a person instead of focusing on the issues. This line of reasoning is illogical because it focuses attention on the person making the argument, sidestepping the argument itself.

Consider the following statement:

> Dr. Thomson, I'm not sure why we should believe anything you have to say about this community health center. Last year, you left your husband for another man.

The preceding attack on Dr. Thomson's character is irrelevant; it has nothing to do with her ideas about the community health center. Sometimes, however, a person's character may have a direct relation to the issue. For example, if Dr. Thomson had invested in a company that supplied medical equipment to the health center, this fact would have been relevant to the issue at hand.

The *ad hominem* fallacy also occurs when you attempt to undermine an argument by associating it with individuals who are easily attacked. For example, consider this statement:

> I think your plan to provide universal health care is interesting. I'm sure Marx and Lenin would agree with you.

Instead of focusing on the specific provisions of the health-care plan, the opposition unfairly associates it with the ideas of Karl Marx and Vladimir Lenin, two well-known Communists.

The Granger Collection

Ad hominem attack against Charles Darwin, originator of the theory of evolution by natural selection.

Creating a Straw Man

This fallacy most likely got its name from the use of straw dummies in military and boxing training. When writers create a **straw man**, they present a weak argument that can easily be refuted. Instead of attacking the real issue, they focus on a weaker issue and give the impression that they have effectively countered an opponent's argument. Frequently, the straw man is an extreme or oversimplified version of the opponent's actual position. For example, during a debate about raising the minimum wage, a senator made the following comment:

> If we raise the minimum wage for restaurant workers, the cost of a meal will increase. Soon, the average person won't be able to afford a cup of soup.

Instead of focusing on legitimate arguments against the minimum wage, the senator misrepresents an opposing argument and then refutes it. As this example shows, the straw man fallacy is dishonest because it intentionally distorts an opponent's position in order to mislead readers.

Hasty or Sweeping Generalization (Jumping to a Conclusion)

A **hasty or sweeping generalization** (also called **jumping to a conclusion**) occurs when someone reaches a conclusion that is based on too little evidence. Many people commit this fallacy without realizing it. For example, when Richard Nixon was elected president in 1972, film critic Pauline Kael

Soldiers practicing attacks against straw men

SOTK2011/Alamy Stock Photo

is supposed to have remarked, "How can that be? No one I know voted for Nixon!" The general idea behind this statement is that if Kael's acquaintances didn't vote for Nixon, then neither did most other people. This assumption is flawed because it is based on a small sample.

Sometimes people make hasty generalizations because they strongly favor one point of view over another. At other times, a hasty generalization is simply the result of sloppy thinking. For example, it is easier for a student to say that an instructor is an unusually hard grader than to survey the instructor's classes to see if this conclusion is warranted (or to consider other reasons for his or her poor performance in a course).

Either/Or Fallacy (False Dilemma)

The **either/or fallacy** (also called a **false dilemma**) occurs when a person says that there are just two choices when there are actually more. In many cases, the person committing this fallacy tries to force a conclusion by presenting just two choices, one of which is clearly more desirable than the other. (Parents do this with young children all the time: "Eat your carrots, or go to bed.")

Politicians frequently engage in this fallacy. For example, according to some politicians, you are either pro-life or pro-choice, pro–gun control or anti–gun control, pro-stem-cell research or anti-stem-cell research. Many people, however, are actually somewhere in the middle, taking a much more nuanced approach to complicated issues.

Consider the following statement:

> I can't believe you voted against the bill to build a wall along the southern border of the United States. Either you're for protecting our border, or you're against it.

This statement is an example of the either/or fallacy. The person who voted against the bill might be against building the border wall but not against all immigration restrictions. The person might favor loose restrictions for some people (for example, people fleeing political persecution and migrant workers) and strong restrictions for others (for example, drug smugglers and human traffickers). By limiting the options to just two, the speaker oversimplifies the situation and attempts to force the listener to accept a fallacious argument.

Equivocation

The fallacy of **equivocation** occurs when a key term has one meaning in one part of an argument and another meaning in another part. (When a term is used **unequivocally**, it has the same meaning throughout the argument.) Consider the following old joke:

> The sign said, "Fine for parking here," so because it was fine, I parked there.

Obviously, the word *fine* has two different meanings in this sentence. The first time it is used, it means "money paid as a penalty." The second time, it means "good" or "satisfactory."

Most words have more than one meaning, so it is important not to confuse the various meanings. For an argument to work, a key term has to have the same meaning every time It appears in the argument. If the meaning shifts during the course of the argument, then the argument cannot be sound.

Consider the following statement:

> This is supposed to be a free country, but nothing worth having is ever free.

In this statement, the meaning of a key term shifts. The first time the word *free* is used, it means "not under the control of another." The second time, it means "without charge."

Red Herring

This fallacy gets its name from the practice of dragging a smoked fish across the trail of a fox to mask its scent during a fox hunt. As a result, the hounds lose the scent and are thrown off the track. The **red herring fallacy** occurs when a person raises an irrelevant side issue to divert attention from the real issue. Used skillfully, this fallacy can distract an audience and change the focus of an argument.

Political campaigns are good sources of examples of the red herring fallacy. Consider this example from the 2016 presidential race:

> I know that Donald Trump says that he is for the "little guy," but he lives in a three-story penthouse in the middle of Manhattan. How can we believe that his policies will help the average American?

The focus of this argument should have been on Trump's policies, not on the fact that he lives in a penthouse.

Here is another red herring fallacy:

> **She:** I read that the Alexa virtual assistant records your conversations, even when it's off. This is an invasion of privacy.
>
> **He:** That certainly is a first-world problem. Think of all the poor people in Haiti. That should put things in perspective.

Again, the focus of the argument should be on a possible invasion of privacy, not on poverty in Haiti.

Person trying to follow the argument.

The actual issue being argued.

Red herring, a distraction not related to the argument.

Slippery Slope

The **slippery-slope fallacy** occurs when a person argues that one thing will inevitably result from another. (Other names for the slippery-slope fallacy are the **foot-in-the-door fallacy** and the **floodgates fallacy**.) Both these names suggest that once you permit certain acts, you inevitably permit additional acts that eventually lead to disastrous consequences. Typically, the slippery-slope fallacy presents a series of increasingly unacceptable events that lead to an inevitable, unpleasant conclusion. (Usually, there is no evidence that such a sequence will actually occur.)

We encounter examples of the slippery-slope fallacy almost daily. During a debate on same-sex marriage, for example, an opponent advanced this line of reasoning:

> If we allow gay marriage, then there is nothing to stop polygamy. And once we allow this, where will it stop? Will we have to legalize incest—or even bestiality?

Whether or not you support same-sex marriage, you should recognize the fallacy of this slippery-slope reasoning. By the last sentence of the preceding passage, the assertions have become so outrageous that they approach parody. People can certainly debate this issue, but not in such a dishonest and highly emotional way.

You Also (Tu Quoque)

The **you also fallacy** asserts that a statement is false because it is inconsistent with what the speaker has said or done. In other words, a person is attacked for doing what he or she is arguing against. Parents often encounter this fallacy when they argue with their teenage children. By introducing an irrelevant point—"You did it too"—the children attempt to distract parents and put them on the defensive:

- How can you tell me not to smoke when you used to smoke?

- Don't yell at me for drinking. I bet you had a few beers before you were twenty-one.

- Why do I have to be home by midnight? Didn't you stay out late when you were my age?

Arguments such as these are irrelevant. People fail to follow their own advice, but that does not mean that their points have no merit. (Of course, not following their own advice does undermine their credibility.)

Appeal to Doubtful Authority

Writers of research papers frequently use the ideas of recognized authorities to strengthen their arguments. However, the sources offered as evidence need to be both respected and credible. The **appeal to doubtful authority** occurs when people use the ideas of nonexperts to support their arguments.

Not everyone who speaks as an expert is actually an authority on a particular issue. For example, when movie stars or recording artists give their opinions about politics, climate change, or foreign affairs—things they may know little about—they are not speaking as experts; therefore, they have no authority. (They *are* experts, however, when they discuss the film or music industries.) A similar situation occurs with the pundits who appear on television news shows or whose ideas are posted on social media sites. Some of these individuals have solid credentials in the fields they discuss, but others offer opinions even though they know little about the subjects. Unfortunately, many people accept the pronouncements of these "experts" uncritically and think it is acceptable to cite them to support their own arguments.

How do you determine whether a person you read about or hear is really an authority? First, make sure that the person actually has expertise in the field he or she is discussing. You can do this by checking his or her credentials on the internet. Second, make sure that the person is not biased. No one is entirely free from bias, but the bias should not be so extreme that it undermines the person's authority. Finally, make sure that you can confirm what the so-called expert says or writes. Check one or two pieces of information in other sources, such as a basic reference text or encyclopedia. Determine if others—especially recognized experts in the field—confirm this information. If there are major points of discrepancy, dig further to make sure you are dealing with a legitimate authority. Be extremely wary of material that appears on social media sites, such as

Comedian/actor Amy Schumer boosts her credibility on the issue of gun control by appearing with her cousin, Senator Charles Schumer.

Andrew Burton/Getty Images News/Getty Images

Facebook and Twitter, even if it is attributed to experts. Don't use information until you have checked both its authenticity and accuracy.

Misuse of Statistics

The **misuse of statistics** occurs when data are misrepresented. Statistics can be used persuasively in an argument, but sometimes they are distorted—intentionally or unintentionally—to make a point. For example, a classic ad for toothpaste claims that four out of five dentists recommend Crest toothpaste. What the ad neglects to mention is the number of dentists who were questioned. If the company surveyed several thousand dentists, then this statistic would be meaningful. If the company surveyed only ten, however, it would not be.

Misleading statistics can be much subtler (and much more complicated) than the preceding example. For example, one year, there were 16,653 alcohol-related deaths in the United States. According to the National Highway Traffic Safety Administration (NHTSA), 12,892 of these 16,653 alcohol-related deaths involved at least one driver or passenger who was legally drunk. Of the 12,892 deaths, 7,326 were the drivers themselves, and 1,594 were legally drunk pedestrians. The remaining 3,972 fatalities were nonintoxicated drivers, passengers, or nonoccupants. These 3,972 fatalities call the total number into question because the NHTSA does not indicate which drivers were at fault. In other words, if a sober driver ran a red light and killed a legally drunk driver, the NHTSA classified this death as alcohol-related. For this reason, the original number of alcohol-related

Cartoonstock.com

"That's what I want to say. See if you can find some statistics to prove it."

deaths—16,653—is somewhat misleading. (The statistic becomes even more questionable when you consider that a person is automatically classified as intoxicated if he or she refuses to take a sobriety test.)

Post Hoc, Ergo Propter Hoc (*After This, Therefore Because of This*)

The *post hoc* **fallacy** asserts that because two events occur closely in time, one event must cause the other. Professional athletes commit the *post hoc* fallacy all the time. For example, one major league pitcher wears the same shirt every time he has an important game. Because he has won several big games while wearing this shirt, he believes it brings him luck.

Many events seem to follow a sequential pattern even though they actually do not. For example, some people refuse to get a flu shot because they say that the last time they got one, they came down with the flu. Even though there is no scientific basis for this link, many people insist that it is true. (The more probable explanation for this situation is that the flu vaccination takes at least two weeks to take effect, so it is possible for someone to be infected by the flu virus before the vaccine starts working. In addition, no flu vaccine is 100 percent effective, so even with the shot, it is possible to contract the disease.)

Another health-related issue also illustrates the *post hoc* fallacy. Recently, the U.S. Food and Drug Administration (FDA) studied several natural supplements that claim to cure the common cold. Because the study showed that these products were not effective, the FDA ordered the manufacturers to stop making false claims. Despite this fact, however, many people still buy these products. When questioned, they say the medications actually work. Again, the explanation for this phenomenon is simple. Most colds last just a few days. As the FDA pointed out in its report, people who took the medications would have begun feeling better with or without them.

Non Sequitur (It Does Not Follow)

The **non sequitur** **fallacy** occurs when a conclusion does not follow from the premises. Frequently, the conclusion is supported by weak or irrelevant evidence—or by no evidence at all. Consider the following statement:

> Megan drives an expensive car, so she must be earning a lot of money.

Megan might drive an expensive car, but this is not evidence that she has a high salary. She could, for example, be leasing the car or paying it off over a five-year period, or it could have been a gift.

Non sequiturs are common in political arguments. Consider this statement:

> Gangs, drugs, and extreme violence plague today's prisons. The only way to address this issue is to release all nonviolent offenders as soon as possible.

This assessment of the prison system may be accurate, but it doesn't follow that because of this situation, all nonviolent offenders should be released immediately.

Scientific arguments also contain non sequiturs. Consider the following statement that was made during a debate on climate change:

> Recently, the polar ice caps have thickened, and the temperature of the oceans has stabilized. Obviously, we don't need to do more to address climate change.

Even if you accept the facts of this argument, you need to see more evidence before you can conclude that no action against climate change is necessary. For example, the cooling trend could be temporary, or other areas of the earth could still be growing warmer.

Bandwagon Fallacy

The **bandwagon fallacy** occurs when you try to convince people that something is true because it is widely held to be true. It is easy to see the problem with this line of reasoning. Hundreds of years ago, most people believed that the sun revolved around the earth and that the earth was flat. As we know, the fact that many people held these beliefs did not make them true.

The underlying assumption of the bandwagon fallacy is that the more people who believe something, the more likely it is to be true. Without supporting evidence, however, this form of argument cannot be valid. For example, consider the following statement made by a driver who was stopped by the police for speeding:

> Officer, I didn't do anything wrong. Everyone around me was going the same speed.

As the police officer was quick to point out, the driver's argument missed the point: he was doing fifty-five miles an hour in a thirty-five-mile-an-hour zone, and the fact that other drivers were also speeding was irrelevant. If the driver had been able to demonstrate that the police officer was mistaken—that he was driving more slowly or that the speed limit was actually sixty miles an hour—then his argument would have had merit. In this case, the fact that other drivers were going the same speed would be relevant because it would support his contention.

Since most people want to go along with the crowd, the bandwagon fallacy can be very effective. For this reason, advertisers use it all the time. For example, a book publisher will say that a book has been on the *New York Times* best-seller list for ten weeks, and a pharmaceutical company will say that its brand of aspirin outsells other brands four to one. These appeals are irrelevant, however, because they don't address the central questions: Is the book actually worth reading? Is one brand of aspirin really better than other brands?

⊜ EXERCISE 5.10 IDENTIFYING LOGICAL FALLACIES

Determine which of the following statements are logical arguments and which are fallacies. If the statement is not logical, identify the fallacy that best applies.

1. Almost all the students I talked to said that they didn't like the senator. I'm sure he'll lose the election on Tuesday.

2. This car has a noisy engine; therefore, it must create a lot of pollution.

3. I don't know how Professor Resnick can be such a hard grader. He's always late for class.

4. A vote for the bill to limit gun sales in the city is a vote against the Second Amendment.

5. It's only fair to pay your fair share of taxes.

6. I had an internship at a government agency last summer, and no one there worked very hard. Government workers are lazy.

7. It's a clear principle of law that people are not allowed to yell "Fire!" in a crowded theater. By permitting protestors to hold a rally downtown, Judge Cohen is allowing them to do just that.

8. Of course this person is guilty. He wouldn't be in jail if he weren't a criminal.

9. Schools are like families; therefore, teachers (like parents) should be allowed to discipline their kids.

10. Everybody knows that staying out in the rain can make you sick.

11. When we had a draft in the 1960s, the crime rate was low. We should bring back the draft.

12. I'm not a doctor, but I play one on TV. I recommend Vicks Formula 44 cough syrup.

13. Some people are complaining about public schools, so there must be a problem.

14. If you aren't part of the solution, you're part of the problem.

15. All people are mortal. James is a person. Therefore, James is mortal.

16. I don't know why you gave me an *F* for handing in someone else's essay. Didn't you ever copy something from someone else?

17. First, the government stops us from buying assault-style rifles. Then, it tries to limit the number of handguns we can buy. What will come next? Soon, they'll try to take away all our guns.

18. Shakespeare was the world's greatest playwright; therefore, *Macbeth* must be a great play.

19. Last month, I bought a new computer. Yesterday, I installed some new software. This morning, my computer wouldn't start up. The new software must be causing the problem.

20. Ellen DeGeneres and Paul McCartney are against testing pharmaceutical and cosmetics products on animals, and that's good enough for me.

⊜ EXERCISE 5.11 ANALYZING LOGICAL FALLACIES

Read the following essay, and identify as many logical fallacies in it as you can. Make sure you identify each fallacy by name and are able to explain the flaws in the writer's arguments.

This essay is from Buchanan.org, where it appeared on October 31, 1994.

IMMIGRATION TIME-OUT

PATRICK J. BUCHANAN

What do we want the America of the years 2000, 2020, and 2050 to be like? Do 1 we have the right to shape the character of the country our grandchildren will live in? Or is that to be decided by whoever, outside America, decides to come here?

By 2050, we are instructed by the chancellor of the University of California 2 at Berkeley, Chang Lin-Tin, "the majority of Americans will trace their roots to Latin America, Africa, Asia, the Middle East, and Pacific Islands."

Now, any man or woman, of any nation or ancestry can come here—and 3 become a good American.

We know that from our history. But by my arithmetic, the chancellor is 4 saying Hispanics, Asians, and Africans will increase their present number of 65 million by at least 100 million in 60 years, a population growth larger than all of Mexico today.

What will that mean for America? Well, South Texas and Southern 5 California will be almost exclusively Hispanic. Each will have tens of millions of people whose linguistic, historic, and cultural roots are in Mexico. Like Eastern Ukraine, where 10 million Russian-speaking "Ukrainians" now look impatiently to Moscow, not Kiev, as their cultural capital, America could see, in a decade, demands for Quebec-like status for Southern California. Already there is a rumbling among militants for outright secession. A sea of Mexican flags was prominent in that L.A. rally against Prop. 187, and Mexican officials are openly urging their kinsmen in California to vote it down.

If no cutoff is imposed on social benefits for those who breach our borders, 6 and break our laws, the message will go out to a desperate world: America is wide open. All you need do is get there, and get in.

Consequences will ensue. Crowding together immigrant and minority 7 populations in our major cities must bring greater conflict. We saw that in the 1992 L.A. riot. Blacks and Hispanics have lately collided in D.C.'s Adams-Morgan neighborhood, supposedly the most tolerant and progressive section of Washington. The issue: bilingual education. Unlike 20 years ago, ethnic conflict is today on almost every front page.

Before Mr. Chang's vision is realized, the United States will have at least two 8 official languages. Today's steady outmigration of "Anglos" or "Euro-Americans," as whites are now called, from Southern Florida and Southern California, will continue. The 50 states will need constant redrawing of political lines to ensure proportional representation. Already we have created the first "apartheid districts" in America's South.

Ethnic militancy and solidarity are on the rise in the United States; the old institutions of assimilation are not doing

> "Ethnic militancy and solidarity are on the rise." 9

their work as they once did; the Melting Pot is in need of repair. On campuses we hear demands for separate dorms, eating rooms, clubs, etc., by black, white, Hispanic, and Asian students. If this is where the campus is headed, where are our cities going?

If America is to survive as "one nation, one people," we need to call a 10 "time-out" on immigration, to assimilate the tens of millions who have lately arrived. We need to get to know one another, to live together, to learn together America's language, history, culture, and traditions of tolerance, to become a new national family, before we add a hundred million more. And we need soon to bring down the curtain on this idea of hyphenated-Americanism.

If we lack the courage to make the decisions—as to what our country will 11 look like in 2050—others will make those decisions for us, not all of whom share our love of the America that seems to be fading away.

⊖ EXERCISE 5.12 CORRECTING LOGICAL FALLACIES

Choose three of the fallacies that you identified in "Immigration Time-Out" for Exercise 5.11. Rewrite each statement in the form of a logical argument.

How Free Should Free Speech Be?

CPL Archives/Everett Collection, Inc.

Go back to page 127, and reread the At Issue box that gives background on how free free speech should be. As the following sources illustrate, this question has a number of possible answers.

As you read this source material, you will be asked to answer questions and to complete some simple activities. This work will help you understand both the content and the structure of the sources. When you are finished, you will be ready to write an argument—either inductive or deductive—that takes a new position on how free free speech should actually be.

SOURCES

This essay originally appeared on the *Huffington Post* on July 24, 2013.

THE CASE FOR CENSORING HATE SPEECH

SEAN MCELWEE

For the past few years speech has moved online, leading to fierce debates 1
about its regulation. Most recently, feminists have led the charge to purge
Facebook of misogyny that clearly violates its hate speech code. Facebook
took a small step two weeks ago, creating a feature that will remove ads from
pages deemed "controversial." But such a move is half-hearted; Facebook and
other social networking websites should not tolerate hate speech and, in the
absence of a government mandate, adopt a European model of expunging
offensive material.

Stricter regulation of internet speech will not be popular with the 2
libertarian-minded citizens of the United States, but it's necessary. A typical
view of such censorship comes from Jeffrey Rosen, who argues in *The New
Republic* that,

"... given their tremendous size and importance as platforms for free
speech, companies like Facebook, Google, Yahoo, and Twitter shouldn't
try to be guardians of what Waldron calls a 'well-ordered society'; instead,
they should consider themselves the modern version of Oliver Wendell
Holmes's fractious marketplace of ideas—democratic spaces where all values, including civility norms, are always open for debate."

This image is romantic and lovely (although misattributed to Oliver Wendell 3
Holmes, who famously toed both lines on the free speech debate, instead of
John Stuart Mill) but it's worth asking what this actually looks like. Rosen for-
wards one example:

"Last year, after the French government objected to the hash tag '#unbonjuif' —
intended to inspire hateful riffs on the theme 'a good Jew . . .'—Twitter
blocked a handful of the resulting tweets in France, but only because
they violated French law. Within days, the bulk of the tweets carrying the
hashtag had turned from anti-Semitic to denunciations of anti-Semitism,
confirming that the Twittersphere is perfectly capable of dealing with hate
speech on its own, without heavy-handed intervention."

It's interesting to note how closely this idea resembles free market funda- 4
mentalism: simply get rid of any coercive rules and the "marketplace of ideas"
will naturally produce the best result. Humboldt State University compiled a
visual map that charts 150,000 hateful insults aggregated over the course of
11 months in the U.S. by pairing Google's Maps API with a series of the most
homophobic, racist, and otherwise prejudiced tweets. The map's existance

draws into question the notion that the "Twittersphere" can organically combat hate speech; hate speech is not going to disappear from Twitter on its own.

The negative impacts of hate speech do not lie in the responses of third-party observers, as hate speech aims at two goals. First, it is an attempt to tell bigots that they are not alone. Frank Collins—the neo-Nazi prosecuted in *National Socialist Party of America v. Skokie* (1977)—said, "We want to reach the good people, get the fierce anti-Semites who have to live among the Jews to come out of the woodwork and stand up for themselves." 5

The second purpose of hate speech is to intimidate the targeted minority, leading them to question whether their dignity and social status is secure. In many cases, such intimidation is successful. Consider the number of rapes that go unreported. Could this trend possibly be impacted by Reddit threads like /r/rapingwomen or /r/mensrights? Could it be due to the harassment women face when they even suggest the possibility they were raped? The rape culture that permeates Facebook, Twitter, and the public dialogue must be held at least partially responsible for our larger rape culture. 6

Reddit, for instance, has become a veritable potpourri of hate speech; consider Reddit threads like /r/nazi, /r/killawoman, /r/misogny, /r/killing-women. My argument is not that these should be taken down because they are offensive, but rather because they amount to the degradation of a class that has been historically oppressed. Imagine a Reddit thread for /r/lynchingblacks or /r/assassinatingthepresident. We would not argue that we should sit back and wait for this kind of speech to be "outspoken" by positive speech, but that it should be entirely banned. 7

American free speech jurisprudence relies upon the assumption that speech is merely the extension of a thought, and not an action. If we consider it an action, then saying that we should combat hate speech with more positive speech is an absurd proposition; the speech has already done the harm, and no amount of support will defray the victim's impression that they are not truly secure in this society. We don't simply tell the victim of a robbery, "Hey, it's okay, there are lots of other people who aren't going to rob you." Similarly, it isn't incredibly useful to tell someone who has just had their race/gender/sexuality defamed, "There are a lot of other nice people out there." 8

Those who claim to "defend free speech" when they defend the right to post hate speech online, are in truth backwards. Free speech isn't an absolute right; no right is weighed in a vacuum. The court has imposed numerous restrictions on speech. Fighting words, libel, and child pornography are all banned. Other countries merely go one step further by banning speech intended to intimidate vulnerable groups. The truth is that such speech does not democratize speech, it monopolizes speech. Women, LGBTQ individuals, and racial or religious minorities feel intimidated and are left out of the public sphere. On Reddit, for example, women have left or changed their usernames to be more male-sounding lest they face harassment and intimidation for speaking on Reddit about even the most gender-neutral topics. 9

Those who try to remove this hate speech have been criticized from left 10
and right. At *Slate*, Jillian York *writes*, "While the campaigners on this issue
are to be commended for raising awareness of such awful speech on Facebook's platform, their proposed solution is ultimately futile and sets a dangerous precedent for special interest groups looking to bring their pet issue to the
attention of Facebook's censors."

It hardly seems right to qualify a group fighting hate speech as an "interest 11
group" trying to bring their "pet issue" to the attention of Facebook censors.
The "special interest" groups she fears might apply for protection must meet
Facebook's strict community standards, which state:

> While we encourage you to challenge ideas, institutions, events, and prac-
> tices, we do not permit individuals or groups to attack others based on
> their race, ethnicity, national origin, religion, sex, gender, sexual orienta-
> tion, disability, or medical condition.

If anything, the groups to which York refers are nudging Facebook towards 12
actually enforcing its own rules.

People who argue against such rules generally portray their opponents as 13
standing on a slippery precipice, tugging at the question "what next?" We can
answer that question: Canada, England, France, Germany, the Netherlands, South
Africa, Australia, and India all ban hate speech. Yet, none of these countries have
slipped into totalitarianism. In many ways, such countries are more free when you
weigh the negative liberty to express harmful thoughts against the positive liberty
that is suppressed when you allow for the intimidation of minorities.

As Arthur Schopenhauer said, "the 14
freedom of the press should be governed
by a very strict prohibition of all and
every anonymity." However, with the
internet the public dialogue has moved
online, where hate speech is easy and
anonymous.

> "Free speech isn't an
> absolute right; no right is
> weighed in a vacuum."

Jeffrey Rosen argues that norms of civility should be open to discussion, 15
but, in today's reality, this issue has already been decided; impugning someone
because of their race, gender, or orientation is not acceptable in a civil society.
Banning hate speech is not a mechanism to further this debate because the
debate is over.

As Jeremy Waldron argues, hate speech laws prevent bigots from, "trying 16
to create the impression that the equal position of members of vulnerable
minorities in a rights-respecting society is less secure than implied by the society's actual foundational commitments."

Some people argue that the purpose of laws that ban hate speech is merely 17
to avoid offending prudes. No country, however, has mandated that anything
be excised from the public square merely because it provokes offense, but
rather because it attacks the dignity of a group—a practice the U.S. Supreme

Court called in *Beauharnais v. Illinois* (1952) "group libel." Such a standard could easily be applied to Twitter, Reddit, and other social media websites. While Facebook's policy as written should be a model, it's enforcement has been shoddy. Chaim Potok argues that if a company claims to have a policy, it should rigorously and fairly enforce it.

If this is the standard, the internet will surely remain controversial, but 18 it can also be free of hate and allow everyone to participate. A true marketplace of ideas must co-exist with a multi-racial, multi-gender, multi-sexually oriented society, and it can.

⊖ AT ISSUE: HOW FREE SHOULD FREE SPEECH BE?

1. McElwee states his thesis at the end of paragraph 1. Should he have given more background information about the issue before stating his thesis? Why or why not?

2. What evidence does McElwee provide to support his thesis? Should he have provided more evidence? If so, what kind?

3. In paragraph 8, McElwee compares a victim of robbery to a victim of hate speech. How strong is this **analogy**? At what points, if any, does this comparison break down?

4. What opposing arguments does McElwee address? What other opposing arguments could he have addressed?

5. In paragraph 12, McElwee says, "People who argue against such rules generally portray their opponents as standing on a slippery precipice. . . ." What is the "slippery precipice" to which McElwee refers? Is this characterization accurate? Fair?

6. What are the major strengths of McElwee's essay? What are its weaknesses? Overall, how effective is McElwee's argument?

This op-ed originally ran in the *Wall Street Journal* on September 24, 2014.

THE UNFREE SPEECH MOVEMENT

SOL STERN

This fall the University of California at Berkeley is celebrating the 50th anniver- 1
sary of the Free Speech Movement, a student-led protest against campus restrictions on political activities that made headlines and inspired imitators around the
country. I played a small part in the Free Speech Movement, and some of those
returning for the reunion were once my friends, but I won't be joining them.

Though the movement promised greater intellectual and political free- 2
dom on campus, the result has been the opposite. The great irony is that while
Berkeley now honors the memory of the Free Speech Movement, it exercises
more thought control over students than the hated institution that we rose up
against half a century ago.

We early-1960s radicals believed ourselves anointed as a new "tell it like it is" 3
generation. We promised to transcend the "smelly old orthodoxies" (in George
Orwell's phrase) of Cold War liberalism and class-based, authoritarian leftism.
Leading students into the university administration building for the first mass
protest, Mario Savio, the Free Speech Movement's brilliant leader from Queens,
New York, famously said: "There's a time when the operation of the machine
becomes so odious—makes you so sick at heart—that you can't take part. . . .
And you've got to indicate to the people who run it, to the people who own it
that unless you're free, the machine will be prevented from working at all."

The Berkeley "machine" now promotes Free Speech Movement kitsch. 4
The steps in front of Sproul Hall, the central administration building where
more than 700 students were arrested on December 2, 1964, have been
renamed the Mario Savio Steps. One of the campus dining halls is called the
Free Speech Movement Cafe, its walls covered with photographs and memen-
tos of the glorious semester of struggle. The university requires freshmen to
read an admiring biography of Savio, who died in 1996, written by New York
University professor and Berkeley graduate Robert Cohen.

Yet intellectual diversity is hardly embraced. Every undergraduate under- 5
goes a form of indoctrination with a required course on the "theoretical or analytical issues relevant to understanding race, culture, and ethnicity in American
society," administered by the university's Division of Equity and Inclusion.

How did this Orwellian inversion occur? It happened in part because 6
the Free Speech Movement's fight for free speech was always a charade. The
struggle was really about using the campus as a base for radical politics. I was
a 27-year-old New Left graduate student at the time. Savio was a 22-year-old
sophomore. He liked to compare the Free Speech Movement to the civil-rights
struggle—conflating the essentially liberal Berkeley administration with the
Bull Connors of the racist South.

During one demonstration Savio suggested that the campus cops who 7
had arrested a protesting student were "poor policemen" who only "have a job
to do." Another student then shouted out: "Just like Eichmann." "Yeah. Very
good. It's very, you know, like Adolf Eichmann," Savio replied. "He had a job to
do, He fit into the machinery."

I realized years later that this moment may have been the beginning of 8
the 1960s radicals' perversion of ordinary political language, like the spelling
"Amerika" or seeing hope and progress in Third World dictatorships.

Before that 1964–65 academic year, most of us radical students could not 9
have imagined a campus rebellion. Why revolt against an institution that until
then offered such a pleasant sanctuary? But then Berkeley administrators made
an incredibly stupid decision to establish new rules regarding political activities
on campus. Student clubs were no longer allowed to set up tables in front of the
Bancroft Avenue campus entrance to solicit funds and recruit new members.

The clubs had used this 40-foot strip of sidewalk for years on the assump- 10
tion that it was the property of the City of Berkeley and thus constitutionally
protected against speech restrictions. But the university claimed ownership
to justify the new rules. When some students refused to comply, the administration compounded its blunder by resorting to the campus police. Not
surprisingly, the students pushed back, using civil-disobedience tactics learned
fighting for civil rights in the South.

The Free Speech Movement was born on October 1, 1964, when police 11
tried to arrest a recent Berkeley graduate, Jack Weinberg, who was back on
campus after a summer as a civil-rights worker in Mississippi. He had set up a
table on the Bancroft strip for the Berkeley chapter of the Congress of Racial
Equality (CORE). Dozens of students spontaneously sat down around the
police car, preventing it from leaving the campus. A 32-hour standoff ensued,
with hundreds of students camped around the car.

Mario Savio, also back from Mississippi, took off his shoes, climbed onto the
roof of the police car, and launched into
an impromptu speech explaining why the
students had to resist the immoral new
rules. Thus began months of sporadic
protests, the occupation of Sproul Hall
on December 2 (ended by mass arrests),
national media attention, and Berkeley's
eventual capitulation.

> "But others had mas- 12
> tered the new world of
> political theater, under-
> stood the weakness of
> American liberalism,
> and soon turned their
> ire on the Vietnam War."

That should have ended the matter. Savio soon left the political arena, say- 13
ing that he had no interest in becoming a permanent student leader. But others
had mastered the new world of political theater, understood the weakness of
American liberalism, and soon turned their ire on the Vietnam War.

The radical movement that the Free Speech Movement spawned eventually 14
descended into violence and mindless anti-Americanism. The movement
waned in the 1970s as the war wound down—but by then protesters had begun
their infiltration of university faculties and administrations they had once

decried. "Tenured radicals," in *New Criterion* editor Roger Kimball's phrase, now dominate most professional organizations in the humanities and social studies. Unlike our old liberal professors, who dealt respectfully with the ideas advanced by my generation of New Left students, today's radical professors insist on ideological conformity and don't take kindly to dissent by conservative students. Visits by speakers who might not toe the liberal line—recently including former Secretary of State Condoleezza Rice and Islamism critic Ayaan Hirsi Ali—spark protests and letter-writing campaigns by students in tandem with their professors until the speaker withdraws or the invitation is canceled.

On October 1 at Berkeley, by contrast, one of the honored speakers at 15 the Free Speech Movement anniversary rally on Sproul Plaza will be Bettina Aptheker, who is now a feminist-studies professor at the University of California at Santa Cruz.

Writing in the Berkeley alumni magazine about the anniversary, 16 Ms. Aptheker noted that the First Amendment was "written by white, propertied men in the 18th century, who never likely imagined that it might apply to women, and/or people of color, and/or all those who were not propertied, and even, perhaps, not citizens, and/or undocumented immigrants. . . . In other words, freedom of speech is a Constitutional guarantee, but who gets to exercise it without the chilling restraints of censure depends very much on one's location in the political and social cartography. We [Free Speech Movement] veterans were too young and inexperienced in 1964 to know this, but we do now, and we speak with a new awareness, a new consciousness, and a new urgency that the wisdom of a true freedom is inexorably tied to who exercises power and for what ends." Read it and weep—for the Free Speech Movement anniversary, for the ideal of an intellectually open university, and for America.

⊘ AT ISSUE: HOW FREE SHOULD FREE SPEECH BE?

1. In your own words, summarize Stern's thesis. Where does he state it?

2. At what point (or points) in the essay does Stern appeal to *ethos*? How effective is this appeal?

3. In paragraph 4, Stern says, "The Berkeley 'machine' now promotes Free Speech Movement kitsch." First, look up the meaning of *kitsch*. Then, explain what Stern means by this statement.

4. Stern supports his points with examples drawn from his own experience. Is this enough? What other kinds of evidence could he have used?

5. In paragraph 5, Stern says that every undergraduate at Berkeley "undergoes a form of indoctrination." What does he mean? Does Stern make a valid point, or is he **begging the question**?

6. Why does Stern discuss Bettina Aptheker in paragraphs 15–16? Could he be accused of making an *ad hominem* attack? Why or why not?

This code came out of a June 1992 meeting of the American Association of University Professors.

ON FREEDOM OF EXPRESSION AND CAMPUS SPEECH CODES

AMERICAN ASSOCIATION OF UNIVERSITY PROFESSORS

Freedom of thought and expression is essential to any institution of higher 1 learning. Universities and colleges exist not only to transmit existing knowledge. Equally, they interpret, explore, and expand that knowledge by testing the old and proposing the new.

This mission guides learning outside the classroom quite as much as in 2 class, and often inspires vigorous debate on those social, economic, and political issues that arouse the strongest passions. In the process, views will be expressed that may seem to many wrong, distasteful, or offensive. Such is the nature of freedom to sift and winnow ideas.

> "On a campus that is free and open, no idea can be banned or forbidden."

On a campus that is free and open, 3 no idea can be banned or forbidden. No viewpoint or message may be deemed so hateful or disturbing that it may not be expressed.

Universities and colleges are also 4 communities, often of a residential character. Most campuses have recently sought to become more diverse, and more reflective of the larger community, by attracting students, faculty, and staff from groups that were historically excluded or underrepresented. Such gains as they have made are recent, modest, and tenuous. The campus climate can profoundly affect an institution's continued diversity. Hostility or intolerance to persons who differ from the majority (especially if seemingly condoned by the institution) may undermine the confidence of new members of the community. Civility is always fragile and can easily be destroyed.

In response to verbal assaults and use of hateful language some campuses 5 have felt it necessary to forbid the expression of racist, sexist, homophobic, or ethnically demeaning speech, along with conduct or behavior that harasses. Several reasons are offered in support of banning such expression. Individuals and groups that have been victims of such expression feel an understandable outrage. They claim that the academic progress of minority and majority alike may suffer if fears, tensions, and conflicts spawned by slurs and insults create an environment inimical to learning. These arguments, grounded in the need to foster an atmosphere respectful of and welcome to all persons, strike a deeply responsive chord in the academy. But, while we can acknowledge both the weight of these concerns and the thoughtfulness of those persuaded of the need for regulation, rules that ban or punish speech based upon its content cannot be justified. An institution of higher learning fails to fulfill its mission if it asserts the power to proscribe ideas—and racial or ethnic slurs, sexist epithets, or homophobic insults almost always express ideas, however repugnant. Indeed, by proscribing any ideas, a university sets an example that profoundly disserves its academic mission. Some may seek to defend a distinction between the regulation of the content of speech and the regulation of the manner (or style) of speech. We find this distinction untenable in practice because offensive style or opprobrious phrases may in fact have been chosen precisely for their expressive power. As the United States Supreme Court has said in the course of rejecting criminal sanctions for offensive words: Words are often chosen as much for their emotive as their cognitive force. We cannot sanction the view that the Constitution, while solicitous of the cognitive content of individual speech, has little or no regard for that emotive function which, practically speaking, may often be the more important element of the overall message sought to be communicated. The line between substance and style is thus too uncertain to sustain the pressure that will inevitably be brought to bear upon disciplinary rules that attempt to regulate speech. Proponents of speech codes sometimes reply that the value of emotive language of this type is of such a low order that, on balance, suppression is justified by the harm suffered by those who are directly affected, and by the general damage done to the learning environment. Yet a college or university sets a perilous course if it seeks to differentiate between high-value and low-value speech, or to choose which groups are to be protected by curbing the speech of others. A speech code unavoidably implies an institutional competence to distinguish permissible expression of hateful thought from what is proscribed as thoughtless hate. Institutions would also have to justify shielding some, but not other, targets of offensive language—not to political preference, to religious but not to philosophical creed, or perhaps even to some but not to other religious affiliations. Starting down this path creates an even greater risk that groups not originally protected may later demand similar solicitude—demands the institution that began the process of banning some speech is ill equipped to resist.

Distinctions of this type are neither practicable nor principled; their very 6 fragility underscores why institutions devoted to freedom of thought and expression ought not adopt an institutionalized coercion of silence.

Moreover, banning speech often avoids consideration of means more 7 compatible with the mission of an academic institution by which to deal with incivility, intolerance, offensive speech, and harassing behavior:

1. Institutions should adopt and invoke a range of measures that penalize conduct and behavior, rather than speech, such as rules against defacing property, physical intimidation or harassment, or disruption of campus activities. All members of the campus community should be made aware of such rules, and administrators should be ready to use them in preference to speech-directed sanctions.

2. Colleges and universities should stress the means they use best—to educate—including the development of courses and other curricular and

co-curricular experiences designed to increase student understanding and to deter offensive or intolerant speech or conduct. Such institutions should, of course, be free (indeed encouraged) to condemn manifestations of intolerance and discrimination, whether physical or verbal.

3. The governing board and the administration have a special duty not only to set an outstanding example of tolerance, but also to challenge boldly and condemn immediately serious breaches of civility.

4. Members of the faculty, too, have a major role; their voices may be critical in condemning intolerance, and their actions may set examples for understanding, making clear to their students that civility and tolerance are hallmarks of educated men and women.

5. Student personnel administrators have in some ways the most demanding role of all, for hate speech occurs most often in dormitories, locker-rooms, cafeterias, and student centers. Persons who guide this part of campus life should set high standards of their own for tolerance and should make unmistakably clear the harm that uncivil or intolerant speech inflicts.

To some persons who support speech codes, measures like these—relying 8 as they do on suasion rather than sanctions—may seem inadequate. But freedom of expression requires toleration of "ideas we hate," as Justice Holmes put it. The underlying principle does not change because the demand is to silence a hateful speaker, or because it comes from within the academy. Free speech is not simply an aspect of the educational enterprise to be weighed against other desirable ends. It is the very precondition of the academic enterprise itself.

⊘ AT ISSUE: HOW FREE SHOULD FREE SPEECH BE?

1. The writers of this statement rely primarily on deductive reasoning. Construct a syllogism that includes the selection's major premise, minor premise, and conclusion.

2. At what audience is this statement aimed—students, instructors, administrators, or the general public? How do you know?

3. What problem do the writers address? Where do they present their solution?

4. In paragraph 5, the writers discuss the major arguments against their position. Why do they address opposing arguments so early in the selection? How effectively do the writers refute these arguments?

5. Paragraph 7 is followed by a numbered list. What information is in this list? Why did the writers decide to set it off in this way?

6. What do the writers mean when they say that free speech "is the very precondition of the academic exercise itself" (para. 8)?

This essay first appeared in the *Washington Post* on February 20, 2015.

INTIMIDATION IS THE NEW NORMAL

JONATHAN HAIDT

Images of fires, fireworks, and metal barricades crashing through windows 1 made for great television, but the rioters who shut down Milo Yiannopoulos's talk at the University of California at Berkeley didn't just attack property. Fewer cell phone cameras captured the moments when they punched and pepper-sprayed members of the crowd, particularly those who seemed like they might be supporters of Yiannopoulos or Donald Trump.

Although the violence on February 1 was clearly instigated by outside 2 agitators—"black bloc" anarchists who show up at events with their faces masked—at least some of the people behind the masks were Berkeley students who thought it was morally permissible to use violence to stop a lecture from taking place. As one student wrote afterward, "Violence helped ensure the safety of students." Another asked, "When the nonviolent tactics [for stopping the talk] have been exhausted—what is left?"

Still, it was easy for the academic community to think of the riot as a spe- 3 cial case. After all, Yiannopoulos is a professional troll. He came to campus to provoke, not to instruct. And he had exposed vulnerable individuals to danger before, as when he posted the name and photo of a trans woman on-screen while he mocked her.

A month later, on March 2, the violence was harder to justify. After stu- 4 dents shouted down Charles Murray's attempt to give a lecture at Middlebury College, he was moved to a locked room in the student center from which his talk was live-streamed. Angry students pounded on the walls and pulled fire alarms to disrupt the broadcast. As Murray and his faculty host—Allison Stanger, a political-science professor—left the building, they were blocked by an "angry mob" (Stanger's words) including both students and nonstudents. As Stanger and Murray tried to push their way through, with the help of two security guards, several people grabbed and pulled at them, sending her to the hospital with whiplash and a concussion. Stanger later wrote that she had feared for her life.

Perhaps because it was a professor who was injured, Middlebury students 5 did not defend the use of violence in the way that some Berkeley students had. But even the students' coordinated effort to silence Murray is harder to justify than the effort to silence Yiannopoulos. Murray is mild-mannered, came with co-sponsorship from the political-science department, and was there not to provoke but to talk about an issue that is central to students' moral and political concerns: social and economic inequality. When two psychologists, Wendy Williams and Stephen Ceci, asked 70 professors at various colleges to assess the political leaning of Murray's speech—given to them as a transcript with no source attributed—they rated it as "middle of the road," leaning neither left nor right.

But for many students and professors, what Murray intended to say was not 6 relevant. The Southern Poverty Law Center had labeled him a "white suprem- acist" on the basis of his writings, and that was sufficient for many to believe that they had a moral duty to deny a platform to him. So perhaps Murray was a special case, too—some said his mere presence, like Yiannopoulos's at Berkeley, posed a direct danger to students. (I urge readers to see Murray's line-by-line corrections of the Southern Poverty Law Center's entry on him, then read some of his writings and decide for themselves.)

A month after the Middlebury fracas came the Heather Mac Donald 7 shout-down at Claremont McKenna College. But this was no special case. Mac Donald is a typical campus speaker—a journalist and political commen- tator who wrote a book challenging prevailing wisdom on a matter of current concern.

In her 2016 book, *The War on Cops*, she argued that overstated claims 8 about systemic racism among police officers have led police departments in some cities to adopt less assertive tactics, which has led to increased crime, including higher rates of murder, particularly of black men. Her thesis, pop- ularly known as "the Ferguson effect," has been hotly debated, but as the left-leaning sociologist Neil Gross summarized the state of play last September, "there is now some evidence that when all eyes are on police misconduct, crime may edge up. Progressives should acknowledge that this idea isn't far-fetched."

Yet because Mac Donald challenged the dominant narrative and criticized 9 the Black Lives Matter movement, some students at Claremont McKenna decided that she, too, must be denied a platform. They mobilized a mass action via Facebook with a call to "show up wearing black" and "bring your comrades, because we're shutting this down." A mob outside the auditorium, estimated at around 300 people, prevented anyone from entering the building. The college decided to stream Mac Donald's talk live from the nearly empty hall as hundreds of protesters pounded on the windows. Immediately after- ward, she was whisked away through a kitchen exit by the campus police in an unmarked car.

What are we to make of this? There were no reports of violence or prop- 10 erty damage. Yet this event is potentially more ominous than the Berkeley and Middlebury violence, for we are witnessing the emergence of a dangerous new norm for responding to speakers who challenge campus orthodoxy. Anyone offended by the speaker can put out a call on Facebook to bring together stu- dents and locals, including "antifa" (antifascist) and black-bloc activists who explicitly endorse the use of violence against racists and fascists. Because of flagrant "concept creep," however, almost anyone who is politically right of cen- ter can be labeled a racist or a fascist, and the promiscuous use of such labels is now part of the standard operating procedure. The call to shut down Mac Donald's talk asserted, without evidence, that her agenda is "racist, anti-Black, capitalist, imperialist, [and] fascist." As with accusations of witchcraft in earlier centuries, once such labels are attached to someone, few will dare to challenge their accuracy, lest they be accused of the same crimes.

It is crucial to note that at all three colleges—Berkeley, Middlebury, and 11 Claremont McKenna—the crowd included a mix of students and locals, some wearing masks. It is therefore no longer possible to assume that a crowd on a college campus will be nonviolent, as crowds of protesting students were in the fall of 2015. What would have happened to Mac Donald had she tried to enter or exit through the main entrance, without a police escort? From now on, any campus speaker who arouses a protest is at risk of a beating. Can this really be the future of American higher education?

I do not doubt that many students face indignities and insults because of 12 their race, gender, sexual orientation, or ability status. I respect students who take actions motivated by their concern for their fellow students. But these actions reflect choices that have far-reaching and potentially damaging consequences. First, there is the decision to appraise events in ways that amplify their harmfulness. A common feature of recent campus shout-downs is the argument that the speaker "dehumanizes" members of marginalized groups or "denies their right to exist." No quotations or citations are given for such strong assertions; these are rhetorical moves made to strengthen the case against the speaker. But if students come to believe that anyone who offends them has "dehumanized" them, they are setting themselves up for far greater vulnerability and isolation. Life, love, and work are full of small offenses and misunderstandings, many of which will now be experienced as monstrous and unforgivable.

Second, students in the past few years have increasingly opted for collective action to shut down talks by speakers they dislike, rather than taking the two traditional options available to all individuals: Don't go to the talk, or go and engage the speaker in the ques- 13

> "It is no longer possible to assume that a crowd on a college campus will be nonviolent."

tion-and-answer period. The decision to turn so many events into collective moral struggles has profound ramifications for the entire college. Everyone is pressured to take sides. Administrators are pressured to disinvite speakers, or at least to condemn their scholarship and morals while reluctantly noting their right to speak. Petitions are floated, and names of signers (and abstainers) are noted.

The human mind evolved for violent intergroup conflict. It comes easily 14 to us, and it can be so emotionally rewarding that we have invented many ways of engaging in it ritually, such as in team sports. But the tribal mind is incompatible with scholarship, open-minded thinking, toleration of dissent, and the search for truth. When tribal sentiments are activated within an academic community, some members start to believe that their noble collective ends justify almost any means, including the demonization of inconvenient research and researchers, false accusations, character assassination, and sometimes even violence. Anyone not with the movement is against it, and its enemies—students, faculty members, administrators—are often intimidated into acquiescence. This is how professors and students are increasingly describing their campus climate, at least at elite four-year residential colleges.

What can be done to change course? College professors, more than anyone else in the country, have a professional duty to speak up for the freedom of scholars, authors, and journalists to present unpopular ideas, theories, and research findings, free from intimidation and harassment. The next time an unpopular speaker is invited to campus, professors should talk to their classes about the norms of the academy, the benefits of having one's cherished ideas challenged, and the impropriety of making slurs and *ad hominem* arguments. Then they should attend the event themselves—especially if they dislike the speaker.

But while professors are best placed to act as role models, it is only administrators who can set and enforce rules. At New York University, where I teach, the policy on protests is detailed and reasonable. It allows silent protests and brief outbursts within the lecture hall, but it states clearly that "chanting or making other sustained or repeated noise in a manner which substantially interferes with the speaker's communication is not permitted." Most colleges have such policies, but they are rarely enforced, even after the college president offers fine words about freedom of speech. From now on, administrators must ensure that any students who violate protest policies will be disciplined or expelled. There must be zero tolerance for mob rule, intimidation of speakers, and intimidation of political minorities among students as well as faculty members. Alumni can help by making it clear that they will give no further funds to colleges that permit students to shout down speakers with impunity.

And finally, when responsible campus leaders all fail to create a campus where diverse perspectives can be heard and discussed, students who desire such a campus must stand up and make their wishes known. There are encouraging signs on this front. In the wake of the unexpected outcome of the 2016 presidential election, the editors of Harvard's main student newspaper called on administrators and faculty members to "take active steps to ensure that students of all political stripes feel comfortable voicing their ideas, especially in the classroom." More recently, Northwestern University became the first in the country whose student government passed a resolution calling on the administration to promote viewpoint diversity and to enforce its policies against disruptive protests.

This year may become a turning point in the annals of higher education. It may be remembered as the year that political violence and police escorts became ordinary parts of campus life. Or it may be remembered as the year when professors, students, and administrators finally found the moral courage to stand up against intimidation, even when it is aimed at people whose ideas they dislike.

⊙ AT ISSUE: HOW FREE SHOULD FREE SPEECH BE?

1. Haidt begins his essay by devoting eight paragraphs to discussing three violent protests. How does this discussion set the stage for the rest of the essay?

2. At the end of paragraph 6, Haidt urges readers to do some research into Charles Murray's writings and then "decide for themselves" if his presence poses a danger to students. Why doesn't Haidt supply this information? What does he hope to gain by telling people to "decide for themselves"?

3. Is Haidt's argument primarily inductive or deductive? Why do you think he chose the strategy that he uses?

4. Does Haidt ever establish that the situation he describes is widespread enough to be a problem? Could he be accused of setting up a **straw man**? Explain.

5. Haidt begins paragraph 15 by asking a question. What is the function of this question?

6. What does Haidt want to accomplish with his essay? Is his purpose to convince readers of something? To move them to action? What is your reaction to his essay?

TALKING PAST EACH OTHER ON FREE SPEECH

LAURIE ESSIG

College free-speech controversies, I fear, will rage on because opposing sides 1
talk past each other.

On one side are those who insist that speech is simply free—no ifs, ands, 2
or buts. These are often the same people who insist that markets are free, disregarding, in both arenas, that society isn't made up only of individuals but
also of structures and histories that give advantage to the elite while oppressing
poor people and ethnic, racial, religious, and sexual minorities.

Those most disadvantaged by so-called free speech insist that we consider 3
its costs, and they see certain ideas as acts of symbolic violence. They consider blocking it a form of self-defense. When hate crimes are on the rise, when
anti-immigrant and anti-minority sentiment is in the wind, to tolerate bigotry
is to invite brutalization, the reasoning goes.

In fact, everyone—right, left, and center—can see the costs of speech 4
when it is directed at them and their sense of safety in the world.

After all, if the right really believes we should all be hearty enough to con- 5
sider views we find abhorrent, why did it cast off one of its media darlings?
Free speech was the right's mantra with regard to its golden boy Milo
Yiannopoulos, whose tweets were so racist and misogynist that he was kicked
off Twitter. When he came to Berkeley on his "Dangerous Faggot" tour, students protested, black-bloc agitators rioted, and the right-wing Twittersphere
went ballistic over those "precious snow-flake" students too fragile to bear his
provocations.

But free speech, as it turns out, applies only when it doesn't touch on 6
matters one holds especially dear. The right became its own precious snow-
flake when Yiannopoulos talked about teenaged boys as sexual subjects who
could consent to sex with adult men. When his words undermined the idea
that teenagers are children and that children are innocent, the "sticks and
stones will break my bones but words will never hurt me" camp screamed
"Shut him down," and shut him down it did: Yiannopoulos was forced to part
ways with Breitbart News, disinvited to speak at the Conservative Political
Action Conference, and lost his book deal with Simon & Schuster.

Targets of rhetoric like Yiannopoulos's reasonably insist that we acknowl- 7
edge symbolic violence not only in raucous provocations but in seemingly
polite racist, sexist, or homophobic opining as well. Recently the very polite
Charles Murray was invited by a student group to speak at Middlebury
College, where I teach. His 1994 book with Richard J. Herrnstein, *The Bell
Curve*, posited a racial basis of intelligence as measured through IQ tests.

The authors used spurious correlations, as well as a highly problematic measure of intelligence, to trot out old, eugenicist arguments that have oft been debunked.

When Murray came to Middlebury in 2007 to discuss his research, according to some alumni of color, it felt pretty awful to sit in a room and have your intelligence and, by extension, your right to be at Middlebury, publicly debated. Many said they wished they had been more forceful in protesting Murray's presence then. 8

So this time, more than 450 alumni and over 70 faculty members (including me) spoke up. We asked the political-science department to withdraw its cosponsorship of the event, or to at least make it a panel-type discussion so that Murray's views might be contested. We also asked President Laurie Patton not to introduce him. 9

We weren't trying to block Murray from speaking. We were seeking some recognition that words can and do hurt, that they can be a form of symbolic violence, the sort pretty obvious to faculty, students, and staff of color, who are already told, in a million small ways, that they don't belong at Middlebury. They can be made fun of in Halloween costumes or "thug"-themed parties where white bros wear baggy jeans and carry malt liquor, casually using the N-word and laughing if anyone is offended. The white bros "belong" at Middlebury, you see. Many of them have relatives, parents, grandparents, even great-grandparents who went to Middlebury or places like it. No one ever debates *their* intelligence, no matter how little of it they display. 10

The Murray event's organizers encouraged us to debate his ideas and to counter his eugenicist arguments with evidence and pointed questions. To be fair, many at Middlebury, including the president and the political-science faculty, were worried about censorship and committed to the idea that we must be able to hear ideas we find disagreeable. For people who feel threatened in the current political climate, however, polite debate about disagreeable ideas is a luxury they can no longer afford. We live in dangerous times, when immigrants fear expulsion and hate crimes are on the rise. Personal vulnerability drowns out the fear of censorship. 11

By the time Murray arrived on campus, the mood was explosive. Protesters shut down his talk, and Allison Stanger, a political-science professor moderating Murray's appearance, was injured, although the circumstances around that are still murky. 12

Since then commentators in the *Atlantic*, the *New York Times*, and elsewhere have attacked Middlebury for being against free speech. We receive emails and tweets calling us "brown-shirts" who seek to "muzzle" speakers. As I write this, my program, gender, sexuality, and feminist studies, is being trolled on Twitter by Murray's American Enterprise Institute colleague Christina Hoff Sommers. The right-wing website The Daily Wire suggests ludicrously that our curriculum is the reason "many leftist students felt compelled not only to disrupt Murray's speech, but also to rationalize the use of violence 13 to combat ideas that they did not agree with." This is the sort of free speech the right loves: It targets feminist, critical race, postcolonial, and queer scholars in ways that are intimidating and designed to shut us up. It calls our courses "categorically insane."

The notion that our curriculum incited violence isn't just wrong, it's slan- 14 derous. But categorical insanity, differently read, is closer to the truth, for our curriculum does teach students to be critical thinkers, to question dominant ideologies and "common sense." The commonsensical notion that speech is free, for instance, and that we all enter fields of speech as equals is certainly a category of inquiry within our program. That must seem incomprehensible, or "insane," to those who do not want to question why things are the way they are. We expect our students to experience "category crisis" when looking from new vantage points at prevailing ways of seeing.

It is this sort of "categorical insanity," in fact, that might just extricate us all 15 from the speech quagmire. That kind of analysis shows that our ways of seeing the world are shaped by our circumstances: race, gender, sexual orientation, class, and so on. When people on the right say they feel their traditions and livelihoods are threatened, I don't question the strength of their feelings. When those on the left no longer want to bear the pain of having their human worth debated, I recognize their outrage. When those in the middle acknowledge that ostensibly free speech has costs, but that censorship is too high a price to ever pay, I trust their sincerity as well, and I agree with them.

> "If we can't untie these infinite knots, maybe we can at least remember how to live together."

Surely Christina Hoff Sommers, 16 a former philosophy professor, understands the nature and value of such category analysis. A free-speech advocate, as I am, she can no doubt find a critique of my department more articulate and empathetic than her tweeted "Oy vey."

I am a card-carrying member of the free-speech absolutist ACLU. I also 17 believe that when institutions support even polite racism and misogyny, they aggravate deep, ancient wounds, symbolically excluding those who have been historically excluded for many generations. I am truly concerned, too, about censorship, since when it is backed by the state it is usually targeted against the likes of me, not Charles Murray.

This queer inability, this refusal to be labeled, requires that I live with 18 unresolvable contradictions. So must we all. Neither Middlebury nor any other college can resolve them. Trite appeals to civility won't resolve them either, nor will columnists' scolds nor acts of violence.

But if we can't untie these infinite knots, maybe we can at least remem- 19 ber how to live together. Academe, and thoughtful people outside it, can begin to acknowledge not just intellectual but also circumstantial ways of perceiving speech.

Whether you're on the right or the left or in the topsy-turvy anxious mid- 20
dle, take a breath. Recognize the vastness of the gaps between us. Recognize
too the humanity and the life experiences of those you fear and scorn. Knowing that we understand speech, its costs and its freedoms, in radically different
ways isn't a tidy fix, but it is at least a first step toward actually hearing one
another.

⊘ AT ISSUE: HOW FREE SHOULD FREE SPEECH BE?

1. Throughout her essay, Essig accepts certain ideas as self-evident.
   What are they? Do you agree with her? Explain.

2. In paragraph 1, Essig says that the two sides to the free speech debate
   "talk past each other." What are two sides of the debate? Could Essig
   be accused of committing the **either/or fallacy**? Why or why not?

3. Does Essig appeal mainly to *logos*, *pathos*, or *ethos*? Explain.

4. Do Essig's sympathies lie with the protestors or those who wanted to
   give Charles Murray a platform for his ideas? How do you know? Why
   does Essig mention Christina Hoff Summers?

5. In her essay, Essig says that she is concerned about censorship
   because it is usually targeted against people like her. What does she
   mean? How do you know?

6. Essig concludes by saying the problem she has defined cannot be
   easily solved. Does this concession undercut her argument in any
   way? Explain.

VISUAL ARGUMENT: FOOTBALL PLAYERS KNEELING

AP Images/Marcio Jose Sanchez

⊙ AT ISSUE: HOW FREE SHOULD FREE SPEECH BE?

1. What point is this visual making? What course of action do you think it is advocating?

2. What visual elements are included in this picture? How does the arrangement of the people help the visual make its point?

3. How does this visual create an emotion appeal? Does it also appeal to *logos* and to *ethos*? Explain.

4. Write a caption for this visual that communicates its main point. Do you think that taking a knee at a football game is a legitimate form of protest? Do you think this type of protest reinforces or undermines our constitutional right to free speech? Explain.

TEMPLATE FOR WRITING A DEDUCTIVE ARGUMENT

Write a one-paragraph **deductive** argument in which you argue *against* your school imposing speech codes. Follow the template below, filling in the blanks to create your argument.

        One of the basic principles of the United States government is the constitutional guarantee of freedom of speech. With few exceptions, all Americans _____ _____

_____

_____. In college _____

_____.

For example, _____

_____. By having the right to express themselves freely,

_____

_____

_____. Therefore, _____

_____.

Not everyone agrees with this view, however. Some people argue that _____

_____

_____

_____. This argument misses the point. When a university limits the speech of some students because others may be upset by their comments, _____

_____

_____.

For this reason, colleges should _____ _____

_____

_____

_____.

TEMPLATE FOR WRITING AN INDUCTIVE ARGUMENT

Write a one-paragraph **inductive** argument in which you argue *in favor of* your school imposing speech codes. Follow the template below, filling in the blanks to create your argument.

The number of students demanding protection from distasteful ideas is growing yearly. Some students complain that _____
_____
_____. These students want _____
_____.
A number of studies have shown that so-called safe spaces and trigger warnings go a long way toward calming students' fears and creating a hospitable learning environment. For example, some students _____
_____. As a result, _____
_____
_____. The best way for colleges to deal with this problem is to _____
_____.
Free speech advocates, however, argue that _____
_____
_____
_____. Although this may be true, _____
_____
_____.
For this reason, it would make sense to _____
_____
_____.

◆ EXERCISE 5.13 REVISING YOUR ARGUMENT PARAGRAPHS

Interview several of your classmates as well as one or two of your instructors about how free free speech should be. Then, revise the deductive and inductive arguments you wrote using the preceding templates so that they include some of these comments.

◆ EXERCISE 5.14 WRITING DEDUCTIVE OR INDUCTIVE ARGUMENTS

Write an essay in which you take a position on the question, "Should Universities Be Able to Place Limits on Free Speech?" Make sure that your essay is organized primarily as either a deductive argument or an inductive argument. Use the readings on pages 166–185 as source material, and be sure to document all information that you get from these sources. (See Chapter 10 for information on documenting sources.)

◆ EXERCISE 5.15 CHECKING FOR FALLACIES

Review the logical fallacies discussed on pages 162–163. Then, reread the essay you wrote for Exercise 5.14, and check to see if it contains any fallacies. Underline any fallacies you find, and identify them by name. Then, rewrite each statement so it expresses a logical argument. Finally, revise your draft to eliminate any fallacies you found.

◆ EXERCISE 5.16 REVIEWING THE FOUR PILLARS OF ARGUMENT

Review the four pillars of argument discussed in Chapter 1. Does your essay include all four elements of an effective argument? Add anything that is missing. Then, label the key elements of your essay.

The 2016 film *Hidden Figures* adapted the stories of real-life black women who worked in STEM fields at NASA in the 1960s, including mathematician Dorothy Vaughan (played in the film by Octavia Spencer). Dorothy Vaughan: The Picture Art Collection/Alamy. *Hidden Figures:* LEVIATHAN FILMS/CHERNIN ENT/FOX 2000 PICTURES/Album/Alamy Stock Photo

CHAPTER

6

Rogerian Argument, Toulmin Logic, and Oral Arguments

AT ISSUE

Why Are So Few Women in STEM Fields?

Until fairly recently, professions such as medicine, law, dentistry, and veterinary practices were overwhelmingly male. Beginning in the 1970s, however, this began to change, and today we can see a major shift within these professions. For example, in 2017, women outnumbered men in American medical schools for the first time in history. Similar shifts can be seen in other previously male-dominated professions—but not in the disciplines referred to as STEM (science, technology, engineering, and mathematics).

Despite the efforts of high schools and colleges, the percentage of women majoring in computer science and in engineering is below 20 percent. In the workplace, the numbers are even lower: only 10.7 percent of computer hardware engineers and 8 percent of mechanical engineers are women. Many people have tried to find an explanation for this disparity. In 2005, Larry Summers, the president of Harvard University, provoked a furor at a conference by suggesting that prejudice alone cannot explain the gender gap in science and math.

More recently, in 2017, James Damore, an engineer at Google, wrote an internal memo that criticized Google's diversity policy, referring to the company as an "ideological echo chamber." Although Damore asserted that he was opposed to workplace sexism and stereotyping, he went on to claim that the male/female imbalance in STEM fields is at least partly the result of biological differences and cannot be eliminated without resorting to discrimination against men. Damore's memo created an uproar at Google, and as a result, he was fired. Others take a more nuanced view of the situation and look for more complex explanations—for example, discrimination and lifestyle choices—to account for women's underrepresentation in STEM fields.

Later in this chapter, you will be asked to think more about this issue. You will be given several sources to consider and asked to write an argument—using one of the three approaches discussed in this chapter—that takes a position on why women are underrepresented in STEM fields.

191

Understanding Rogerian Argument

The traditional model of argument is **confrontational**—characterized by conflict and opposition. This has been the tradition since Aristotle wrote about argument in ancient Greece. The end result of this model of argument is that someone is a winner and someone is a loser or someone is right and someone is wrong.

Arguments do not always have to be confrontational, however. In fact, the twentieth-century psychologist Carl Rogers contended that in many situations, this method of arguing can actually be counterproductive, making it impossible for two people to reach agreement. According to Rogers, attacking opponents and telling them that they are wrong or misguided puts them on the defensive. The result of this tactic is frequently ill will, anger, hostility, and conflict. If you are trying to negotiate an agreement or convince someone to do something, these are exactly the responses that you do not want. To solve this problem, Rogers developed a new approach to argument—one that emphasizes cooperation and consensus over confrontation.

Rogerian argument begins with the assumption that people of good will can find solutions to problems that they have in common. Rogers recommends that you consider those with whom you disagree as colleagues, not opponents. Instead of entering into the adversarial relationship that is assumed in classical argument, Rogerian argument encourages you to enter into a cooperative relationship in which both you and your readers search for **common ground**—points of agreement about a problem. By taking this approach, you are more likely to find a solution that will satisfy everyone.

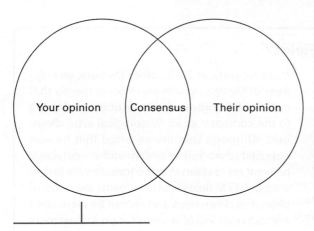

Rogerian argument as a Venn diagram

Structuring Rogerian Arguments

Consider the following situation. Assume that you bought a video game console that stopped working one week after the warranty expired. Also assume that the manager of the store where you purchased the game console has refused to exchange it for another console. His point is that because the warranty has expired, the store has no obligation to take the product back. As a last resort, you write a letter to the game console's manufacturer. If you were writing a traditional argument, you would state your thesis—"It is clear that I should receive a new game console"—and then present arguments to support your position. You would also refute opposing arguments, and you would end your letter with a strong concluding statement.

Because Rogerian arguments begin with different assumptions, however, they are structured differently from classical arguments. In a Rogerian argument, you would begin by establishing common ground—by pointing out the concerns you and the video game console's manufacturer share. For example, you could say that as a consumer, you want to buy merchandise that will work as advertised. If the company satisfies your needs, you will continue to buy its products. This goal is shared by the manufacturer. Therefore, instead of beginning with a thesis statement that demands a yes or no response, you would point out that you and the manufacturer share an interest in solving your problem.

Next, you would describe *in neutral terms*—using impartial, unbiased language—the manufacturer's view of the problem, defining the manufacturer's concerns and attempting to move toward a compromise position. For example, you would explain that you understand that the company wants to make a high-quality product that will satisfy customers. You would also say that you understand that despite the company's best efforts, mistakes sometimes happen.

In the next section of your letter, you would present your own view of the problem fairly and objectively. This section plays a major role in convincing the manufacturer that your position has merit. Here, you should also try to concede the strengths of the manufacturer's viewpoint. For example, you can say that although you understand that warranties have time limits, your case has some unique circumstances that justify your claim.

Then you would explain how the manufacturer would benefit from granting your request. Perhaps you could point out that you have been satisfied with other products made by this manufacturer and expect to purchase more in the future. You could also say that instead of requesting a new game console, you would be glad to send the console back to the factory to be repaired. This suggestion shows that you are fair and willing to compromise.

Finally, your Rogerian argument would reinforce your position and end with a concluding statement that emphasizes the idea that you are certain that the manufacturer wants to settle this matter fairly.

⊙ EXERCISE 6.1 IDENTIFYING COMMON GROUND

Read through the At Issue topics listed in this book's table of contents. Choose one topic, and then do the following:

1. Summarize your own position on the issue.

2. In a few sentences, summarize the main concerns of someone who holds the opposite position.

3. Identify some common ground that you and someone who holds the opposite position might have.

4. Write a sentence that explains how your position on the issue might benefit individuals (including those who hold opposing views) or society in general.

Writing Rogerian Arguments

Rogerian arguments are typically used to address issues that are open to compromise. By making it clear that you understand and respect the opinions of others, you avoid an "I win/you lose" situation and demonstrate empathy and respect for all points of view. In this sense, Rogerian arguments are more like negotiations than classical arguments. Thus, in a Rogerian argument, you spend a good deal of time defining the common ground that exists between you and those with whom you disagree. Ideally, you demonstrate that it is possible to reach a consensus, one that represents the common ground that exists between opposing sides. The more successful you are in accomplishing this goal, the more persuasive your argument will be. Of course with some issues—usually the most polarizing—a consensus is difficult or even impossible to achieve. In these cases, the best you can hope for is to convince people to agree on just one or two points. With other issues, however, you will be able to demonstrate to readers how they would benefit by moving toward your position.

> **NOTE**
>
> Although the Rogerian approach to argument can be used to develop a whole essay, it can also be part of a more traditional argument. In this case, it frequently appears in the refutation section, where opposing arguments are addressed.

In general, a Rogerian argument can be structured in the following way:

INTRODUCTION	Introduces the problem, pointing out how both the writer and reader are affected (establishes common ground)
BODY	Presents the reader's view of the problem
	Presents the writer's view of the problem (includes evidence to support the writer's viewpoint)
	Shows how the reader would benefit from moving toward the writer's position (includes evidence to support the writer's viewpoint)
	Lays out possible compromises that would benefit both reader and writer (includes evidence to support the writer's viewpoint)
CONCLUSION	Strong concluding statement reinforces the thesis and emphasizes compromise

⊃ EXERCISE 6.2 ANALYZING A ROGERIAN ARGUMENT

The following student essay includes all the elements of a Rogerian argument. This essay was written in response to the question, "Is it fair for instructors to require students to turn off their cell phones in class?" After you read the essay, answer the questions on page 198, consulting the preceding outline if necessary.

WHY CELL PHONES DO NOT BELONG IN THE CLASSROOM

ZOYA KAHN

Some college students think it is unfair for instructors to require them to turn off their cell phones during class. Because they are accustomed to constant cell phone access, they don't understand how such a rule is justified. Granted, a strict, no-exceptions policy requiring that cell phones be turned off all over campus is not fair, but neither is a policy that prevents instructors from imposing restrictions. Both students and instructors know that cell phone use—including texting—during class can be disruptive. In addition, most would agree that the primary goal of a university is to create a respectful learning environment and that cell phone use during class undercuts this goal. For this reason, it is in everyone's interest for instructors to institute policies that require students to turn off cell phones during class.

1

Common ground

Thesis statement

Many students believe that requiring them to turn off their cell phones is unfair because it makes them feel less safe. Students are understandably concerned that, with their phones turned off, they will be unreachable during an emergency. For example, text message alerts are part of the emergency response system for most universities. Similarly, cell phones are a way for friends and family to contact students if there is an emergency. For these reasons, many students think that they should be free to make their own decisions concerning cell use. They believe that by turning their phones to vibrate or silent mode, they are showing respect for their classmates. Moreover, students need to learn how to regulate their own technology use, which will extend well beyond academia and graduation. As Dinesha Johnson, a student at

2

Reader's view of the problem

Henry Ford College notes in an opinion column, "Allowing students to have the freedom to practice self-discipline with their personal phone usage is necessary because when they are allowed such freedoms in the workplace they will handle it responsibly" (Johnson). Most students are honest, responsible, and courteous. However, those few students who cannot control themselves or are simply determined to misuse their phones will do so, regardless of the school's phone policy.

Writer's view of the situation

To protect the integrity of the school's learning environment, 3 instructors are justified in requiring students to turn off their phones. Studies over the past several years have shown how distracting cell phones can be during a class. For example, a ringing cell phone significantly impairs students' performance, and a vibrating phone can be just as distracting (End et al. 56–57). In addition, texting in class decreases students' ability to focus, lowers test performance, and lessens students' retention of class material (Tindell and Bohlander 2). More recent research suggests that more daily use of cell phones correlate with lower grade point averages among high school students (Barnwell). Even more disturbing, cell phones enable some students to cheat. Students can use cell phones to text test questions and answers, to search the web, and to photograph exams. Although asking students to turn off their phones will not prevent all these problems, it will reduce the abuses, and this will benefit the majority of students.

Benefits for reader of writer's position

Even though students have good reasons for wanting to keep their 4 phones on, there are even better reasons for accepting some reasonable restrictions. First, when students use cell phones during class, they distract themselves (as well as their classmates) and undermine everyone's ability to learn. Second, having their cell phones on gives students a false sense of security. A leading cell phone company has found that cell phones can actually "detract from school safety and crisis preparedness" in numerous ways. For example, the use of cell phones during a crisis can overload the cell phone system and make it useless. In addition, cell phones make it easy for students to spread rumors and, in some cases, cell phone use has created more panic than the incidents that actually caused the rumors ("Cell Phones").

Possible compromise

One possible compromise is for instructors to join with students to 5 create cell phone policies that take into consideration various situations and settings. For example, instructors could require students to turn off their phones only during exams. Instructors could also try to find ways to engage students by using cell phone technology in the classroom. For example, in some schools teachers take advantage of the various functions available on most cell phones—calculators, cameras, dictionaries, and internet browsers ("Cell Phones"). In addition, schools should consider implementing alternative emergency alert systems. Such compromises would ensure safety, limit possible disruptions, reduce the potential for academic dishonesty, and enhance learning. They also would have a better chance of succeeding because students would have to buy-in to the policies. As Anita Charles, the director of Secondary Teacher Education at Bates College and a researcher who has studied this topic, states, "Negotiation, when [students] feel that they're being listened to, benefits everybody, because the teacher finds that students become more cooperative" (McConville).

It is understandable that students want instructors to permit the use of cell phones during class, but it is also fair for instructors to ask students to turn them off. Although instructors should be able to restrict cell phone use, they should also make sure that students understand the need for this policy. It is in everyone's best interest to protect the integrity of the classroom and to make sure that learning is not compromised by cell phone use. To ensure the success of their education, students should be willing to turn off their phones.

6

Concluding statement

Works Cited

Barnwell, Paul. "Should Smartphones Be Banned from Classrooms?" *The Atlantic*, Atlantic Media Company, 27 Apr. 2016, www.theatlantic .com/education/archive/2016/04/do-smartphones-have-a-place-in-the -classroom/480231/.

"Cell Phones and Text Messaging in Schools." *National School Safety and Security Services*, 2012, www.schoolsecurity.org/trends/cell-phones -and-text-messaging-in-schools/.

End, Christian M., Shaye Worthman, Mary Bridget Mathews, and Katharina Wetterau. "Costly Cell Phones: The Impact of Cell Phone Rings on Academic Performance." *Teaching of Psychology*, vol. 37, no. 1, 2010, pp. 55–57. *Academic Search Complete*, doi: 10.1080/00986280903425912.

Johnson, Dinesh A. Mirror News. "Why Students Should Be Using Their
Phones in Class." *Mirror News.* Henry Ford College, 29 Jan. 2018,
mirrornews.hfcc.edu/news/2018/01-29/why-students-should-be
-using-their-phones-class.

McConville, Emily. "Why Banning Cellphones in Schools Misses the
Point." Bates Wordmark, Bates College, 23 Mar. 2018, www.bates
.edu/news/2018/03/23/why-banning-cellphones-in-schools
-misses-the-point.

Tindell, Deborah R., and Robert W. Bohlander. "The Use and Abuse of
Cell Phones and Text Messaging in the Classroom: A Survey of
College Students." *College Teaching,* vol. 60, no. 1, 2012, pp. 1–9.
ERIC Institute of Education Services, eric.ed.gov/?id=EJ951966.

Identifying the Elements of a Rogerian Argument

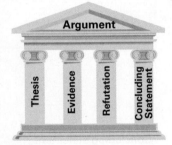

1. How does the writer attempt to establish common ground? Do you think she is successful?

2. What evidence does the writer supply to support her position?

3. Other than reinforcing the writer's position, what else is the conclusion trying to accomplish?

4. How does the concluding statement reinforce agreement and compromise?

5. How would this essay be different if it were written as a traditional argument (as opposed to a Rogerian argument)?

Understanding Toulmin Logic

Another way of describing the structure of argument was introduced by the philosopher Stephen Toulmin in his book *The Uses of Argument* (1958). Toulmin observed that although formal logic is effective for analyzing classical arguments, it is inadequate for describing the arguments that occur in everyday life. Although Toulmin was primarily concerned with the structures of arguments at the level of sentences or paragraphs, his model is also useful when dealing with longer arguments.

In its simplest terms, a **Toulmin argument** has three parts—the *claim*, the *grounds*, and the *warrant*. The **claim** is the main point of the essay— usually stated as the thesis. The **grounds** are the evidence that a writer uses to support the claim. The **warrant** is the **inference**—either stated or implied—that connects the claim to the grounds.

A basic argument using Toulmin logic would have the following structure.

CLAIM	Online education should be a part of all students' education.
GROUNDS	Students who take advantage of online education get better grades and report less stress than students who do not.
WARRANT	Online education is a valuable educational option.

Notice that the preceding three-part structure resembles the **syllogism** that is the backbone of classical argument. (See pp. 130–133 for a discussion of syllogisms.)

> **NOTE**
>
> When you use Toulmin logic to construct an argument, you still use deductive and inductive reasoning. You arrive at your claim inductively from facts, observations, and examples, and you connect the grounds and the warrant to your claim deductively.

Constructing Toulmin Arguments

Real arguments—those you encounter in print or online every day—are not as simple as the preceding three-part model implies. To be convincing, arguments often contain additional parts. To account for the demands of everyday debates, Toulmin expanded his model to include the following six interconnected elements.

CLAIM	The **claim** is the main point of your essay. It is a debatable statement that the rest of the essay will support.
	Online education should be a part of all students' education.
GROUNDS	The **grounds** are the concrete evidence that a writer uses to support the claim. These are the facts and observations that support the thesis. They can also be the opinions of experts that you locate when you do research.
	Studies show that students who take advantage of online education often get better grades than students who do not.
	Research indicates that students who take advantage of online education are under less stress than those who do not.

WARRANT

The **warrant** is the inference that links the claim with the grounds. The warrant is often an unstated assumption. Ideally, the warrant should be an idea with which your readers will agree. (If they do not agree with it, you will need to supply **backing**.)

Online education is a valuable educational option.

BACKING

The **backing** consists of statements that support the warrant.

My own experience with online education was positive. Not only did it enable me to schedule classes around my job but it also enabled me to work at my own pace in my courses.

QUALIFIERS

The **qualifiers** are statements that limit the claim. For example, they can be the real-world conditions under which the claim is true. These qualifiers can include words such as *most, few, some, sometimes, occasionally, often,* and *usually.*

Online education should be a required part of most students' education.

REBUTTALS

The **rebuttals** are exceptions to the claim. They are counterarguments that identify the situations where the claim does not hold true.

Some people argue that online education deprives students of an interactive classroom experience, but a course chat room can give students a similar opportunity to interact with their classmates.

⊝ EXERCISE 6.3 PLANNING A TOULMIN ARGUMENT

Look through this book's table of contents, and select an At Issue topic that interests you (ideally, one that you know something about). Write a sentence that states your position on this issue. (In terms of Toulmin argument, this statement is the *claim*.)

Then, supply as many of the expanded Toulmin model elements as you can, consulting the preceding description of these elements.

Claim: _____

_____

Grounds: _____

_____

_____

_____

Warrant: _____

_____

_____

Backing: _____

_____

Qualifiers: _____

_____

_____

Rebuttals: _____

_____

Writing Toulmin Arguments

One of the strengths of the Toulmin model is that it recognizes that effective arguments often involve more than stating ideas in absolute terms. Unlike the classical model of argument, the Toulmin model encourages writers to make realistic and convincing points by including claims and qualifiers and by addressing opposing arguments in down-to-earth and constructive ways. In a sense, this method of constructing an argument reminds writers that arguments do not exist in a vacuum. They are often quite subtle and are aimed at real readers who may or may not agree with them.

In general, a Toulmin argument can be organized in the following way:

INTRODUCTION	Introduces the problem
	States the claim (and possibly the qualifier)
BODY	Possibly states the warrant
	Presents the backing that supports the warrant
	Presents the grounds that support the claim
	Presents the conditions of rebuttal
	States the qualifiers
CONCLUSION	Brings the argument to a close
	Strong concluding statement reinforces the claim

➲ EXERCISE 6.4 ANALYZING A TOULMIN ARGUMENT

The following student essay, which includes all the elements of a Toulmin argument, was written in response to the question, "Are cheerleaders athletes?" After you read the essay, answer the questions on page 204, consulting the preceding outline if necessary.

COMPETITIVE CHEERLEADERS ARE ATHLETES

JEN DAVIS

Recently, the call to make competitive cheerleading an official   1
college sport and to recognize cheerleaders as athletes has gotten
stronger. Critics of this proposal maintain that cheerleading is simply
entertainment that occurs on the sidelines of real sporting events.
According to them, although cheerleading may show strength and
skill, it is not a competitive activity. This view of cheerleading, however,
misses the point. Because competitive cheerleading pits teams against
each other in physically and technically demanding athletic contests, it

Claim and qualifier should be recognized as a sport. For this reason, those who participate
in the sport of competitive cheerleading should be considered athletes.

Warrant Acknowledging them as athletes gives them the respect and   2
Backing support they deserve. Many people associate cheerleading with
pom-poms and short skirts and ignore the strength and skill that the
Grounds competitive version requires. After all, cheerleaders are supposed to
be cheering on boys and men who play "real" sports, right? Part of
the problem is a stereotype from cheerleading in the National Football
League, which "essentially comprises of dance routines performed by
scantily clad women in glittery boots" (Pant). Not surprisingly then
(and much like athletes in other female-dominated sports), cheerleaders have had to fight to be taken seriously. For example, Title IX, the
law that mandates gender equity in college sports, does not recognize
competitive cheerleading as a sport. This situation assumes a very
narrow definition of sports, one that needs to be updated. For example,
note how women's versions of long-accepted men's sports—such as
basketball, soccer, and track—are easy for people to respect and to

support. Competitive cheerleading, however, departs from this model and is not seen as a sport even though those who compete in it are skilled, accomplished athletes. Moreover, they do so at considerable physical risk: while overall injuries in the sport are low, college cheerleaders have the highest catastrophic injury rate (Lundy)

Recent proposals to rename competitive cheerleading "stunt" or   3   Backing
"team acrobatics and tumbling" are an effort to reshape people's ideas
about what cheerleaders actually do. Although some cheerleading   Grounds
squads have kept to their original purpose—to lead fans in cheering on
their teams—competitive teams practice rigorously, maintain impressive
levels of physical fitness, and risk serious injuries. Like other sports,
competitive cheerleading involves extraordinary feats of strength and
skill. Cheerleaders perform elaborate floor routines and ambitious
stunts, including flips from multilevel human pyramids. Competitive
cheerleaders also do what all athletes must do: they enter competitive
contests, are judged, and emerge as winners or losers.

Those in authority, however, are slow to realize that cheerleading is   4   Rebuttal
a sport. In 2010, a federal judge declared that competitive cheerleading
was "too underdeveloped and disorganized" to qualify as a legitimate
varsity sport under Title IX (Tigay). This ruling was shortsighted. Before
competitive cheerleading can develop as a sport, it needs to be *acknowledged* as a sport. Without their schools' financial support, cheerleading teams cannot recruit, offer scholarships, or host competitions. To
address this situation, several national groups are asking the National
Collegiate Athletic Association (NCAA) to designate competitive cheerleading as an "emerging sport." By doing this, the NCAA would show
its support and help competitive cheerleading to develop and eventually to flourish. This does not mean, however, that all cheerleaders are
athletes or that all cheerleading is a sport. In addition, the NCAA does
have reason to be cautious when it comes to redefining competitive
cheerleading. Some schools have taken sideline cheerleading teams
and recategorized them just so they could comply with Title IX. These   Qualifiers
efforts to sidestep the purpose of the law are, as one expert puts it,
"obviously transparent and unethical" (Tigay). Even so, fear of possible
abuse should not keep the NCAA from doing what is right and giving
legitimate athletes the respect and support they deserve.

Competitive cheerleaders are athletes in every sense of the word. 5
They are aggressive, highly skilled, physically fit competitors. For this
reason, they deserve to be acknowledged as athletes under Title IX and
supported by their schools and by the NCAA. Biased and outdated ideas
about what is (and what is not) a sport should not keep competitive
cheerleading from being recognized as the sport it is. As one proponent
puts it, "If someone tries to tell you that cheerleading is not a sport,
send [him or her] to a college-level competition and ask if their favorite
Concluding statement   professional athlete could do that" (Ruder). It is time to give competitive
cheerleaders the support and recognition they deserve.

Works Cited

Lundy, John. "'A Risk You Take': Cheerleaders Face Possibility of
   Catastrophic Injuries." *West Central Tribune*, 8 Feb. 2018, www
   .wctrib.com/sports/other/4399147-risk-you-take-cheerleaders-face
   -possibility-catastrophic-injuries.

Pant, Bhavya. "To Cheer or Not to Cheer." *Massachusetts Daily
   Collegian*, University of Massachusetts, 3 Apr. 2018, dailycollegian
   .com/2018/04/to-cheer-or-not-to-cheer/.

Ruder, Rebecca. "Cheerleading Is a Sport." *Western Courier*, 15 Sept.
   2017, westerncourier.com/38687/opinions/cheerleading-is-a-sport/.

Tigay, Chanan. "Is Cheerleading a Sport Protected by Title IX?" *CQ
   Researcher*, 25 Mar. 2011, p. 276. library.cqpress.com/cqresearcher
   /document.php?id=cqresrre2011032500.

Identifying the Elements of a Toulmin Argument

1. Summarize the position this essay takes as a three-part argument
   that includes the claim, the grounds, and the warrant.

2. Do you think the writer includes enough backing for her claim? What
   other supporting evidence could she have included?

3. Find the qualifier in the essay. How does it limit the argument? How
   else could the writer have qualified the argument?

4. Do you think the writer addresses enough objections to her claim?
   What other arguments could she have addressed?

5. Based on your reading of this essay, what advantages do you think
   Toulmin logic offers to writers? What disadvantages does it present?

Understanding Oral Arguments

Many everyday arguments—in school, on the job, or in your community—are presented orally. In many ways, an oral argument is similar to a written one: it has an introduction, a body, and a conclusion, and it addresses and refutes opposing points of view. In other, more subtle ways, however, an oral argument is different from a written one. Before you plan and deliver an oral argument, you should be aware of these differences.

The major difference between an oral argument and a written one is that an audience cannot reread an oral argument to clarify information. Listeners have to understand an oral argument the first time they hear it. To help your listeners, you need to design your presentation with this limitation in mind, considering the following guidelines:

- **An oral argument should contain verbal signals that help guide listeners.** Transitional phrases such as "My first point," "My second point," and "Let me sum up" are useful in oral arguments, where listeners do not have a written text in front of them. They alert listeners to information to come and signal shifts from one point to another.

- **An oral argument should use simple, direct language and avoid long sentences.** Complicated sentences that contain elevated language and numerous technical terms are difficult for listeners to follow. For this reason, your sentences should be straightforward and easy to understand.

- **An oral argument should repeat key information.** A traditional rule of thumb for oral arguments is, "Tell listeners what you're going to tell them; then tell it to them; finally, tell them what you've told them." In other words, in the introduction of an oral argument, tell your listeners what they are going to hear; in the body, discuss your points, one at a time; and finally, in your conclusion, restate your points. This intentional repetition ensures that your listeners follow (and remember) your points.

- **An oral argument should include visuals.** Visual aids can make your argument easier to follow. You can use visuals to identify your points as you discuss them. You can also use visuals—for example, charts, graphs, or tables—to clarify or reinforce key points as well as to add interest. Carefully selected visuals help increase the chances that what you are saying will be remembered.

Planning an Oral Argument

The work you do to plan your presentation is as important as the presentation itself. Here is some advice to consider as you plan your oral argument:

1. **Choose your topic wisely.** Select a topic that is somewhat controversial so listeners will want to hear your views. You can create interest in

a topic, but it is easier to appeal to listeners if they are already interested in what you have to say. In addition, try to choose a topic that you know something about. Even though you will probably have to do some research, the process will be much easier if you are already familiar with the basic issues.

2. **Know your audience.** Consider your audience and its needs before you begin to plan your presentation. For example, how much do listeners already know about your topic? Are they well informed, or do they know little about it? If listeners are unfamiliar with your topic, you will have to supply background information and definitions of key terms. If they already know a lot, you can dispense with this material and discuss your subject in more depth. Also, assess your audience members' likely response to your presentation. Will they be receptive? Hostile? Neutral? The answers to these questions will help you decide which arguments will most likely be effective (and which will not).

3. **Know your time limit.** Most oral presentations have a time limit. If you run over your allotted time, you risk boring or annoying your listeners. If you finish too soon, it will seem as if you don't know much about your subject. As you prepare your argument, include all the information that you can cover within your time limit. Keep in mind that you will not be able to go into as much detail in a short speech as you will in a long speech, so plan accordingly.

Visual aids can help listeners follow an oral presentation.

kasto80/iStock/Getty Images

4. **Identify your thesis statement.** Like a written argument, an oral argument should have a debatable thesis statement. Keep this statement simple, and make sure that it clearly conveys your position. Remember that in an oral argument, your listeners have to understand your thesis the first time they hear it. (See Chapter 7 for more on developing a thesis statement.)

5. **Gather support for your thesis.** Assume that your listeners are **skeptical**, that is, that they are not easily convinced. Even if you think that your audience is friendly, you still need to make a persuasive case. Don't make the mistake of thinking that listeners will automatically accept all your ideas just because they agree with your main point. For this reason, you need to support your thesis with compelling evidence if you expect listeners to conclude that your position is valid. Supporting evidence can be in the form of facts, observations, expert opinion, and statistics. Some of your support can come from your own experiences, but most will come from your research.

6. **Acknowledge your sources.** Remember that all of the information you get from your research needs to be acknowledged. As you deliver your presentation, let listeners know where the information you are using comes from—for example, "According to a 2020 editorial in the *New York Times* . . ." or "As Kenneth Davis says in his book *America's Hidden History.* . . ." This strategy enhances your credibility by showing that you are well informed about your topic. (Including source information also helps you protect yourself from unintentional **plagiarism**. See Chapter 11.)

7. **Prepare your speaking notes.** Effective speakers do not read their speeches. Instead, they prepare **speaking notes**—often on index cards—that list the points they want to make. (Microsoft's PowerPoint, as well as some other presentation software packages, has a section on each slide for speaking notes. Although the notes are displayed on the computer screen, they are not visible to the audience.) These notes guide you as you speak, so you should make sure that there are not too many of them and that they contain just key information. (If you use note cards, it is a good idea to number them so that you can be sure that they are in the correct order.)

8. **Prepare visual aids.** Visual aids help you to communicate your thesis and your supporting points more effectively. Visuals increase interest in your presentation, and they also strengthen your argument by reinforcing your points and making them easier for listeners to follow and to understand. In addition, visuals can help establish your credibility and thus improve the persuasiveness of your argument.

You can use the following types of visual aids in your presentations:

- Diagrams
- Photographs
- Slides
- Smartboards, flip charts
- Overhead transparencies
- Document cameras
- Handouts, objects

In order moving clockwise from top left: deomis/Shutterstock.com; Petr Vaclavek/ Shutterstock.com; Tarapong Siri/ Shutterstock.com; Brian A Jackson/ Shutterstock.com

In addition to these kinds of visual aids, you can also use **presentation software**, such as Microsoft's PowerPoint or the web-based application Prezi (Prezi.com). With presentation software, you can easily create visually appealing and persuasive slides. You can insert scanned photographs or drawings into slides, or you can cut and paste charts, graphs, and tables into them. You can even include YouTube videos and MP3 files. Keep in mind, however, that the images, videos, or sound files that you use must support your thesis; if they are irrelevant, they will distract or confuse your listeners. (See pp. 216–218 for examples of PowerPoint slides.)

9. **Practice your presentation.** As a general rule, you should spend as much time rehearsing your speech as you do preparing it. In other words, practice, practice, practice. Be sure you know the order in which you will present your points and when you will move from one visual to another. Rehearse your speech aloud with your speaking notes and your visuals until you are confident that you can get through your presentation effectively. Try to anticipate any problems that may arise with your visuals, and solve them at this stage of the process. If possible, practice your speech in the room in which you will actually deliver it. Bring along a friend, and ask for feedback. Finally, cut or add material as needed until you are certain that you can stay within your time limit.

CHECKLIST

Designing and Displaying Visuals

☐ Use images that are large enough for your audience to see and that will reproduce clearly.

- ☐ Make lettering large enough for your audience to see. Use 40- to 50-point type for titles, 25- to 30-point type for major points, and 20- to 25-point type for less important points.
- ☐ Use bulleted lists, not full sentences or paragraphs.
- ☐ Put no more than three or four points on a single visual
- ☐ Make sure there is a clear contrast between your lettering and the background.
- ☐ Don't show your listeners the visual before you begin to speak about it. Display the visual only when you discuss it.
- ☐ Face your listeners when you discuss a visual. Even if you point to the screen, always look at your listeners. Never turn your back on your audience.
- ☐ Introduce and discuss each visual. Don't simply show or read the visual to your audience. Always tell listeners more than they can read or see for themselves.
- ☐ Don't use elaborate visuals or special effects that will distract your audience.

❍ EXERCISE 6.5 PLANNING AN ORAL ARGUMENT

Look through the table of contents of this book, and select three At Issue topics that interest you. Imagine that you are planning to deliver an oral argument to a group of college students on each of these topics. For each topic, list three visual aids you could use to enhance your presentation.

Delivering Oral Arguments

Delivery is the most important part of a speech. The way you speak, your interaction with the audience, your posture, and your eye contact all affect your overall presentation. In short, a confident, controlled speaker will have a positive impact on an audience, while a speaker who fumbles with note cards, speaks in a shaky voice, or seems disorganized will lose credibility. To make sure that your listeners see you as a credible, reliable source of information, follow these guidelines:

1. **Accept nervousness.** For most people, nervousness is part of the speech process. The trick is to convert this nervousness into energy that you channel into your speech. The first step in dealing with nervousness is to make sure that you have rehearsed enough. If you have prepared adequately, you will probably be able to handle any problem you may encounter. If you make a mistake, you can correct it. If you forget something, you can fit it in later.

DEALING WITH NERVOUSNESS

If nervousness is a problem, the following strategies can help you to relax:

- **Breathe deeply.** Take a few deep breaths before you begin speaking. Research has shown that increased oxygen has a calming effect on the brain.

- **Use visualization.** Imagine yourself delivering a successful speech, and fix this image in your mind. It can help dispel anxiety.

- **Empty your mind.** Consciously try to eliminate all negative thoughts. Think of your mind as a room full of furniture. Imagine yourself removing each piece of furniture until the room is empty.

- **Drink water.** Before you begin to speak, take a few sips of water. Doing so will eliminate the dry mouth that is a result of nervousness. Don't, however, drink water during your speech.

- **Keep things in perspective.** Remember, your speech is a minor event in your life. Nothing that you do or say will affect you significantly.

2. **Look at your audience.** When you speak, look directly at the members of your audience. At the beginning of the speech, make eye contact with a few audience members who seem to be responding positively. As your speech progresses, look directly at as many audience members as you can. Try to sweep the entire room. Don't focus excessively on a single person or on a single section of your audience.

3. **Speak naturally.** Your presentation should sound like a conversation, not a performance. This is not to suggest that your presentation should include slang, ungrammatical constructions, or colloquialisms; it should conform to the rules of standard English. The trick is to maintain the appearance of a conversation while following the conventions of public speaking. Achieving this balance takes practice, but it is a goal worth pursuing.

4. **Speak slowly.** When you give a presentation, you should speak more slowly than you do in normal conversation. This strategy gives listeners time to process what they hear—and gives you time to think about what you are saying.

5. **Speak clearly and correctly.** As you deliver your presentation, speak clearly. Do not drop tense endings, and be careful to pronounce words correctly. Look up the pronunciation of unfamiliar words in a dictionary, or ask your instructor for help. If you go through an entire speech

pronouncing a key term or a name incorrectly, your listeners will question your competence.

6. **Move purposefully.** As you deliver your speech, don't pace, move your hands erratically, or play with your note cards. Try to stand in one spot, with both feet flat on the floor. Move only when necessary—for example, to point to a visual or to display an object. If you intend to distribute printed material to your listeners, do so only when you are going to discuss it. (Try to arrange in advance for someone else to give out your handouts.) If you are not going to refer to the material in your presentation, wait until you have finished your speech before you distribute it. Depending on the level of formality of your presentation and the size of your audience, you may want to stand directly in front of your audience or behind a podium.

7. **Be prepared for the unexpected.** Don't get flustered if things don't go exactly as you planned. If you forget material, work it in later. If you make a mistake, correct it without apologizing. Most of the time, listeners will not realize that something has gone wrong unless you call attention to it. If someone in the audience looks bored, don't worry. You might consider changing your pace or your volume, but keep in mind that the person's reaction might have nothing to do with your presentation. He or she might be tired, preoccupied, or just a poor listener.

8. **Leave time for questions.** End your presentation by asking if your listeners have any questions. As you answer questions, keep in mind the following advice:

   - *Be prepared.* Make sure you have anticipated the obvious counterarguments to your position, and be prepared to address them. In addition, prepare a list of websites or other resources that you can refer your audience to for more information.

   - *Repeat a question before you answer it.* This technique enables everyone in the audience to hear the question, and it also gives you time to think of an answer.

   - *Keep control of interchanges.* If a questioner repeatedly challenges your answer or monopolizes the conversation, say that you will be glad to discuss the matter with him or her after your presentation is finished.

   - *Be honest.* Answer questions honestly and forthrightly. If you don't know the answer to a question, say so. Tell the questioner you will locate the information that he or she wants and send it by email. Above all, do not volunteer information that you are not sure is correct.

   - *Use the last question to summarize.* When you get to the last question, end your answer by restating the main point of your argument.

Remember to project
confidence and
control as you speak.

Wavebreak Media/AGE Fotostock

Composing an Oral Argument

The written text of an oral argument is organized just as any other argument is: it has an introduction that gives the background of the issue and states the thesis, it has a body that presents evidence that supports the thesis, it identifies and refutes arguments against the thesis, and it ends with a concluding statement.

In general, an oral argument can be structured in the following way:

INTRODUCTION	Presents the background of the issue
	States the thesis
BODY	Presents evidence: Point 1 in support of the thesis
	Presents evidence: Point 2 in support of the thesis
	Presents evidence: Point 3 in support of the thesis
	Refutes opposing arguments
CONCLUSION	Brings the argument to a close
	Concluding statement restates thesis
	Speaker asks for questions

⊖ EXERCISE 6.6 ANALYZING AN ORAL ARGUMENT

The following oral argument was presented by a student in a speech course in response to the assignment, "Argue for or against the advantages of a 'gap year' between high school and college." (Her PowerPoint slides appear at the end of the speech.) After you read this argument, answer the questions on page 219, consulting the preceding outline if necessary.

AN ARGUMENT IN SUPPORT OF THE "GAP YEAR"

CHANTEE STEELE

College: even the word sounded wonderful when I was in high   1
school. Everyone told me it would be the best time of my life. They
told me that I would take courses in exciting new subjects and that
I'd make lifelong friends. [Show slide 1.] What they didn't tell me was
that I would be anxious, confused, and uncertain about my major and
about my future. Although this is only my second year in college, I've
already changed my major once, and to be honest, I'm still not sure I've
made the right decision. But during the process of changing majors,
my adviser gave me some reading material that included information
about a "gap year." A gap year is a year off between high school and
college when students focus on work or community service and learn
about themselves—something that would have benefited me. Although
gaining popularity in the United States, the gap year still suggests
images of spoiled rich kids who want to play for a year before going to
college. According to educator Christina Wood, however, in the United
Kingdom a gap year is common; it is seen as a time for personal growth
that helps students mature (Wood 36). [Show slide 2.] In fact, 230,000
British students take a gap year before going to college. As the rest of
my speech will show, a well-planned gap year gives students time to   **Thesis statement**
mature, to explore potential careers, and to volunteer or travel.

[Show slide 3.] Apparently I'm not alone in my uncertainty about   2   **Evidence: Point 1 in**
my major or about my future. The Educational Advisory Board estimates   **support of thesis**
that between 75 percent and 85 percent of college students will switch
majors at least once (Venit). As they go from high school to college,
most students have little time to think about what to do with their lives.
A gap year before college would give them time to learn more about
themselves. According to Abigail Falik and Linda Frey, "The gap year
has become increasingly popular with admissions leaders, who have
witnessed firsthand its positive impact on students and campus culture"
(Falik and Frey). A year off provides many students with the perspective
they need to mature and to feel more confident about their decisions.
It's also a choice that very few students regret, as those who take time

off overwhelmingly report that the experience increased their maturity and confidence (Hirsch).

Evidence: Point 2 in support of thesis

The gap year gives students many options to explore before going 3 to college. [Show slide 4] This slide shows just some of the resources students can use as they prepare for their gap year. As you can see, they can explore opportunities for employment, education, and volunteer work. There are even resources for students who are undecided. The key is to make the year both "purposeful and practical" (Falik and Frey). Ideally, it should be challenging and allow students to build new skills; it should also include elements of service to others, as well as a balance between freedom and guidance from a mentor (Falik and Frey). That may include studying abroad in an exchange program or even working a full-time job to save money for tuition (Jones).

Evidence: Point 3 in support of thesis

Taking a gap year can also help students to get into better colleges. 4 According to an article by the dean of admissions at Harvard, "Occasionally students are admitted to Harvard or other colleges in part because they accomplished something unusual during a year off" (Fitzsimmons, McGrath, and Ducey). Depending on the scope of their service or work, a gap year could enable students to earn scholarships that they were not eligible for before. In fact, some colleges actually recommend that students take time off after high school. Harvard is one of several U.S. colleges that "encourages admitted students to defer enrollment for one year to travel, pursue a special project or activity, work, or spend time in another meaningful way" (Fitzsimmons, McGrath, and Ducey). Furthermore, evidence shows that a gap year can help students to be more successful after they begin in college. One Middlebury College admissions officer has calculated that "a single gap semester was the strongest predictor of academic success at his school" (Bull 7). Given this support for the gap year and given the resources that are now available to help students plan it, the negative attitudes about it in the United States are beginning to change.

Refutation of opposing arguments

In spite of these benefits, parental concerns about "slackerdom" and 5 money are common. Supporters of the gap year acknowledge that students have to be motivated to make the most of their experiences. Clearly, the gap year is not for everyone. For example, students who are not self-motivated may not benefit from a gap year. In addition, parents worry about how much money the gap year will cost them. This is a real concern when you add the year off to the expense of four years of college (Wood 37). However, if finances are a serious concern, students can spend their gap year working in their own communities or taking advantage of a paid experience like AmeriCorps—which, as the AmeriCorps website shows, covers students' room and board *and* offers an educational stipend after students complete the program. [Show slide 5.] Additionally, parents and students should consider the time and money that is wasted when a student who is not ready for college starts school and then drops out.

After considering the benefits of a gap year, I have concluded that more students should postpone college for a year. Many students (like me) are uncertain about their goals. We welcome new opportunities and are eager to learn from new experiences and may find a year of service both emotionally and intellectually rewarding. Given another year to mature, many of us would return to school with a greater sense of purpose, focus, and clarity. In some cases, the gap year could actually help us get into better schools and possibly get more financial aid. If we intend to take the college experience seriously, spending a gap year learning about our interests and abilities would help us to become better, more confident, and ultimately more focused students. [Show slide 6.]

Are there any questions?

6

Concluding statement

Works Cited

Bull, Holly. "Navigating a Gap Year." *TeenLife*, Feb. 2011, pp. 6–9.

Falik, Abigail, and Linda Frey. *The Chronicle of Higher Education*, 3 June 2018, www.chronicle.com/article/The-Best-Freshman-Year-Is-a/243563.

Fitzsimmons, William, et al. "Time Out or Burn Out for the Next Generation." *Harvard College Office of Admissions*, 2011, college .harvard.edu/admissions/preparing-college/should-i-take-time.

Hirsch, Leni M. G. "Ready, Set, Don't Go." *The Harvard Crimson*, 15 Apr. 2016, www.thecrimson.com/article/2016/4/15/take-a-gap-year/.

Venit, Ed. "How Late Is Too Late? Myths and Facts about the Consequences of Switching College Majors." *Student Success Collaborative, Education Advisory Board*, 29 Aug. 2018, www.eab.com/-/media /EAB/Technology/Student-Success-Collaborative/Success-Pages /EAB_Major%20Switching%20Myths%20and%20Facts.pd.

Wood, Christina. "Should You Take a 'Gap Year'?" *Careers and Colleges,* Fall 2007, pp. 36–37.

Slide 1

AnaBGD/iStock/Getty Images

Slide 2

230,000 students between 18 and 25 take a Gap
Year in the U.K.

—Tom Griffiths, founder and director
of GapYear.com

(qtd. in Christina Wood, "Should You Take a 'Gap Year'?,"
Careers and Colleges, Fall 2007)

Slide 3

> **50%** of students change their major at least once.
> —National Research Center for College
> and University Admissions

Slide 4

A Few Links for the Potential "Gapster"

(links from Holly Bull, "The Possibilities of the Gap Year," *Chronicle of Higher Education* 52.44 [2006])

Employment

Cool Works: CoolWorks.com (domestic jobs)

Working Abroad: WorkingAbroad.org (jobs overseas)

Education

Global Routes: GlobalRoutes.org (semester-long courses)

Sea-mester: Seamester.com (sea voyage programs)

Volunteer Work

AmeriCorps: AmeriCorps.gov

City Year: CityYear.org

Thoughtful Texts for Fence Sitters

Karl Haigler and Rae Nelson, *The Gap-Year
  Advantage* (Macmillan, 2005)

Colin Hall, *Taking Time Off* (Princeton Review, 2003)

Charlotte Hindle and Joe Bindloss, *The Gap Year
  Book* (Lonely Planet, 2005)

Slide 5

Corporation for National and Community Service.

Slide 6

In order moving clockwise from the top left: © Roger Cracknell 01/classic/Alamy Stock Photo; © Steve Stock/Alamy Stock Photo; David Cordner/Getty Images; Sportstock/E+/Getty Images

Identifying the Elements of an Oral Argument

1. Where does this oral argument include verbal signals to help guide readers?

2. Does this oral argument use simple, direct language? What sections of the speech, if any, could be made simpler?

3. Where does this oral argument repeat key information for emphasis? Is there any other information that you think should have been repeated?

4. What opposing arguments does the speaker identify? Does she refute them convincingly?

5. How effective are the visuals that accompany the text of this oral argument? Are there enough visuals? Are they placed correctly? What other information do you think could have been displayed in a visual?

6. What questions would you ask this speaker at the end of her speech?

Why Are So Few Women in STEM Fields?

Dorothy Vaughan: The Picture Art Collection/Alamy. *Hidden Figures:* LEVIATHAN FILMS/CHERNIN ENT/FOX 2000 PICTURES/ Album/Alamy Stock Photo.

Go back to page 191, and reread the At Issue box, which gives background about whether online education is better than classroom instruction. As the following sources illustrate, this question has a number of possible answers.

After you review the sources listed below, you will be asked to answer some questions and to complete some simple activities. This work will help you to understand both the content and the structure of the sources. When you are finished, you will be ready to develop an argument—using one of the three alternative approaches to argument discussed in this chapter—that takes a position on whether online education is better than classroom learning.

SOURCES

 Olivia Nicholas, "What Are You Going to Do with That Major?," page 221

 Olga Khazan, "The More Gender Equality, the Fewer Women in STEM," page 224

 Stuart Reges, "Why Women Don't Code," page 227

 Rosalind C. Barnett and Caryl Rivers, "We've Studied Gender and STEM for 25 Years. The Science Doesn't Support the Google Memo," page 237

 Barbara Oakley, "Why Do Women Shun STEM? It's Complicated," page 242

 Visual Argument: STEM PSA, page 245

The following essay appeared in the *Whitman Wire*, the student newspaper of Whitman College, on February 8, 2018.

WHAT ARE YOU GOING TO DO WITH THAT MAJOR?

OLIVIA NICHOLAS

The problem is not that we have too few women in STEM; it is that we have too 1
few men in the humanities. Increasing women's access to STEM is an important and worthy cause, but in our efforts to improve access, we have devalued the humanities. Somehow, for once in our lives, we have forgotten to ask: what about the men?

We've known for a while that there is a gender divide in academic disci- 2
plines. The national response was to strive to increase the number of women in STEM. In 2011 First Lady Michelle Obama made a speech on the subject: "We need all hands on deck, and that means clearing hurdles for women and girls as they navigate careers in science, technology, engineering, and math." This call to action is warranted, since many women have certainly been dissuaded from studying STEM, but why is no one talking about increasing the number of men studying the humanities? Because, whether we acknowledge it or not, we have concluded that STEM is more important than the humanities.

At liberal arts colleges, majors are often segmented along gender lines. 3
Women make up a disproportionate share of the humanities majors at liberal arts colleges, while men make up the majority in the hard sciences and mathematics. According to the U.S. Department of Education's most recent statistics, in 2008, engineering ranked third on the list of most popular majors for men in the United States and 83.2 percent of engineering students were male. Men also make up 82.4 percent of computer and information science majors. Meanwhile, men only made up about 33.8 percent of all liberal arts and sciences, humanities and general studies majors.

Whitman follows this trend. Considering currently declared majors by per- 4
centage and eliminating majors with fewer than five people, those with the highest number of men at Whitman are computer science (90 percent male), physics (73 percent), economics (72 percent) and chemistry (71 percent). Meanwhile, the majors with the lowest number of men include race and ethnic studies (0 percent), environmental science-sociology (7 percent), French (11 percent) and English (21 percent). Nine out of the top ten woman-dominated majors at Whitman are in the humanities (with the exception being sociology, which is a social science). Meanwhile, only two of the top ten male-dominated majors at Whitman are in the humanities: philosophy and German.

Paula England and Li Su in an essay from the 2010 book *Gender &* 5
Society, find that women have contributed to the decrease in major segregation

through their decisions to enter male-dominated fields of study, while very few men have chosen to enter woman-dominated fields. So, where are the men?

> "The arts and humanities are devalued precisely because women study them."

Evelyn Fox Keller offers one explanation in her 1985 book *Reflections on Gender and Science*, where she states that people often associate masculinity with objectivity and femininity with subjectivity. Those fields that are objective and therefore seen as masculine are viewed as more legitimate and worthy, while fields that are subjective and therefore seen as feminine are devalued. The arts and humanities, in other words, are devalued precisely because women study them. One might argue that perhaps men are simply more interested in more objective fields and the fact that society places greater importance on these fields is a mere coincidence. However, England and Li's findings suggest otherwise. They found that when women do enter previously male-dominated fields, men begin to leave those fields. Men do not want to study fields that women study, not because they are not rigorous or interesting, but because they believe that what interests women is decidedly unimportant.

Currently, women are the majority in American higher education. The 7 U.S. Department of Education states that women make up 56 percent of college students enrolled this fall 2017. As women increase in numbers in higher education, their decisions about disciplinary focus have a greater and greater impact on the colleges and universities they attend. Women's steady decline in the humanities in favor of social sciences and STEM presents the humanities with the threat of extinction. Women's turn away from the humanities could very likely be their kiss of death. So, again, I ask: what about the men?

⊘ AT ISSUE: WHY ARE SO FEW WOMEN IN STEM FIELDS?

1. Nicholas begins her essay by saying, "The problem is not that we have too few women in STEM; it is that we have too few men in the humanities" (para. 1). Is this statement an example of the **either/or fallacy**? Explain.

2. According to Nicholas, men are not going into the humanities because they "have concluded that STEM is more important than the humanities" (2). What other explanations might there be for men not studying the humanities?

3. In this essay, where does the claim appear? How is the claim qualified? How does the qualifier set up the rest of the essay?

4. Is Nicholas's argument aimed primarily at an audience of women in STEM fields or a general audience? How do you know?

5. Throughout her essay, Nicholas supports her argument with statistics. How effective is this support?

6. Consider the following facts:

   ■ Computer science, biophysics, and physics tend to be male dominated.

   ■ Neurobiology, environmental biology, and biology of global health tend to be female dominated.

   ■ Social work, English, and psychology tend to be female dominated.

   ■ History, economics, and finance tend to be male dominated.

   How would Nicholas explain these disparities? How do you?

7. Where does Nicholas address opposing arguments? How effectively does she refute them?

This piece first appeared online at TheAtlantic.com on February 18, 2018.

THE MORE GENDER EQUALITY, THE FEWER WOMEN IN STEM

OLGA KHAZAN

Though their numbers are growing, only 27 percent of all students taking the 1 AP Computer Science exam in the United States are female. The gender gap only grows worse from there: Just 18 percent of American computer-science college degrees go to women. This is in the United States, where many college men proudly describe themselves as "male feminists" and girls are taught they can be anything they want to be.

Meanwhile, in Algeria, 41 percent of college graduates in the fields of 2 science, technology, engineering, and math—or "STEM," as it's known—are female. There, employment discrimination against women is rife and women are often pressured to make amends with their abusive husbands.

According to a report I covered a few years ago, Jordan, Qatar, and the 3 United Arab Emirates were the only three countries in which boys are significantly *less* likely to feel comfortable working on math problems than girls are. In all of the other nations surveyed, girls were more likely to say they feel "helpless while performing a math problem."

So what explains the tendency for nations that have traditionally *less* 4 gender equality to have *more* women in science and technology than their gender-progressive counterparts do?

According to a new paper published in *Psychological Science* by the 5 psychologists Gijsbert Stoet, at Leeds Beckett University, and David Geary, at the University of Missouri, it could have to do with the fact that women in countries with higher gender inequality are simply seeking the clearest possible path to financial freedom. And often, that path leads through STEM professions.

The issue doesn't appear to be girls' aptitude for STEM professions. In 6 looking at test scores across 67 countries and regions, Stoet and Geary found that girls performed about as well or better than boys did on science in most countries, and in almost all countries, girls would have been capable of college-level science and math classes if they had enrolled in them.

But when it comes to their *relative* strengths, in almost all the countries— 7 all except Romania and Lebanon—boys' best subject was science, and girls' was reading. (That is, even if an average girl was as good as an average boy at science, she was still likely to be even better at reading.) Across all countries, 24 percent of girls had science as their best subject, 25 percent of girls' strength was math, and 51 percent excelled in reading. For boys, the percentages were 38 for science, 42 for math, and 20 for reading. And the more gender-equal the country, as measured by the World Economic Forum's Global Gender Gap Index, the larger this gap between boys and girls in having science as their best subject. (The most gender-equal countries are the typical snowy utopias you hear about, like Sweden, Finland, and Iceland. Turkey and the United Arab Emirates rank among the least equal, according to the Global Gender Gap Index.)

The gap in reading "is related at least in part to girls' advantages in basic 8 language abilities and a generally greater interest in reading; they read more and thus practice more," Geary told me.

What's more, the countries that minted the most female college graduates 9 in fields like science, engineering, or math were also some of the least gender-equal countries. They posit that this is because the countries that empower women also empower them, indirectly, to pick whatever career they'd enjoy most and be best at.

"Countries with the highest gender equality tend to be welfare states," they 10 write, "with a high level of social security." Meanwhile, less gender-equal countries tend to also have less social support for people who, for example, find themselves unemployed. Thus, the authors suggest, girls in those countries might be more inclined to choose STEM professions, since they offer a more certain financial future than, say, painting or writing.

When the study authors looked at the "overall life satisfaction" rating of 11 each country—a measure of economic opportunity and hardship—they found that gender-equal countries had more life satisfaction. The life-satisfaction ranking explained 35 percent of the variation between gender equality and women's participation in STEM. That correlation echoes past research showing that the genders are actually more segregated by field of study in more economically developed places.

The upshot of this research is neither especially feminist nor especially sad: It's not that gender equality discourages girls from pursuing science. It's that it allows them not to if they're not interested. The findings will likely seem controversial, since the idea that men and women have different inherent

> "There's something in even the most liberal societies that's nudging women away from math and science." 12

abilities is often used as a reason, by some, to argue we should forget trying to recruit more women into the STEM fields. But, as the University of Wisconsin gender-studies professor Janet Shibley Hyde, who wasn't involved with the study, put it to me, that's not quite what's happening here.

"Some would say that the gender STEM gap occurs not because girls can't 13 do science, but because they have other alternatives, based on their strengths in verbal skills," she said. "In wealthy nations, they believe that they have the freedom to pursue those alternatives and not worry so much that they pay less."

Instead, this line of research, if it's replicated, might hold useful takeaways 14 for people who do want to see more Western women entering STEM fields. In this study, the percentage of girls who did excel in science or math was still larger than the number of women who were graduating with STEM degrees.

That means there's something in even the most liberal societies that's nudging women away from math and science, even when those are their best subjects. The women-in-STEM advocates could, for starters, focus their efforts on those would-be STEM stars.

Then again, it could just be that, feeling financially secure and on equal 15 footing with men, some women will always choose to follow their passions, rather than whatever labor economists recommend. And those passions don't always lie within science.

⊙ AT ISSUE: WHY ARE SO FEW WOMEN IN STEM FIELDS?

1. A *paradox* is an absurd or self-contradictory statement that could possibly be true. In what sense is Khazan's thesis a paradox?

2. In paragraph 4, Khazan asks a question. What function does this question have in her essay?

3. Speaking of the research done by Gijsbert Stoet and David Geary, Khazan says, "The upshot of this research is neither especially feminist nor especially sad" (para. 12). What does she mean? Why, according to Khazan, are their findings controversial?

4. Should Khazan have provided more details about Stoet and Geary's study? For example, how many children did they interview? Were the samples randomly chosen? How did they measure "overall life satisfaction" (11)? Explain.

5. In her concluding paragraphs, Kazan uses the following phrases:

   ■ "Some would say. . . ." (13)

   ■ "Instead, this line of research, if it's replicated. . . ." (14)

   ■ "Then again, it could just be that. . . ." (15)

   What do these phrases indicate about Khazan's assessment of Stoet and Geary's study?

6. Suppose Khazan wanted to present her ideas in a speech. What parts of the essay would you suggest she expand? What parts would you advise her to condense or delete? What visuals would you suggest she use?

7. Use Toulmin logic to analyze Khazan's essay, identifying the argument's claim, its grounds, and its warrant. Does Khazan appeal only to *logos*, or does she appeal to *pathos* and *ethos*? Explain.

This essay was posted to the online magazine *Quillette* on June 19, 2018.

WHY WOMEN DON'T CODE

STUART REGES

Ever since Google fired James Damore for "advancing harmful gender stereo- 1
types in our workplace," those of us working in tech have been trying to figure
out what we can and cannot say on the subject of diversity. You might imagine
that a university would be more open to discussing his ideas, but my experience suggests otherwise.

For the last ten months I have been discussing this issue at the Allen 2
School of Computer Science & Engineering where I work. I have tried to
understand why Damore's opinions generated such anger and have struggled to decide what I want to do in response. As a result of my attempts to
discuss this, our mailing list known as "diversity-allies" is now a moder-
ated list to prevent "nuanced, and potentially hurtful, discussion." Instead,
I have been encouraged to participate in face-to-face meetings that have
often been tense, but which have helped me to understand where others are
coming from.

I embarked on this journey because I worry that tech companies and uni- 3
versities are increasingly embracing an imposed silence, in which one is not
permitted to question the prevailing wisdom on how to achieve diversity goals.
I intend to fight this imposed silence and I encourage others to do the same.
We can't allow the Damore incident to establish a precedent. Damore's Twitter
handle briefly claimed that he had been "fired for truth," but really he was fired
for honesty. Those of us who disagree with current diversity efforts need to
speak up and share our honest opinions, even if doing so puts us at risk.

Saying controversial things that might get me fired is nothing new for me. 4
I've been doing it most of my adult life and usually my comments have generated a big yawn. I experienced a notable exception in a 1991 case that received
national attention, when I was fired from Stanford University for "violating
campus drug policy" as a means of challenging the assumptions of the war
on drugs. My attitude in all of these cases has been that I need to speak up
and give my honest opinion on controversial issues. Most often nothing comes
of it, but if I can be punished for expressing such ideas, then it is even more
important to speak up and try to make the injustice plain.

So let me go once more unto the breach by stating publicly that I believe 5
that women are less likely than men to want to major in computer science and
less likely to pursue a career as a software engineer and that this difference
between men and women accounts for most of the gender gap we see in computer science degree programs and in Silicon Valley companies.

My Diversity Work

My friends advise me that only someone who has fought for diversity can dis- 6 cuss the state of the movement, so let me describe some details of my 32-year career teaching computer science. I worked for ten years at Stanford managing introductory computer science courses, receiving the Dinkelspiel Award for Outstanding Service to Undergraduate Education along the way. I spent eight years at the University of Arizona doing similar work where I won the College of Science Distinguished Teaching Award and the Honors College Outstanding Advisor Award. For the last fourteen years I have worked at the University of Washington where I manage introductory computer science courses, winning the Distinguished Teaching Award in 2014.

I have been a champion of using undergraduate TAs in introductory 7 programming classes. I set up undergraduate TA programs at Stanford and Arizona that continue to this day and we have a thriving program at UW. I was co-author of an IEEE article entitled, "Broadening Participation: The Why and the How." My work with introductory courses and undergraduate TAs factored into the selection in 2015 of UW as the inaugural winner of the Excellence in Promoting Women in Undergraduate Computing prize awarded by NCWIT (the National Center for Women & Information Technology).

In my years of teaching nothing has brought me more joy and sense of 8 accomplishment than helping young people discover a love of computer science. Many of them have been men but more often they have been women. I have helped hundreds of women to learn to love computer science and for most it has been life changing.

As a result, I am absolutely convinced that for many years there have 9 been—and even today still are—many women who have not yet discovered the bright future they can have in the field of computer science. Half of the women in our undergraduate major are "interest changers," which means they weren't intending to apply to the major when they started our first course. For men the figure is closer to 20 percent, so there is a big gender gap.

In short, I have always been and continue to be a strong advocate of many 10 aspects of the diversity agenda.

The Equality Agenda versus the Equity Agenda

Arguments over diversity have been going on for decades at universities with 11 bitter fights along the way over affirmative action, political correctness, and speech codes. These arguments have acquired renewed urgency as major tech companies have joined the fray in response to increased scrutiny from the media about the lack of diversity in their workforce.

No company has done more than Google to create and share resources 12 in this space. They developed a popular workshop on unconscious bias that has been copied by many other organizations, and they extended those ideas to create a second workshop called "Bias Busters" that many universities have also adopted.

Like most of us who work in tech, I heard mention of these things but didn't take the time to investigate them. But when Damore was fired, I started looking more closely at the content of these workshops and I found much to criticize. In talking to professional staff who work in this area and students and faculty who are deeply committed to this issue, I have found that there are two visions of diversity and inclusion. 13

I favor what I call the "equality agenda" in computer science. Advocates of the equality agenda want to see the most talented and passionate individuals joining us regardless of their life circumstances or unalterable characteristics. For us, diversity has its usual dictionary definition of having a variety of individuals, which implies racial, ethnic, and gender diversity but also political and religious diversity. Inclusion involves welcoming a broad range of individuals to consider pursuing computer science as a career. The equality agenda, then, is about encouragement and removal of artificial barriers. 14

Professionals and activists who work in this area tend to see it differently. For them, diversity involves a commitment to righting the wrongs of the past. Political and religious diversity are not on their list because they don't represent the immutable characteristics previously used to justify discrimination. They may concede that Damore's claim that Google has become an echo chamber might be an issue worth addressing, but they will deny that this is a diversity issue. By contrast, working with the LGBTQ community is important because of the historical oppression they have experienced even though there is no evidence that LGBTQ individuals are currently discriminated against in the field. 15

Their understanding of inclusion is also quite different. Inclusion is about culture, and in a twist worthy of Orwell, inclusion often demands the exclusion of ideas and opinions. Google's Bias Busters workshop trains people to intervene when they hear examples of bias. Microaggression training fosters inclusion by preparing people to recognize and eliminate small slights that could make some people uncomfortable. Google CEO Sundar Pichai used the word in this sense when he justified Damore's firing with the observation that, "It's important for the women at Google, and all the people at Google, that we want to make an inclusive environment." 16

The word "equity" has the most variability in how it is understood. For example, Steven Pinker uses the term "equity feminism" to refer to something similar to what I am calling the equality agenda. But among professionals and activists, "equity" has the specific meaning of working to dismantle existing power structures as a way to redress privilege. 17

I refer to this combination of ideas as the "equity agenda." While the equality agenda focuses on equality of opportunity, the equity agenda is concerned with outcomes. Its proponents don't demand equal outcomes but instead use unequal outcomes as evidence that there is more work to be done. So, unless or until we reach perfect gender parity, they will continue to argue for more diversity programs for women. 18

Why So Much Anger?

When I tried to discuss Damore at my school, I found it almost impossible. 19 As a thought experiment, I asked how we could make someone like Damore feel welcome in our community. The pushback was intense. My question was labeled an "inflammatory example" and my comments were described as "hurtful" to women. When I mentioned that perhaps we could invite Damore to speak at UW, a faculty member responded, "If he comes here, we'll hurt him." She was joking, but the sentiment was clear.

One faculty member gave a particularly cogent response. She said, "Is 20 it our job to make someone with those opinions feel welcome? I'm not sure whether academic freedom dictates that." She argued that because we know that women have traditionally been discriminated against, perhaps it is more important to support them because the environment will not be sufficiently inclusive if they have to deal with someone like Damore. She said it "is up to us" to decide, but that, "choosing to hold a viewpoint does not necessarily give you the right to feel comfortable."

As Damore mentions in his essay, this issue has acquired a moral dimen- 21 sion, which is why the response is often anger. Jonathan Haidt, author of *The Righteous Mind*, has described this as elevating certain ideas to a sacred status. In this case, suggesting that men and women are different either in interests or abilities is considered blasphemy. So let me commit some blasphemy.

Men and Women Are Different

As Sundar Pichai said in his memo to employees explaining why he fired 22 Damore, "To suggest a group of our colleagues have traits that make them less biologically suited to that work is offensive and not OK." This is a fairly egregious misrepresentation of what Damore actually wrote, but fortunately we don't need to turn to biology or Damore for evidence that men and women are different. The gender diversity movement itself has spent the better part of 30 years cataloguing differences between men and women. Indeed, the entire goal of achieving gender diversity makes no sense unless you believe that men and women work in fundamentally different ways.

One of the earliest ideas I encountered was that men believe in their suc- 23 cesses and discount their failures while women believe in their failures and discount their successes. If you attend almost any diversity event today you will hear that "stereotype threat" and "imposter syndrome" should be discussed with our students because women disproportionately suffer from these problems. Lack of confidence, therefore, is held to be a particular problem for women.

The diversity literature also discusses how men and women have different 24 priorities, as in this passage from the seminal book *Unlocking the Clubhouse* by Jane Margolis and Allan Fisher:

> A critical part of attracting more girls and women to computer science is providing multiple ways to "be in" computer science. Concern for people, family, "balance in life," novels, and a good night's sleep should not come

at the cost of success in computer science. But the full acceptance of this proposition cuts across the dominant culture of the field.

They claim that men have created a culture that matches their values and inter- 25 ests. How is that possible if men and women don't differ in fundamental ways?

Diversity advocates have also started claiming that diverse teams perform 26 better. In a CNBC interview discussing her book *Own It: The Power of Women at Work*, Wall Street veteran Sallie Krawcheck said, "It's the qualities that women bring to the workforce—not better than the men, but somewhat different than the men—where our holistic decision making, our risk awareness, our relationship orientation skills that we tend to bring are becoming actually more valuable going forward, not less valuable."

The Oppression Narrative

A dangerous narrative has been taking hold in recent years that the gender gap is 27 mostly the fault of men and the patriarchal organizations they have built to serve their interests. Emily Chang's new book *Brotopia* asserts that, "the environment in the tech industry has become toxic for women," and that, "women have been systematically excluded from the greatest wealth creation in the history of the world and denied a voice in the rapid remolding of our global culture."

Chang and I clearly know different people because the women I talk to 28 who are working in Silicon Valley are enjoying their experiences as software engineers. Certainly there are bad actors and companies where the culture is broken, but the vast majority of women work at companies that make significant efforts to provide a supportive work experience.

Another example of this false narrative comes from NPR's *Planet Money*, 29 which produced a segment entitled "When Women Stopped Coding." They identify 1984 as the year that "something changed" and they highlight a theory that around that time the personal computer revolution was affecting college campuses. Young men were arriving who had used personal computers young women lacked because families disproportionately bought computers for boys. NPR claims that, "As personal computers became more common, computer science professors increasingly assumed that their students had grown up playing with computers at home," and includes an anecdote from a woman who had a bad experience in her introductory programming class. I don't doubt that this woman had a bad experience, but the claim that computer science faculty were gearing their courses towards men with prior experience is simply not true.

I ran the introductory programming courses at Stanford in the 1980s and 30 I met regularly with faculty who taught introductory programming at other schools. We were on a mission to make CS1 a universal course taken by a broad range of students. We loved Rich Pattis's 1981 book, *Karel the Robot*, because it was, as it's subtitle claimed, "A Gentle Introduction to the Art of Computer Programming." Many schools were experimenting with new courses, new textbooks, and new programming environments, all of which were intended to make it easier for novices to learn how to program.

231

The NPR piece also noted that we have experienced a slow but steady 31 decrease in women majoring in computer science since 1984. Even as women were taking a greater share of slots in medicine, law, and the physical sciences, they represented a decreasing percentage of computer science degrees. This is consistent with the idea that women simply chose to pursue other interests, but NPR chose to highlight the suggestion that professors teaching introductory courses were creating courses unfriendly to women.

It's Complicated

The more I study the gender gap in computer science the more I become con- 32 vinced that there are no simple answers. When I hear a claim or encounter a graph, I find that it takes a great deal of effort to drill down into the details and I almost always end up concluding, "It's complicated." This article would become a book if I were to drill down on everything, but the NPR graph provides a nice example of what you find when you dig into the data.

To better understand the level of interest by gender, I used data from the 33 same source, the Digest of Education Statistics put out annually by the National Center for Education Statistics. I computed separate statistics for the percentage of men and women obtaining computing degrees, comparing men against other men and women against other women.

Graphing the data this way allows us to see a phenomenon that those of us 34 who lived through these years understand all too well. Computer science has gone through two major boom and bust cycles in the last 40 years. The idea that men drove women from the field is not supported by the data. There has been no period of time when men have been increasing while women have been decreasing. In 48 of the last 50 years the trend was the same for men and women with the percentage of women going up at the same time that the percentage of men went up and the percentage of women going down when the percentage of men went down. But while the trend has been the same, the magnitude of the response has differed significantly.

In both cycles, men disproportionately reacted to the boom part of the 35 cycle and women disproportionately reacted to the bust. And as the graph illustrates, men are once again responding faster and more forcefully to the new boom we are experiencing today. The cumulative effect of these differences has been devastating for the goal of increasing the participation of women in computer science.

We don't yet understand why men rush in during the boom years and why 36 women turn away during the bust years, but it seems likely that multiple factors are at work. Men disproportionately respond to economic incentives, so they are more likely to respond favorably to reports of high salaries for tech workers. Women tend, on average, to be more risk averse, and are more likely to respond strongly to negative stories about dwindling job prospects in tech. Perhaps women also react differently to changes in messaging as departments desperate to meet demand during the boom part of the cycle shift from an attitude of welcoming prospective students to one of pushing them away.

The Free Choice Explanation

I suggest a variation of Hanlon's Razor that one should never attribute to oppres- 37
sion that which is adequately explained by free choice. If men and women are
different, then we should expect them to make different choices. In 2010, the
National Academy of Sciences published a paper entitled "Understanding
Current Causes of Women's Under-Representation in Science." As in the NPR
piece, the authors describe the great success women have had in other fields:

> Since 1970, women have made dramatic gains in science. Today, half of all
> MD degrees and 52 percent of PhDs in life sciences are awarded to women,
> as are 57 percent of PhDs in social sciences, 71 percent of PhDs to psychol-
> ogists, and 77 percent of DVMs to veterinarians. Forty years ago, women's
> presence in most of these fields was several orders of magnitude less; e.g., in
> 1970 only 13 percent of PhDs in life sciences went to women. In the most
> math-intensive fields, however, women's growth has been less pronounced.

But they reject discrimination as an explanation: 38

> We conclude that past initiatives to combat discrimination against women
> in science appear to have been highly successful. Women's current under-
> representation in math-intensive fields is not caused by discrimination
> in these domains, but rather to sex differences in resources, abilities, and
> choices (whether free or constrained).

In 2013, *Psychological Science* published a paper that explored this ques- 39
tion further entitled "Not Lack of Ability but More Choice: Individual and Gender Differences in Choice of Careers in Science, Technology, Engineering, and
Mathematics." The authors included Jacquelynne Eccles who is well known for
a career spanning decades studying student motivation and gender differences.

They concluded that women may choose non-STEM careers because they 40
have academic strengths that many men lack. They found that individuals
with high math ability but only moderate verbal ability were the most likely
to choose a career in STEM (49 percent) and that this group included more
men than women (70 percent men). By contrast, individuals with both high
math ability and high verbal ability were less likely to pursue a career in STEM
(34 percent) and this group had more women than men (63 percent women).
They write that, "Our study provides evidence that it is not lack of ability that
causes females to pursue non-STEM careers, but rather the greater likelihood
that females with high math ability also have high verbal ability and thus can
consider a wider range of occupations."

In 2018, another paper explored the same question from a different per- 41
spective using international data from the PISA survey (the Programme for
International Student Assessment). Olga Khazan summarized the paper well
in an article for the *Atlantic*:

> The issue doesn't appear to be girls' aptitude for STEM professions. In
> looking at test scores across 67 countries and regions, Stoet and Geary

found that girls performed about as well or better than boys did on science in most countries, and in almost all countries, girls would have been capable of college-level science and math classes if they had enrolled in them.

But when it comes to their *relative* strengths, in almost all the countries—all except Romania and Lebanon—boys' best subject was science, and girls' was reading. (That is, even if an average girl was as good as an average boy at science, she was still likely to be even better at reading.) Across all countries, 24 percent of girls had science as their best subject, 25 percent of girls' strength was math, and 51 percent excelled in reading. For boys, the percentages were 38 for science, 42 for math, and 20 for reading.

The study found that gender differences increased in countries that have greater gender equality as measured by the World Economic Forum's annual *Global Gender Gap* Report. They noted that countries with the highest gender equality tend to be "welfare states . . . with a high level of social security for all its citizens," which they believe can (influence women's choices. They describe this as a paradox because it implies that the more progress we make towards achieving the equality agenda, the further we are likely to be from achieving the equity agenda. As Khazan says in the conclusion to her article, "it could just be that, feeling financially secure and on equal footing with men, some women will always choose to follow their passions, rather than whatever labor economists recommend. And those passions don't always lie within science." 42

I was curious to see how this relates to computing degrees, so I checked out the data for the top ten countries in terms of gender equality. Of the eight countries that include statistics for undergraduate degrees, the average percentage of women majoring in computing was 1.9 percent versus 8.2 percent for men. Taking into account the higher number of undergraduate degrees received by women, the Nordic countries which have the highest scores for gender equality (Iceland, Norway, and Finland) are producing computing graduates who are 18.6 percent, 17 percent, and 15.9 percent female, respectively. These percentages are very close to what we see in the United States. 43

Where Do We Go from Here?

I believe we have reached a significant crossroads in the campaign to increase the representation of women in tech. We have harvested the low-hanging fruit by eliminating overt discrimination and revamping policies and procedures that favored men. Now we more often focus on minutia such as replacing *Star Trek* posters with travel posters. And yet, the campaign has stalled. 44

At the University of Washington, we have managed over the last ten years to increase the percentage of women taking our first course from 26 percent to 41 percent and to increase the percentage taking the second course from 18 percent to 31 percent. In the early years, we were able to go from 16 percent women in our major to 30 percent, but we have made no additional progress since. I have heard from friends at Stanford that they have been stalled for several 45 years at 30 percent and a colleague at Princeton reports that they are stuck in the mid-30s for percentages of women. CMU and Harvey Mudd have reported percentages at or above 50 percent, but they have a highly selective student body and have put special emphasis on tweaking admissions criteria and creating special programs for women in computing.

The sad truth is that UW, Stanford, and Princeton are among the best 46 performing schools and part of that success is likely due to being a top-10 department. For most schools, the percentage of women is much lower. Over the last ten years the percentage of undergraduate computing degrees going to women nationwide has bounced around in a tight range, varying from 17.6 percent to 18.7 percent.

Computer science departments have never put more attention and resources into the diversity campaign than they have in the last few years, and we have 47

> "Women *can* code, but often they don't *want* to."

seen a small but steady increase in the percentage of women choosing a computing major, going from 0.9 percent in 2008 to 1.1 percent in 2017. But at the same time, and with no special encouragement from us, the percentage of men choosing a computing major has also increased, going from 5.3 percent in 2008 to 6.4 percent in 2017.

I worry that lack of progress will make us more likely to switch from pos- 48 itive messages about women succeeding in tech to negative stories about men behaving badly in tech, which I think will do more harm than good. Women will find themselves wondering if they should resent men and men will feel guilty for sins committed by other men. Women are not going to find this message appealing and men will find themselves feeling even more awkward around women than they would be otherwise.

Our community must face the difficult truth that we aren't likely to make 49 further progress in attracting women to computer science. Women *can* code, but often they don't *want* to. We will never reach gender parity. You can shame and fire all of the Damores you find, but that won't change the underlying reality.

It's time for everyone to be honest, and my honest view is that having 50 20 percent women in tech is probably the best we are likely to achieve. Accepting that idea doesn't mean that women should feel unwelcome. Recognizing that women will be in the minority makes me even more appreciative of the women who choose to join us.

Obviously many people will disagree with my assessment. I have already 51 been told that expressing such ideas is hurtful to women. But it is exactly because I care so much about diversity that I value honesty above politeness. To be effective, we have to commit ourselves to a search for the truth and that search can succeed only if everyone feels comfortable sharing their honest opinions.

In the last ten months I have taken the time to talk to those who dis- 52 agree with me. I welcome such conversations. I have strong opinions, but I also realize that I could be wrong. The big question is whether there is room in tech for a James Damore or for me when we question basic tenets of the equity agenda. I believe that the uproar over Damore's firing underscores how extreme his case was. This article will probably produce a big yawn like most of my other controversial stands over the years. If so, then I encourage all of the closet Damores out there to join the discussion and to let people know what you really think.

⊘ AT ISSUE: WHY ARE SO FEW WOMEN IN STEM FIELDS?

1. Reges begins his essay by asserting his need to address controversial ideas. He goes on to describe his "32-year career teaching computer science" (para. 6). Why do you think he includes this information before he begins to discuss the gender gap in computer science?

2. In paragraph 13, Reges says that there are "two visions of diversity and inclusion." What are they? Which one does he favor? Why?

3. In paragraph 21, Reges says that he is going to commit "blasphemy." To what idea is he referring? Why does he consider this idea blasphemy?

4. What is Reges's opinion of James Damore? What is his opinion of those who disagree with Damore? What does he think of Sundar Pichai's decision to fire him? How do you know?

5. Draw a **rhetorical triangle** (p. 19) that represents the relative importance of various appeals in this essay. Which appeal does the longest side of the triangle represent? What does the shortest side represent? Do you think this is a good balance?

6. What evidence does Reges present to support his thesis? How convincing is this evidence? Explain.

7. Suppose Reges wanted to present his ideas as a Rogerian argument. How would he have to change his essay?

This essay was posted to the technology news website *Recode* on August 11, 2017.

WE'VE STUDIED GENDER AND STEM FOR 25 YEARS. THE SCIENCE DOESN'T SUPPORT THE GOOGLE MEMO.

ROSALIND C. BARNETT AND CARYL RIVERS

A Google engineer who was fired for posting an online claim that women's biology makes them less able than men to work in technology jobs has charged that he is being smeared and is a victim of political correctness.

James Damore, 28, questioned the company's diversity policies and claimed that scientific data backed up his assertions. Google CEO Sundar Pichai wrote that Damore's 3,300-word manifesto crossed the line by "advancing harmful gender stereotypes" in the workplace. Pichai noted that "To suggest a group of our colleagues have traits that make them less biologically suited to that work is offensive and not OK."

Damore argued that many men in the company agreed with his sentiments. That's not surprising, since the idea that women just can't hack it in math and science has been around for a very long time. It has been argued that women's lack of a "math gene," their brain structures and their inherent psychological traits put most of them out of the game.

Some critics sided with Damore. For example, columnist Ross Douthat of the *New York Times* found his scientific arguments intriguing.

But are they? What are the real facts? We have been researching issues of gender and STEM (science, technology, engineering, and math) for more than 25 years. We can say flatly that there is no evidence that women's biology makes them incapable of performing at the highest levels in any STEM fields.

Many reputable scientific authorities have weighed in on this question, including a major paper in the journal *Science* debunking the idea that the brains of males and females are so different that they should be educated in single-sex classrooms. The paper was written by eight prominent neuroscientists, headed by professor Diane Halpern of Claremont McKenna College, past president of the American Psychological Association. They argue that "There is no well-designed research showing that single-sex education improves students' academic performance, but there is evidence that sex segregation increases gender stereotyping and legitimizes institutional sexism."

They add, "Neuroscientists have found few sex differences in children's brains beyond the larger volume of boys' brains and the earlier completion of girls' brain growth, neither of which is known to relate to learning."

Several major books have debunked the idea of important brain differences between the sexes. Lise Eliot, associate professor in the Department of Neuroscience at the Chicago Medical School, did an exhaustive review of the

237

scientific literature on human brains from birth to adolescence. She concluded, in her book *Pink Brain, Blue Brain*. that there is "surprisingly little solid evidence of sex differences in children's brains."

Rebecca Jordan-Young, a sociomedical scientist and professor at Barnard 9 College, also rejects the notion that, there are pink and blue brains, and that the differing organization of female and male brains is the key to behavior. In her book *Brain Storm: The Flaws in the Science of Sex Differences*, she says that this narrative misunderstands the complexities of biology and the dynamic nature of brain development.

And happily, the widely held belief that boys are naturally better than girls at 10 math and science is unraveling among serious scientists. Evidence is mounting that girls are every bit as competent as boys in these areas. Psychology professor Janet Hyde of the University of Wisconsin–Madison has strong U.S. data showing no meaningful differences in math performance among more than seven million boys and girls in grades 2 through 12.

Also, several large-scale international testing programs find girls closing 11 the gender gap in math, and in some cases outscoring the boys. Clearly, this huge improvement over a fairly short time period argues against biological explanations.

Much of the data that Damore provides in his memo is suspect, outdated, 12 or has other problems.

In his July memo, titled "Google's Ideological Echo Chamber: How bias 13 clouds our thinking about diversity and inclusion," Damore wrote that women on average have more "openness directed towards feelings and aesthetics rather than ideas." And he stated that women are more inclined to have an interest in "people rather than things, relative to men."

Damore cites the work of Simon Baron-Cohen, who argues in his widely 14 reviewed book *The Essential Difference* that boys are biologically programmed to focus on objects, predisposing them to math and understanding systems, while girls are programmed to focus on people and feelings. The British psychologist claims that the male brain is the "systematizing brain" while the female brain is the "empathizing" brain.

This idea was based on a study of day-old babies, which found that the 15 boys looked at mobiles longer and the girls looked at faces longer. Male brains, Baron-Cohen says, are ideally suited for leadership and power. They are hardwired for mastery of hunting and tracking, trading, achieving and maintaining power, gaining expertise, tolerating solitude, using aggression, and taking on leadership roles.

The female brain, on the other hand, is specialized for making friends, 16 mothering, gossip, and "reading" a partner. Girls and women are so focused on others, he says, that they have little interest in figuring out how the world works.

But Baron-Cohen's study had major problems. It was an "outlier" study. 17 No one else has replicated these findings, including Baron-Cohen himself. It is so flawed as to be almost meaningless. Why?

The experiment lacked crucial controls against experimenter bias and was 18 badly designed. Female and male infants were propped up in a parent's lap and shown, side by side, an active person or an inanimate object. Since newborns can't hold their heads up independently, their visual preferences could well have been determined by the way their parents held them.

"Media stories continue to promote the idea of very different brains on little evidence." 19

There is much literature that flat-out contradicts Baron-Cohen's study, providing evidence that male and female infants tend to respond equally to people and objects, notes Elizabeth Spelke, co-director of Harvard's Mind Brain Behavior Interfaculty Initiative. But media stories continue to promote the idea of very different brains on little evidence.

Damore also claims that women experience more stress and anxiety 20 than men, and that "This may contribute to the higher levels of anxiety women report on Googlegeist and to the lower number of women in high-stress jobs."

He implies that stress and anxiety are personality traits inherent in 21 females, but more likely they are due to the pressures and discrimination women face on the job that men do not. For example, a 2008 report sponsored by major companies, "The Athena Factor," found that women in high positions in male-dominated fields, such as tech, suffer harsher penalties than men when they slip up. Women don't get second chances. Men do.

One of the report's authors, Sylvia Ann Hewlett, founding president of 22 the Center for Work-Life Policy in New York, notes in the *Harvard Business Review* that in tech firms, "the way to get promoted is to do a diving catch. Some system is crashing in Bulgaria, so you get on the plane in the middle of the night and dash off and spend the weekend wrestling with routers and come back a hero."

But what if you don't make the catch? "Women have a hard time taking 23 on those assignments because you can dive and fail to catch. If a man fails, his buddies dust him off and say, 'It's not your fault; try again next time.' A woman fails and is never seen again."

Add to that conundrum the fact that just getting in the door is harder for a 24 woman than it is for a man.

Her résumé may look exactly like his, but because her name is Mary and not 25 John, she may not get a second look. A review of studies of U.S. decision makers who have the power to hire candidates found that clearly competent men were rated higher than equally competent women. This bias is especially rampant in the high-tech industry. One study, conducted by professors at Columbia, Northwestern, and the University of Chicago, found that two-thirds of managers selected male job candidates, even when the men did not perform as well as the women on math problems that were part of the application process.

Throw in the facts that, according to research, competent men are seen 26 as likeable, while competent women are seen as bitchy, that women get less credit for their accomplishments than men do, that men are often promoted on promise while women get elevated only on the basis of performance, and that sexual harassment is a constant problem for women in tech.

All of these are issues that males simply do not have to face. The "anxiety 27 gap" exists for a reason, and it is not about biology.

Many of Damore's controversial conclusions rest heavily on one recent 28 study and much older, now-discredited research, ignoring reams of data that tell a very different story. The argument that men, especially affluent men, are more focused on their "male" breadwinner role than on their more "female" family roles, does not reflect either research data or observational data.

For example:

■ Over the past two decades, men in the U.S. are spending more and more time on housework and childcare on both workdays and weekends. Indeed, their time spent on such tasks is close to that spent by their wives, according to the National Study of the Changing Workforce.

■ The psychological well-being of employed married fathers is as closely linked to their family as to their employee roles, according to a study directed by Dr. Barnett.

■ Today, companies are offering more and more paternity leave, because male employees are clamoring for it. Generous leave policies are seen as a recruitment tool, as companies are in an arms race with competitors to attract millennials and retain their best talent.

■ In 2016, Mark Zuckerberg, CEO of Facebook, caused banner headlines when his daughter was born and he took a two-month paternity leave. He set an example for his employees and those of other companies.

And they seem to have noticed. According to SmartAsset.com, "in just the past 29 year . . . at least 17 big employers have either introduced or expanded paid-leave options for new dads." They include Hilton, Netflix, Spotify, Microsoft, and Fidelity.

"The rate of expansion is unprecedented," said Ellen Bravo, executive 30 director of Family Values @ Work.

But many men who would opt for paternity leave hesitate, not because of 31 innate biological dispositions, but because of fear of retribution. Cultural stereotypes exert a powerful effect, punishing men for the caring, family-oriented behavior that they desire. Damore's article may make it even harder for such men to take the paternity leave they so clearly crave.

The recent history of Sweden's legislation on paternity leave highlights 32 dramatically the overwhelming role of cultural stereotypes on male parental behavior. It's not biology at work here, but laws mandating at least two months of the nation's well-paid, 13-month parental leave exclusively for fathers that have created profound social change.

"In perhaps the most striking example of social engineering, a new defini- 33 tion of masculinity is emerging," notes the *New York Times*. Birgitta Ohlsson,

European affairs minister, put it this way: "Machos with dinosaur values don't make the top-10 lists of attractive men in women's magazines anymore. Now men can have it all—a successful career and being a responsible daddy. It's a new kind of manly. It's more wholesome."

Damore, on the other hand, argues for downplaying empathy in American companies.   34

Creating more dinosaurs doesn't seem like a healthy way to go.   35

⊙ AT ISSUE: WHY ARE SO FEW WOMEN IN STEM FIELDS?

1. Why do Barnett and Rivers wait until paragraph 5 to state their thesis? What information do they provide before stating it? Why is this information necessary?

2. At what point in their essay do Barnett and Rivers appeal to *ethos*? What do they hope to establish with this appeal?

3. According to Barnett and Rivers, "the 'anxiety gap' exists for a reason" (para. 27). What do they mean?

4. In paragraph 5 Barnett and Rivers say, "there is no evidence that women's biology makes them incapable of performing at the highest levels in any STEM field." Do they include enough facts and examples to support this assertion? Could they be accused of making a **sweeping generalization**? Why or why not?

5. Much of this essay is devoted to refuting James Damore's Google memo. How do Barnett and Rivers characterize this memo? How effectively do they refute its assertions? (If you wish, go online and read Damore's memo.)

6. Barnett and Rivers end their essay by saying, "Creating more dinosaurs doesn't seem like a healthy way to go" (41). To what are they referring? How fair is this statement?

7. Is Barnett and Rivers's argument primarily inductive or deductive? Why do you think that they chose this structure?

This essay first appeared in the July 13, 2018, issue of the *Wall Street Journal.*

WHY DO WOMEN SHUN STEM? IT'S COMPLICATED

BARBARA OAKLEY

Why do relatively few women work in science, technology, engineering, and 1 mathematics? University of Washington lecturer Stuart Reges—in a provocative essay, "Why Women Don't Code"—suggests that women's verbal and analytical skills lead to career choices outside STEM. Mr. Reges's critics say he is making women feel inferior by implying they aren't interested in tech. I'm a female engineering professor with decades of experience as well as a background in the humanities and social sciences, so perhaps I can lend some perspective to the controversy.

I've observed that women tend to choose disciplines other than STEM, 2 often for the reasons Mr. Reges mentions. Yet his argument is incomplete. An important but often neglected factor is the attitudes of undergraduate professors. Not STEM professors, but professors in the humanities and social sciences.

Professors have profound influence over students' career choices. I'm 3 sometimes flabbergasted at the level of bias and antagonism toward STEM from professors outside scientific fields. I've heard it all: STEM is only for those who enjoy "rote" work. Engineering is not creative. There's only one right answer. You'll live your life in a cubicle. It's dehumanizing. You'll never talk to anyone. And, of course, it's sexist. All this from professors whose only substantive experience with STEM is a forced march through a single statistics course in college, if that.

My colleagues in the humanities unthinkingly malign STEM in front of 4 me. Their bias has become so deeply ingrained that they don't think twice. My students tell me it's worse when I'm not around. With joking asides during class or more-pointed conversations about careers, the STEM disciplines are caricatured as a gulag for creative types. Even a few untoward remarks like this to students can have profound effects. It's too bad, because science, technology, engineering, and math can be among the most creative and satisfying disciplines.

Many studies, including a critical review by Elizabeth Spelke in *American Psychologist*, have shown that on average men and women have the same abilities in math and science. But as Mr. Reges notes, women tend to do better than men verbally—a consequence of early developmental advantages.

How does this alter career choice? A student named Bob might get 6 a C in physics 101 but a D in English composition. His English professor probably won't try to recruit him into the field. Bob's choice to become an engineer makes sense because he's less likely to be good at the social sciences or humanities.

Women who are average in physics classes, on the other hand, are often 7 better at other subjects. When Sara has a C in physics 101, she's more likely to have a B or even an A in English composition. Her English professor is more likely to recruit her. And, crucially, the "STEM is only for uncreative nerds" characterization can play well here. It can provide a mental boost for Sara to hear a powerful figure like her professor denigrate the subject she's struggling with.

Even when a professor isn't working to recruit Sara to the social sciences or humanities, she might be recruiting herself. Grades mean something; if Sara's working hard to get a C in calculus, but she earns an A in English with less effort, she's going to experience a powerful pull toward the humanities. 8

"Jerks exist in every workplace."

Consider a student who gets an A in every subject. Let's call her Nadine. 9 She's the type of student who could excel in whatever she chooses. Her engineering professors might be telling her that an electrical engineering degree is a great career choice that will open doors and pay well. But her non-STEM professors may be telling her something completely different: "You won't use your fantastic writing skills. And besides, you'll just sit in a cubicle crunching numbers." Nadine can begin to feel she's untrue to her full set of talents if she picks engineering. So Nadine jumps the STEM ship.

What about the women who go into STEM and discover bias in the work- 10 place? Jerks exist in every workplace. Bullying is so prevalent in nursing, for example, that it's the subject of dozens of studies. "Bullying behaviors fall on a continuum ranging from eye-rolling and exclusion to humiliation, withholding information, scapegoating, intimidation, and backstabbing," a 2016 article in *American Nurse Today* notes. "The bully sets out to destroy the victim's confidence and credibility as a way to gain power and control."

If I drew a Venn diagram to see the intersection between a jerk and a 11 sexist, it would show almost total overlap—in male-dominated disciplines, that is. It can be easy for a woman who has landed in a toxic software-development environment to say, "There's horrible bias here!" And she'd be right. But there are toxic pockets in every discipline or field. STEM is no different.

I have experienced bias in my career, but I also would not be where I am 12 today without the strong support of many wonderful men. Women are vitally important to STEM. Professors outside these disciplines should stop mischaracterizing to poach the best students, who are often women. And it's time for everyone to step back, take a breath, and acknowledge that good and bad bosses and co-workers exist everywhere.

⊘ AT ISSUE: WHY ARE SO FEW WOMEN IN STEM FIELDS?

1. Explain the essay's title.

2. Regarding STEM, how does Oakley characterize students? How does she characterize instructors? Based on your experience, are these characterizations fair? Accurate? Explain.

3. In paragraph 2, Oakley concedes an opposing argument. Why? What weakness does she go on to identify?

4. In her essay, Oakley discusses three hypothetical students. What point (or points) does she make about each one? How effective is this rhetorical strategy? Would her argument have been stronger had she used the experiences of actual students to support her argument? What other kinds of evidence could she have used?

5. Addressing the fact that women in STEM workplaces experience bias, Oakley says, "Jerks exist in every workplace" (para. 10). Should she have done more to address this issue? Explain.

6. Oakley begins her essay by saying that she is a female engineer "with decades of experience" (1). She ends her essay by saying, "I have experienced bias in my career" (12). What does she hope to accomplish by including this personal information?

7. What preconceptions about women in STEM fields does Oakley assume her readers have? How do you know?

VISUAL ARGUMENT: STEM PSA

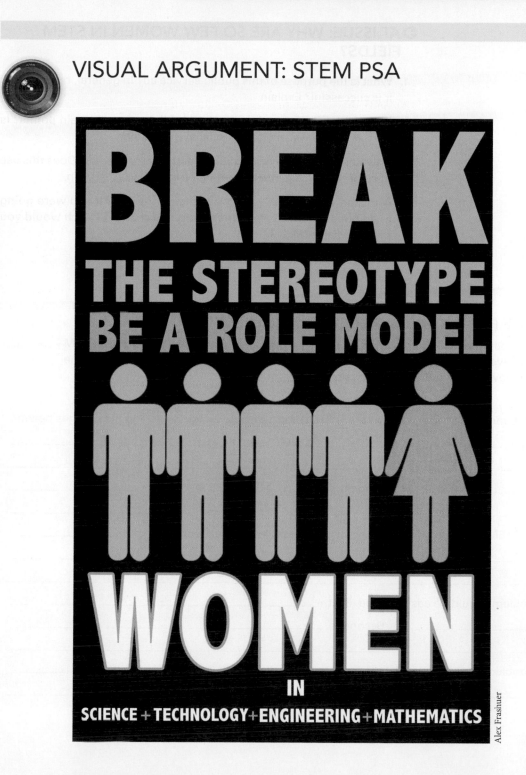

Alex Frashuer

⊙ **AT ISSUE: WHY ARE SO FEW WOMEN IN STEM FIELDS?**

1. What is the purpose of this public-service ad? In general, do you think it is successful? Explain.

2. How do the variations in type size highlight the ad's main points? Is the use of this visual element effective? Explain.

3. How does the ad use color to emphasize its main point? Does this use of color reinforce gender stereotypes in any way? Explain.

4. Is this ad easy to read, or does it seem crowded? If you were going to edit this ad, which elements would you change? Which would you keep the same? Why?

TEMPLATE FOR WRITING A ROGERIAN ARGUMENT

Write a one-paragraph **Rogerian** argument in which you argue that the drawbacks of STEM education have to be addressed before it can appeal to the majority of women. Follow the template below, filling in the blanks to create your argument.

With more and more women taking STEM courses, both the students and the colleges benefit.

For example, _____

_____

_____. In addition, _____

_____.

However, STEM education does have some drawbacks for women. For instance, _____

_____

_____.

These problems could be easily solved. First, _____

_____. Second, _____

_____.

If these problems are addressed, both students and colleges would benefit because _____

_____.

TEMPLATE FOR WRITING A TOULMIN ARGUMENT

Write a one-paragraph **Toulmin** argument in which you argue in favor of changes to STEM education. Follow the template below, filling in the blanks to create your argument.

Many colleges and universities have instituted programs to encourage women to consider STEM majors. These programs are the best way _____

_____.

If colleges are going to meet the rising demand for STEM graduates, they _____

_____

_____.

The science and math courses I took _____

_____

_____.

Recent studies show that _____

_____. In addition, _____

_____. However, some people argue that _____

_____   _____

_____.They also say that _____

_____.

These arguments _____

_____

For this reason, STEM education is _____

_____

_____

⬀ EXERCISE 6.7 DISCUSSING AN ARGUMENT

Discuss your ideas about STEM education with one or two of your class-mates. Consider both the strengths and the limitations of these courses. What classes do you think women avoid? Why do you think this is so? What changes could be made to make majoring in STEM more appeal-ing? Then, edit the Rogerian and Toulmin arguments that you wrote on the previous templates so that they include some of these comments.

➔ EXERCISE 6.8 WRITING AN ARGUMENTATIVE ESSAY

Write an argumentative essay on the topic, "Why are so few women in STEM fields?" Use the principles of either Rogerian argument or Toulmin logic to structure your essay. Cite sources in the Reading and Writing about the Issue section on pages 221–246, and be sure to document the sources you use and to include a works-cited page. (See Chapter 10 for information on documenting sources.)

➔ EXERCISE 6.9 CONSIDERING THE FOUR PILLARS OF ARGUMENT

Review the four pillars of argument that are discussed in Chapter 1. Does your essay include all four elements of an effective argument? Add anything that is missing. Then, label the elements of your argument.

➔ EXERCISE 6.10 CONSTRUCTING AN ORAL ARGUMENT

Assume that you have been asked to present the information in the essay you wrote for Exercise 6.8 as an oral argument. What information would you include? What information would you eliminate? Find two or three visuals that you would use when you deliver your speech. Then, make an outline of your speech and indicate at what points you would display these visuals.

Writing an Argumentative Essay

Planning, Drafting, and Revising an Argumentative Essay

Should All College Campuses Go Green?

In recent years, more and more American colleges and universities have become "green campuses," emphasizing **sustainability**—the use of systems and materials that will not deplete the earth's natural resources. Various schools have taken steps such as the following:

- Placing an emphasis on recycling and reducing nonbiodegradable waste
- Creating green buildings and using eco-friendly materials in construction projects
- Instituting new curricula in environmental science
- Monitoring their greenhouse gas emissions and evaluating their carbon footprint
- Growing crops on campus to feed students
- Hiring full-time "sustainability directors"
- Encouraging students to use bikes instead of cars
- Purchasing wind-generated electricity to supply the campus's energy
- Eliminating trays in college cafeterias

Although many schools continue to launch ambitious programs and projects to reduce their energy dependence, some have been more cautious, citing the high cost of such programs and the need to allocate resources elsewhere. Moreover, some critics of the green movement object to the notion that colleges should help to make students "sustainability literate." Such critics consider the green movement to be an expression of political correctness that at best does no more than pay lip service to the problem and at worst threatens academic freedom by furthering a political agenda.

The question remains whether the green movement that is spreading rapidly across college campuses is here to stay or just a fad—or something between these two extremes. This chapter takes you through the process of writing an argumentative essay on the topic of whether all college campuses should go green. (Exercises guide you through the process of writing your own argumentative essay on a topic of your choice.)

Before you can write a convincing argumentative essay, you need to understand the **writing process**. You are probably already familiar with the basic outline of this process, which includes *planning, drafting,* and *revising.* This chapter reviews this familiar process and explains how it applies to the specific demands of writing an argumentative essay.

Choosing a Topic

The first step in planning an argumentative essay is to choose a topic you can write about. Your goal is to select a topic that you have some emotional stake in—not simply one that interests you. If you are going to spend hours planning, writing, and revising an essay, you should care about your topic. At the same time, you should be able to keep an open mind about your topic and be willing to consider various viewpoints. Your topic also should be narrow enough to fit the boundaries of your assignment—the time you have to work on the essay and its length and scope.

Typically, your instructor will give you a general assignment, such as the following.

> **Assignment**
> Write a three- to five-page argumentative essay on a topic related to college services, programs, facilities, or curricula.

The first thing you need to do is narrow this general assignment to a topic, focusing on one particular campus service, program, facility, or curriculum. You could choose to write about any number of topics—financial aid, the writing center, athletics, the general education curriculum—taking a position, for example, on who should receive financial aid, whether to expand the mission of the writing center, whether college athletes should receive a salary, or why general education requirements are important for business majors.

If you are interested in environmental issues, however, you might decide to write about the green movement that has been spreading across college campuses, perhaps using your observations of your own campus's programs and policies to support your position.

> **Topic**
> The green movement on college campuses

Topics to Avoid

Certain kinds of topics are not appropriate for argumentative essays.

- **Topics that are statements of fact.** Some topics are just not arguable. For example, you could not write an argumentative essay on a statement of fact, such as the fact that many colleges saw their endowments decline after the financial crisis of 2008. (A fact is not debatable, so there can be no argument.)

- **Topics that have been overused.** Some familiar topics also present problems. These issues—the death penalty, abortion rights, and so on—are important (after all, that's why they are written about so often), but finding an original argument on either side of the debate can be a challenge. For example, you might have a hard time finding something new to say that would convince some readers that the death penalty is immoral or that abortion is a woman's right. In many people's minds, these issues are "settled." When you write on topics such as these, some readers' strong religious or cultural beliefs are likely to prevent them from considering your arguments, however well supported they might be.

- **Topics that rely on subjective judgments.** Some very narrow topics depend on subjective value judgment, often taking a stand on issues readers simply will not care much about, such as whether one particular video game or TV reality show is more entertaining than another. Such topics are unlikely to engage your audience (even if they seem compelling to you and your friends).

⊘ EXERCISE 7.1 CHOOSING A TOPIC

In response to the boxed assignment on the previous page, list ten topics that you could write about. Then, cross out any that do not meet the following criteria:

- The topic interests you.

- You know something about the topic.

- You care about the topic.

- You are able to keep an open mind about the topic.

- The topic fits the boundaries of your assignment.

Now, decide on one topic to write an essay about.

Thinking about Your Topic

Before you can start to develop a thesis statement or plan the structure of your argument, you need to think a bit about the topic you have chosen. You can use *invention strategies*—such as **freewriting** (writing without stopping for a predetermined time), **brainstorming** (making quick notes on your topic), or **clustering** (creating a diagram to map out your thoughts)—to help you discover ideas you might write about. You can also explore ideas in a writing journal or in conversations with friends, classmates, family members, or instructors.

Freewriting

> People say green is good, but I'm not sure why. Do we really need a separate, smelly container for composting? Won't the food decompose just as fast in a landfill? In middle school, we learned about the "three Rs" to save the environment—one was Recycle, but I forget the other two. Renew? Reuse? Remember? Whatever. OK, I know not to throw trash on the ground, and I know we're supposed to separate trash and recycling, etc. I get that. But does all this time and effort really do any good?

Brainstorming

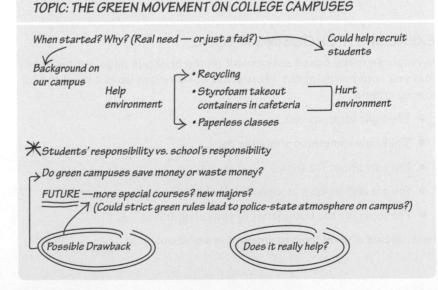

TOPIC: THE GREEN MOVEMENT ON COLLEGE CAMPUSES

When started? Why? (Real need — or just a fad?) — Could help recruit students

Background on our campus

Help environment — • Recycling / • Styrofoam takeout containers in cafeteria / • Paperless classes — Hurt environment

*Students' responsibility vs. school's responsibility

Do green campuses save money or waste money?

FUTURE —more special courses? new majors? (Could strict green rules lead to police-state atmosphere on campus?)

Possible Drawback   Does it really help?

Clustering

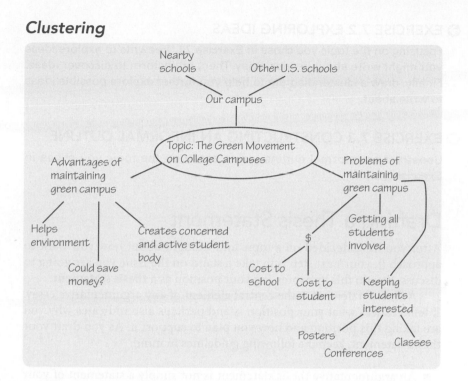

When you finish exploring ideas, you should be able to construct a quick **informal outline** that lists the ideas you plan to discuss.

Informal Outline

Topic: The Green Movement on College Campuses
   History/background
      National
      Our campus
   Positive aspects
      Helps environment
      Attracts new students
   Negative aspects
      Cost
      Enforcement
   Future

By grouping your ideas and arranging them in a logical order, an informal outline like the preceding one can help lead you to a thesis statement that expresses the position you will take on the issue.

⮕ **EXERCISE 7.2 EXPLORING IDEAS**

Focusing on the topic you chose in Exercise 7.1, freewrite to explore ideas you might write about in your essay. Then, brainstorm to discover ideas. Finally, draw a cluster diagram to help you further explore possible ideas to write about.

⮕ **EXERCISE 7.3 CONSTRUCTING AN INFORMAL OUTLINE**

Construct an informal outline for an essay on the topic you chose in Exercise 7.1.

Drafting a Thesis Statement

After you have decided on a topic and thought about how you want to approach it, your next step is to take a stand on the issue you are going to discuss. You do this by expressing your position as a **thesis statement**.

A thesis statement is the central element of any argumentative essay. It tells readers what your position is and perhaps also indicates why you are taking this position and how you plan to support it. As you draft your thesis statement, keep the following guidelines in mind:

- An argumentative thesis statement is not simply a statement of your topic; rather, it expresses the point you will make about your topic.

TOPIC	The green movement on college campuses
THESIS STATEMENT	College campuses should go green.

- An argumentative thesis statement should be specific, clearly indicating to readers exactly what position you will take in your essay.

TOO GENERAL	Colleges need to do more to get students involved in environmental issues.
REVISED	Colleges should institute programs and classes to show students the importance of using sustainable resources.

- An argumentative thesis statement should get right to the point, avoiding wordy, repetitive language.

WORDY	Because issues that revolve around the environment are so crucial and important, colleges should do more to increase student involvement in campus projects that are concerned with sustainability.

REVISED   Because environmental issues are so important, colleges should take steps to involve students in campus sustainability projects.

- Many argumentative thesis statements include words such as *should* and *should not*.

  - College campuses should _____.

  - Because _____, colleges should _____.

  - Even though _____, colleges should not _____.

> **NOTE**
>
> At this point, any thesis that you come up with is tentative. As you think about your topic and perhaps read about it, you will very likely modify your thesis statement, perhaps expanding or narrowing its scope, rewording it to make it more precise, or even changing your position. Still, the thesis statement that you decide on at this point can give you some focus as you explore your topic.

TENTATIVE THESIS STATEMENT

College campuses should go green.

⊘ EXERCISE 7.4 DEVELOPING A THESIS STATEMENT

List five possible thesis statements for the topic you chose in Exercise 7.1. (To help you see your topic in several different ways, you might experiment by drafting at least one thesis statement that evaluates, one that considers causes and/or effects, and one that proposes a solution to a problem.) Which thesis statement seems to suggest the most promising direction for your essay? Why?

Understanding Your Purpose and Audience

When you write an argument, your primary purpose is to convince your audience to accept your position. Sometimes you will have other goals as well. For example, you might want to change readers' ideas about an issue, perhaps by challenging a commonly held assumption. You might even want to move readers to take some action in support of your position.

To make the best possible case to your audience, you need to understand who your audience is—what knowledge, values, beliefs, and opinions your readers might have. You will also need to have some idea whether your audience is likely to be receptive, hostile, or neutral to the ideas you propose.

In most cases, it makes sense to assume that your readers are receptive but **skeptical**—that they have open minds but still need to be convinced. However, if you are writing about a topic that is very controversial, you will need to assume that at least some of your readers will not support your position and may, in fact, be hostile to it. If this is the case, they will be scrutinizing your arguments very carefully, looking for opportunities to argue against them. Your goal in this situation is not necessarily to win readers over but to make them more receptive to your position—or at least to get them to admit that you have made a good case even though they may disagree with you. At the same time, you also have to work to convince those who probably agree with you or those who are neutral (perhaps because the issue you are discussing is something they haven't thought much about).

An audience of first-year college students who are used to the idea that sound environmental practices make sense might find the idea of a green campus appealing—and, in fact, natural and obvious. An audience of faculty or older students might be more skeptical, realizing that the benefits of green practices might be offset by the time and expense they could involve. College administrators might find the long-term goal of a green campus attractive (and see it as a strong recruitment tool), but they might also be somewhat hostile to your position, anticipating the considerable expense that would be involved. If you wrote an argument on the topic of green campuses, you would need to consider these positions—and, if possible, address them.

● EXERCISE 7.5 CONSIDERING YOUR AUDIENCE

Consider how different audiences might respond to the thesis statement you found the most promising in Exercise 7.3. Identify five possible groups of readers on your college campus—for example, athletes, history majors, or part-time faculty. Would you expect each group to be receptive, hostile, or neutral to your position? Why?

Gathering Evidence

After you have a sense of who your audience will be and how these readers might react to your thesis, you can begin to collect **evidence** to support your thesis. As you look for evidence, you need to evaluate the usefulness and relevance of each of your sources, and you need to be alert for possible bias.

Evaluating the Evidence in Your Sources

As you read each potential source, consider the quality of the supporting evidence that the writer marshals to support his or her position. The more compelling the evidence, the more willing you should be to accept the writer's ideas—and, perhaps, to integrate these ideas into your own essay.

> **NOTE**
>
> Don't forget that if you use any of your sources' ideas, you must document them. See Chapter 10 for information on MLA documentation format and Appendix B for information on APA documentation format.

To be convincing, the evidence that is presented in the sources you review should be *accurate*, *relevant*, *representative*, and *sufficient*:

- **Accurate** evidence comes from reliable sources that are quoted carefully—and not misrepresented by being quoted out of context.

- **Relevant** evidence applies specifically (not just tangentially) to the topic under discussion.

- **Representative** evidence is drawn from a fair range of sources, not just those that support the writer's position.

- **Sufficient** evidence is enough facts, statistics, expert opinion, and so on to support the essay's thesis.

(For more detailed information on evaluating sources, see Chapter 8.)

> **NOTE**
>
> Remember, the evidence you use to support your own arguments should also satisfy the four criteria listed above.

Detecting Bias in Your Sources

As you select sources, you should be alert for **bias**—a writer's use of preconceived ideas (rather than factual evidence) as support for his or her arguments. A writer who demonstrates bias may not be trustworthy, and you should approach such a writer's arguments with skepticism. To determine whether a writer is biased, follow these guidelines:

- *Consider what a writer explicitly tells you* about his or her beliefs or opinions. For example, if a writer mentions that he or she is a lifelong member of the Sierra Club, a vegan, and the owner of a house heated by solar energy, then you should consider the possibility that he or she might downplay (or even disregard) valid arguments against maintaining a green campus rather than presenting a balanced view.

- *Look for slanted language.* For example, a writer who mocks supporters of environmental issues as "politically correct" or uses pejorative terms such as *hippies* for environmentalists should not earn your trust.

- *Consider the supporting evidence* the writer chooses. Does the writer present only examples that support his or her position and ignore valid opposing arguments? Does the writer quote only those experts who agree with his or her position—for example, only pro- (or only anti-) environmental writers? A writer who does this is presenting an unbalanced (and therefore biased) case.

- *Consider the writer's tone.* A writer whose tone is angry, bitter, or sarcastic should be suspect.

- *Consider any overtly offensive statements or characterizations* that a writer makes. A writer who makes negative assumptions about college students (for example, characterizing them as selfish and self-involved and therefore dismissing their commitment to campus environmental projects) should be viewed with skepticism.

> **NOTE**
>
> As you develop your essay, be alert for any biases you hold that might affect the strength or logic of your own arguments. See "Being Fair," page 267.

➲ EXERCISE 7.6 EXAMINING YOUR BIASES

In writing an essay that supports the thesis statement you have been working with in this chapter, you might find it difficult to remain objective. What biases do you have that you might have to watch for as you research and write about your topic?

➲ EXERCISE 7.7 GATHERING EVIDENCE

Now, gather evidence to support the thesis statement you decided on in Exercise 7.3, evaluating each source carefully (and consulting Chapter 8 as necessary). Be on the lookout for bias in your sources.

USING VISUALS AS EVIDENCE

As you draft your essay, you might want to consider adding a **visual**—such as a chart, graph, table, photo, or diagram—to help you make a point more forcefully. For example, in a paper on the green campus movement, you could include anything from photos of students recycling to a chart comparing energy use at different schools. Sometimes a visual can be so specific, so attractive, or so dramatic that its impact will be greater than words would be; in such cases, the image itself can constitute a visual argument. At other times, a visual can expand and support a written argument.

You can create a visual yourself, or you can download one from the internet, beginning your search with Google Images. If you download a visual and paste it into your paper, be sure to include a reference to the visual in your discussion to explain the argument it makes—or to show readers how it supports your argument.

NOTE

Don't forget to label any visuals with a figure number, to use proper documentation, and to include a caption explaining what the visual shows, as the student essay that begins on page 278 does. (For information on documentation, see Chapter 10.)

Refuting Opposing Arguments

As you plan your essay and explore sources that might supply your supporting evidence, you will encounter evidence that contradicts your position. You may be tempted to ignore this evidence, but if you do, your argument will not be very convincing. Instead, as you review your sources, identify the most convincing arguments against your position and prepare yourself to **refute** them (that is, to disprove them or call them into question), showing them to be illogical, unfair, or untrue. Indicating to readers that you are willing to address these arguments—and that you can respond effectively to them—will help convince them to accept your position.

Of course, simply saying that your opponent's position is "wrong" or "stupid" is not convincing. You need to summarize opposing arguments accurately and clearly identify their weaknesses. In the case of a strong opposing argument, be sure to concede its strengths (that is, acknowledge that it is a valid position) before you refute it; if you do not, readers may see you as uninformed or unfair. For example, you could refute the argument that maintaining a green campus is too expensive by acknowledging that although expenditures are high at first, in the long run, a green campus is not all that costly considering its benefits.

In assessing the strength of an opposing argument, you should always try to identify its limitations. Even a strong opposing argument may be addressing only one part of the problem. For example, an argument might focus on students' reluctance to comply with campus environmental guidelines and ignore efforts by the school's administration to overcome that reluctance. Or, an argument might focus on the current lack of green buildings on campus and ignore the school's requirement that green materials be used in all campus construction projects.

Also be careful not to create a **straw man**—that is, do not distort an opposing argument by oversimplifying it so it can be easily refuted (for example, claiming that environmentalists believe that sustainability should always be a college's first priority in its decisions about allocating resources). This unfair tactic will discourage readers from trusting you and thus will undermine your credibility.

Strategies for Refuting Opposing Arguments

In order to do a convincing job of refuting an argument that challenges your position, you need to consider where such an argument might be weak and on what basis you could refute it.

WEAKNESS IN OPPOSING ARGUMENT	REFUTATION STRATEGY
Factual errors or contrary-to-fact statements	Identify and correct the errors, perhaps explaining how they call the writer's credibility into question.
Insufficient support	Point out that more facts and examples are needed; note the kind of support (for example, statistics) that is missing.
Illogical reasoning	Identify fallacies in the writer's argument, and explain why the logic is flawed. For example, is the writer setting up a straw man or employing the either/or fallacy? (See Chapter 5 for more on logic.)
Exaggerated or overstated claims	Identify exaggerated statements, and explain why they overstate the case.
Biased statements	Identify biased statements, and show how they exhibit the writer's bias. (See page 259, "Detecting Bias in Your Sources.")
Irrelevant arguments	Identify irrelevant points and explain why they are not pertinent to the writer's argument.

⊘ EXERCISE 7.8 EVALUATING OPPOSING ARGUMENTS

Read paragraphs 7 and 8 of the student essay on page 278. Summarize the opposing argument presented in each of these paragraphs. Then, consulting the preceding list, identify the specific weakness of each opposing argument. Finally, explain the strategy the student writer uses to refute the argument.

Revising Your Thesis Statement

Before you can begin to draft your argumentative essay, and even before you can start to arrange your ideas, you need to revise your tentative thesis statement so it says exactly what you want it to say. After you have gathered and evaluated evidence to support your position and considered the merits of opposing ideas, you are ready to refocus your thesis and state it in more precise terms. Although a tentative thesis statement such as "College campuses should go green" is a good start, the thesis that guides your essay's structure should be more specific. In fact, it will be most useful as a guide if its phrasing actually acknowledges opposing arguments.

> ### REVISED THESIS STATEMENT
>
> Colleges should make every effort to create and sustain green campuses because by doing so they will not only improve their own educational environment but also ensure their institutions' survival and help solve the global climate crisis.

⊘ EXERCISE 7.9 REVISING YOUR THESIS STATEMENT

Consulting the sources you gathered in Exercise 7.7, list all the arguments against the position you express in your thesis statement. Then, list possible refutations of each of these arguments. When you have finished, revise your thesis statement so that it is more specific, acknowledging the most important argument against your position.

After you have revised your thesis statement, you will have a concise blueprint for the essay you are going to write. At this point, you will be ready to plan your essay's structure and write a first draft.

Structuring Your Essay

As you learned in Chapter 1, an argumentative essay, like other essays, includes an introduction, a body, and a conclusion. In the introduction of an argumentative essay, you state your thesis; in the body paragraphs, you present evidence to support your thesis and you acknowledge and refute opposing arguments; and in your conclusion, you bring your argument to a close and reinforce your thesis with a strong concluding statement. As you have seen, these four elements—thesis, evidence, refutation, and concluding statement—are like the four pillars of the ancient Greek temple, supporting your argument so that it will stand up to scrutiny.

SUPPLYING BACKGROUND INFORMATION

Depending on what you think your readers know—and what you think they need to know—you might decide to include a background paragraph that supplies information about the issue you are discussing. For example, in an essay about green campuses, you might briefly sum up the history of the U.S. environmental movement and trace its rise on college campuses. If you decide to include a background paragraph, it should be placed right after your introduction, where it can prepare readers for the discussion to follow.

Understanding basic essay structure can help you as you shape your essay. You should also know how to use induction and deduction, how to identify a strategy for your argument, and how to construct a formal outline.

Using Induction and Deduction

Many argumentative essays are structured either **inductively** or **deductively**. (See Chapter 5 for explanations of induction and deduction.) For example, the body of an essay with the thesis statement that is shown on page 263 could have either of the following two general structures:

INDUCTIVE STRUCTURE

- Colleges have been taking a number of steps to follow green practices.

- Through these efforts, campuses have become more environmentally responsible, and their programs and practices have had a positive impact on the environment.

- Because these efforts are helping to save the planet, they should be expanded.

DEDUCTIVE STRUCTURE

- Saving the planet is vital.

- Green campuses are helping to save the planet.

- Therefore, colleges should continue to develop green campuses.

These structures offer two options for arranging material in your essay. Many argumentative essays, however, combine induction and deduction or use other strategies to organize their ideas.

Identifying a Strategy for Your Argument

There are a variety of different ways to structure an argument, and the strategy you use depends on what you want your argument to accomplish. In this text, we discuss five options for presenting material: *definition arguments, cause-and-effect arguments, evaluation arguments, ethical arguments,* and *proposal arguments.* (See p. 390 for more on these options.)

Any of the five options listed above could guide you as you develop an essay on green campuses:

- You could structure your essay as a **definition argument**, explaining the concept of a green campus and giving examples to show its positive (or negative) impact.

- You could structure your essay as a **cause-and-effect argument**, showing how establishing a green campus can have positive results for students and for the campus—or how it might cause problems.

- You could structure your essay as an **evaluation argument**, assessing the strengths and weaknesses of various programs and policies designed to create and sustain a green campus.

- You could structure your essay as an **ethical argument**, explaining why maintaining a green campus is the right thing to do from a moral or ethical standpoint.

- You could structure your essay as a **proposal argument**, recommending a particular program, service, or course of action and showing how it can support a green campus.

Constructing a Formal Outline

If you like, you can construct a **formal outline** before you begin your draft. (Later on, you might also construct an outline of your finished paper to check the logic of its structure.) A formal outline, which is more detailed and more logically organized than the informal outline shown on page 255, presents your main points and supporting details in the order in which you will discuss them.

A formal outline of the first body paragraph (para. 2) of the student essay on page 278 would look like this:

I. Background of the term *green*
   A. 1960s environmental movement
      1. Political agenda
      2. Environmental agenda

B. Today's movements
  1. Eco-friendly practices
  2. Green values

Following a formal outline makes the drafting process flow smoothly, but many writers find it hard to predict exactly what details they will use for support or how they will develop their arguments. In fact, your first draft is likely to move away from your outline as you develop your ideas. Still, if you are the kind of writer who prefers to know where you are going before you start on your way, you will probably consider the time you devote to outlining to be time well spent.

⊜ EXERCISE 7.10 CONSTRUCTING A FORMAL OUTLINE

Look back at the thesis you decided on earlier in this chapter, and review the evidence you collected to support it. Then, construct a formal outline for your argumentative essay.

Establishing Credibility

Before you begin drafting your essay, you need to think about how to approach your topic and your audience. The essay you write will use a combination of logical, emotional, and ethical appeals, and you will have to be careful to use these appeals reasonably. (See pp. 15–21 for information on these appeals.) As you write, you will concentrate on establishing yourself as well informed, reasonable, and fair.

Being Well Informed

If you expect your readers to accept your ideas, you will need to establish yourself as someone they should believe and trust. Achieving this goal depends upon showing your audience that you have a good command of your material—that is, that you know what you are talking about.

If you want readers to listen to what you are saying, you need to earn their respect by showing them that you have done your research, that you have collected evidence that supports your argument, and that you understand the most compelling arguments against your position. For example, discussing your own experiences as a member of a campus or community environmental group, your observations at a Greenpeace convention, and essays and editorials that you have read on both sides of the issue will encourage your audience to accept your ideas on the subject of green campuses.

Being Reasonable

Even if your evidence is strong, your argument will not be convincing if it does not seem reasonable. One way to present yourself as a reasonable person is to **establish common ground** with your readers, stressing possible points of agreement instead of attacking those who might disagree with your position. For example, saying, "We all want our planet to survive" is a more effective strategy than saying, "Those who do not support the concept of a green campus are out to destroy our planet." (For more on establishing common ground, see the discussion of Rogerian argument in Chapter 6.)

Another way to present yourself as a reasonable person is to **maintain a reasonable tone**. Try to avoid absolutes (words like *always* and *never*); instead, use more conciliatory language (*in many cases, much of the time,* and so on). Try not to use words and phrases like *obviously* or *as anyone can see* to introduce points whose strength may be obvious only to you. Do not brand opponents of your position as misguided, uninformed, or deluded; remember, some of your readers may hold opposing positions and will not appreciate your unfavorable portrayal of them.

Finally, be very careful to treat your readers with respect, addressing them as your intellectual equals. Avoid statements that might insult them or their beliefs ("Although some ignorant or misguided people may still think . . ."). And never assume that your readers know less about your topic than you do; they may actually know a good deal more.

Being Fair

If you want readers to respect your point of view, you need to demonstrate respect for them by being fair. It is not enough to support your ideas convincingly and maintain a reasonable tone. You also need to avoid unfair tactics in your argument and take care to avoid **bias**.

In particular, you should be careful not to *distort evidence, quote out of context, slant evidence, make unfair appeals,* or *use logical fallacies.* These unfair tactics may influence some readers in the short term, but in the long run such tactics will alienate your audience.

- **Do not distort evidence. Distorting** (or misrepresenting) **evidence** is an unfair tactic. It is not ethical or fair, for example, to present your opponent's views inaccurately or to exaggerate his or her position and then argue against it. If you want to argue that expanding green programs on college campuses are a good idea, it is not fair to attack someone who expresses reservations about their cost by writing, "Mr. McNamara's concerns about cost reveal that he has basic doubts about saving the planet." (His concerns reveal no such thing.) It is, however, fair to acknowledge your opponent's reasonable concerns about cost and then go on to argue that the long-term benefits of such programs justify their expense.

- **Do not quote out of context.** It is perfectly fair to challenge someone's stated position. It is not fair, however, to misrepresent that position by quoting out of context—that is, by taking the words out of the original setting in which they appeared. For example, if a college dean says, "For schools with limited resources, it may be more important to allocate resources to academic programs than to environmental projects," you are quoting the dean's remarks out of context if you say, "According to Dean Levering, it is 'more important to allocate resources to academic programs than to environmental projects.'"

- **Do not slant evidence.** An argument based on slanted evidence is not fair. **Slanting** involves choosing only evidence that supports your position and ignoring evidence that challenges it. This tactic makes your position seem stronger than it actually is. Another kind of slanting involves using biased language to unfairly characterize your opponents or their positions—for example, using a dismissive term such as *tree hugger* to describe a concerned environmentalist.

- **Do not make unfair appeals.** If you want your readers to accept your ideas, you need to avoid **unfair appeals** to the emotions, such as appeals to your audience's fears or prejudices. For example, if you try to convince readers of the importance of using green building materials by saying, "Construction projects that do not use green materials doom future generations to a planet that cannot sustain itself," you are likely to push neutral (or even receptive) readers to skepticism or to outright hostility.

- **Do not use logical fallacies.** Using **logical fallacies** (flawed arguments) in your writing is likely to diminish your credibility and alienate your readers. (See Chapter 5 for information about logical fallacies.)

MAINTAINING YOUR CREDIBILITY

Be careful to avoid phrases that undercut your credibility ("Although this is not a subject I know much about") and to avoid apologies ("This is just my opinion"). Be as clear, direct, and forceful as you can, showing readers you are confident as well as knowledgeable. And, of course, be sure to proofread carefully: grammatical and mechanical errors and typos will weaken your credibility.

Drafting Your Essay

Once you understand how to approach your topic and your audience, you will be ready to draft your essay. At this point, you will have selected the sources you will use to support your position as well as identified the strongest arguments against your position (and decided how to refute them). You may also have prepared a formal outline (or perhaps just a list of points to follow).

As you draft your argumentative essay, keep the following guidelines in mind:

- **Follow the general structure of an argumentative essay.** State your thesis in your first paragraph, and discuss each major point in a separate paragraph, moving from least to most important point to emphasize your strongest argument. Introduce each body paragraph with a clearly worded topic sentence. Discuss each opposing argument in a separate paragraph, and be sure your refutation appears directly after your mention of each opposing argument. Finally, don't forget to include a strong concluding statement in your essay's last paragraph.

- **Decide how to arrange your material.** As you draft your essay, you may notice that it is turning out to be an ethical argument, an evaluation argument, or another kind of argument that you recognize. If this is the case, you might want to ask your instructor how you can arrange your material so it is consistent with this type of argument (or consult the relevant chapter in Part 5, "Strategies for Argument").

- **Use evidence effectively.** As you make your points, select the evidence that supports your argument most convincingly. As you write, **summarize** or **paraphrase** relevant information from your sources, and respond to this information in your own voice, supplementing material that you find in your sources with your own original ideas and conclusions. (For information on finding and evaluating sources, see Chapter 8; for information on integrating source material, see Chapter 9.)

- **Use coordination and subordination to make your meaning clear.** Readers shouldn't have to guess how two points are connected; you should use coordination and subordination to show them the relationship between ideas.

Choose **coordinating conjunctions**—*and*, *but*, *or*, *nor*, *for*, *so*, and *yet*—carefully, making sure you are using the right word for your purpose. (Use *and* to show addition; *but*, *for*, or *yet* to show contradiction; *or* to present alternatives; and *so* to indicate a causal relationship.)

Choose **subordinating conjunctions**—*although*, *because*, and so on—carefully, and place them so that your emphasis will be clear.

Consider the two ideas expressed in the following sentences.

> Achieving a green campus is vitally important. Creating a green campus is expensive.

If you want to stress the idea that green measures are called for, you would connect the sentences like this:

> Although creating a green campus is expensive, achieving a green campus is vitally important.

If, however, you want to place emphasis on the high cost, you would connect the sentences as follows:

> Although achieving a green campus is vitally important, creating a green campus is expensive.

- **Include transitional words and phrases.** Be sure you have enough transitions to guide your readers through your discussion. Supply signals that move readers smoothly from sentence to sentence and paragraph to paragraph, and choose signals that make sense in the context of your discussion.

SUGGESTED TRANSITIONS FOR ARGUMENT

- To show causal relationships: *because, as a result, for this reason*

- To indicate sequence: *first, second, third; then; next; finally*

- To introduce additional points: *also, another, in addition, furthermore, moreover*

- To move from general to specific: *for example, for instance, in short, in other words*

- To identify an opposing argument: *however, although, even though, despite*

- To grant the validity of an opposing argument: *certainly, admittedly, granted, of course*

- To introduce a refutation: *however, nevertheless, nonetheless, still*

- **Define your terms.** If the key terms of your argument have multiple meanings—as *green* does—be sure to indicate what the term means in the context of your argument. Terms like *environmentally friendly, climate change, environmentally responsible, sustainable,* and *sustainability literacy* may mean very different things to different readers.

- **Use clear language.** An argument is no place for vague language or wordy phrasing. If you want readers to understand your points, your writing should be clear and direct. Avoid vague words like *good, bad, right,* and *wrong,* which are really just unsupported judgments that do nothing to help you make your case. Also avoid wordy phrases such as *revolves around* and *is concerned with,* particularly in your thesis statement and topic sentences.

GRAMMAR IN CONTEXT

Using Parallelism

As you draft your argumentative essay, you should express corresponding words, phrases, and clauses in **parallel** terms. The use of matching parts of speech to express corresponding ideas strengthens your argument's impact because it enables readers to follow your line of thought.

   In particular, use parallelism in sentences that highlight *paired items* or *items in a series*.

- **Paired Items**

   UNCLEAR   Maintaining a green campus is important because <u>it sets</u> an example for students and the <u>environment will be protected</u>.

   PARALLEL   Maintaining a green campus is important because it <u>sets</u> an example for students and <u>protects</u> the environment.

- **Items in a Series**

   UNCLEAR   Students can do their part to support green campus initiatives in four ways—by <u>avoiding</u> bottled water, use of electricity <u>should be limited</u>, and they <u>can recycle</u> packaging and also <u>educating</u> themselves about environmental issues is a good strategy.

   PARALLEL   Students can do their part to support green campus initiatives in four ways—by <u>avoiding</u> bottled water, by <u>limiting</u> use of electricity, by <u>recycling</u> packaging, and by <u>educating</u> themselves about environmental issues.

- **Finally, show your confidence and your mastery of your material.** Avoid qualifying your statements with phrases such as *I think*, *I believe*, *it seems to me*, and *in my opinion*. These qualifiers weaken your argument by suggesting that you are unsure of your material or that the statements that follow may not be true.

⊘ EXERCISE 7.11 DRAFTING YOUR ARGUMENTATIVE ESSAY

Keeping the preceding guidelines in mind, write a draft of an argumentative essay that develops the thesis statement you have been working with. If you like, include a visual to support your argument.

Revising Your Essay

After you have written a draft of your essay, you will need to revise it. **Revision** is "re-seeing"—looking carefully and critically at the draft you have written. Revision is different from editing and proofreading, which focus on grammar, punctuation, mechanics, and the like. In fact, revision can involve substantial reworking of your essay's structure and content. The strategies discussed on the pages that follow can help you revise your arguments.

Asking Questions

Asking some basic questions, such as those in the three checklists that follow, can help you to focus on the individual elements of your essay as you revise.

CHECKLIST

Questions about Your Essay's Purpose and Audience

☐ What was your primary purpose in writing this essay? What other purposes did you have?

☐ What appeals, strategies, and evidence did you use to accomplish your goals?

☐ Who is the audience for your essay? Do you see your readers as receptive, hostile, or neutral to your position?

☐ What basic knowledge do you think your readers have about your topic? Have you provided enough background for them?

☐ What biases do you think your readers have? Have you addressed these biases in your essay?

☐ What do you think your readers believed about your topic before reading your essay?

☐ What do you want readers to believe now that they have read your essay?

CHECKLIST

Questions about Your Essay's Structure and Style

☐ Does your essay have a clearly stated thesis?

☐ Are your topic sentences clear and concise?

☐ Have you provided all necessary background and definitions?

☐ Have you refuted opposing arguments effectively?

☐ Have you included enough transitional words and phrases to guide readers smoothly through your discussion?

☐ Have you avoided vague language and wordy phrasing?

☐ Does your essay have a strong concluding statement?

CHECKLIST

Questions about Your Essay's Supporting Evidence

☐ Have you supported your opinions with *evidence*—facts, observations, examples, statistics, expert opinion, and so on?

☐ Have you included enough evidence to support your thesis?

☐ Do the sources you rely on present information accurately and without bias?

☐ Are your sources' discussions directly relevant to your topic?

☐ Have you consulted sources that represent a wide range of viewpoints, including sources that challenge your position?

☐ Have you included one or more visuals to support your argument?

The answers to the questions in the checklists may lead you to revise your essay's content, structure, and style. For example, you may want to look for additional sources that can provide the kind of supporting evidence you need, or you may want to add visuals or replace a visual with one that more effectively supports your argument. Then, you may notice you need to revise the structure of your essay, perhaps rearranging your points so that the most important point is placed last, for emphasis. You may also want to revise your essay's introduction and conclusion, sharpening your thesis statement or adding a stronger concluding statement. Finally, you may decide to add more background material to help your readers understand the issue you are writing about or to help them take a more favorable view of your position.

Using Outlines and Templates

To check the logic of your essay's structure, you can prepare a revision outline or consult a template.

- To make sure your essay's key points are arranged logically and supported convincingly, you can construct a **formal outline** of your draft. (See pp. 265–66 for information on formal outlines.) This outline will indicate whether you need to discuss any additional points, add supporting evidence, or refute an opposing argument more fully. It will also show you if paragraphs are arranged in a logical order.

- To make sure your argument flows smoothly from thesis statement to evidence to refutation of opposing arguments to concluding statement, you can refer to one of the paragraph **templates** that appear throughout this book. These templates can help you to construct a one-paragraph summary of your essay.

Getting Feedback

After you have done as much as you can on your own, it is time to get feedback from your instructor and (with your instructor's permission) from your school's writing center or from other students in your class.

Instructor Feedback You can get feedback from your instructor in a variety of different ways. For example, your instructor may ask you to email a draft of your paper to him or her with some specific questions ("Do I need paragraph 3, or do I have enough evidence without it?" "Does my thesis statement need to be more specific?"). The instructor will then reply with corrections and recommendations. If your instructor prefers a traditional face-to-face conference, you may still want to email your draft ahead of time to give him or her a chance to read it before your meeting.

Writing Center Feedback You can also get feedback from a writing center tutor, who can be either a student or a professional. The tutor can give you another point of view about your paper's content and organization and also help you focus on specific questions of style, grammar, punctuation, and mechanics. (Keep in mind, however, that a tutor will not edit or proofread your paper for you; that is your job.)

Peer Review Finally, you can get feedback from your classmates. **Peer review** can be an informal process in which you ask a classmate for advice, or it can be a more structured process, involving small groups working with copies of students' work. Peer review can also be conducted electronically. For example, students can exchange drafts by email or respond to one another's drafts that are posted on the course website. They can also use Word's comment tool, as illustrated in the following example.

DRAFT

Colleges and universities have no excuse for ignoring the threat of global climate change. Campus leaders need to push beyond efforts to recycle or compost and instead become models of sustainability. Already, many universities are hard at work demonstrating that reducing their institution's environmental impact is not only possible but worthwhile. They are overhauling their entire infrastructure, their buildings, systems, and even curriculum. While many students, faculty, staff, and administrators are excited by these new challenges, some still question this need to go green. Is it worth the money? Is it promoting "a moral and behavioral agenda rather than an educational one" (Butcher)? In fact, greening will ultimately save institutions money while providing their students with a good education. Colleges should make every effort to create green campuses because by doing so they will help solve the global climate crisis.

Comment [LB]: Your first two sentences are a little abrupt. Maybe you could ease into your argument more slowly?

Comment [KS]: I like these two questions. They really got me thinking.

Comment [PL]: Could you be more specific? I'm not sure what you mean.

Comment [PL]: You definitely talk about this in your paper, but you also talk about other reasons to go green. You might consider revising this thesis statement so it matches your argument.

FINAL VERSION

In recent years, the pressure to go green has led colleges and universities to make big changes. The threats posed by global climate change are inspiring campus leaders to push beyond efforts to recycle to become models of sustainability. Today, in the interest of reducing their environmental impact, many campuses are seeking to overhaul their entire infrastructure—their buildings, their systems, and even their curriculum. While many students, faculty, staff, and administrators are excited by these new challenges, some question this need to go green. Is it worth the money? Is it promoting "a moral and behavioral agenda rather than an educational one" (Butcher)? In fact, greening will ultimately save institutions money while providing their students with the educational opportunities necessary to help them solve the crisis of their generation. Despite the expense, colleges should make every effort to create and sustain green campuses because by doing so they will not only improve their own educational environment but also ensure their institutions' survival and help solve the global climate crisis.

GUIDELINES FOR PEER REVIEW

Remember that the peer-review process involves *giving* feedback as well as receiving it. When you respond to a classmate's work, follow these guidelines:

- Be very specific when making suggestions, clearly identifying errors, inconsistencies, redundancy, or areas that need further development.

- Be tactful and supportive when pointing out problems.

- Give praise and encouragement whenever possible.

- Be generous with your suggestions for improvement.

➲ EXERCISE 7.12 REVISING YOUR ARGUMENTATIVE ESSAY

Following the guidelines for revision discussed earlier, get some feedback from others, and then revise your argumentative essay.

Polishing Your Essay

The final step in the writing process is putting the finishing touches on your essay. At this point, your goal is to make sure that your essay is well organized, convincing, and clearly written, with no distracting grammatical or mechanical errors.

Editing and Proofreading

When you **edit** your revised draft, you review your essay's overall structure, style, and sentence construction, but you focus on grammar, punctuation, and mechanics. Editing is an important step in the writing process because an interesting, logically organized argument will not be convincing if readers are distracted by run-ons and fragments, confusingly placed modifiers, or incorrect verb forms. (Remember, your grammar checker will spot some grammatical errors, but it will miss many others.)

When you **proofread** your revised and edited draft, you carefully read every word, trying to spot any remaining punctuation or mechanical errors, as well as any typographical errors (typos) or misspellings that your spellchecker may have missed. (Remember, a spellchecker will not flag a correctly spelled word that is used incorrectly.)

Choosing a Title

After you have edited and proofread your essay, you need to give it a title. Ideally, your title should create interest and give readers clear information about the subject of your essay. It should also be appropriate for your topic. A serious topic calls for a serious title, and a thoughtfully presented argument deserves a thoughtfully selected title.

GRAMMAR IN CONTEXT

Contractions versus Possessive Pronouns

Be especially careful not to confuse the contractions *it's, who's, they're,* and *you're* with the possessive forms *its, whose, their,* and *your.*

| INCORRECT | <u>Its</u> not always clear <u>who's</u> responsibility it is to promote green initiatives on campus. |
| CORRECT | <u>It's</u> not always clear <u>whose</u> responsibility it is to promote green initiatives on campus. |

A title does not need to surprise or shock readers. It also should not be long and wordy or something many readers will not understand. A simple statement of your topic ("Going Green") or of your position on the issue ("College Campuses Should Go Green") is usually all that is needed. If you like, you can use a quotation from one of your sources as a title ("Green Is Good").

⊙ EXERCISE 7.13 EVALUATING POSSIBLE ESSAY TITLES

Evaluate the suitability and effectiveness of the following titles for an argumentative essay on green campuses. Be prepared to explain the strengths and weaknesses of each title.

- Green Campuses
- It's Not Easy Being Green
- The Lean, Clean, Green Machine
- What Students Can Do to Make Their Campuses More Environmentally Responsible
- Why All Campuses Should Be Green Campuses
- Planting the Seeds of the Green Campus Movement
- The Green Campus: An Idea Whose Time Has Come

Checking Format

Finally, make sure that your essay follows your instructor's guidelines for documentation style and manuscript format. (The student paper on p. 278 follows MLA style and manuscript format. For additional sample essays illustrating MLA and APA documentation style and manuscript format, see Chapter 10 and Appendix B, respectively.)

⊙ The following student essay, "Going Green," argues that colleges should make every effort to create green campuses.

GOING GREEN

SHAWN HOLTON

In recent years, the pressure to go green has led colleges and universities to make big changes. The threats posed by climate change are encouraging campus leaders to push beyond early efforts, such as recycling, to become models of sustainability. Today, in the interest of reducing their environmental impact, many campuses are seeking to overhaul their entire infrastructure. Although many students, faculty, staff, and administrators are excited by these new challenges, some question this need to go green. Is it worth the money? Is it promoting "a moral and behavioral agenda rather than an educational one" (Butcher)? In fact, greening will ultimately save institutions money while providing their students with the educational opportunities necessary to help them solve the crisis of their generation. Despite the expense, colleges should make every effort to create and sustain green campuses because by doing so they will not only improve their own educational environment but also ensure their institutions' survival and help solve the global climate crisis.

1

Although the green movement has been around for many years, *green* has become a buzzword only relatively recently. Green political parties and groups began forming in the 1960s to promote environmentalist goals ("Environmentalism"). These groups fought for "grassroots democracy, social justice, and nonviolence" in addition to environmental protections and were "self-consciously activist and unconventional" in their strategies ("Environmentalism"). Today, however, *green* denotes much more than a political movement; it has become a catchall word for anything eco-friendly. People use *green* to describe everything from fuel-efficient cars to fume-free house paint. Green values have become more mainstream in response to evidence that human activities, particularly those that result in greenhouse-gas emissions, may be causing global warming at a dramatic rate ("Call for Climate Leadership" 4). To fight this climate change, many individuals, businesses, and organizations have chosen to go green, making sustainability and preservation of the environment a priority.

2

Greening a college campus means moving toward a sustainable campus that works to conserve the earth's natural resources. It means reducing the university's carbon footprint by focusing on energy efficiency in every aspect of campus life. This is no small task. Although replacing incandescent lightbulbs with compact fluorescent ones and offering more locally grown food in dining halls are valuable steps, meaningful sustainability requires more comprehensive changes. For example, universities also need to invest in alternative energy sources, construct new buildings and remodel old ones, and work to reduce campus demand for nonrenewable products. Although these changes will eventually save universities money, in most cases, the institutions will need to spend money now to reduce costs in the long term. To achieve this transformation, many colleges—individually or in cooperation with other schools—have established formal "climate commitments," set specific goals, and developed tools to track their investments and evaluate their progress.

Despite these challenges, there are many compelling reasons to act now. Saving money on operating costs, thus making the school more competitive in the long term, is an appealing incentive. In fact, many schools have made solid and sometimes immediate gains by greening some aspect of their campus. For example, by changing its parking and transit systems to encourage more carpooling, biking, and walking, Cornell University has saved 417,000 gallons of fuel and cut costs by $36 million over the last twelve years ("Call for Climate Leadership" 10). By installing geothermal wells and replacing its old power plant with a geothermal pump system, the University of Central Missouri (UCM) is saving 31 percent in energy costs, according to a case study in *Climate Neutral Campus Report* (Trane). These changes were not merely a social, or even a political, response, but a necessary part of updating the campus. Betty Roberts, the UCM vice president for administration, was faced with the problem of how to "make a change for the benefit of the institution . . . with no money." After saving several million dollars by choosing to go green, Roberts naturally reported that the school was "very happy!" with its decision (qtd. in Trane). There is more to be gained than just savings, however. Oberlin College not only saves money by generating its own solar energy (as shown in Fig. 1) but also makes money by selling its excess electricity back to the local power company (Petersen). Many other schools have taken similar steps, with similarly positive results.

3 Body paragraph: Definition of *green* as it applies to colleges

4 Body paragraph: First argument in support of thesis

Body paragraph:
Second argument
in support of
thesis

AP Images/The Morning Journal/Paul M. Walsh

Fig. 1. Solar panels on the roof of
the Adam Joseph Lewis Center for
Environmental Studies, Oberlin
College. 2008. Oberlin.edu.

Attracting the attention of the   5
media, donors, and—most significantly—
prospective students is another practical
reason for schools to go green. As one
researcher explains, "There is enough
evidence nationwide to detect an arms-
race of sorts among universities competing for green status" (Krizek et al. 27).
The *Princeton Review* now includes a
"green rating," and according to recent
studies, more than two thirds of college
applicants say that they consider green
ratings when choosing a school (Krizek
et al. 27). A school's commitment to the
environment can also bring in large private donations. For example, Carnegie
Mellon University attracted $1.7 million
from the National Science Foundation for
its new Center for Sustainable Engineering (Egan). The University of California,
Davis, will be receiving up to $25 million
from the Chevron Corporation to research biofuel technology ("Call for
Climate Leadership" 10). While greening certainly costs money, a green
commitment can also help a school remain financially viable.

Body paragraph: Third
argument in support of
thesis

In addition to these practical reasons for going green, universi-   6
ties also have another, perhaps more important, reason to promote
and model sustainability: doing so may help solve the climate crisis.
Although an individual school's reduction of emissions may not notice-
ably affect global warming, its graduates will be in a position to make
a huge impact. College is a critical time in most students' personal and
professional development. Students are making choices about what kind
of adults they will be, and they are also receiving the training, education,
and experience that they will need to succeed in the working world. If
universities can offer time, space, and incentives—both in and out of the
classroom—to help students develop creative ways to live sustainably,
these schools have the potential to change the thinking and habits of a
whole generation.

Many critics of greening claim that becoming environmentally friendly is too expensive and will result in higher tuition and fees. However, often a very small increase in fees, as little as a few dollars a semester, can be enough to help a school institute significant change. For example, at the University of Colorado–Boulder, a student-initiated $1 increase in fees allowed the school to purchase enough wind power to reduce its carbon emissions by 12 million pounds ("Call for Climate Leadership" 9). Significantly, the students were the ones who voted to increase their own fees to achieve a greener campus. Although university faculty and administrators' commitment to sustainability is critical for any program's success, few green initiatives will succeed without the enthusiastic support of the student body. Ultimately, students have the power. If they think their school is spending too much on green projects, then they can make a change or choose to go elsewhere.

7 Refutation of first opposing argument

Other critics of the trend toward greener campuses believe that schools with commitments to sustainability are dictating how students should live rather than encouraging free thought. As one early critic has claimed, "Once [sustainability literacy] is enshrined in a university's public pronouncements or private articles, then the institution has diminished its commitment to academic inquiry" (Butcher). This kind of criticism overlooks the fact that figuring out how to achieve sustainability requires and will continue to require rigorous critical thinking and creativity. Why not apply the academic skills of inquiry, analysis, and problem solving to the biggest problem of our day? Not doing so would be irresponsible and would confirm the perception that universities are ivory towers of irrelevant knowledge. In fact, the presence of sustainability as both a goal and a subject of study has the potential to reaffirm academia's place at the center of civil society.

8 Refutation of second opposing argument

Creating a green campus is a difficult task, but universities must rise to the challenge or face the consequences. If they do not commit to changing their ways, they will become less and less able to compete for students and for funding. If they refuse to make a comprehensive commitment to sustainability, they also risk irrelevance at best and institutional collapse at worst. Finally, by not rising to the challenge, they will be giving up the opportunity to establish themselves as leaders in addressing the climate crisis. As the coalition of American College and University Presidents states in its Climate Commitment, "No other institution has the influence,

9 Conclusion

Concluding statement

the critical mass and the diversity of skills needed to successfully reverse global warming" ("Call for Climate Leadership" 13). Now is the time for schools to make the choice and pledge to go green.

Works Cited

Butcher, Jim. "Keep the Green Moral Agenda off Campus." *Times Higher Education*, 19 Oct. 2007, www.timeshighereducation.com/news/keep -the-green-moral-agenda-off-campus/310853.article.

"A Call for Climate Leadership." *American College and University Presidents Climate Commitment*, Aug. 2009, www2.presidentsclimatecommitment .org/html/documents/ACUPCC_InfoPacketv2.pdf.

Egan, Timothy. "The Greening of America's Campuses." *New York Times*, 8 Jan. 2006, www.nytimes.com/2006/01/08/education/edlife/egan _environment.html?scp=1&amp%3Bsq=The&_r=0.

"Environmentalism." *Encyclopaedia Britannica Online*, 2015, www.britannica .com/topic/environmentalism.

Krizek, Kevin J., Dave Newport, James White, and Alan R. Townsend. "Higher Education's Sustainability Imperative: How to Practically Respond?" *International Journal of Sustainability in Higher Education*, vol. 13, no. 1, 2012, pp. 1–33. DOI: 10.1108/14676371211190281.

Petersen, John. "A Green Curriculum Involves Everyone on Campus." *Chronicle of Higher Education*, vol. 54, no. 41, 2008, p. A25. *ERIC Institute of Education Services*, eric.ed.gov/?id=EJ801316.

Trane. "University of Central Missouri." *Climate Neutral Campus Report*, Kyoto Publishing, 14 Aug. 2009, secondnature.org/wp-content /uploads/09-8-14_ClimateNeutralCampusReportReleased.pdf.

⊘ EXERCISE 7.14 PREPARING A FINAL DRAFT

Edit and proofread your essay, paying special attention to parenthetical documentation and to your works-cited page, and check to make sure your essay's format is consistent with your instructor's requirements. When you have finished, give your essay a title, and print out a final copy.

⊘ EXERCISE 7.15 EVALUATING VISUAL ARGUMENTS

Write a paragraph in which you evaluate the visual in the student essay on pages 278–82. Does it add valuable support to the essay, or should it be deleted or replaced? Can you suggest a visual that could serve as a more convincing argument in support of green campuses?

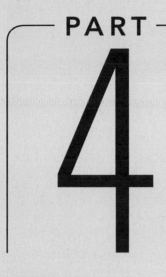

PART

4

Using Sources to Support Your Argument

Finding and Evaluating Sources

Is Technology a Serious Threat to Our Privacy?

The internet and social media have become deeply woven into our lives, to the point where Facebook has over 2.23 billion users worldwide. Not surprisingly, social media sites have become a primary tool for people—from marketers to cybercriminals—who want to access personal information, for better and for worse. High profile data breaches have raised concerns too. Facebook faced a scandal in 2018 when it revealed that over 87 million of its users' data had been shared with Cambridge Analytica, a political consulting firm that sought data on American political behavior.

Most people agree that such breaches are bad and that protecting privacy is important. But they disagree over approaches to the problem. Some want stricter government regulation; others think free markets will address the issue; still, others argue that the only way to ensure privacy is for individuals to avoid sharing personal information online.

Later in this chapter, you will evaluate several sources to determine whether they are acceptable for an argumentative essay about technology and privacy. In Chapter 9, you will learn how to integrate sources into an essay on this topic. In Chapter 10, you will see an MLA paper on one aspect of the topic: whether it is ethical for employers to access information posted on job applicants' social-networking sites. Finally, in Chapter 11, you will learn how to use sources responsibly while considering the question, "Where should we draw the line with plagiarism?"

Finding Sources

In some argumentative essays, you can use your own ideas as evidence in support of your position. In many others, however, you have to do **research**—collect information (in both print and electronic form) from magazines, newspapers, books, journals, and other sources—to supplement your own ideas.

The obvious question is, "How does research help you to construct better arguments?" The answer is that research enables you to explore the ideas of others, consider multiple points of view, and expand your view of your subject. By doing so, you get a better understanding of the issues surrounding your topic, and as a result, you are able to develop a strong thesis and collect the facts, examples, statistics, quotations, and expert opinion that you will need to support your points. In addition, by taking the time to find reliable, up-to-date sources, you demonstrate to readers that your discussion is credible and that you are someone worth listening to. In short, doing research enables you to construct intelligent, authoritative, and convincing arguments.

As you do research, keep in mind that your argumentative essay should not be a collection of other people's ideas. It should present an original thesis that you develop with your own insights and opinions. You use the information you get from your research to provide additional support for your thesis and to expand your discussion. In other words, your voice, not the voices of your sources, should control the discussion.

Finding Information in the Library

When most students do research, they immediately go to the internet. Unfortunately, by doing this, they ignore the most reliable source of high-quality information available to them: their college library.

Your college library contains both print and electronic resources that you cannot find anywhere else. Although the internet gives you access to an almost unlimited amount of material, it does not offer the consistently high level of reliable information found in your college library. For this reason, you should always begin your research by surveying the resources of the library.

The best way to access your college library is to visit its website, which is the gateway to a great deal of information—for example, its online catalog, electronic databases, and reference works.

> **The Online Catalog:** The **online catalog** lists all the books, journals, newspapers, magazines, and other material housed in the library. Once you gain access to this catalog, you can type in keywords that will lead you to sources related to your topic.

> **NOTE**
>
> Many libraries have a **discovery service** that enables you to use a single search box to access a wide variety of content—for example, the physical items held by a library as well as content from e-books, journal articles, government documents, and electronic databases. Most discovery services return high-quality results quickly and (like Google) rank them according to relevancy.

Online Databases: All college libraries subscribe to **databases**—collections of digital information that you access through a keyword search. The library's online databases enable you to retrieve bibliographic citations as well as the full text of articles from hundreds of publications. Some of these databases—for example, *Expanded Academic ASAP* and *Proquest Research Library*—provide information on a wide variety of topics. Others—for example, *Business Source Premier* and *Sociological Abstracts*—provide information on a particular subject area. Before selecting a database, check with the reference librarian to determine which will be most useful for your topic.

Reference Works: All libraries contain **reference works**—sources of accurate and reliable information such as dictionaries, encyclopedias, and almanacs. These reference works are available both in print and in electronic form. **General encyclopedias**—such as the *New Encyclopaedia Britannica* and the *Columbia Encyclopedia*—provide general information on a wide variety of topics. **Specialized reference works**—such as *Facts on File* and the *World Almanac*—and **special encyclopedias**—such as the *Encyclopedia of Law and Economics*—offer detailed information on specific topics.

> **NOTE**
>
> Although a general encyclopedia (print or electronic) can provide an overview of your topic, encyclopedia articles do not usually treat topics in enough depth for college-level research. Be sure to check your instructor's guidelines before you use a general encyclopedia in your research.

Finding Information on the Internet

Although the internet gives you access to a vast amount of information, it has its limitations. For one thing, because anyone can publish on the web, you cannot be sure if the information found there is trustworthy, timely, or authoritative. Of course, there are reliable sources of information on the web. For example, the information on your college library's website is reliable. In addition, Google Scholar provides links to some scholarly sources that are as good as those found in a college library's databases. Even so, you have to approach this material with caution; some articles accessed through Google Scholar are pay-per-view, and others are not current or comprehensive.

USING GOOGLE SCHOLAR

Google Scholar is a valuable research resource. If you use it, however, you should be aware of its drawbacks:

■ It includes some non-scholarly publications. Because it does not accurately define scholar, some material may not conform to academic standards of reliability.

■ It does not index all scholarly journals. Many academic journals are available only through a library's databases and are not accessible on the internet.

■ Google Scholar is uneven across scholarly disciplines—that is, it includes more information from some disciplines than others. In addition, Google Scholar does not perform well for publications before 1990.

■ Google Scholar does not screen for quality. Because Google Scholar uses an algorithm, not a human being, to select sources, it does not always filter out junk journals.

■ Some of the articles in Google Scholar are pay-per-view. Before you pay to download an article, check to see if your college library gives you free access.

A **search engine**—such as Google—helps you to locate and to view documents that you search for with keywords. Different types of search engines are suitable for different purposes:

■ **General-Purpose Search Engines: General-purpose search engines** retrieve information on a great number of topics. They cast the widest possible net and bring in the widest variety of information. The disadvantage of general-purpose search engines is that you get a great deal of irrelevant material. Because each search engine has its own unique characteristics, you should try a few of them to see which you prefer. The most popular general-purpose search engines are Google, Bing, Yahoo!, and Ask.com.

- **Specialized Search Engines: Specialized search engines** focus on specific subject areas or on a specific type of content—for example, business, government, or health services. The advantage of specialized search engines is that they eliminate the need for you to wade through pages of irrelevant material. By focusing your search on a specific subject area, you are more likely to locate information on your particular topic. You can find a list of specialized search engines on the Search Engine List (thesearchenginelist.com).

- **Metasearch Engines:** Because each search engine works differently, results can (and do) vary. For this reason, if you limit yourself to a single search engine, you can miss a great deal of useful information. **Metasearch engines** solve this problem by taking the results of several search engines and presenting them in a simple, no-nonsense format. The most popular metasearch engines are Dogpile, ixquick, MetaGer, MetaCrawler, and Sputtr.

klaikungwon/Shutterstock

Sources must be evaluated carefully.

Evaluating Sources

When you **evaluate** a source, you assess the objectivity of the author, the credibility of the source, and its relevance to your argument. Whenever you locate a source—print or electronic—you should always take the time to evaluate it.

Although a librarian or an instructor has screened the print and electronic sources in your college library for general accuracy and trustworthiness, you cannot simply assume that these sources are suitable for your particular writing project. Material that you access online presents particular problems. Although some material on the internet (for example, journal articles that are published in both print and digital format) is reliable, other material (for example, personal websites and blogs) may be unreliable and unsuitable for your research. Remember, if you use an untrustworthy source, you undercut your credibility.

To evaluate sources, you use the same process that you use when you evaluate anything else. For example, if you are thinking about buying a laptop computer, you use several criteria to help you make your decision—for example, price, speed, memory, reliability, and availability of technical support. The same is true for evaluating research sources. You can use the following criteria to decide whether a source is appropriate for your research.

- Accuracy
- Credibility
- Objectivity
- Currency
- Comprehensiveness
- Authority

The illustrations on page 291 show where to find information that can help you evaluate a source.

Accuracy A source is **accurate** when it is factual and free of errors. One way to judge the accuracy of a source is to compare the information it contains to that same information in several other sources. If a source has factual errors, then it probably includes other types of errors as well. Needless to say, errors in spelling and grammar should also cause you to question a source's general accuracy.

You can also judge the accuracy of a source by checking to see if the author cites sources for the information that is discussed. Documentation can help readers determine both the quality of information in a source and the range of sources used. It can also show readers what sources a writer has failed to consult. (Failure to cite an important book or article should cause you to question the writer's familiarity with a subject.) If possible, verify the legitimacy of some of the books and articles that a writer cites by seeing what you can find out about them online. If a source has caused a great deal of debate or if it is disreputable, you will probably be able to find information about the source by researching it on Google.

Credibility A source is **credible** when it is believable. You can begin checking a source's credibility by determining where a book or article was published. If a university press published the book, you can be reasonably certain that it was **peer reviewed**—read by experts in the field to confirm the accuracy of the information. If a commercial press published the book, you will have to consider other criteria—the author's reputation and the date of publication, for example—to determine quality. If your source is an article, see if it appears in a **scholarly journal**—a periodical aimed at experts in a particular field—or in a **popular magazine**—a periodical aimed at general readers. Journal articles are almost always acceptable

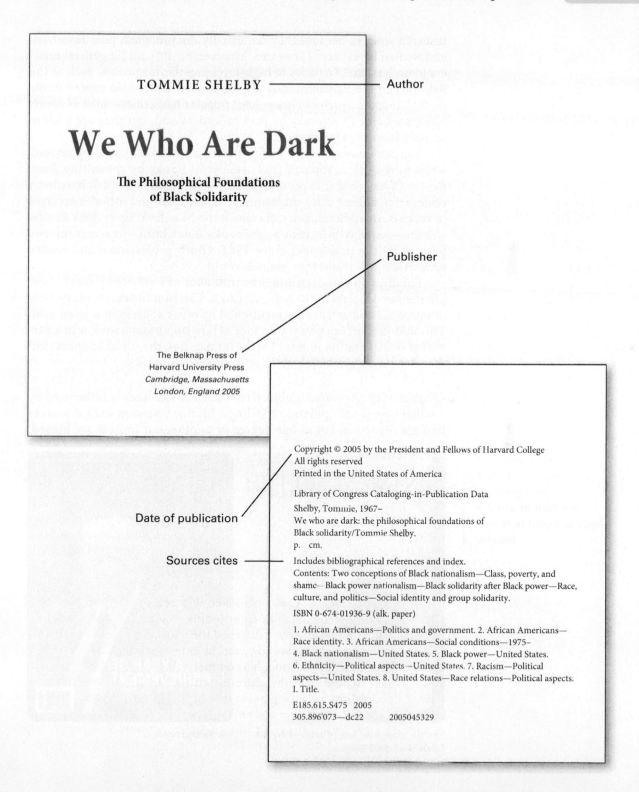

TOMMIE SHELBY ——————————— Author

We Who Are Dark

**The Philosophical Foundations
of Black Solidarity**

Publisher

The Belknap Press of
Harvard University Press
Cambridge, Massachusetts
London, England 2005

Date of publication

Sources cites

Copyright © 2005 by the President and Fellows of Harvard College
All rights reserved
Printed in the United States of America

Library of Congress Cataloging-in-Publication Data

Shelby, Tommie, 1967–
We who are dark: the philosophical foundations of
Black solidarity/Tommie Shelby.
p. cm.

Includes bibliographical references and index.
Contents: Two conceptions of Black nationalism—Class, poverty, and
shame— Black power nationalism—Black solidarity after Black power—Race,
culture, and politics—Social identity and group solidarity.

ISBN 0-674-01936-9 (alk. paper)

1. African Americans—Politics and government. 2. African Americans—
Race identity. 3. African Americans—Social conditions—1975–
4. Black nationalism—United States. 5. Black power—United States.
6. Ethnicity—Political aspects—United States. 7. Racism—Political
aspects—United States. 8. United States—Race relations—Political aspects.
I. Title.

E185.615.S475 2005
305.896'073—dc22   2005045329

research sources because they are usually documented, peer reviewed, and written by experts. (They can, however, be difficult for general readers to understand.) Articles in high-level popular magazines, such as the *Atlantic* and the *Economist*, may also be suitable—provided experts wrote them. However, articles in lower-level popular magazines—such as *Sports Illustrated* and *Time*—may be easy to understand, but they are seldom acceptable sources for research.

You can determine how well respected a source is by reading reviews written by critics. You can find reviews of books by consulting *Book Review Digest*—either in print or online—which lists books that have been reviewed in at least three magazines or newspapers and includes excerpts of reviews. In addition, you can consult the *New York Times Book Review* website—www.nytimes.com/pages/books/index.html—to access reviews printed by the newspaper since 1981. (Both professional and reader reviews are also available at Amazon.com.)

Finally, you can determine the influence of a source by seeing how often other scholars in the field refer to it. **Citation indexes** indicate how often books and articles are mentioned by other sources in a given year. This information can give you an idea of how important a work is in a particular field. Citation indexes for the humanities, the social sciences, and the sciences are available both in print and electronically.

Objectivity A source is **objective** when it is not unduly influenced by a writer's personal opinions or feelings. Ideally, you want to find sources that are objective, but to one degree or another, all sources are **biased**.

The covers of the liberal and conservative magazines shown here suggest different biases.

The New Yorker cover, June 19, 2017 by Barry Blitt, Conde Nast Publications, Inc.

The National Review

In short, all sources—especially those that take a stand on an issue—reflect the opinions of their authors, regardless of how hard they may try to be impartial. (Of course, an opinion is perfectly acceptable—as long as it is supported by evidence.)

As a researcher, you should recognize that bias exists and ask yourself whether a writer's assumptions are justified by the facts or are simply the result of emotion or preconceived ideas. You can make this determination by looking at a writer's choice of words and seeing if the language is slanted or by reviewing the writer's points and seeing if his or her argument is one-sided. Get in the habit of asking yourself whether you are being offered a legitimate point of view or simply being fed propaganda.

Currency   A source is **current** when it is up to date. (For a book, you can find the date of publication on the copyright page, as shown on page 291. For an article, you can find the date on the front cover of the magazine or journal.) If you are dealing with a scientific subject, the date of publication can be very important. Older sources might contain outdated information, so you want to use the most up-to-date source that you can find. For other subjects—literary criticism, for example—the currency of the information may not be as important as it is in the sciences.

Comprehensiveness   A source is **comprehensive** when it covers a subject in sufficient depth. The first thing to consider is whether the source deals specifically with your subject. (If it treats your subject only briefly, it will probably not be useful.) Does it treat your subject in enough detail? Does the source include the background information that you need to understand the discussion? Does the source mention other important sources that discuss your subject? Are facts and interpretations supported by the other sources you have read, or are there major points of disagreement? Finally, does the author include documentation?

How comprehensive a source needs to be depends on your purpose and audience as well as on your writing assignment. For a short essay for an introductory course, editorials from the *New York Times* or the *Wall Street Journal* might give you enough information to support your argument. If you are writing a longer essay, however, you might need to consult journal articles (and possibly books) about your subject.

Authority   A source has **authority** when a writer has the expertise to write about a subject. Always try to determine if the author is a recognized authority or simply a person who has decided to write about a particular topic. For example, what other books or articles has the author written? Has your instructor ever mentioned the author's name? Is the author mentioned in your textbook? Has the author published other works on the same subject or on related subjects? (You can find this information on Amazon.com.)

You should also determine if the author has an academic affiliation. Is he or she a faculty member at a respected college or university? Do other established scholars have a high opinion of the author? You can often find this information by using a search engine such as Google or by consulting one of the following directories:

Contemporary Authors

Directory of American Scholars

International Who's Who

National Faculty Directory

Who's Who in America

Wilson Biographies Plus Illustrated

⊜ EXERCISE 8.1 EVALUATING SOURCES

Assume that you are preparing to write an argumentative essay on the topic of whether information posted on social-networking sites threatens privacy. Read the sources that follow, and evaluate each source for accuracy, credibility, objectivity, currency, comprehensiveness, and authority.

■ Zeynep Tufekci, "The Privacy Debacle"

■ David N. Cicilline and Terrell McSweeny, "Competition Is at the Heart of Facebook's Privacy Problem"

■ Daniel Lyons, "Facebook: Privacy Problems and PR Nightmare"

This essay appeared in the January 30, 2018 issue of the *New York Times*.

THE PRIVACY DEBACLE

ZEYNEP TUFEKCI

Did you make a New Year's resolution to exercise more? Perhaps you down- 1 loaded a fitness app to help track your workouts, maybe one that allows you to share that data online with your exercise buddies?

If so, you probably checked a box to accept the app's privacy policy. For 2 most apps, the default setting is to share data with at least the company; for many apps the default is to share data with the public. But you probably didn't even notice or care. After all, what do you have to hide?

For users of the exercise app Strava, the answer turns out to be a lot more 3 than they realized. Since November, Strava has featured a global "heat map" showing where its users jogged or walked or otherwise traveled while the app was on. The map includes some three trillion GPS data points, covering more than 5 percent of the earth. Over the weekend, a number of security analysts showed that because many American military service members are Strava users, the map inadvertently reveals the locations of military bases and the movements of their personnel.

Perhaps more alarming for the military, similar patterns of movement 4 appear to possibly identify stations or airstrips in locations where the United States is not known to have such operations, as well as their supply and logistics routes. Analysts noted that with Strava's interface, it is relatively easy to identify the movements of individual soldiers not just abroad but also when they are back at home, especially if combined with other public or social media data.

> "Data privacy is not like a consumer good."

Apart from chastening the cybersecurity experts in the Pentagon, 5 the Strava debacle underscores a crucial misconception at the heart of the system of privacy protection in the United States. The privacy of data cannot be managed person-by-person through a system of individualized informed consent.

Data privacy is not like a consumer good, where you click "I accept" and 6 all is well. Data privacy is more like air quality or safe drinking water, a public good that cannot be effectively regulated by trusting in the wisdom of millions of individual choices. A more collective response is needed.

Part of the problem with the ideal of individualized informed consent 7 is that it assumes companies have the ability to inform us about the risks we are consenting to. They don't. Strava surely did not intend to reveal the GPS coordinates of a possible Central Intelligence Agency annex in Mogadishu, Somalia—but it may have done just that. Even if all technology companies meant well and acted in good faith, they would not be in a position to let you know what exactly you were signing up for.

Another part of the problem is the increasingly powerful computational 8 methods called machine learning, which can take seemingly inconsequential data about you and, combining them with other data, can discover facts about you that you never intended to reveal. For example, research shows that data as minor as your Facebook "likes" can be used to infer your sexual orientation, whether you use addictive substances, your race and your views on many political issues. This kind of computational statistical inference is not 100 percent accurate, but it can be fairly close—certainly close enough to be used to profile you for a variety of purposes.

A challenging feature of machine learning is that exactly how a given system works is opaque. Nobody—not even those who have access to the code and data—can tell what piece of data came together with what other piece of data to result in the finding the program made. This further undermines the notion of informed consent, as we do not know which data results in what privacy consequences. What we do know is that these algorithms work better the more data they have. This creates an incentive for companies to collect and store as much data as possible, and to bury the privacy ramifications, either in legalese or by playing dumb and being vague.

What can be done? There must be strict controls and regulations con- 10 cerning how all the data about us—not just the obviously sensitive bits—is collected, stored and sold. With the implications of our current data practices unknown, and with future uses of our data unknowable, data storage must move from being the default procedure to a step that is taken only when it is of demonstrable benefit to the user, with explicit consent and with clear warnings about what the company does and does not know. And there should also be significant penalties for data breaches, especially ones that result from under-investment in secure data practices, as many now do.

Companies often argue that privacy is what we sacrifice for the super- 11 computers in our pockets and their highly personalized services. This is not true. While a perfect system with no trade-offs may not exist, there are technological avenues that remain underexplored, or even actively resisted by big companies, that could allow many of the advantages of the digital world without this kind of senseless assault on our privacy.

With luck, stricter regulations and a true consumer backlash will force our 12 technological overlords to take this issue seriously and let us take back what should be ours: true and meaningful informed consent, and the right to be let alone.

This editorial was published in *WIRED* on April 24, 2018.

COMPETITION IS AT THE HEART OF FACEBOOK'S PRIVACY PROBLEM

DAVID N. CICILLINE AND TERRELL McSWEENY

Our data are being turned against us. Data powers disinformation campaigns 1 attacking democratic institutions. It is used to foment division and turn us against one another. Cambridge Analytica harvested the personal information of approximately 87 million Facebook users not just to target would-be vot-ers with campaign ads but, as former Cambridge Analytica staffer Christopher Wylie put it to the *New York Times*, to "fight a culture war in America."

Consumers are trusting companies with vast amounts of intimate data and 2 receiving very little assurance that it will be properly handled and secured. In turn, our data are used to power the connected services we use, and depending on the platform or app, are sold to advertisers. Sometimes, as in the case of Facebook, we receive services for free in exchange for our data.

But in this system individuals bear the risk that their data will be handled 3 properly—and have little recourse when it is not.

It is time for a better deal. Americans should have rights to and control over 4 their data. If we don't like a service, we should be free to move our data to another.

But Facebook's control of consumers' information and attention is 5 substantial and durable. There are more than 200 million monthly active Facebook users in the United States, and the company already owns two potential competitors—Instagram, a social photo-sharing company, and WhatsApp, a messaging service. Facebook also collects and mines consumers' data across the internet, even for consumers without Facebook accounts.

It is also difficult and time-consuming to move data between platforms.   6

The ability to control this data isn't just part of Facebook's business model; 7 it's also a vital component of creating choice, competition, and innovation online. The value of Facebook's network grows and depends on the number of people who are on it.

But unlike other networks—such as your phone company, which is required 8 to let you keep your existing phone number when switching service providers and make calls regardless of the carrier you use—Facebook and other technology companies also have the final say over whether you can take your key information to a competing service or communicate across different platforms.

The result of this asymmetry in control? The same network effect that 9 creates value for people on Facebook can also lock them into Facebook's walled garden by creating barriers to competition. People who may want to leave Facebook are less likely to do so if they aren't able to seamlessly rebuild their network of contacts, photos, and other social graph data on a competing service or communicate across services.

This friction effectively blocks new competitors—including platforms 10 that might be more protective of consumers' privacy and give consumers more control over their data—from entering the market. That's why we need pro-competitive policies that give power back to Americans through more rights and control over their data.

> "It is critical that we restore Americans' control over their data."   11

Privacy and competition are becoming increasingly interdependent conditions for protecting rights online. It is critical that we restore Americans' control over their data through data portability and interoperability requirements.

Data portability would reduce barriers to entry online by giving people 12 tools to export their network—rather than merely downloading their data—to competing platforms with the appropriate privacy safeguards in place.

Before it was acquired by Facebook, Instagram owed much of its immense 13 growth to the open APIs that allowed users of Twitter and Facebook to import their friend networks to a new, competing service.

And today, you can already use your Facebook account to import your 14 profile and contacts on Spotify and some other social apps.

Interoperability would facilitate competition by enabling communication 15 across networks in the way the Open Internet was designed to work.

The bottom line: Unless consumers gain meaningful control over their 16 personal information, there will continue to be persistent barriers to competition and choice online.

Of course, there need to be guardrails in place to protect the privacy and 17 security of users.

Legislators and regulators also need to more extensively reform data secu- 18 rity and privacy law to improve privacy, transparency, and accountability online—particularly among data brokers and credit reporting agencies like Equifax—and create more transparency in political advertisements and spending online.

But at a minimum, Americans should have real control over their data. 19 A procompetitive solution to reducing barriers to entry online will encourage platforms to compete on providing better privacy, control, and rights for consumers.

This essay was published by *Newsweek* on May 25, 2010.

FACEBOOK: PRIVACY PROBLEMS AND PR NIGHTMARE

DANIEL LYONS

Facebook's 26-year-old founder and CEO Mark Zuckerberg may be a brilliant 1 software geek, but he's lousy at public relations. In fact the most amazing thing about Facebook's current crisis over user privacy is how bad the company's PR machine is.

Instead of making things better, Facebook's spin doctors just keep making 2 things worse. Instead of restoring trust in Facebook, they just make the company seem more slippery and sneaky. Best example is an op-ed that Zuckerberg published earlier this week in the *Washington Post*, a classic piece of evasive corporate-speak that could only have been written by PR flacks.

In the op-ed, Zuckerberg pretends to believe that the biggest concern users 3 have is how complicated Facebook's privacy controls are. He vows to remedy that by making things simpler.

> "The problem is the privacy policy itself."

But the real problem isn't the com- 4 plexity of Facebook's privacy controls. The problem is the privacy policy itself. Of course Zuckerberg knows this. He's many things, but stupid isn't one of them. The real point of his essay, in fact, was that Facebook has no intention of rolling back the stuff that people are really upset about.

The company did revise its privacy policy this week, and some privacy 5 experts were appeased, while others said Facebook still has more work to do. For one thing, if you want to keep Facebook from sharing your info with Facebook apps and connected websites, you have to opt out—meaning, the default setting is you're sharing. From my perspective a better policy would just to have everything set to private, by default.

But at this point the details of the policy aren't even the real issue. The real 6 issue is one of perception, which is that sure, Facebook made some changes, but only because they had no choice. The perception is that Facebook got caught doing something wrong, and sheepishly backed down. That is the narrative that will be attached to this latest episode, and it's not a good one for Facebook.

As for that vapid op-ed earlier in the week, Facebook might also have 7 thought twice about publishing the piece in the *Washington Post*, since Donald E. Graham, chairman of the *Post*, also sits on Facebook's board of directors and has been an important mentor to Zuckerberg.

Everyone involved, including Graham himself, says nobody pulled any 8 strings, that Facebook just submitted the piece to the *Post* without Graham's knowledge, and the *Post* chose to run it because it was of interest to readers.

In other words we are asked to believe that though Graham and 9 Zuckerberg are close friends, and presumably Zuckerberg has been consulting with Graham (and other board members) over the privacy crisis, Zuckerberg and his team never mentioned to Graham the fact that Facebook was going to publish an op-ed in Graham's newspaper.

Okay. Maybe that's true. Nevertheless, of all the newspapers in the world, 10 why choose the one that's owned by one of your board members? Chalk up another clunker for the Facebook PR team.

Facebook's real problem now is that Zuckerberg and his PR reps have 11 made so many ludicrous statements that it's hard to believe anything they say. They've claimed that they're only changing privacy policies because that is what members want. They've said, when the current crisis began, that there was nothing wrong with the policy itself—the problem was simply that Facebook hadn't explained it well enough.

One gets the impression that Facebook doesn't take any of this stuff very 12 seriously. It just views the complaints as little fires that need to be put out. The statements Facebook issues aren't meant to convey any real information— they're just blasts from a verbal fire extinguisher, a cloud of words intended not to inform, but to smother.

Just keep talking, the idea seems to be, and it doesn't matter what you say. 13 In fact the more vapid and insincere you can be, the better. Eventually the world will get sick of the sound of your voice, and the whiners will give up and go away.

Of course Facebook wouldn't need to do any of this spinning if it would 14 just fix its privacy policy. It could, for example, go back to the policy it used in 2005, which said your info would only be shared with your friends.

No doubt Zuckerberg has performed a bunch of calculations, weighing 15 the cost of the bad publicity against the benefit of getting hold of all that user data. And he's decided to push on and endure the black eye.

Which tells you all you need to know about Mark Zuckerberg, and the 16 value of the information that Facebook is collecting.

⮕ EXERCISE 8.2 WRITING AN EVALUATION

Write a one- or two-paragraph evaluation of each of the three sources you read for Exercise 8.1. Be sure to support your evaluation with specific references to the sources.

Evaluating Websites

The internet is like a freewheeling frontier town in the old West. Occasionally, a federal marshal may pass through, but for the most part, there is no law and order, so you are on your own. On the internet, literally anything goes—exaggerations, misinformation, errors, and even complete fabrications. Some websites contain reliable content (for example, journal articles that are published in both print and digital format), but many do not. The main reason for this situation is that there is no authority—as there is in a college library—who evaluates sites for accuracy and trustworthiness. That job falls to you, the user.

Another problem is that websites often lack important information. For example, a site may lack a date, a sponsoring organization, or even the name of the author of the page. For this reason, it is not always easy to evaluate the material you find there.

ACCEPTABLE VERSUS UNACCEPTABLE INTERNET SOURCES

Before you use an internet source, you should consider if it is acceptable for college-level work:

Acceptable Sources

- Websites sponsored by reliable organizations, such as academic institutions, the government, and professional organizations

- Websites sponsored by academic journals and reputable magazines or newspapers

- Blogs by recognized experts in their fields

- Research forums

Unacceptable Sources

- Information on anonymous websites

- Information found in chat rooms or on discussion boards

- Personal blogs written by authors of questionable expertise

- Information on personal web pages

- Poorly written web pages

When you evaluate a website (especially when it is in the form of a blog or a series of posts), you need to begin by viewing it skeptically—unless you know for certain that it is reliable. In other words, assume that its information is questionable until you establish that it is not. Then apply the same criteria you use to evaluate any sources—*accuracy*, *credibility*, *objectivity*, *currency*, *comprehensiveness*, and *authority*.

The web page pictured on page 302 shows where to find information that can help you evaluate a website.

Accuracy Information on a website is **accurate** when it is factual and free of errors. Information in the form of facts, opinions, statistics, and interpretations is everywhere on the internet, and in the case of Wiki sites, this information is continually being rewritten and revised. Given the volume and variety of this material, it is a major challenge to determine its accuracy. You can assess the accuracy of information on a website by asking the following questions:

- **Does the site contain errors of fact?** Factual errors—inaccuracies that relate directly to the central point of the source—should immediately disqualify a site as a reliable source.

- **Does the site contain a list of references or any other type of documentation?** Reliable sources indicate where their information comes from. The authors know that people want to be sure that the information they are using is accurate and reliable. If a site provides no documentation, you should not trust the information it contains.

- **Does the site provide links to other sites?** Does the site have links to reliable websites that are created by respected authorities or sponsored by trustworthy institutions? If it does, then you can conclude that your source is at least trying to maintain a certain standard of quality.

- **Can you verify information?** A good test for accuracy is to try to verify key information on a site. You can do this by checking it in a reliable print source or on a good reference website such as Encyclopedia.com.

Credibility Information on a website is **credible** when it is believable. Just as you would not naively believe a stranger who approached you on the street, you should not automatically believe a site that you randomly encounter on the web. You can assess the credibility of a website by asking the following questions:

- **Does the site list authors, directors, or editors?** Anonymity—whether on a website or on a blog—should be a red flag for a researcher who is considering using a source.

- **Is the site refereed?** Does a panel of experts or an advisory board decide what material appears on the website? If not, what standards are used to determine the suitability of content?

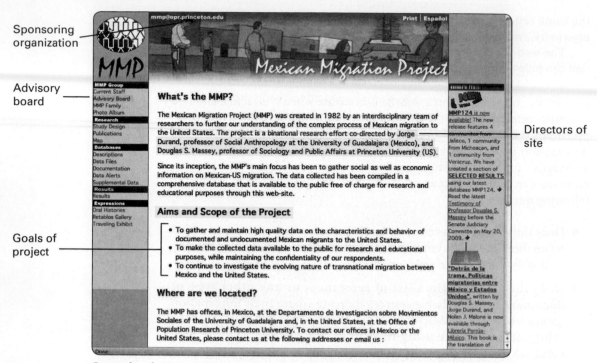

Sponsoring organization

Advisory board

Goals of project

Directors of site

Courtesy from the Mexican Migration Project, mmp.opr.princeton.edu

- **Does the site contain errors in grammar, spelling, or punctuation?** If it does, you should be on the alert for other types of errors. If the people maintaining the site do not care enough to make sure that the site is free of small errors, you have to wonder if they will take the time to verify the accuracy of the information presented.

- **Does an organization sponsor the site?** If so, do you know (or can you find out) anything about the sponsoring organization? Use a search engine such as Google to determine the purpose and point of view of the organization.

Objectivity Information on a website is **objective** when it limits the amount of **bias** that it displays. Some sites—such as those that support a particular political position or social cause—make no secret of their biases. They present them clearly in their policy statements on their home pages. Others, however, try to hide their biases—for example, by referring only to sources that support a particular point of view and not mentioning those that do not.

Keep in mind that bias does not automatically disqualify a source. It should, however, alert you to the fact that you are seeing only one side of an issue and that you will have to look further to get a complete picture. You can assess the objectivity of a website by asking the following questions:

- **Does advertising appear on the site?** If the site contains advertising, check to make sure that the commercial aspect of the site does not affect its objectivity. The site should keep advertising separate from content.

- **Does a commercial entity sponsor the site?** A for-profit company may sponsor a website, but it should not allow commercial interests to determine content. If it does, there is a conflict of interest. For example, if a site is sponsored by a company that sells organic products, it may include testimonials that emphasize the virtues of organic products and ignore information that is skeptical of their benefits.

- **Does a political organization or special-interest group sponsor the site?** Just as you would for a commercial site, you should make sure that the sponsoring organization is presenting accurate information. It is a good idea to check the information you get from a political site against information you get from an educational or a reference site— Ask.com or Encyclopedia.com, for example. Organizations have specific agendas, and you should make sure that they are not bending the truth to satisfy their own needs.

- **Does the site link to strongly biased sites?** Even if a site seems trustworthy, it is a good idea to check some of its links. Just as you can judge people by the company they keep, you can also judge websites by the sites they link to. Links to overly biased sites should cause you to reevaluate the information on the original site.

USING A SITE'S URL TO ASSESS ITS OBJECTIVITY

A website's **URL** (uniform resource locator) can give you information that can help you assess the site's objectivity.

Look at the domain name to identify sponsorship. Knowing a site's purpose can help you determine whether a site is trying to sell you something or just trying to provide information. The last part of a site's URL can tell you whether a site is a commercial site (.com and .net), an educational site (.edu), a nonprofit site (.org), or a governmental site (.gov, .mil, and so on).

See if the URL has a tilde (~) in it. A tilde in a site's URL indicates that information was published by an individual and is unaffiliated with the sponsoring organization. Individuals can have their own agendas, which may be different from the agenda of the site on which their information appears or to which it is linked.

AVOIDING CONFIRMATION BIAS

Confirmation bias is a tendency that people have to accept information that supports their beliefs and to ignore information that does not. For example, people see false or inaccurate information on websites, and because it reinforces their political or social beliefs, they forward it to others. Eventually, this information becomes so widely distributed that people assume that it is true. Numerous studies have demonstrated how prevalent confirmation bias is. Consider the following examples:

- A student doing research for a paper chooses sources that support her thesis and ignores those that take the opposite position.

- A prosecutor interviews witnesses who establish the guilt of a suspect and overlooks those who do not.

- A researcher includes statistics that confirm his hypothesis and excludes statistics that do not.

When you write an argumentative essay, do not accept information just because it supports your thesis. Realize that you have an obligation to consider all sides of an issue, not just the side that reinforces your beliefs.

Currency Information on a website is **current** when it is up-to-date. Some sources—such as fiction and poetry—are timeless and therefore are useful whatever their age. Other sources, however—such as those in the hard sciences—must be current because advances in some disciplines can quickly make information outdated. For this reason, you should be aware of the shelf life of information in the discipline you are researching and choose information accordingly. You can assess the currency of a website by asking the following questions:

- **Does the website include the date when it was last updated?** As you look at web pages, check the date on which they were created or updated. (Some websites automatically display the current date, so be careful not to confuse this date with the date the page was last updated.)

- **Are all links on the site live?** If a website is properly maintained, all the links it contains will be **live**—that is, a click on the link will take you to other websites. If a site contains a number of links that are not live, you should question its currency.

- **Is the information on the site up to date?** A site might have been updated, but this does not necessarily mean that it contains the most up-to-date information. In addition to checking when a website was last updated, look at the dates of the individual articles that appear on the site to make sure they are not outdated.

Comprehensiveness Information on a website is **comprehensive** when it covers a subject in depth. A site that presents itself as a comprehensive source should include (or link to) the most important sources of information that you need to understand a subject. (A site that leaves out a key source of information or that ignores opposing points of view cannot be called comprehensive.) You can assess the comprehensiveness of a website by asking the following questions:

- **Does the site provide in-depth coverage?** Articles in professional journals—which are available both in print and online—treat subjects in enough depth for college-level research. Other types of articles— especially those in popular magazines and in general encyclopedias, such as Wikipedia—are often too superficial (or untrustworthy) for college-level research.

- **Does the site provide information that is not available elsewhere?** The website should provide information that is not available from other sources. In other words, it should make a contribution to your knowledge and do more than simply repackage information from other sources.

- **Who is the intended audience for the site?** Knowing the target audience for a website can help you to assess a source's comprehensiveness. Is it aimed at general readers or at experts? Is it aimed at high school students or at college students? It stands to reason that a site that is aimed at experts or college students will include more detailed information than one that is aimed at general readers or high school students.

Authority Information on a website has **authority** when you can establish the legitimacy of both the author and the site. You can determine the authority of a source by asking the following questions:

- **Is the author an expert in the field that he or she is writing about?** What credentials does the author have? Does he or she have the expertise to write about the subject? Sometimes you can find this information on the website itself. For example, the site may contain an "About the Author" section or links to other publications by the author. If this information is not available, do a web search with the author's name as a keyword. If you cannot confirm the author's expertise (or if the site has no listed author), you should not use material from the site.

- **What do the links show?** What information is revealed by the links on the site? Do they lead to reputable sites, or do they take you to sites that suggest that the author has a clear bias or a hidden agenda? Do other reliable sites link back to the site you are evaluating?

- **Is the site a serious publication?** Does it include information that enables you to judge its legitimacy? For example, does it include a statement of purpose? Does it provide information that enables you to determine the criteria for publication? Does the site have a board of advisers? Are those advisers experts? Does the site include a mailing address and a phone number? Can you determine if the site is the domain of a single individual or the effort of a group of individuals?

- **Does the site have a sponsor?** If so, is the site affiliated with a reputable institutional sponsor, such as a governmental, educational, or scholarly organization?

⊙ EXERCISE 8.3 CONSIDERING TWO HOME PAGES

Consider the following two home pages—one from the website for the *Chronicle of Higher Education*, a publication aimed at college instructors and administrators, and the other from the website for *Glamour*, a publication aimed at general readers. Assume that on both websites, you have found articles about privacy and social-networking sites. Locate and label the information on each home page that would enable you to determine the suitability of using information from the site in your paper.

CULTURE

Miss Universe Is Making History With the Pageant's First Openly Trans Contestant

HERE'S A TIP

This Is Exactly How Much You Should Tip When You Stay at a Hotel

UNLIKELY EXPERTS

The Best Beauty Gifts to Give, According to QVC Experts

➔ EXERCISE 8.4 CONSIDERING TWO MISSION STATEMENTS

Here are the **mission statements**—statements of the organizations' purposes—from the websites for the *Chronicle of Higher Education* and *Glamour*, whose home pages you considered in Exercise 8.3. What

The Chronicle of Higher Education

The Chronicle of Higher Education has the nation's largest newsroom dedicated to covering colleges and universities. As the unrivaled leader in higher education journalism, we serve our readers with indispensable real-time news and deep insights, plus the essential tools, career opportunities, and knowledge to succeed in a rapidly changing world.

Our award-winning journalism is well-known at colleges and universities: More than 2 million people visit our website every month, and 1,650 organizations across the country make our journalism available to every one of their employees and students. Our newsroom is home to top experts in higher education who contribute to the ongoing conversation on the issues that matter.

The Chronicle, a privately owned, independent news and information organization, was founded in 1966 and originally owned by a nonprofit, Editorial Projects in Education. EPE sold The Chronicle in 1978 to Jack Crowl and Corbin Gwaltney, and The Chronicle of Higher Education Inc. was formed. Gwaltney bought the entire company in 1990, and he is co-chair of its board of directors, along with his wife, Pamela Gwaltney. The Chronicle of Higher Education Inc. publishes *The Chronicle of Higher Education, The Chronicle of Philanthropy, Arts & Letters Daily,* and *The Chronicle Review.*

Learn More About:

Account & Subscription FAQ

Community Guidelines

Copyright and Reprints

Submissions

Privacy Policy

How to Pitch Us

More Information

Advertise

Contact Us

Employment Opportunities

Internships

Newsletters

Subscribe

The Chronicle Store

The Chronicle of Philanthropy

The Chronicle of Philanthropy is an independent news organization that has been serving leaders, fundraisers, grant makers, and others involved in the philanthropic enterprise for almost 30 years. It offers a robust advice section to help nonprofit workers do their jobs as well as one of the biggest listings of career opportunities.

The Chronicle updates its website throughout the day and appears 12 times per year in print.

GLAMOUR

About Glamour

glamour.com

Glamour is one of the biggest fashion and beauty media brands in the world, currently reaching an all-time high of one out of eight American women, with 9.7 million print readers, more than 11 million unique monthly users online, and over 14 million followers across social media platforms. Glamour believes in the power of women being themselves and stands with women as they do their own thing: honestly, authentically, and awesomely. Across every platform, Glamour is the ultimate authority for the next generation of changemakers.

Editor-in-Chief
Samantha Barry

Chief Business Officer
Susan Plagemann

additional information can you get from these mission statements? How do they help you to evaluate the sites as well as the information that might appear on the sites?

⊙ EXERCISE 8.5 EVALUATING MATERIAL FROM WEBSITES

Each of the following sources was found on a website: Bart Lazar, "Why We Need a Privacy Label on the Internet," page 308; Douglass Rushkoff, "You Are Not Facebook's Customer," page 309; and Igor Kuksov, "All Ears: The Dangers of Voice Assistants," page 309.

Assume that you are preparing to write an essay on the topic of whether information posted on social-networking sites threatens privacy. First, visit the websites on which the articles below appear, and evaluate each site for accuracy, credibility, objectivity, currency, comprehensiveness, and authority. Then, using the same criteria, evaluate each source.

This piece appeared on Politico on April 25, 2018.

WHY WE NEED A PRIVACY LABEL ON THE INTERNET

BART LAZAR

As Facebook and other internet companies deal with the fallout from security 1 lapses before and after the presidential election, lawmakers are increasingly concerned that lax oversight is resulting in major violations of Americans' privacy. When Facebook CEO Mark Zuckerberg testified before two committees earlier this month, even GOP lawmakers typically opposed to regulations said new rules to restrict the actions of Facebook and other internet companies may be necessary.

To finish reading this article and evaluate its source, Google search for Bart 2
Lazar's "Why We Need a Privacy Label on the Internet" or go to: https://www
.politico.com/agenda/story/2018/04/25/internet-privacy-label-000656.

This article was posted to Douglass Rushkoff's personal website.

YOU ARE NOT FACEBOOK'S CUSTOMER

DOUGLASS RUSHKOFF

The ire and angst accompanying Facebook's most recent tweaks to its interface 1
are truly astounding. The complaints rival the irritation of AOL's dial-up users
back in the mid-'90s, who were getting too many busy signals when they tried
to get online. The big difference, of course, is that AOL's users were paying
customers. In the case of Facebook, which we don't even pay to use, we aren't
the customers at all.

To continue reading this article and evaluate its source, Google search 2
for Douglass Rushkoff's "You Are Not Facebook's Customer" or go to:
www.rushkoff.com/you-are-not-facebooks-customer/.

This article originally appeared on Kaspersky Lab's website on February 28, 2017.

ALL EARS: THE DANGERS OF VOICE ASSISTANTS

IGOR KUKSOV

Nowadays the proverb "the walls have ears" is not as metaphoric as it used 1
to be.

"The telescreen received and transmitted simultaneously. Any sound that 2
Winston made, above the level of a very low whisper, would be picked up by
it. . . . There was of course no way of knowing whether you were being watched
at any given moment." That is George Orwell's description of Big Brother's
spying devices in the novel *1984*.

To continue reading this article and evaluate its source, Google search 3
for Igor Kuksov's "All Ears: The Dangers of Voice Assistants" or go to:
www.kaspersky.com/blog/voice-recognition-threats/14134/.

⊘ EXERCISE 8.6 EVALUATING A BLOG POST

Read the blog post below and then answer the questions on page 311.

This article first appeared on Mashable.com on February 6, 2012.

SHOULD ATHLETES HAVE SOCIAL MEDIA PRIVACY? ONE BILL SAYS YES

SAM LAIRD

Should universities be allowed to force student athletes to have their Facebook 1 and Twitter accounts monitored by coaches and administrators?

No, says a bill recently introduced into the Maryland state legislature. 2

The bill would prohibit institutions "from requiring a student or an appli- 3 cant for admission to provide access to a personal account or service through an electronic communications device"—by sharing usernames, passwords, or unblocking private accounts, for example.

Introduced on Thursday, Maryland's 4 Senate Bill 434 would apply to all students but particularly impact college sports. Student-athletes' social media accounts are frequently monitored by authority figures for instances of indecency or impropriety, especially in high-profile sports like football and men's basketball.

> "Student-athletes' social media accounts are frequently monitored."

In one example, a top football recruit reportedly put his scholarship hopes 5 in jeopardy last month after a series of inappropriate tweets.

The bill's authors say that it is one of the first in the country to take on the 6 issue of student privacy in the social media age, according to the *New York Times*.

Bradley Shear is a Maryland lawyer whose work frequently involves sports 7 and social media. In a recent post to his blog, Shear explained his support for Senate Bill 434 and a similar piece of legislation that would further extend students' right to privacy on social media.

"Schools that require their students to turn over their social media user 8 names and/or content are acting as though they are based in China and not in the United States," Shear wrote.

But legally increasing student-athletes' option to social media privacy 9 could also help shield the schools themselves from potential lawsuits.

On his blog, Shear uses the example of Yardley Love, a former Univer- 10 sity of Virginia women's lacrosse player who was allegedly murdered by her ex-boyfriend, who played for the men's lacrosse team.

If the university was monitoring the lacrosse teams' social media accounts 11 and missed anything that could have indicated potential violence, it "may have had significant legal liability for negligent social media monitoring because it failed to protect Love," Shear wrote.

On the other hand, if the school was only monitoring the accounts of its 12 higher-profile football and basketball players, Shear wrote, then that could have been considered discrimination and the university "may have been sued for not monitoring the electronic content of all of its students."

Do you think universities should be allowed to force their athletes into 13 allowing coaches and administrators to monitor their Facebook and Twitter accounts?

Questions

1. What steps would you take to determine whether Laird's information is accurate?

2. How could you determine whether Laird is respected in his field?

3. Is Laird's blog written for an audience that is knowledgeable about his subject? How can you tell?

4. Do you think this blog post is a suitable research source? Why or why not?

5. This blog post was written in 2012. Do you think it is still relevant today? Why or why not?

...privacy is a function of liberty.

-Edward Snowden

This installation on Alcatraz Island from artist Ai Weiwei features a quotation from Edward Snowden, who became a notorious figure after leaking classified information about potentially privacy-invading surveillance programs to the public. AP Images/Eric Risberg

CHAPTER

9

Summarizing, Paraphrasing, Quoting, and Synthesizing Sources

AT ISSUE

Is Technology a Serious Threat to Our Privacy? (continued)

In Chapter 8, you learned how to evaluate sources for an essay about the dangers of posting personal information online. In this chapter, you will learn how to take notes from sources that address this issue.

As you saw in Chapter 8, before you can decide what material to use to support your arguments, you need to evaluate a variety of potential sources. After you decide which sources you will use, you can begin thinking about where you might use each source. Then, you will need to consider how to integrate information from the sources you have chosen into your essay in the form of *summary*, *paraphrase*, and *quotation*. When you actually write your argument, you will *synthesize* source material into your essay, blending information from your sources with your own ideas and interpretations (as the student writer did when she wrote the MLA research paper in Chapter 10).

Summarizing Sources

A **summary** restates the main idea of a passage (or even of an entire book or article) in concise terms. Because a summary does not include the examples or explanations in the source, and because it omits the original source's rhetorical strategies and stylistic devices, it is always much shorter than the original. Usually, in fact, it consists of just a sentence or two.

WHEN TO SUMMARIZE

Summarize when you want to give readers a general sense of a passage's main idea or a source's position on an issue.

When you summarize information, you do not include your own opinions, but you do use your own words and phrasing, not those of your source. If you want to use a particularly distinctive word or phrase from your source, you may do so—but you must always place such words in quotation marks and **document** them. If you do not, you will be committing **plagiarism**. (See Chapter 10 for information on documenting sources; see Chapter 11 for information on avoiding plagiarism by using sources responsibly.)

The following paragraph appeared in a newspaper opinion essay.

ORIGINAL SOURCE

When everyone has a blog, a MySpace page, or Facebook entry, everyone is a publisher. When everyone has a cellphone with a camera in it, everyone is a paparazzo. When everyone can upload video on YouTube, everyone is a filmmaker. When everyone is a publisher, paparazzo, or filmmaker, everyone else is a public figure. We're all public figures now. The blogosphere has made the global discussion so much richer—and each of us so much more transparent. ("The Whole World Is Watching," Thomas L. Friedman, *New York Times*, June 27, 2007, p. 23)

The following effective summary conveys a general but accurate sense of the original paragraph without using the source's phrasing or including the writer's own opinions. (One distinctive and hard-to-reword phrase is placed in quotation marks.) Parenthetical documentation identifies the source of the material.

EFFECTIVE SUMMARY

The popularity of blogs, social-networking sites, cell phone cameras, and YouTube has enhanced the "global discussion" but made it very hard for people to remain anonymous (Friedman 23).

Notice that this one-sentence summary is much shorter than the original passage and that it does not include all the original's examples. Still, it accurately communicates a general sense of the original paragraph's main idea.

The following summary is not acceptable. Not only does it express the student writer's opinion, but it also uses the source's exact words without putting them in quotation marks or providing documentation. (This constitutes plagiarism.)

> **UNACCEPTABLE SUMMARY**
>
> It seems to me that nowadays blogs, social-networking sites, cell phone cameras, and YouTube are everywhere, and what this means is that we're all public figures now.

SUMMARIZING SOURCES

Do

- Convey the main idea of the original passage.

- Be concise.

- Use your own original words and phrasing.

- Place any distinctive words borrowed from your source in quotation marks.

- Include documentation.

Do not

- Include your own analysis or opinions.

- Include digressions.

- Argue with your source.

- Use your source's syntax or phrasing (unless you are quoting).

⊘ EXERCISE 9.1 WRITING A SUMMARY

Write a two-sentence summary of the following passage. Then, edit your summary so that it is only one sentence long. Be sure your summary conveys the main idea of the original passage and includes proper documentation (see Chapter 10).

> Make sure you represent your best self on any social network. On LinkedIn, that means crafting a professional persona. On Facebook, Snapchat, Instagram, and Twitter, even if you're mainly interacting with friends, don't forget that posts may still be public.
>
> According to a CareerBuilder.com survey, 60 percent of employers research job candidates on social media, and over half are reluctant to hire candidates with no online presence. They're mainly looking for professionalism, whether you're a fit for the company and proof of qualifications.

If your social media profiles show you in that light, you're golden. (Alice Underwood, "9 Things to Avoid on Social Media While Looking for a New Job," *Glassdoor*, 3 Jan., 2018)

Paraphrasing Sources

A **paraphrase** is different from a summary. While a summary gives a general overview of the original, a paraphrase presents the source's ideas in detail, including its main idea, its key supporting points, and perhaps even its examples. For this reason, a paraphrase is longer than a summary. (In fact, it may be as long as the original.)

WHEN TO PARAPHRASE

Paraphrase when you want to communicate the key points discussed in a source—particularly a complex or complicated passage—in clear, accessible language.

Like a summary, a paraphrase uses your own words and phrasing, not the language and syntax of the original. Any distinctive words or phrases from your source must be placed in quotation marks. When you paraphrase, you may not always follow the order of the original source's ideas, but you should try to convey the writer's emphasis and most important points.

The following paragraph is from an editorial that appeared in a student newspaper.

ORIGINAL SOURCE

Additionally, as graduates retain their Facebook accounts, employers are increasingly able to use Facebook as an evaluation tool when making hiring decisions. Just as companies sometimes incorporate social functions into their interview process to see if potential hires can handle themselves responsibly, they may also check out a student's Facebook account to see how the student chooses to present him or herself. This may seem shady and underhanded, but one must understand that social networks are not anonymous; whatever one chooses to post will be available to all. Even if someone goes to great pains to keep an employer-friendly profile, his or her friends may still tag pictures of him or her which will be available to whoever wants to see them. Not only can unexpected Facebook members get information by viewing one's profile, but a user's personal information can also leak out by merely registering for the service. Both the user agreement and the privacy policy indicate that Facebook can give information to third parties and can supplement its data with information from newspapers, blogs, and instant messages. ("Beware What You Post on Facebook," *The Tiger*, Clemson University, August 4, 2006)

The following paraphrase reflects the original paragraph's emphasis and clearly communicates its key points.

EFFECTIVE PARAPHRASE

As an editorial in *The Tiger* observes, because students keep their accounts at social-networking sites after they graduate, potential employers can use the information they find there to help them evaluate candidates' qualifications. This process is comparable to the way a company might evaluate an applicant in person in a social situation. Some people may see the practice of employers checking applicants' Facebook pages as "shady and underhanded," but these sites are not intended to be anonymous or private. For example, a person may try to maintain a profile that will be appropriate for employers, but friends may post inappropriate pictures. Also, people can reveal personal information not only in profiles but also simply by registering with Facebook. Finally, as Facebook states in its membership information, it can supply information to others as well as provide data from other sources. ("Beware")

Notice that this paraphrase includes many of the details presented in the original passage and quotes a distinctive phrase, but its style and sentence structure are different from those of the original.

The following paraphrase is not acceptable because its phrasing and sentence structure are too close to the original. It also borrows words and phrases from the source without attribution and does not include documentation.

UNACCEPTABLE PARAPHRASE

As more and more college graduates keep their Facebook accounts, employers are increasingly able to use them as evaluation tools when they decide whom to hire. Companies sometimes set up social functions during the interview process to see how potential hires handle themselves; in the same way, they can consult a Facebook page to see how an applicant presents himself or herself. This may seem underhanded, but after all, Facebook is not anonymous; its information is available to all. Many people try to keep their profiles employer friendly, but their friends sometimes tag pictures of them that employers will be able to see. Besides, students' personal information is available not just on their profiles but also in the form they fill out when they register. Finally, according to their user agreement and their privacy policy, Facebook can give information to third parties and also add data from other sources.

PARAPHRASING SOURCES

Do

- Convey the source's ideas fully and accurately.

- Use your own words and phrasing.

- Convey the emphasis of the original.

- Simplify and clarify complex language and syntax.

- Put any distinctive words borrowed from the source in quotation marks.

- Include documentation.

Do not

- Use the exact words or phrasing of your source (unless you are quoting).

- Include your own analysis or opinions.

- Argue with or contradict your source.

- Wander from the topic of the source.

⊜ EXERCISE 9.2 COMPARING SUMMARY AND PARAPHRASE

Write a paraphrase of the passage you summarized in Exercise 9.1. How is your paraphrase different from your summary?

⊜ EXERCISE 9.3 WRITING A PARAPHRASE

The following paragraph is from the same Clemson University student newspaper article that was excerpted on pages 316–17. Read the paragraph, and then write a paraphrase that communicates its key ideas. Before you begin, circle any distinctive words and phrases that might be difficult to paraphrase, and consider whether you should quote them. Be sure to include documentation. (See Chapter 10.)

> All these factors make clear the importance of two principles: Responsibility and caveat emptor. First, people should be responsible about how they portray themselves and their friends, and employers, authorities, and the owners must approach this information responsibly and fairly. Second, "let the buyer beware" applies to all parties involved. Facebook users need to understand the potential consequences of the information they share, and outside viewers need to understand that the material on Facebook is often only a humorous, lighthearted presentation of one aspect of a person. Facebook is an incredibly valuable communications tool that will link the college generation more tightly than any before it, but users have to understand that, like anything good in life, they have to be aware of the downsides.

Quoting Sources

When you **quote** words from a source, you need to quote accurately—that is, every word and every punctuation mark in your quotation must match the source *exactly*. You also need to be sure that your quotation conveys the meaning its author intended and that you are not distorting the meaning by **quoting out of context** or by omitting an essential part of the passage you are quoting.

WHEN TO QUOTE

Quote a source's words only in the following situations:

- Quote when your source's words are distinctive or memorable.

- Quote when your source's words are so direct and concise that a paraphrase would be awkward or wordy.

- Quote when your source's words add authority or credibility to your argument (for example, when your source is a well-known expert on your topic).

- Quote a point when you will go on to refute it.

Remember, quoting from a source adds interest to your paper—but only when the writer's words are compelling. Too many quotations—especially long quotations—distract readers and make it difficult for them to follow your discussion. Quote only when you must. If you include too many quotations, your paper will be a patchwork of other people's words, not an original, unified whole.

QUOTING SOURCES

Do

- Enclose borrowed words in quotation marks.
- Quote accurately.
- Include documentation.

Do not

- Quote out of context.
- Distort the source's meaning.
- Include too many quotations.

⊘ EXERCISE 9.4 IDENTIFYING MATERIAL TO QUOTE

Read the following paragraphs from a newspaper column. (The full text of this column appears in Exercise 9.5.) If you were going to use these paragraphs as source material for an argumentative essay, which particular words or phrases do you think you might want to quote? Why?

> How do users not know that a server somewhere is recording where you are, what you ate for lunch, how often you post photos of your puppy, what you bought at the supermarket for dinner, the route you drove home, and what movie you watched before you went to bed?
>
> So why do we act so surprised and shocked about the invasion of the privacy we so willingly relinquish, and the personal information we forfeit that allows its captors to sell us products, convict us in court, get us fired, or produce more of the same banality that keeps us logging on?
>
> We, all of us, are digital captives. (Shelley Fralic, "Don't Fall for the Myths about Online Privacy," *Calgary Herald*, October 17, 2015.)

⊘ EXERCISE 9.5 SUMMARY AND PARAPHRASE: ADDITIONAL PRACTICE

Read the newspaper column that follows, and highlight it to identify its most important ideas. (For information on highlighting, see Chapter 2.) Then, write a summary of one paragraph and a paraphrase of another paragraph. Assume that this column is a source for an essay you are writing on the topic, "Is Technology a Serious Threat to Our Privacy?" Be sure to include documentation.

This column is from the *Calgary Herald*, where it appeared on page 1 on October 17, 2015.

DON'T FALL FOR THE MYTHS ABOUT ONLINE PRIVACY

SHELLEY FRALIC

[handwritten note: 7-9 billion?]

If you are a Facebooker—and there are 1.5 billion of us on the planet, so chances are about one in five that you are—you will have noticed yet another round of posts that suggest in quasi-legalese that you can somehow block the social network's invasion of your privacy.

This latest hoax cautions that Facebook will now charge $5.99 to keep privacy settings private, and the copyright protection disclaimers making the rounds this week typically begin like this: "As of date-and-time here, I do not give Facebook or any entities associated with Facebook permission to use my pictures, information, or posts, both past and future. By this statement, I give notice to Facebook it is strictly forbidden to disclose, copy, distribute, or take any other action against me based on this profile and/or its contents. The content of this profile is private and confidential information."

Well, no, it's not. 3

This is a new-age version of an old story, oft-told. No one reads the fine 4 print. Not on contracts, not on insurance policies, and not on social media sites that are willingly and globally embraced by perpetually plugged-in gossipmongers, lonely hearts, news junkies, inveterate sharers, and selfie addicts.

Facebook's fine print, like that of many internet portals, is specific and 5 offers users a variety of self-selected "privacy" options.

But to think that any interaction with it, and its ilk, is truly private is 6 beyond absurd.

How can there still be people out there who still don't get that Netflix and 7 Facebook, Instagram and Twitter, Google and Tinder, and pretty much every keystroke or communication we register on a smartphone or laptop, not to mention a loyalty card and the GPS in your car, are constantly tracking and sifting and collating everything we do?

How do users not know that a server somewhere is recording where you 8 are, what you ate for lunch, how often you post photos of your puppy, what you bought at the supermarket for dinner, the route you drove home, and what movie you watched before you went to bed?

So why do we act so surprised and shocked about the invasion of the 9 privacy we so willingly relinquish, and the personal information we forfeit that allows its captors to sell us products, convict us in court, get us fired, or produce more of the same banality that keeps us logging on?

We, all of us, are digital captives. 10

But do we have to be so stupid about it? 11

And the bigger question is this: If we, the adults who should know better, 12 don't get it, what are we teaching our kids about the impact and repercussions of their online lives? What are they learn-ing about the voluntary and wholesale abandonment of their privacy? What are we teaching them about "sharing" with strangers?

> "We, all of us, are digital captives."

Worried about future generations not reading books or learning how to 13 spell properly or write in cursive? Worry more, folks, that internet ignorance is the new illiteracy.

Meantime, when another Facebook disclaimer pops up with a plea 14 to share, consider this clever post from a user who actually read the fine print:

"I hereby give my permission to the police, the NSA, the FBI and CIA, 15 the Swiss Guard, the Priory of Scion, the inhabitants of Middle Earth, Agents Mulder and Scully, the Goonies, ALL the Storm Troopers and Darth Vader, the Mad Hatter, Chuck Norris, S.H.I.E.L.D., The Avengers, The Illuminati . . . to view all the amazing and interesting things I publish on Facebook. I'm aware that my privacy ended the very day that I created a profile on Facebook."

Yes, it did. 16

Working Source Material into Your Argument

When you use source material in an argumentative essay, your goal is to integrate the material smoothly into your discussion, blending summary, paraphrase, and quotation with your own ideas.

To help readers follow your discussion, you need to indicate the source of each piece of information clearly and distinguish your own ideas from those of your sources. Never simply drop source material into your discussion. Whenever possible, introduce quotations, paraphrases, and summaries with an **identifying tag** (sometimes called a *signal phrase*), a phrase that identifies the source, and always follow them with documentation. This practice helps readers identify the boundaries between your own ideas and those of your sources.

It is also important that you include clues to help readers understand why you are using a particular source and what the exact relationship is between your source material and your own ideas. For example, you may be using a source to support a point you are making or to contradict another source.

Using Identifying Tags

Using identifying tags to introduce your summaries, paraphrases, or quotations will help you to accomplish the goals discussed above (and also help you to avoid accidental plagiarism).

SUMMARY WITH IDENTIFYING TAG
<u>According to Thomas L. Friedman</u>, the popularity of blogs, social-networking sites, cell phone cameras, and YouTube has enhanced the "global discussion" but made it hard for people to remain anonymous (23).

Note that you do not always have to place the identifying tag at the beginning of the summarized, paraphrased, or quoted material. You can also place it in the middle or at the end:

IDENTIFYING TAG AT THE BEGINNING
<u>Thomas L. Friedman notes</u> that the popularity of blogs, social-networking sites, cell phone cameras, and YouTube has enhanced the "global discussion" but made it hard for people to remain anonymous (23).

IDENTIFYING TAG IN THE MIDDLE
The popularity of blogs, social-networking sites, cell phone cameras, and YouTube, <u>Thomas L. Friedman observes</u>, has enhanced the "global discussion" but made it hard for people to remain anonymous (23).

IDENTIFYING TAG AT THE END
The popularity of blogs, social-networking sites, cell phone cameras, and YouTube has enhanced the "global discussion" but made it hard for people to remain anonymous, <u>Thomas L. Friedman points out (23)</u>.

TEMPLATES FOR USING IDENTIFYING TAGS

To avoid repeating phrases like *he says* in identifying tags, try using some of the following verbs to introduce your source material. (You can also use "According to . . . ," to introduce a source.)

For Summaries or Paraphrases

[Name of writer]	notes	acknowledges	proposes	that <u>[summary or paraphrase]</u>.
The writer	suggests	believes	observes	
The article	explains	comments	warns	
The essay	reports	points out	predicts	
	implies	concludes	states	

For Quotations

As [name of writer]	notes,	acknowledges,	proposes,	"_____[quotation]_____."
As the writer	suggests,	believes,	observes,	
As the article	warns,	reports,	points out,	
As the essay	predicts,	implies,	concludes,	
	states,	explains,		

Working Quotations into Your Sentences

When you use quotations in your essays, you may need to edit them—for example, by adding, changing, or deleting words—to provide context or to make them fit smoothly into your sentences. If you do edit a quotation, be careful not to distort the source's meaning.

Adding or Changing Words When you add or change words in a quotation, use **brackets** to indicate your edits.

ORIGINAL QUOTATION
"Twitter, Facebook, Flickr, FourSquare, Fitbit, and the SenseCam give us a simple choice: participate or fade into a lonely obscurity" (Cashmore).

WORDS ADDED FOR CLARIFICATION

As Cashmore observes, "Twitter, Flickr, FourSquare, Fitbit, and the SenseCam [as well as similar social-networking sites] give us a simple choice: participate or fade into a lonely obscurity."

ORIGINAL QUOTATION

"The blogosphere has made the global discussion so much richer—and each of us so much more transparent" (Friedman 23).

WORDS CHANGED TO MAKE VERB TENSE LOGICAL

As Thomas L. Friedman explains, increased access to cell phone cameras, YouTube, and the like continues to "[make] the global discussion so much richer—and each of us so much more transparent" (23).

Deleting Words When you delete words from a quotation, use **ellipses**—three spaced periods—to indicate your edits. However, never use ellipses to indicate a deletion at the beginning of a quotation.

ORIGINAL QUOTATION

"Just as companies sometimes incorporate social functions into their interview process to see if potential hires can handle themselves responsibly, they may also check out a student's Facebook account to see how the student chooses to present him or herself" ("Beware").

UNNECESSARY WORDS DELETED

"Just as companies sometimes incorporate social functions into their interview process, . . . they may also check out a student's Facebook account . . ." ("Beware").

DISTORTING QUOTATIONS

Be careful not to distort a source's meaning when you add, change, or delete words from a quotation. In the following example, the writer intentionally deletes material from the original quotation that would weaken his argument.

Original Quotation

"This incident is by no means an isolated one. Connecticut authorities are investigating reports that seven girls were sexually assaulted by older men they met online" ("Beware").

Distorted

"This incident is by no means an isolated one. [In fact,] seven girls were sexually assaulted by older men" they met online ("Beware").

⊖ EXERCISE 9.6 INTEGRATING QUOTED MATERIAL

Look back at "Don't Fall for the Myths about Online Privacy" (p. 320). Select three quotations from this essay. Then, integrate each quotation into an original sentence, taking care to place the quoted material in quotation marks. Be sure to acknowledge your source in an identifying tag and to integrate the quoted material smoothly into each sentence.

⊖ EXERCISE 9.7 INTEGRATING SUMMARIES AND PARAPHRASES

Reread the summary you wrote for Exercise 9.1 and the paraphrase you wrote for Exercise 9.3. Add three different identifying tags to each, varying the verbs you use and the position of the tags. Then, check to make sure you have used correct parenthetical documentation. (If the author's name is included in the identifying tag, it should not also appear in the parenthetical citation.)

Synthesizing Sources

When you write a **synthesis**, you combine summary, paraphrase, and quotation from several sources with your own ideas to support an original conclusion. You use a synthesis to identify similarities and differences among ideas, indicating where sources agree and disagree and how they support or challenge one another's ideas. In a synthesis, transitional words and phrases should identify points of similarity (*also, like, similarly,* and so on) or difference (*however, in contrast,* and so on). Identifying tags and parenthetical documentation should identify each piece of information from a source and distinguish your sources' ideas from one another and from your own ideas.

The following effective synthesis is excerpted from the student paper in Chapter 10. Note how the synthesis blends information from three sources with the student's own ideas to support her point about how the internet has affected people's concepts of "public" and "private."

EFFECTIVE SYNTHESIS

Part of the problem is that the internet has fundamentally altered our notions of "private" and "public" in ways that we are only just beginning to understand. As Shelley Fralic observes in "Don't Fall for the Myths about Online Privacy," Facebook's privacy options do not really protect its users' privacy. On sites like Facebook, people often reveal intimate details of their lives to hundreds—perhaps even thousands—of strangers. This situation is unprecedented and, at least for the foreseeable future, irreversible. The French artist, film producer, and fashion designer Maripol has noted, "Andy Warhol said that everyone will be famous for fifteen minutes, but with social

— Student's original point

— Paraphrase

— Student's own ideas

— Quotation

Student's evaluation
of source

Quotation

media, everyone is famous all of the time" (qtd. in Hanra). In essence, we are all exhibitionists now, to some degree and our private lives are on display as never before. Given the changes in our understanding of privacy and the public nature of the internet, the suggestion that we should live our lives by the same rules we lived by thirty years ago simply does not make sense. As *New York Times* columnist Thomas Friedman noted prophetically in 2007, in the internet age, more and more of "what you say or do or write will end up as a digital fingerprint that never gets erased" (23).

Compare the effective synthesis above with the following unacceptable synthesis.

UNACCEPTABLE SYNTHESIS

"The sheer volume of personal information that people are publishing online—and the fact that some of it could remain visible permanently—is changing the nature of personal privacy." On sites like Facebook, people can reveal the most intimate details of their lives to millions of total strangers. This development is unprecedented and, at least for the foreseeable future, irreversible. "When everyone has a blog . . . or Facebook entry, everyone is a publisher. . . . When everyone is a publisher, paparazzo, or filmmaker, everyone else is a public figure" (Friedman 23). Given the changes in our understanding of privacy and the essentially public nature of the internet, the analogy that David Hall makes in an essay about online behavior and workplace discrimination between an online post and a private conversation seems to be of limited use. In the internet age, more and more of "what you say or do or write will end up as a digital fingerprint that never gets erased."

Unlike the effective synthesis, the preceding unacceptable synthesis does not begin with a topic sentence that introduces the point the source material in the paragraph will support. Instead, it opens with an out-of-context quotation whose source (an essay by Alison George in *New Scientist*) is not identified. This quotation could have been paraphrased—its wording is not particularly memorable—and, more important, it should have been accompanied by documentation. (If source information is not provided, the writer is committing plagiarism even if the borrowed material is set in quotation marks.) The second quotation, although it includes parenthetical documentation (Friedman 23), is dropped into the paragraph without an identifying tag; the third quotation, also from the Friedman article, is not documented at all, making it appear to be from Hall. All in all, the paragraph is not a smoothly connected synthesis but a string of unconnected ideas. It does not use sources effectively and responsibly, and it does not cite them appropriately.

SYNTHESIZING SOURCES

Do

- Combine summary, paraphrase, and quotations from sources with your own ideas.

- Place borrowed words and phrases in quotation marks.

- Introduce source material with identifying tags.

- Document material from your sources.

Do not

- Drop source material into your synthesis without providing context.

- String random pieces of information together without supplying transitions to connect them.

- Cram too many pieces of information into a single paragraph; in most cases, two or three sources per paragraph (plus your own comments) will be sufficient.

⊘ EXERCISE 9.8 WRITING A SYNTHESIS

Write a synthesis that builds on the paraphrase you wrote for Exercise 9.2. Add your own original ideas—examples and opinions—to the paraphrase, and also blend in information from one or two of the other sources that appear in this chapter. Use identifying tags and parenthetical documentation to introduce your sources and to distinguish your own ideas from ideas expressed in your sources.

⊘ EXERCISE 9.9 INTEGRATING VISUAL ARGUMENTS

Suppose you were going to use this chapter's opening image of the Ai Weiwei art installation (p. 312) as a visual argument in an essay about whether technology poses a threat to our privacy, possibly taking into account the artist's personal history. Write a paragraph in which you introduce the image, briefly describe it, and explain its relevance to your essay's topic and how it supports your position.

10

Documenting Sources: MLA

When you are building an argument, you use sources for support. To acknowledge the material you borrow and to help readers evaluate your sources, you need to supply documentation. In other words, you need to tell readers where you found your information. If you use documentation responsibly, you will also avoid **plagiarism**, an ethical offense with serious consequences. (See Chapter 11 for more on plagiarism.)

WHY DOCUMENT SOURCES?

- To acknowledge the debt that you owe to your sources
- To demonstrate that you are familiar with the conventions of academic discourse
- To enable readers to judge the quality of your research
- To avoid plagiarism
- To make your argument more convincing

MLA documentation consists of two parts: **parenthetical references** in the text of your paper and a **works-cited list** at the end of the paper. (The references are keyed to the works-cited list.)

Using Parenthetical References

The basic parenthetical citation consists of the author's last name and a page number:

(Fielding 213)

If the author is referred to in the sentence, include only the page number in the parenthetical reference.

> According to environmental activist Brian Fielding, the number of species affected is much higher (213).

Here are some other situations you may encounter:

- When referring to a work by two authors, include both authors' names.

  (Stange and Hogarth 53)

- When citing a work with no listed author, include a short version of the title.

  ("Small Things" 21)

- When citing a source that is quoted in another source, indicate this by including the abbreviation *qtd. in.*

  According to Kevin Kelly, this narrow approach is typical of the "hive mind" (qtd. in Doctorow 168).

- When citing two or more works by the same author, include a short title after the author's name.

  (Anderson, *Long Tail* 47)

- If a source does not include page numbers, or if you are referring to the entire source rather than to a specific page, cite the author's name in the text of your paper rather than in a parenthetical reference.

You must document *all* information that is not **common knowledge**, whether you are summarizing, paraphrasing, or quoting. (See p. 357 for an explanation of common knowledge.) With direct quotations, include the parenthetical reference and a period *after* the closing quotation marks.

> According to Doctorow, this is "authorship without editorship. Or authorship fused with editorship" (166).

When quoting a passage of more than four lines, indent the entire passage half an inch from the left margin, and do not use quotation marks. Place the parenthetical reference *after* the final punctuation mark.

Doctorow points out that Wikipedia's history pages can be extremely informative:

> This is a neat solution to the problem of authority—if you want to know what the fully rounded view of opinions on any controversial subject looks like, you need only consult its entry's history page for a blistering eyeful of thorough debate on the subject. (170)

Preparing the Works-Cited List

Start your works-cited list on a new page following the last page of your paper. Center the heading Works Cited at the top of the page. List entries alphabetically by the author's last name—or by the first word (other than an article such as *a* or *the*) of the title if an author is not given. Double-space within and between entries. Each entry should begin at the left-hand margin, with subsequent lines indented one-half inch. (This format can be automatically generated if you use the "hanging indent" option in your word processing program.)

Citations need to identify elements of what MLA documentation refers to as a source's "container." If a source is part of a larger whole, that larger source is considered the container. When citing a chapter in a book, for example, the book itself would be considered the container. Not every work is held by a container, however. If you were citing a movie watched in a movie theater, the movie is the source and it has no container. But if the same movie is watched as part of a DVD boxed set, that set is the container. Other examples include songs, which are contained on an album; or individual blog posts, which are contained on a blog.

The following information should be included in the citation, in this order and when available: the *title of the container*; the *name of contributors* such as editors or translators; the *version or edition*; the *volume and issue numbers*; the *publisher*; the *date of publication*; and a *location* such as the page number, DOI, permalink, or URL. Which of these elements will be relevant or available for citation will depend on the container.

When you have completed your list, double-check your parenthetical references to make sure they match the items in your works-cited list.

The following models illustrate the most common kinds of references.

Periodicals

For periodical articles found online or through a full-text database, see page 339.

Guidelines for Citing a Periodical Article

To cite a print article in MLA style, include the following:

1. Author, last name first

2. Title of the article, in quotation marks

3. Title of the periodical, in italics

4. Volume and issue numbers

5. Date or year of publication

6. Page number(s) of the article

   (See images on page 333.)

Carton, Evan. "American Scholars: Ralph Waldo Emerson, Joseph Smith, John Brown, and the Springs of Intellectual Schism." *New England Quarterly,* vol. 85, no. 1, 2012, pp. 5–37.

Journals

Journals are periodicals published for experts in a field. Cite both volume number and issue number when available. In cases where only an issue number is available, cite just the issue.

Minkler, Lanse. "Economic Rights and Political Decision-Making." *Human Rights Quarterly*, vol. 31, no. 2, 2009, pp. 369–93.

Picciotto, Joanna. "The Public Person and the Play of Fact." *Representations*, no. 105, 2009, pp. 85–132.

Magazines

Magazines are periodicals published for a general audience. Do not include a magazine's volume and issue number, but do include the date (day, month, and year for weekly publications; month and year for those published less frequently). If pages are not consecutive, give the first page followed by a plus sign.

Lansky, Sam. "Science fiction knows the future is female." *Time*, 26 Feb. 2018, pp. 95–97.

Sancton, Tom. "Visionnaire." *Vanity Fair*, May 2018, pp. 92–99.

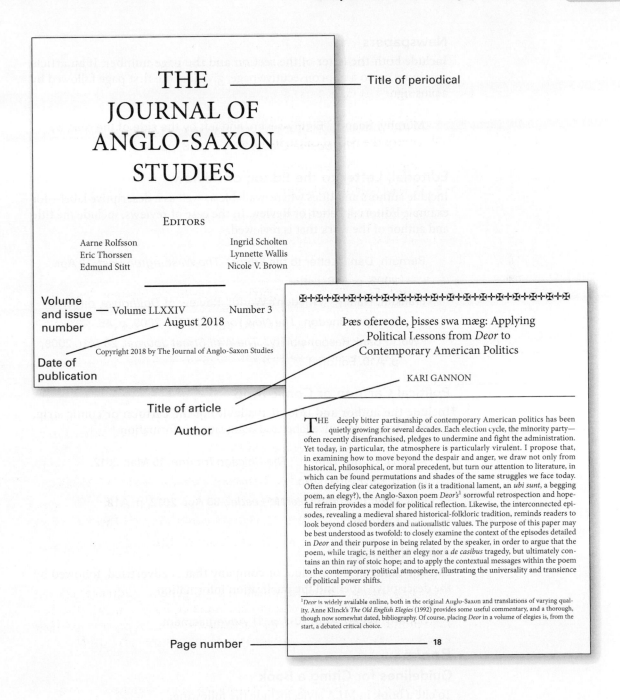

Title of periodical

THE
JOURNAL OF
ANGLO-SAXON
STUDIES

EDITORS

Aarne Rolfsson   Ingrid Scholten
Eric Thorssen   Lynnette Wallis
Edmund Stitt   Nicole V. Brown

Volume
and issue
number — Volume LLXXIV   Number 3
           August 2018

Copyright 2018 by The Journal of Anglo-Saxon Studies

Date of
publication

Title of article

Author

Þæs ofereode, þisses swa mæg: Applying
Political Lessons from *Deor* to
Contemporary American Politics

KARI GANNON

THE deeply bitter partisanship of contemporary American politics has been
quietly growing for several decades. Each election cycle, the minority party—
often recently disenfranchised, pledges to undermine and fight the administration.
Yet today, in particular, the atmosphere is particularly virulent. I propose that,
in examining how to move beyond the despair and anger, we draw not only from
historical, philosophical, or moral precedent, but turn our attention to literature, in
which can be found permutations and shades of the same struggles we face today.
Often defying clear categorization (is it a traditional lament, an *ubi sunt*, a begging
poem, an elegy?), the Anglo-Saxon poem *Deor's*[1] sorrowful retrospection and hope-
ful refrain provides a model for political reflection. Likewise, the interconnected episodes, revealing a medieval shared historical-folkloric tradition, reminds readers to
look beyond closed borders and nationalistic values. The purpose of this paper may
be best understood as twofold: to closely examine the context of the episodes detailed
in *Deor* and their purpose in being related by the speaker, in order to argue that the
poem, while tragic, is neither an elegy nor a *de casibus* tragedy, but ultimately contains an thin ray of stoic hope; and to apply the contextual messages within the poem
to the contemporary political atmosphere, illustrating the universality and transience
of political power shifts.

[1]*Deor* is widely available online, both in the original Anglo-Saxon and translations of varying quality. Anne Klinck's *The Old English Elegies* (1992) provides some useful commentary, and a thorough,
though now somewhat dated, bibliography. Of course, placing *Deor* in a volume of elegies is, from the
start, a debated critical choice.

Page number — 18

Newspapers

Include both the letter of the section and the page number. If an article continues on to a nonconsecutive page, give just the first page followed by a plus sign.

> Murphy, Sean P. "Eighty-seven, and left by the side of the road by
> Uber." *The Boston Globe*, 2 Nov. 2018, pp. A1+.

Editorial, Letter to the Editor, or Review

Include authors and titles where available as well as a descriptive label—for example Editorial, Letter, or Review. In the case of reviews, include the title and author of the work that is reviewed.

> Bernath, Dan. "Letter to the Editor." *The Washington Post*, 12 Apr.
> 2009, p. A16. Letter.
>
> Franklin, Nancy. "Whedon's World." Review of *Dollhouse*, directed
> by Joss Whedon. *The New Yorker*, 2 Mar. 2009, p. 45.
>
> "World Bank Responsibility." *The Wall Street Journal*, 28 Mar. 2009,
> p. A10. Editorial.

Political Cartoon or Comic Strip

Include the author and title (if available) of the cartoon or comic strip, followed by a descriptive label and publication information.

> Adams, Scott. "Dilbert." *The Chicago Tribune,* 10 Mar. 2012,
> p. C9. Comic strip.
>
> Pett, Joel. *Lexington Herald-Leader,* 30 Apr. 2012, p. A12.
> Cartoon.

Advertisement

Cite the name of the product or company that is advertised, followed by the descriptive label and the publication information.

> Subaru. *Wired*, Aug. 2017, p. 11. Advertisement.

Books

Guidelines for Citing a Book

To cite a book in MLA style, include the following:

1. Author, last name first

2. Title, in italics

3. Full publisher's name

4. Date of publication

```
   ┌───1───┐ ┌────2────┐ ┌──────3──────┐ ┌─4─┐
   McKibben, Bill. Oil and Honey. St. Martin's Griffin, 2014.
```

Text stock contains 20% post-consumer waste recycled fiber

OIL AND HONEY. Copyright © 2013, 2014 by Bill McKibben. All rights reserved. ⟶ **Date of Publication**
Printed in the United States of America. For information, address
St. Martin's Press, 175 Fifth Avenue, New York, N. Y. 10010.

WWW.stmartins.com

Designed by Kelly S. Too

The Library of Congress has cataloged the Henry Holt edition as follows:

McKibben, Bill.
   Oil and honey : the education of an unlikely activist / Bill McKibben.
      p. cm.
   ISBN 978-0-8050-9284-4 (hardcover)
   ISBN 978-0-8050-9838-9 (e-book)
   1. McKibben, Bill.   2. Environmentalism—United States.   3. Climatic changes—
Environmental aspects.   4. Petroleum industry and trade—Environmental
aspects.   5. Petroleum industry and trade—Political aspects—United States.
6. Environmentalists—United States—Biography.   7. Beekeepers—United States—
Biography. 1. Title.
   GE197.M356 2013
   363.70092—dc23
   [B]   2013010995

ISBN 978-1-250-04871-4 (trade paperback)

St. Martin's Griffin books may be purchased for educational, business, or
promotional use. For information on bulk purchases, please contact Macmillan
Corporate and Premium Sales Department at 1-800-221-7945, extension 5442,
or write specialmarkets@macmillan.com

First published in hardcover by Times Books, an imprint of
Henry Holt and Company

First St. Martins's Griffin Edition: August 2014

10 9 8 7 6 5 4 3 2 1

Title of book ⟶ OIL AND HONEY

THE EDUCATION OF
AN UNLIKELY ACTIVIST

Author ⟶ BILL McKIBBEN

Publisher

TIMES BOOKS   HENRY HOLT AND COMPANY   NEW YORK

Jiri Hera/Shutterstock

Book by One Author

List the author, last name first, followed by the title (italicized). Include the full publisher's name, abbreviated when called for, and end with the date of publication.

> Goodwin, Doris Kearns. *Leadership*. Simon & Schuster, 2018.

Book by Two Authors

List authors in the order in which they are listed on the book's title page. List the first author with last name first, but list the second author with first name first.

> Singer, Peter, and Jim Mason. *The Way We Eat: Why Our Food Choices Matter*. Rodale, 2006.

Book by Three or More Authors

List only the first author, last name first, followed by the abbreviation et al. ("and others").

> Gould, Harvey, et al. *Advanced Computer Simulation Methods*. Pearson Education, 2009.

Two or More Books by the Same Author

List the entries alphabetically by title. In each entry after the first, substitute three unspaced hyphens, followed by a period, for the author's last name.

> Friedman, Thomas L. *Hot, Flat, and Crowded: Why We Need a Green Revolution—and How It Can Renew America*. Farrar, Strauss and Giroux, 2008.
>
> ---. *The World Is Flat: A Brief History of the Twenty-First Century*. Farrar, Strauss and Giroux, 2005.

Edited Book

If your focus is on the *author*, include the name of the editor (or editors) after the title, preceded by the abbreviation *Ed.* (for "edited by"). If the book is an edited collection of essays by different authors, treat it as an anthology.

> Whitman, Walt. *The Portable Walt Whitman*. Ed. by Michael Warner, Penguin Classics, 2004.

If your focus is on the *editor*, begin with the editor's name followed by editor or editors.

> Michael Warner, editor. *The Portable Walt Whitman*. Penguin
>   Classics, 2004.

Translation

> Bolaño, Roberto. *The Savage Detectives*. Translated by Natasha
>   Wimmer, Picador, 2008.

Revised Edition

> Smith, Steven S., et al., *The American Congress*. 4th ed., Cambridge
>   UP, 2006.

Anthology

Include the name of the editor (or editors) of the anthology, followed by editor or editors.

> Browning, John Edgar, and Caroline Joan S. Picart, editors.
>   *Speaking of Monsters*, Palgrave, 2012.

Work in an Anthology

> Malone, Dan. "Immigration, Terrorism, and Secret Prisons."
>   *Keeping Out the Other: Immigration Enforcement Today*,
>   edited by David C. Brotherton and Philip Kretsedemas,
>   Columbia UP, 2008, pp. 44–62.

More Than One Work in the Same Anthology

To avoid repeating the entire anthology entry, you may provide a cross-reference from individual essays to the entire anthology.

> Adelson, Glenn et al., editors. *Environment: An Interdisciplinary
>   Anthology*, Yale UP, 2008.
> Lesher, Molly. "Seeds of Change." Adelson, pp. 131–37.
> Marshall, Robert. "The Problem of the Wilderness." Adelson,
>   pp. 288–92.

Section or Chapter of a Book

> Tirado, Linda. "I'm Not Angry So Much as I'm Really Tired."
> *Hand to Mouth: Living in Bootstrap America*, Berkeley,
> 2014, pp. 69–86.

Introduction, Preface, Foreword, or Afterword

> Christiano, Thomas, and John Christman. Introduction.
> *Contemporary Debates in Political Philosophy*. Edited by
> Thomas Christiano and John Christman, Wiley, 2009,
> pp. 1–20.

Multivolume Work

> McNeil, Peter, editor. *Fashion: Critical and Primary Sources*. Berg
> Publishers, 2009. 4 vols.

Article in a Reference Work

A **reference work** is a book (print or electronic)—such as an encyclopedia, a dictionary, a bibliography, an almanac, or a handbook—that contains factual information. If the entries in a reference work are arranged alphabetically, do not include page numbers or volumes. When citing a familiar encyclopedia that publishes new editions regularly, include only the edition (if given) and year. If the article's author is given, include that as well. For less well-known reference encyclopedias, include publication information.

> "Human Rights." *Encyclopedia Americana*. 2003 ed.
> "Seagrass Beds." *Ocean: A Visual Encyclopedia*. DK Publishing,
> 2015.

> **NOTE**
>
> Keep in mind that many instructors do not consider encyclopedia articles acceptable research sources. Before including a citation for an encyclopedia article in your works-cited list, check with your instructor.

Audiovisual Sources

TV Show

> "Dance Dance Resolution." *The Good Place*, written by Megan
> Amram, directed by Drew Goddard, NBC, 20 Sept. 2017.

Film

> *Get Out*. Directed by Jordan Peele, performances by Daniel
> Kaluuya, Allison Williams, and Bradley Whitford, Universal
> Pictures, 2017.

Internet Sources

Citing internet sources can be problematic because they sometimes lack basic information—for example, dates of publication or authors' names. When citing internet sources, include all the information you can find.

- For sites that are online editions of printed works, include as much of the original print information as is available, as well as the URL.

- For sites that exist only online, include (when available) the author, title, overall website title (if part of a larger project), the date it was last updated, and the URL.

- For works that are accessed through a library database, include the name of the database (in italics) and the URL or Digital Object Identifier (DOI). A DOI is a unique series of numbers assigned to electronic documents. The DOI remains the same regardless of where on the internet a document is located.

For particularly long URLs (three lines or greater), you may use the URL for the main website on which you found the content instead of the URL for the specific page which you are referencing. However, your instructor may not require a URL, so be sure to confirm their preference. It is always a good idea, however, to keep a record of the URLs for yourself in case you need to revisit your source.

If you type a URL into a works-cited entry that carries over to the next line, make sure that you break it at an appropriate place—for example, after a slash or a hyphen. If you paste a URL into a works-cited entry, Word will do this for you.

Guidelines for Citing a Website

To cite a website in MLA style, follow these guidelines:

1. Author (if any)

2. Title (if any)

3. Name of website or sponsor

4. Date the site was last updated

5. DOI or URL

Author

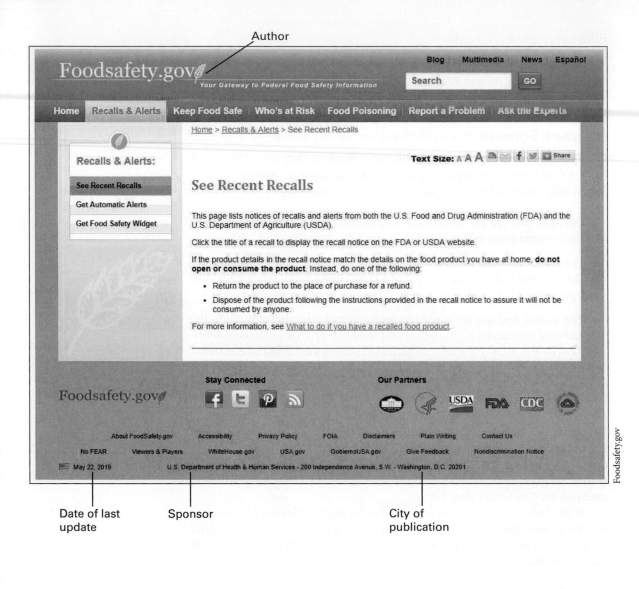

Date of last update   Sponsor   City of publication

—— 1 —— —————— 2 ——————
Foodsafety.gov. "UBC Food Distributors Recalls Hot Curry Powder

—————————————— ———— 3 ————
and Curry Powder due to Lead." US Dept of Health and

———————— 4 ——— ———— 5 ————
Human Services, 30 Oct. 2018. www.fda.gov/Safety/Recalls/

—— 5 ——
ucm624397.htm

Entire Website

Include (if available) the author, title of the website, date of last update, and the URL.

Document within a Website

"Uniform Impunity: Mexico's Misuse of Military Justice to
Prosecute Abuses in Counternarcotics and Public
Security Operations." *Human Rights Watch*, Apr. 2009,
www.hrw.org/report/2009/04/29/uniform-impunity
/mexicos-misuse-military-justice-prosecute-abuses
-counternarcotics.

Online Video

Baggs, Amanda. "In My Language." *YouTube*, 14 Jan. 2007,
www.youtube.com/watch?v=JnylM1hl2jc.

Blog Posts and Blog Comments

Cimons, Marlene. "Why Cities Could Be the Key to Solving
the Climate Crisis." *Thinkprogress.org*, Center for American
Progress Action Fund, 10 Dec. 2015, thinkprogress.org
/climate/2015/12/10/3730938/cities-key-to-climate-crisis/.

Parks, Tim. "Why Translation Deserves Scrutiny." *NYR Daily*,
NYREV, 23 Oct. 2018, www.nybooks.com/daily/2018/10/23
/why-translation-deserves-scrutiny/.

Tweet

Begin with the author's real name, followed by the user name in parentheses. Include only the user name if the real name is unknown. Next, include the entire text of the tweet in quotation marks, followed by the date, the time, and the medium (Tweet).

Barack Obama (@POTUS44). "Thank you for everything. My last
ask is the same as my first. I'm asking you to believe—not in
my ability to create change, but in yours." *Twitter*, 11 Jan. 2017,
12:52 a.m., twitter.com/POTUS44/status/819044196371800065.
Tweet.

Podcast

Koenig, Sarah. "A Bird in Jail Is Worth Two on the Street." *Serial,* Chicago Public Radio, 3 Oct. 2018, serialpodcast.org /season-one/1/the-alibi.

Ogg, Erica. "Google Tries to Rehab Its Antitrust Image." *CNET News Daily Podcast*, CBS Interactive, 8 May 2009, www.cnet.com /news/cnet-news-daily-podcast-google-tries-to-rehab-its -antitrust-image/.

Online Book

Doctorow, Cory. *Content: Selected Essays on Technology, Creativity, Copyright, and the Future of the Future,* Tachyon, 2008. *Craphound.com.*

Part of an Online Book

Zittrain, Jonathan L. "The Lessons of Wikipedia." *The Future of the Internet and How to Stop It,* Yale UP, 2008. *futureoftheinternet.org.*

Article in an Online Scholarly Journal

Johnston, Rebecca. "Salvation or Destruction: Metaphors of the Internet." *First Monday*, vol. 14, no. 4, 2009, firstmonday.org /article/view/2370/2158.

Magazine Article Accessed Online

Winter, Jessica. "Why Aren't Mothers Worth Anything to Venture Capitalists?." *The New Yorker*, 25 Sept. 2018, www.newyorker.com/business/currency/why-arent -mothers-worth-anything-to-venture-capitalists.

Newspaper Article Accessed Online

Twilley, Nicola. "With Bugs, You're Never Alone." *The New York Times*, 29 Oct. 2018, www.nytimes.com/2018/10/29/science /spider-insect-survey.html.

Article from a Library Database

Hartley, Richard D. "Sentencing Reform and the War on Drugs: An
Analysis of Sentence Outcomes for Narcotics Offenders
Adjudicated in the US District Courts on the Southwest Border."
Criminal Justice Policy Review, vol. 19, no. 4, 2008, pp. 414–37.
Sage Premier, doi: 10.1177/1043986208323264.

Legal Case

When citing a court opinion, provide the plaintiffs' names, the legal citation (volume, abbreviation of the source, page numbers), the name of the
court, the year of the decision, and any relevant information about where
you found it. In many cases, online versions of the opinions will include
only the first page; in those cases, supply that page number followed by a
plus sign.

Miranda v. Arizona, 384 US 436+. Supreme Court of the US. 1966.
FindLaw, Thompson Reuters, caselaw.findlaw.com
/us-supreme-court/384/436.html.

Government Document

Include the government agency or body issuing the document, followed by
publication information.

United States, Department of Homeland Security, *Estimates
of the Unauthorized Immigrant Population Residing in
the United States, Office of Immigration Policy*, Feb. 2009,
www.dhs.gov/sites/default/files/publications/ois_ill_pe_
2011_0.pdf.

MLA PAPER GUIDELINES

- An MLA paper should have a one-inch margin all around and be double-spaced.

- Indent the first line of every paragraph. Number all pages, including the first, consecutively. Type your name, followed by the page number, in the upper right-hand corner.

- An MLA paper does not typically have a title page. Type the following information at the top of the paper, one inch from the left-hand margin:

    Name

    Instructor

    Course

    Date submitted

- Center the title of the paper. Capitalize all important words of the title, except prepositions, articles, coordinating conjunctions, and the *to* in infinitives—unless the word is the first or last word of the title. Titles should never be italicized, underlined, or followed by a period.

- Begin the **works-cited list** on a new numbered page, after the body of the paper. (See page 331 for a discussion of the works-cited list.)

- Citations should follow MLA documentation style.

NOTE

In the student essay that follows, note that the blue annotations explain the student's choice of sources and the purple annotations highlight features of the student's use of documentation.

⬇ The following student research paper, "Should Data Posted on Social-Networking Sites Be 'Fair Game' for Employers?" by Erin Blaine, follows MLA documentation style as outlined in the preceding pages.

Blaine 1

Erin Blaine

Professor Adams

Humanities 101

4 March 2020

Should Data Posted on Social-Networking Sites

Be "Fair Game" for Employers?

The popularity of social-networking sites such as

Facebook, Instagram, LinkedIn, and Twitter has increased dra-

matically over the last several years, especially among college

students and young professionals. These sites provide valuable

opportunities for networking and for connecting socially. At the

same time, however, potential employers, human resources

professionals, and even college admissions officers routinely

use these sites to evaluate applicants. Because it is so easy

to access social-networking sites and because they provide

valuable information, this practice is certain to continue. Some

people concerned about this development argue that social-

networking sites should be off-limits because potential employ-

ers are seeing information out of context and are unable to

properly evaluate it. As long as applicants have freely posted

information in a public forum, however, there is no reason for

an employer not to consider it during the hiring process.

The number of employers and universities using

social-networking sites to evaluate candidates is growing

every year. A 2017 survey found that 35 percent of college

admissions officers acknowledged visiting sites like Facebook

to learn more about applicants, and 40 percent said that the

information they found "negatively impacted the applicant's

admissions chances" (Gurram). This practice also occurs in

the business world, where the numbers are even more

striking. One study found that 70 percent of employers use to

help them evaluate potential employees (Driscoll). The practice

This source and the following one supply statistics that support the main point of the paragraph.

Parenthetical reference identifies the source, which is included in the works-cited list.

Blaine 2

Citations from Driscoll and Preston add credibility.

of checking social media is so common that some employers use outside companies, such as Social Intelligence Corp., to do internet background checks on job candidates (Preston).

Not everyone is happy with this practice, though, and some have strong objections. Becca Bush, a college student in Chicago, argues that employers should not have the right to use social media to evaluate potential employees. "It's a violation of privacy," she says. "Twenty years ago, people still did the same things as now," but the information "wasn't as widespread" (qtd. in Cammenga). Marc S. Rotenberg, president of the Electronic Privacy Information Center, agrees, saying, "Employers should not be judging what people in their private lives do away from the workplace." Rotenberg goes on to say that privacy settings on sites like Facebook are often misunderstood. According to him, "People are led to believe that there is more limited disclosure than there actually is" (qtd. in Preston). Some people mistakenly think that looking at an applicant's Facebook page is illegal (Cammenga). Even though it is not, this practice can lead to discrimination, which *is* illegal. An online search can reveal characteristics that an applicant is not required to disclose to employers—for example, race, age, religion, sex, national origin, marital status, or disability (Preston).

Parenthetical documentation containing *qtd. in* indicates a source quoted in another source.

Quotes from Rotenberg are summarized here to present an opposing viewpoint.

Given the realities of the digital age, however, admissions committees and job recruiters are acting reasonably when they access social-networking sites. As a practical matter, it would be almost impossible to prevent employers from reviewing online sites as part of informal background and reference checks. Moreover, those who believe that it is unethical for recruiters to look at the online profiles of prospective job candidates seem willing to accept the benefits of social-networking sites but unwilling to acknowledge that these new technologies bring new responsibilities and liabilities. Finally, the problems associated with employers' use of social-networking sites would not

3

4

Blaine 3

be an issue in the first place if users of social-networking sites took full advantage of the available measures to protect themselves.

Part of the problem is that the internet has fundamentally altered our notions of "private" and "public" in ways that we are only just beginning to understand. As Shelley Fralic observes in "Don't Fall for the Myths about Online Privacy," Facebook's privacy options do not really protect its users' privacy, and thinking they do "is beyond absurd" (1). On sites like Facebook, people can reveal intimate details of their lives to millions of strangers. This situation is unprecedented and, at least for the foreseeable future, irreversible. The French artist, film producer, and fashion designer Maripol has noted, "Andy Warhol said that everyone will be famous for fifteen minutes, but with social media, everyone is famous all of the time" (qtd. in Hanra). In essence, we are all exhibitionists now, to some degree and our private lives are on display as never before. Given the changes in our understanding of privacy and the public nature of the internet, the suggestion that we should live our lives by the same rules we lived by thirty years ago simply does not make sense. As *New York Times* columnist Thomas Friedman noted prophetically in 2007, in the internet age, more and more of "what you say or do or write will end up as a digital fingerprint that never gets erased" (23).

Rather than relying on outdated notions of privacy, students and job seekers should accept these new conditions and take steps to protect themselves. Most college and career counseling services have easy-to-follow recommendations for how to maintain a positive online reputation. First on almost everyone's list is adjusting privacy settings. Understanding and employing these settings is a user's responsibility; misunderstanding such protections is no excuse. As Mariel Loveland suggests, those who want extra help can hire an online reputation-management company such as Reputation.com or Integrity Defenders or use services

5

6

Because the source and the author are named in an identifying tag, only the page numbers are needed parenthetically.

Distinctive key phrases are quoted directly.

Including a recognized authority, such as Friedman, adds credibility.

Internet source includes no page number in the parenthetical documentation.

Blaine 4

such as those offered by Reppler. According to Sameer Somal, because many people judge a person solely on the basis of his or her online presence, it is important to make sure that your digital footprint is positive. Online reputation management companies identify questionable material across different social networks and take steps to protect your reputation.

The most important way for people to protect themselves against the possible misuse of personal information is for them to take responsibility for the information they post online. According to a recent article in *Education Week*, even middle school students should keep their future college and career plans in mind when they post information online ("Online Behavior"). In preparing students to apply for college, many high school counselors stress the "golden rule": "students should never post anything online they wouldn't want their parents to see" ("Online Behavior"). Students and job seekers must realize that a commonsense approach to the internet requires that they develop good "digital grooming" habits (Bond). For example, one self-described "cautious internet user" says that she "goes through the information on her [Facebook] account every few weeks and deletes statuses, messages, and other things" (Bond). She understands that a potential employer coming across an applicant's membership in a Facebook group such as "I Sold My Grandma for Crack-Cocaine!" or a picture of a student posing with an empty liquor bottle may not understand the tone, the context, or the joke. Students should also be careful about "friends" who have access to their online social networks, asking themselves whether these people really know them and would have good things to say about them if a prospective employer contacted them for a reference. According to one high school principal, 75 percent of the students at his school admitted to accepting a friend request from someone

7

Not every summary or paraphrase needs to include a quotation.

Brackets indicate that a quotation has been edited for clarity.

Paraphrasing provides readers with the key points of a source.

Blaine 5

they did not know ("Online Behavior"). Getting students to consider the repercussions of this kind of choice is central to many social-media education programs.

Although social-networking sites have disadvantages, they [8] also have advantages. These sites provide an excellent opportunity for job seekers to connect with potential employers and to get their names and résumés in circulation. For example, a job seeker can search the LinkedIn networks of a company's executives or human resources staff for mutual connections. In addition, a job seeker can post information calculated to appeal to potential employers. Recruiters are just as likely to hire candidates based on social-media screening as they are to reject them. A national survey conducted by Harris Poll on behalf of CareerBuilder found that more than 57 percent of employers are less likely to interview a candidate they can't find online. The majority of companies will dig through social profiles, but find it even more suspect if they see nothing at all (Driscoll). Another article reports the following:

> However, one third (33 percent) of employers who research candidates on social networking sites say they've found content that made them more likely to hire a candidate. What's more, nearly a quarter (23 percent) found content that directly led to them hiring the candidate, up from 19 percent last year. ("Number of Employers")

In today's job market, people should think of their networks as extensions of themselves. They need to take an active role in shaping the image they want to project to future employers. So even though students and job seekers should be careful [9] when posting information online, they should not miss the opportunity to take advantage of the many opportunities that social-networking sites offer.

A quotation of more than four lines of text is double-spaced, indented one inch from the left margin, and typed as a block, without quotation marks. Parenthetical documentation comes after the final punctuation.

Blaine 6

Works Cited

The works-cited list includes full information for all sources cited in the paper.

Bond, Michaelle. "Facebook Timeline a New Privacy Test." *USA Today*, 2 Nov. 2011, www.usatoday.com/tech/news /internetprivacy/story/2011-11-02/facebook-timeline -privacy/51047658/1.

Cammenga, Michelle. "Facebook Might Be the Reason You Don't Get That Job." *Hub Bub*, Loyola University Chicago's School of Communication, 23 Feb. 2012, blogs.luc.edu/hubbub /reporting-and-writing/employers-screen-facebook/.

Driscoll, Kara. "Employers Less Likely to Hire Applicants with No Social Media Presence." Dayton Daily News, 14 July 2017, www.mydaytondailynews.com/business/employers -less-likely-hire-applicants-with-social-media-presence /MALOhAY4en0kok5WJfpVoK/.

Fralic, Shelley. "Don't Fall for the Myths about Online Privacy." *Calgary Herald*, 17 Oct. 2015, p. 1.

Friedman, Thomas L. "The Whole World Is Watching." *The New York Times,* 27 June 2007, p. A23.

Gurram, Mugdha. "Study Shows College Admissions Evaluate Applicant's Social Media." *The Daily Free Press*, Boston University, 20 Oct. 2017, dailyfreepress.com/blog/2017/10/20 /study-shows-college-admissions-evaluate-applicants -social-media/.

Hanra, Hanna. "Maripol: 'Did I Discover Madonna? She Discovered Me!'" *The Guardian*, Guardian News and Media, 20 Mar. 2015, www.theguardian.com/fashion/2015/mar/20 /maripol-madonna-photographer-stylist-polaroids-exhibition.

Loveland, Mariel. "Reppler Launches 'Reppler Image Score,' Rates Social Network Profile Content for Potential Employers." *Scribbal*, 27 Sept. 2011, www.scribbal.com /reppler-launches-rates-social-network-profile-content-09-27-11/.

Blaine 7

"Number of Employers Passing on Applicants Due to
Social Media Posts Continues to Rise." *CareerBuilder*,
26 June 2014, www.careerbuilder.com/share/aboutus
/pressreleasesdetail.aspx?sd=6%2F26%2F2014&id
=pr829&ed=12%2F31%2F2014.

"Online Behavior Jeopardizing College Plans; Admissions Officers
Checking Social-Networking Sites for Red Flags."
Education Week, 14 Dec. 2011, p. 11. *Academic One File*,
www.edweek.org/ew/articles/2011/12/08/14collegeadmit
.h31.html.

Preston, Jennifer. "Social Media History Becomes a New Job
Hurdle." *The New York Times*, 20 July 2011, www.nytimes.com
/2011/07/21/technology/social-media-history-becomes
-a-new-job-hurdle.html?_r=0.

Somal, Sameer. "Digital Reputation Management 101." *Medium*,
12 Apr. 2018, medium.com/@SameerSomal
/digital-reputation-management-101-5506eceb02cb.

Underwood, Alice. "9 Things to Avoid on Social Media While
Looking for a New Job." *Glassdoor*, 3 Jan. 2018,
www.glassdoor.com/blog/things-to-avoid-on-social
-media-job-search/

Be sure that
your data
comes from
recent sources.

The New York Times

FRIDAY, AUGUST 24, 2018

Printed in De

Trump Tweet Echoes Agenda Of Supremacy

A Racist Narrative for South African Farms

By JULIE HIRSCHFELD DAVIS and NORIMITSU ONISHI

WASHINGTON — Like so many of President Trump's late-night tweets, this one was in-spired by a segment on his favor-ite cable channel, Fox News.

But when Mr. Trump an-nounced Wednesday night that he was directing his sec-state to scrutinize was the targ- for lan-

PRES AT JU SESSIO

PLEA DEAL

Trump's Lega Feed Attack Attorney

CHAPTER

11

Using Sources Responsibly

AT ISSUE

Where Should We Draw the Line with Plagiarism?

In recent years, a number of high-profile plagiarism cases have put a spotlight on how much "borrowing" from other sources is acceptable. Some critics—and many colleges and universities—draw little distinction between intentional and unintentional plagiarism, arguing that any unattributed borrowing is theft. Others are more forgiving, accepting the fact that busy historians or scientists (or students) might not realize that a particular sentence in their notes was not their original idea or might accidentally incorporate a source's exact words (or its unique syntax or phrasing) into their own work without attribution.

In the age of the internet, with its "cut-and-paste" culture, plagiarism has become easier to commit; however, with the development of plagiarism-detection software, it is also now much easier to detect. Still, some colleges and

universities are uncomfortable with the idea of using such software, arguing that it establishes an atmosphere of distrust.

On college campuses, as in the professional world, many are questioning and reevaluating the concept of plagiarism. What exactly constitutes plagiarism? How serious a matter is it? Is there a difference between intentional and unintentional plagiarism? Why do people commit plagiarism? What should be done to prevent it? How should it be punished? What are its short- and long-term consequences?

These are some (although by no means all) of the questions to consider as you explore the sources at the end of this chapter. After reading these sources, you will be asked to write an argumentative essay that takes a position on the issue of what exactly constitutes plagiarism and how it should be dealt with.

Understanding Plagiarism

Plagiarism is the act of using the words or ideas of another person without attributing them to their rightful author—that is, presenting those borrowed words and ideas as if they are your own. When you plagiarize, you fail to use sources ethically or responsibly.

TWO DEFINITIONS OF PLAGIARISM

From *MLA Handbook,* Eighth Edition (2016)

Merriam-Webster's Collegiate Dictionary defines plagiarizing as committing "literary theft." Plagiarism is presenting another person's ideas, information, expressions, or entire work as one's own. It is thus a kind of fraud: deceiving others to gain something of value. While plagiarism only sometimes has legal repercussions (e.g., when it involves copyright infringement—violating an authors' exclusive legal right to publication), it is always a serious moral and ethical offense.

From *Publication Manual of the American Psychological Association,* Sixth Edition (2009)

Researchers do not claim the words and ideas of another as their own; they give credit where credit is due (APA Ethics Code Standard 8.11, Plagiarism). Quotation marks should be used to indicate the exact words of another. *Each time* you paraphrase another author (i.e., summarize a passage or rearrange the order of a sentence and change some of the words), you need to credit the source in the text.

The key element of this principle is that authors do not present the work of another as if it were their own work. This can extend to ideas as well as written words. If authors model a study after one done by someone else, the originating author should be given credit. If the rationale for a study was suggested in the Discussion section of someone else's article, that person should be given credit. Given the free exchange of ideas, which is very important to the health of intellectual discourse, authors may not know where an idea for a study originated. If authors do know, however, they should acknowledge the source; this includes personal communications.

For many people, defining plagiarism is simple: it is not "borrowing" but stealing, and it should be dealt with severely. For others, however, it is a more slippery term, seen as considerably more serious if it is intentional than if it is accidental (for example, the result of careless research methods). Most colleges and universities have guidelines that define plagiarism strictly and have penalties in place for those who commit it.

To avoid committing unintentional plagiarism, you need to understand exactly what it is and why it occurs. You also need to learn how to use sources responsibly and to understand what kind of information requires documentation and what kind does not.

Avoiding Unintentional Plagiarism

Even if you do not intentionally misuse the words or ideas of a source, you are still committing plagiarism if you present the work of others as your own. To avoid unintentional plagiarism, you need to maintain control over your sources, keeping track of all the material you use so that you remember where you found each piece of information.

As you take notes, be careful to distinguish your sources' ideas from your own. If you are copying a source's words into your notes, put them in quotation marks. (If you are taking notes by hand, circle the quotation marks; if you are typing your notes, put the quotation marks in boldface or in color.) If you photocopy material, write the full source information on the first page, and staple the pages together. When you download material from the internet, be sure the URL appears on every page. Finally, never cut and paste material from a source directly into your paper.

As you draft your paper, be sure to quote your sources' words accurately (even punctuation must be reproduced exactly as it appears in the source). Be careful not to quote out of context, and be sure that you are presenting your sources' ideas accurately when you summarize or paraphrase. (For information on quoting, paraphrasing, and summarizing source material, see Chapter 9.)

The most common errors that lead to unintentional plagiarism—and how to avoid them—are listed below.

COMMON ERROR	HOW TO AVOID IT
No source information is provided for borrowed material (including statistics).	Always include full parenthetical documentation and a works-cited list that make the source of your information clear to readers. (See Chapter 10.)
A source's ideas are presented as if they are your own original ideas.	Keep track of the sources you consult, and always keep full source information with your sources. Never cut and paste material from an electronic source directly into your paper.
The boundaries of borrowed material are unclear.	Be sure to use an identifying tag *before* and parenthetical documentation *after* borrowed material. (See Chapter 9.)

(Continued)

COMMON ERROR	HOW TO AVOID IT
The language of paraphrases or summaries is too close to that of the original source.	Be careful to use original phrasing and syntax when you write summaries and paraphrases. (See Chapter 9.)
A friend's or tutor's words or ideas appear in your paper.	Be sure that any help you receive is in the form of suggestions, not additions.
Material you wrote for another course is used in your paper.	Always get permission from *both* instructors if you want to reuse work you did for another course, and be sure the material you use is substantially revised.

INTERNET SOURCES AND PLAGIARISM

The internet presents a particular challenge for students as they try to avoid plagiarism. Committing plagiarism (intentional or unintentional) with electronic sources is easy because it is simple to cut and paste material from online sources into a paper. However, inserting even a sentence or two from an internet source (including a blog, an email, or a website) into a paper without quotation marks and documentation constitutes plagiarism.

It is also not acceptable to use a visual found on the internet without acknowledging its source. This includes:

- Graphs
- Charts
- Tables
- Photographs

Finally, even if an internet source does not identify its author, the words or ideas you find there are not your own original material, so you must identify their source.

INTENTIONAL PLAGIARISM

Deliberately plagiarizing from a source, handing in another student's paper as your own, or buying a paper from an internet site is never acceptable. Such acts constitute serious violations of academic integrity. Creating your own original work is an important part of the educational experience, and misrepresenting someone else's work as your own undermines the goals of education.

Knowing What to Document

Documentation is the practice of identifying borrowed material and providing the proper bibliographic information for each source. Different academic disciplines require different formats for documentation—for example, English uses MLA, and psychology uses APA. For this reason, you should be sure to check with your instructor to find out what documentation style to use. (For information on MLA and APA documentation formats, see Chapter 10 and Appendix B, respectively.)

Regardless of the discipline, the following kinds of information should always be documented:

- Quotations from a source

- Summaries of a source's main points

- Paraphrases of a source's original ideas

- Opinions, judgments, and conclusions that are not your own

- Statistics from a source

- Visuals from a source

- Data from charts or graphs in a source

The following kinds of information, however, do not require documentation:

- **Common knowledge**—that is, factual information that can be found in several different sources. Examples of different sources include the following:
  - A writer's date of birth
  - A scientific fact
  - The location of a famous battle

■ Familiar quotations—anything from proverbs to frequently quoted lines from Shakespeare's plays—that you expect readers will recognize

■ Your own original opinions, judgments, and conclusions

⊜ EXERCISE 11.1 DECIDING WHAT TO DOCUMENT

Which of the following statements requires documentation, and why?

1. Doris Kearns Goodwin is a prize-winning historian.

2. Doris Kearns Goodwin's *The Fitzgeralds and the Kennedys* is a 900-page book with about 3,500 footnotes.

3. In 1994, Lynne McTaggart accused Goodwin of borrowing material from a book that McTaggart wrote.

4. My own review of the background suggests that Goodwin's plagiarism was unintentional.

5. Still, these accusations left Goodwin to face the "slings and arrows" of media criticism.

6. As Goodwin explains, "The more intensive and far-reaching a historian's research, the greater the difficulty of citation."

7. In her defense, Goodwin argued that the more research a historian does, the harder it is to keep track of sources.

8. Some people still remain convinced that Goodwin committed plagiarism.

9. Goodwin believes that her careful research methods, which she has described in exhaustive detail, should have prevented accidental plagiarism.

10. Some of Goodwin's critics have concluded that her reputation as a historian was hurt by the plagiarism charges.

⊜ EXERCISE 11.2 KNOWING WHEN TO DOCUMENT

Assume you are using the following editorial as a source. Identify two pieces of information you would need to document (for example, statistics). Then, identify two pieces of information you would *not* need to document (for example, common knowledge).

This editorial was first published on May 1, 2013.

WHEN BEYONCÉ'S INSPIRATION TURNS INTO IMITATION

ERIKA RAMIREZ

They say imitation is the sincerest form of flattery, but what if the person 1 imitating is a polarizing icon that should be doing otherwise—someone like Beyoncé?

On Monday (April 29), pop singer Kerli posted a side-by-side photo on her 2 Facebook page of her and Beyoncé donning the same Amato Haute Couture dress. The photo of Beyoncé comes from the pages of her 2013 *Mrs. Carter Show* tour book.

Except, it's not just the Furne One designed dress—which also Nicki Minaj 3 wore in her "Va Va Voom" video—that's similar in the photo. Both singers can be seen painted in white, from head to toe, and stylistically posed as sculptures.

No one owns a look, image, dance move (after all, how many artists have 4 pulled out signature Michael Jackson moves?), or in this case, an experimental costume. They're not copyrighted property, but filed as intellectual property.

Any artist, including Beyoncé, can wear whatever another artist wore, 5 but that multiplicity gets suspicious and easily pegged as stealing. And understandably so, when it's not only the look of the artist that is being traced, but his or her entire idea.

Beyoncé first caught flak for working up a dance similar to Josephine 6 Baker's iconic banana dance in her "Deja Vu" video, then was seen sporting a skirt with dangling bananas when performing the "B'Day" track. But let's be honest: that wasn't *that* serious, at least not at that point in her 20-year plus career. She later borrowed from Bob

> "There's a difference between inspiration and imitation."

Fosse's routine, "Mexican Breakfast," in the video for her girls anthem, "Single Ladies (Put a Ring on It)." There are also references to "Rich Man's Frug" scene (of Bob Fosse's "Sweet Charity") in Bey's "Get Me Bodied" video.

There's a difference between inspiration and imitation. "Countdown" is 7 a good example of Beyoncé doing both in one piece of work. She references Audrey Hepburn's *Funny Face* dancing and both Hepburn and Peggy Moffitt's late 50's/early 60's fashion, then elaborates with color schemes and pairs the choreography perfectly with the pace of the soundscapes. She also samples Boyz II Men's countdown from their song, "Uhh Ahh."

As the video continues, we see Bey using the same choreography, cinema- 8 tography, and costumes that Belgian choreographer and dancer, Anne Teresa De Keersmaeker, used in "Rosas Danst Rosas." It's one thing to be inspired by someone else's work and revamp with one's personal style, but it's another to duplicate exact movements, which is ultimately violating the artist's intellectual property. Context matters.

Before the debut of "Countdown," Beyoncé was criticized for nearly repli- 9
cating Italian singer Lorella Cuccarini's live performance with her performance
of "Run the World (Girls)" at the 2011 Billboard Music Awards. She later stated
that she had hired the same choreographers that had worked on Cuccarini's
performance, but it's still puzzling as to why she didn't work with them to create a groundbreaking concept of her own.

The choreography, seen in the performance and the song's accompany- 10
ing music video, comes from Mozambique dance troupe Tofo Tofo. Instead of
thanking them for the inspiration after the fact, as she's done with Cuccarini
and Keersmaeker, Beyoncé brought them to the U.S. and hired them to dance
alongside her in the "Run the World (Girls)" video.

The 2011 song, off her fourth studio album *4* swipes the beat from Major 11
Lazer's 2009 "Pon De Floor." According to Diplo, one half of Major Lazer,
the making of "Run the World (Girls)" started out as a "joke" (whatever that
means).

Beyoncé's "1 + 1" video features scenes similar to the unfinished French 12
film, *Le'Enfer*, while her "Love On Top" video has dancing scenes much the
same as those in New Edition's "If It Isn't Love" video.

But more bothersome than Bey's inspiration-turned-imitation act—and 13
less subtle as her career progresses—is that she's playing off the risks that other
artists have been brave enough to take (and appropriately praised for) instead
of challenging herself and taken some herself.

Perhaps visual and dance concepts don't come as naturally to her as vocal 14
prowess, but I'm doubtful that she can recruit those for which it does. No
shots at Frank Gatson Jr. (but shots?) who is a director, visual artist developer,
creative director, and choreographer who's worked closely with greats like
Diana Ross, Mariah Carey, Tina Turner, and consecutively with Beyoncé.

Even as a vocal performer, Beyoncé is more of a canvas than a creator. 15
The majority of her discography was written (yes, some co-written) by other
singer-songwriters, from the likes of Ne-Yo to The-Dream. But the formula works
for her: she holds 19 top 10s on Hot R&B/Hip-Hop Songs chart with six No. 1s.

The bittersweet side of Beyoncé stealing imitable art is that when she does, 16
she does it well. Perhaps it's why we give the diva a pass, or two, and will in the
future. Let's also not forget that voice of hers and stage stamina that hypnotizes
many into disregarding such acts—after all, words and imagery can only strike
a chord or transcend to a degree if they're executed with astounding talent.

Revising to Eliminate Plagiarism

As you revise your papers, scrutinize your work carefully to be sure you
have not inadvertently committed plagiarism. To help you understand the
most common situations in which accidental plagiarism is likely to occur,
read this paragraph from page 1 of "Don't Fall for the Myths about Online
Privacy," by Shelley Fralic, which appears in Chapter 9 (p. 320).

Facebook's fine print, like that of many internet portals, is specific and offers a variety of self-selected "privacy" options.

But to think that any interaction with it, and its ilk, is truly private is beyond absurd.

How can there still be people out there who still don't get that Netflix and Facebook, Instagram and Twitter, Google and Tinder, and pretty much every keystroke or communication we register on a smartphone or laptop, not to mention a loyalty card and the GPS in your car, are constantly tracking and sifting and collating everything we do?

To avoid unintentional plagiarism when using material from this paragraph in an essay of your own, follow these four guidelines:

1. **Be sure you have identified your source and provided appropriate documentation.**

   PLAGIARISM

   Even though Facebook users can select from various privacy options, it makes no sense to assume that engaging with Facebook and similar sites guarantees privacy.

This student writer does not quote directly from Fralic's discussion, but his summary of her comments does not represent her original ideas and therefore needs to be documented.

The following correct use of source material includes both an **identifying tag** (a phrase that identifies Fralic as the source of the ideas) and a page number that directs readers to the exact location of the material the student is summarizing. (Full source information is provided in the works-cited list.)

   CORRECT

   According to Shelley Fralic, even though Facebook users can select from among various privacy options, it makes no sense to assume that engaging with Facebook and similar sites guarantees privacy (1).

2. **Be sure you have placed quotation marks around borrowed words.**

   PLAGIARISM

   According to Shelley Fralic, it is hard to imagine that people still don't understand that Facebook and similar sites are constantly tracking and sifting and collating everything we do (1).

Although the preceding sentence provides parenthetical documentation and includes an identifying tag indicating the source of its ideas, it uses Fralic's exact words without placing them in quotation marks.

To avoid committing plagiarism, the student needs to either place quotation marks around Fralic's words or paraphrase her comments.

CORRECT (BORROWED WORDS IN QUOTATION MARKS)

According to Shelley Fralic, it is hard to imagine that people still don't understand that Facebook and similar sites "are constantly tracking and sifting and collating everything we do" (1).

CORRECT (BORROWED WORDS PARAPHRASED)

According to Shelley Fralic, it is hard to imagine that people still don't understand that Facebook and similar sites are always following our posts (1).

3. **Be sure you have indicated the boundaries of the borrowed material.**

PLAGIARISM

Although Facebook users can select from among various privacy options, engaging with Facebook is not private. It is hard to imagine that anyone still believes that Facebook is not "constantly tracking and sifting and collating everything we do" (1).

In the preceding passage, the student correctly places Fralic's words in quotation marks and includes appropriate parenthetical documentation. However, she does not indicate that other ideas in the passage, although not quoted directly, are also Fralic's.

To avoid committing plagiarism, the student needs to use identifying tags to indicate the boundaries of the borrowed material, which goes beyond the quoted words.

CORRECT

According to Shelley Fralic, although Facebook users can select from among various privacy options, engaging with Facebook is not private. It is hard to imagine, Fralic observes, that anyone still believes that Facebook is not "constantly tracking and sifting and collating everything we do" (1).

4. Be sure you have used your own phrasing and syntax.

PLAGIARISM

As Shelley Fralic observes, Facebook's fine print offers various self-selected "privacy" options. However, she believes that it is beyond absurd to think that interacting with Facebook and its ilk is truly private. She questions how there can still be people who don't realize that sites like Netflix, Facebook, and Instagram—and pretty much every keystroke on our smartphones or laptops, and even our loyalty cards and GPS—are constantly tracking and sifting and collating everything we do (1).

The student who wrote the paragraph above does provide an identifying tag and parenthetical documentation to identify the source of his ideas. However, his paragraph's phrasing and syntax are almost identical to Fralic's.

In the following paragraph, the writer correctly paraphrases and summarizes Friedman's ideas, quoting a few distinctive passages. (See Chapter 9 for information on paraphrase and summary.)

CORRECT

According to Shelley Fralic, although Facebook does permit its users to choose among various privacy options, using the site is by no means a private activity. Fralic wonders how anyone can still not understand that the sites we visit—not just Facebook, but also Instagram, Twitter, and the rest—as well as "pretty much every keystroke or communication we register on a smartphone or laptop . . . are constantly tracking and sifting and collating everything we do" (1).

EXERCISE 11.3 SYNTHESIZING SOURCES RESPONSIBLY

The following student paragraph synthesizes information from two different sources (which appear on pp. 364–65, following the student paragraph), but the student writer has not used sources responsibly. (For information on synthesis, see Chapter 9.) Read the sources and the paragraph, and then make the following changes:

- Insert quotation marks where the student has quoted a source's words.
- Edit paraphrased and summarized material if necessary so that its syntax and phrasing are not too close to those of a source.

- Add parenthetical documentation where necessary to acknowledge the use of a source's words or original ideas.

- Add identifying tags where necessary to clarify the scope of the borrowed material or to differentiate material from the two sources.

- Check every quoted passage once more to see if the quotation adds something vital to the paragraph. If it does not, summarize or paraphrase the source's words instead.

STUDENT PARAGRAPH

In recent years, psychologists have focused on the idea that girls (unlike boys) face a crisis of self-esteem as they approach adolescence. Both Carol Gilligan and Mary Pipher did research to support this idea, showing how girls lose their self-confidence in adolescence because of sexist cultural expectations. Women's groups have expressed concern that the school system favors boys and is biased against girls. In fact, boys are often regarded not just as classroom favorites but also as bullies who represent obstacles on the path to gender justice for girls. Recently, however, this impression that boys are somehow privileged while girls are shortchanged is being challenged.

Source 1

That boys are in disrepute is not accidental. For many years women's groups have complained that boys benefit from a school system that favors them and is biased against girls. "Schools shortchange girls," declares the American Association of University Women. . . . A stream of books and pamphlets cite research showing not only that boys are classroom favorites but also that they are given to schoolyard violence and sexual harassment.

In the view that has prevailed in American education over the past decade, boys are resented, both as the unfairly privileged sex and as obstacles on the path to gender justice for girls. This perspective is promoted in schools of education, and many a teacher now feels that girls need and deserve special indemnifying consideration. "It is really clear that boys are Number One in this society and in most of the world," says Patricia O'Reilly, a professor of education and the director of the Gender Equity Center, at the University of Cincinnati.

The idea that schools and society grind girls down has given rise to an array of laws and policies intended to curtail the advantage boys have and to redress the harm done to girls. That girls are treated as the second sex in school and consequently suffer, that boys are accorded privileges and consequently benefit—these are things everyone is presumed to know. But they are not true.

—Christina Hoff Sommers, "The War against Boys"

Source 2

Girls face an inevitable crisis of self-esteem as they approach adolescence. They are in danger of losing their voices, drowning, and facing a devastating dip in self-regard that boys don't experience. This is the picture that Carol Gilligan presented on the basis of her research at the Emma Willard School, a private girls' school in Troy, N.Y. While Gilligan did not refer to genes in her analysis of girls' vulnerability, she did cite both the "wall of Western culture" and deep early childhood socialization as reasons.

Her theme was echoed in 1994 by the clinical psychologist Mary Pipher's surprise best seller, *Reviving Ophelia* (Putnam, 1994), which spent three years on the *New York Times* best-seller list. Drawing on case studies rather than systematic research, Pipher observed how naturally outgoing, confident girls get worn down by sexist cultural expectations. Gilligan's and Pipher's ideas have also been supported by a widely cited study in 1990 by the American Association of University Women. That report, published in 1991, claimed that teenage girls experience a "free-fall in self-esteem from which some will never recover."

The idea that girls have low self-esteem has by now become part of the academic canon as well as fodder for the popular media. But is it true? No.

—Rosalind C. Barnett and Caryl Rivers, "Men Are from Earth, and So Are Women. It's Faulty Research That Sets Them Apart"

Where Should We Draw the Line with Plagiarism?

dennizn/Alamy Stock Photo

Reread the At Issue box on page 353. Then, read the sources on the following pages. As you read these sources, you will be asked to answer questions and to complete some activities. This work will help you to understand the content and structure of the material you read. When you have read the sources, you will be ready to write an argumentative essay in which you take a position on the topic, "Where Should We Draw the Line with Plagiarism?"

SOURCES

 Trip Gabriel, "Plagiarism Lines Blur for Students in Digital Age," page 367

 Jennifer Mott-Smith, "Bad Idea about Writing: Plagiarism Deserves to Be Punished," page 371

 Richard A. Posner, "The Truth about Plagiarism," page 375

 Helen Rubinstein, "When Plagiarism Is a Plea for Help," page 378

 Dan Ariely, "Essay Mills: A Coarse Lesson in Cheating," page 382

 Visual Argument: Term Papers for Sale Advertisement (web page), page 385

This article is from the August 1, 2010, edition of the *New York Times*.

PLAGIARISM LINES BLUR FOR STUDENTS IN DIGITAL AGE

TRIP GABRIEL

At Rhode Island College, a freshman copied and pasted from a website's fre- 1
quently asked questions page about homelessness—and did not think he
needed to credit a source in his assignment because the page did not include
author information.

At DePaul University, the tip-off to one student's copying was the purple 2
shade of several paragraphs he had lifted from the web; when confronted by
a writing tutor his professor had sent him to, he was not defensive—he just
wanted to know how to change purple text to black.

And at the University of Maryland, a student reprimanded for copy- 3
ing from Wikipedia in a paper on the Great Depression said he thought its
entries—unsigned and collectively written—did not need to be credited since
they counted, essentially, as common knowledge.

Professors used to deal with plagiarism by admonishing students to give 4
credit to others and to follow the style guide for citations, and pretty much left
it at that.

But these cases—typical ones, according to writing tutors and officials 5
responsible for discipline at the three schools who described the plagiarism—
suggest that many students simply do not grasp that using words they did not
write is a serious misdeed.

It is a disconnect that is growing in the internet age as concepts of intel- 6
lectual property, copyright, and originality are under assault in the unbridled
exchange of online information, say educators who study plagiarism.

Digital technology makes copying and pasting easy, of course. But that is 7
the least of it. The internet may also be redefining how students—who came
of age with music file-sharing, Wikipedia, and web-linking—understand the
concept of authorship and the singularity of any text or image.

"Now we have a whole generation of students who've grown up with infor- 8
mation that just seems to be hanging out there in cyberspace and doesn't seem
to have an author," said Teresa Fishman, director of the Center for Academic
Integrity at Clemson University. "It's possible to believe this information is just
out there for anyone to take."

Professors who have studied plagiarism do not try to excuse it—many are 9
champions of academic honesty on their campuses—but rather try to understand why it is so widespread.

In surveys from 2006 to 2010 by Donald L. McCabe, a co-founder of the 10
Center for Academic Integrity and a business professor at Rutgers University, about 40 percent of 14,000 undergraduates admitted to copying a few
sentences in written assignments.

367

Perhaps more significant, the number who believed that copying from the 11 web constitutes "serious cheating" is declining—to 29 percent on average in recent surveys from 34 percent earlier in the decade.

Sarah Brookover, a senior at the Rutgers campus in Camden, N.J., said 12 many of her classmates blithely cut and paste without attribution.

"This generation has always existed in a world where media and intellec- 13 tual property don't have the same gravity," said Ms. Brookover, who at 31 is older than most undergraduates. "When you're sitting at your computer, it's the same machine you've downloaded music with, possibly illegally, the same machine you streamed videos for free that showed on HBO last night."

Ms. Brookover, who works at the 14 campus library, has pondered the differ- ences between researching in the stacks and online. "Because you're not walking into a library, you're not physically hold- ing the article, which takes you closer to 'this doesn't belong to me,'" she said. Online, "everything can belong to you really easily."

> "Online, 'everything can belong to you really easily.'"

A University of Notre Dame anthropologist, Susan D. Blum, disturbed by 15 the high rates of reported plagiarism, set out to understand how students view authorship and the written word, or "texts" in Ms. Blum's academic language.

She conducted her ethnographic research among 234 Notre Dame under- 16 graduates. "Today's students stand at the crossroads of a new way of conceiving texts and the people who create them and who quote them," she wrote last year in the book *My Word! Plagiarism and College Culture*, published by Cornell University Press.

Ms. Blum argued that student writing exhibits some of the same qualities 17 of pastiche that drive other creative endeavors today—TV shows that con- stantly reference other shows or rap music that samples from earlier songs.

In an interview, she said the idea of an author whose singular effort 18 creates an original work is rooted in Enlightenment ideas of the individual. It is buttressed by the Western concept of intellectual property rights as secured by copyright law. But both traditions are being challenged. "Our notion of authorship and originality was born, it flourished, and it may be waning," Ms. Blum said.

She contends that undergraduates are less interested in cultivating a unique 19 and authentic identity—as their 1960s counterparts were—than in trying on many different personas, which the web enables with social networking.

"If you are not so worried about presenting yourself as absolutely unique, 20 then it's O.K. if you say other people's words, it's O.K. if you say things you don't believe, it's O.K. if you write papers you couldn't care less about because they accomplish the task, which is turning something in and getting a grade," Ms. Blum said, voicing student attitudes. "And it's O.K. if you put words out there without getting any credit."

The notion that there might be a new model young person, who freely 21 borrows from the vortex of information to mash up a new creative work, fueled a brief brouhaha earlier this year with Helene Hegemann, a German teenager whose best-selling novel about Berlin club life turned out to include passages lifted from others.

Instead of offering an abject apology, Ms. Hegemann insisted, "There's 22 no such thing as originality anyway, just authenticity." A few critics rose to her defense, and the book remained a finalist for a fiction prize (but did not win).

That theory does not wash with Sarah Wilensky, a senior at Indiana 23 University, who said that relaxing plagiarism standards "does not foster creativity, it fosters laziness."

"You're not coming up with new ideas if you're grabbing and mixing and 24 matching," said Ms. Wilensky, who took aim at Ms. Hegemann in a column in her student newspaper headlined "Generation Plagiarism."

"It may be increasingly accepted, but there are still plenty of creative 25 people—authors and artists and scholars—who are doing original work," Ms. Wilensky said in an interview. "It's kind of an insult that that ideal is gone, and now we're left only to make collages of the work of previous generations."

In the view of Ms. Wilensky, whose writing skills earned her the role of 26 informal editor of other students' papers in her freshman dorm, plagiarism has nothing to do with trendy academic theories.

The main reason it occurs, she said, is because students leave high school 27 unprepared for the intellectual rigors of college writing.

"If you're taught how to closely read sources and synthesize them into 28 your own original argument in middle and high school, you're not going to be tempted to plagiarize in college, and you certainly won't do so unknowingly," she said.

At the University of California, Davis, of the 196 plagiarism cases referred 29 to the disciplinary office last year, a majority did not involve students ignorant of the need to credit the writing of others.

Many times, said Donald J. Dudley, who oversees the discipline office on 30 the campus of 32,000, it was students who intentionally copied—knowing it was wrong—who were "unwilling to engage the writing process."

"Writing is difficult, and doing it well takes time and practice," he said.   31

And then there was a case that had nothing to do with a younger gener- 32 ation's evolving view of authorship. A student accused of plagiarism came to Mr. Dudley's office with her parents, and the father admitted that he was the one responsible for the plagiarism. The wife assured Mr. Dudley that it would not happen again.

⊘ AT ISSUE: SOURCES FOR UNDERSTANDING PLAGIARISM

1. Gabriel begins inductively, presenting three paragraphs of evidence before he states his thesis. Is this the best strategy, or should these examples appear later in his discussion? Explain.

2. In paragraph 5, Gabriel notes that "many students simply do not grasp that using words they did not write is a serious misdeed." Is this his thesis statement? Does he take a position, or is he just presenting information?

3. Why, according to Gabriel, is plagiarism so widespread? Do you think the reasons he cites in any way excuse plagiarism—at least accidental plagiarism? Does Gabriel seem to think they do?

4. What is *pastiche* (para. 17)? What is a collage (25)? How does the concept of pastiche or collage apply to plagiarism? Do you see the use of pastiche in TV shows or popular music (17) as different from its use in academic writing? Why or why not?

5. Summarize Sarah Wilensky's views (23–28) on the issue Gabriel discusses. Do you agree with her? Do you agree with Helene Hegemann's statement, "There's no such thing as originality anyway, just authenticity" (22)?

6. Do you think the anecdote in paragraph 32 is a strong ending for this article? Does the paragraph need a more forceful concluding statement? Explain.

This article appeared in *Insider Higher Education* on May 23, 2017.

BAD IDEA ABOUT WRITING: PLAGIARISM DESERVES TO BE PUNISHED

JENNIFER MOTT-SMITH

"College Plagiarism Reaches All-Time High"
"Studies Find More Students Cheating, With High Achievers No Exception"

Headlines like these from *the Huffington Post* and *the New York Times* scream at 1 us about an increase in plagiarism. As a society, we feel embattled, surrounded by falling standards; we bemoan the increasing immorality of our youth. Plagiarism, we know, is an immoral act, a simple case of right and wrong, and as such, deserves to be punished.

However, nothing is simple about plagiarism. In fact, the more we exam- 2 ine plagiarism, the more inconsistencies we find, and the more confusion.

How we think about the issue of plagiarism is clouded by the fact that it is 3 often spoken of as a crime. Plagiarism is not only seen as immoral; it is seen as stealing—the stealing of ideas or words. In his book *Free Culture*, Stanford law professor Lawrence Lessig questions what it can possibly mean to steal an idea.

> "I understand what I am taking when I take the picnic table you put in your backyard. I am taking a thing, the picnic table, and after I take it, you don't have it. But what am I taking when I take the good idea you had to put a picnic table in the backyard—by, for example, going to Sears, buying a table, and putting it in my backyard? What is the thing that I am taking then?"

Lessig gets at the idea that, when a person borrows an idea, no harm is 4 done to the party from whom it was taken. But what about loss in revenues as a form of harm? Surely there is no loss of revenues when a student plagia-rizes a paper. From Lessig's metaphor we can see that theft, and even copyright infringement, are not entirely apt ways to think about plagiarism.

But Lessig's metaphor does not help us understand that, in academic 5 writing, acknowledgment of sources is highly valued. Neither does it reveal that taking ideas and using them in your own writing, with conventional attri-bution, is a sophisticated skill that requires a good deal of practice to master.

There are at least three important things to understand about the com- 6 plexity of using sources. First, ideas are often a mixture of one's own ideas, those we read and those we discuss with friends—making it hard or even impossible to sort out who owns what. Second, writers who are learning a new field often "try out" ideas and phrases from other writers in order to master the field. That process, which allows them to learn, involves little or no deceit. And third, expectations for citing sources vary among contexts and readers, making it not only confusing to learn the rules but impossible to satisfy them all.

It is quite hard to separate one's ideas from those of others. When we read, 7 we always bring our own knowledge to what we're reading. Writers cannot say everything; they have to rely on readers to supply their own contribution to make meaning. One difficulty arises when you read an argument with unnamed steps. As a good reader, you fill them in so you can make sense of the argument. Now, if you were to write about those missing steps, would they be your ideas or those of your source?

Writers may reuse the ideas of others, but surely they know when they 8 reuse words, so should they attribute them? Perhaps not. Words are not discrete entities that can be recombined in countless ways, rather, they fall into patterns that serve certain ways of thinking, the very ways of thinking or habits of mind that we try to instill in students.

The fact is that language is formulaic, meaning that certain words com- 9 monly occur together. There are many idioms, such as "toe the line" or "cut corners" that need not be attributed. There are also many co-occurring words that don't quite count as idioms, such as "challenge the status quo," "it should also be noted that . . ." and "The purpose of this study is to . . ." that similarly do not require attribution. Those are called collocations. Student writers need to acquire and use a great number of them in academic writing. What this means is that not every verbatim reuse is plagiarism.

"Much research has shown that patchwriting is not deceitful and therefore should not be punished."

Moreover, imposing strict rules 10 against word reuse may function to prevent student writers from learning to write in their fields. When student writers reuse patterns of words without attribution in an attempt to learn how to sound like a journalist, say, or a biologist, or a literary theorist, it is called *patchwriting*. In fact, not only student writers but all writers patch together pieces of text from sources, using their own language to sew the seams, in order to learn the language of a new field.

Because of the complex way in which patchwriting mixes text from var- 11 ious sources, it can be extremely difficult to cite one's sources. Despite this lack of attribution, much research has shown that patchwriting is not deceitful and therefore should not be punished. In fact, some scholars are interested in exploring how writing teachers could use the concept of patchwriting to help student writers develop their own writing skills.

The third reason that it is not always easy to acknowledge sources is that 12 expectations for referencing vary widely and what counts as plagiarism depends on context. If, for instance, you use a piece of historic information in a novel, you don't have to cite it, but if you use the same piece of information in a history paper, you do. Journalists typically do not supply citations, although they have fact checkers making sure their claims are accurate. In business, people often start their reports by cutting and pasting earlier reports without attribution. And in the academy, research has shown that the reuse of words in science articles is much more common and accepted than it is in the humanities.

In high school, student writers probably used textbooks that did not con- 13 tain citations, and once in college, they may observe their professors giving lectures that come straight from the textbook without citation, cribbing one another's syllabi and cutting and pasting the plagiarism policy into their syllabi. They may even notice that their university lifted the wording of its plagiarism policy from another institution!

In addition to those differing standards for different genres or fields of 14 study, research has also shown that individual "experts" such as experienced writers and teachers do not agree whether or not a given piece of writing counts as plagiarism. Given such wide disagreement over what constitutes plagiarism, it is quite difficult, perhaps impossible, for student writers to meet everyone's expectations for proper attribution. Rather than assuming that they are trying to pass off someone else's work as their own and therefore deserve punishment, we should recognize the complexity of separating one's ideas from those of others, mastering authoritative phrases and meeting diverse attribution standards.

While most people feel that plagiarism deserves punishment, some under- 15 stand that plagiarism is not necessarily deceitful or deserving censure. Today, many writers and writing teachers reject the image of the writer as working alone, using (God-given) talent to produce an original piece of work. In fact, writers often do two things that are proscribed by plagiarism policies: they recombine ideas in their writing and they collaborate with others.

Interestingly, the image of the lone, divinely inspired writer is only a few 16 hundred years old, a European construct from the Romantic era. Before the eighteenth century or so, writers who copied were respected as writers. Even today, rather than seeing copying as deceitful, we sometimes view it as a sign of respect or free publicity.

Today, millennial students often copy without deceitful intent. Reposting 17 content on their Facebook pages and sharing links with their friends, they may not cite because they are making an allusion; readers who recognize the source without a citation share the in-joke.

In school, millennials may not cite because they are not used to doing so 18 or they believe that having too many citations detracts from their authority. In either case, these are not students trying to get away with passing someone else's work off as their own, and, in fact, many studies have concluded that plagiarism, particularly that of second-language student writers, is not done with the intent to deceive.

Despite these complexities of textual reuse, most faculty members never- 19 theless expect student writers to do their "own work." In fact, student writers are held to a higher standard and punished more rigorously than established writers.

What is even more troublesome is that teachers' determinations of when 20 plagiarism has occurred is more complicated than simply noting whether a student has given credit to sources or not. Research has shown that teachers let inadequate attribution go if they feel the overall sophistication or authority of the paper is good, whereas they are stricter about citing rules when the sophistication or authority is weak. Furthermore, they tend to more readily recognize authority in papers written by students who are members of a powerful group (e.g., whites, native English speakers or students whose parents went to college). Thus, in some instances, plagiarism may be more about social inequity than individual deceit.

As we come to realize that writers combine their ideas with those of others 21 in ways that cannot always be separated out for the purposes of attribution, that writers often reuse phrases in acceptable ways, that citing standards themselves vary widely and are often in the eye of the beholder, and that enforcement of plagiarism rules is an equity issue, the studies and articles panicking over plagiarism make less and less sense. In looking at plagiarism from the different perspectives offered by collaborative writers and today's millennial student writers, we can see that much plagiarism is not about stealing ideas or deceiving readers.

Unless plagiarism is out-and-out cheating, like cutting and pasting an 22 entire paper from the internet or paying someone to write it, we should be cautious about reacting to plagiarism with the intent to punish. For much plagiarism, a better response is to relax and let writers continue to practice the difficult skill of using sources.

❂ AT ISSUE: SOURCES FOR UNDERSTANDING PLAGIARISM

1. Many people, like law professor Lawrence Lessig (quoted in paragraph 3), see plagiarism as theft, but Mott-Smith disagrees. Why?

2. In paragraph 6, Mott-Smith introduces three key concepts to explain "the complexity of using sources." In your own words, summarize these three ideas.

3. What does Mott-Smith mean when she says that language is "formulaic" (para. 9)? Why does she believe this characterization explains—or even excuses—some plagiarism?

4. Mott-Smith points out that expectations for citing sources can vary from one situation to another. For example, different instructors and different kinds of writing tasks may have different citation standards. Do you believe that the fact that there is so little agreement about what constitutes plagiarism means that some kinds of plagiarism should not be punished? Is this what Mott-Smith believes?

5. How are Mott-Smith's ideas about student plagiarism like and unlike Richard Posner's ideas (p. 375) about plagiarism in professional settings?

6. According to Mott-Smith, what is the difference between "out-and-out cheating" (22) and the kind of casual, inadvertent plagiarism that occurs more widely? How does she believe each of these two kinds of plagiarism should be dealt with? What do you think?

This essay appeared in *Newsday* on May 18, 2003.

THE TRUTH ABOUT PLAGIARISM

RICHARD A. POSNER

Plagiarism is considered by most writers, teachers, journalists, scholars, and even 1
members of the general public to be the capital intellectual crime. Being caught
out in plagiarism can blast a politician's career, earn a college student expulsion,
and destroy a writer's, scholar's, or journalist's reputation. In recent days, for example, the *New York Times* has referred to "widespread fabrication and plagiarism"
by reporter Jayson Blair as "a low point in the 152-year history of the newspaper."

In James Hynes' splendid satiric novella of plagiarism, *Casting the Runes*, 2
the plagiarist, having by black magic murdered one of the historians whom he
plagiarized and tried to murder a second, is himself killed by the very same
black magic, deployed by the widow of his murder victim.

There is a danger of overkill. Plagiarism 3
can be a form of fraud, but it is no accident that,
unlike real theft, it is not a crime. If a thief steals
your car, you are out the market value of the car,

> "There is a
> danger of overkill."

but if a writer copies material from a book you wrote, you don't have to replace
the book. At worst, the undetected plagiarist obtains a reputation that he does
not deserve (that is the element of fraud in plagiarism). The real victim of his
fraud is not the person whose work he copies, but those of his competitors who
scruple to enhance their own reputations by such means.

The most serious plagiarisms are by students and professors, whose unde- 4
tected plagiarisms disrupt the system of student and scholarly evaluation.
The least serious are those that earned the late Stephen Ambrose and Doris
Kearns Goodwin such obloquy° last year. Popular historians, they jazzed   *Abusive language*
up their books with vivid passages copied from previous historians without
quotation marks, though with footnote attributions that made their "crime"
easy to detect. (One reason that plagiarism, like littering, is punished heavily,
even though an individual act of plagiarism usually does little or no harm, is
that it is normally very difficult to detect—but not in the case of Ambrose and
Goodwin.) Competing popular historians might have been injured, but I'm
not aware of anyone actually claiming this.

Confusion of plagiarism with theft is one reason plagiarism engenders 5
indignation; another is a confusion of it with copyright infringement. Wholesale copying of copyrighted material is an infringement of a property right, and
legal remedies are available to the copyright holder. But the copying of brief
passages, even from copyrighted materials, is permissible under the doctrine
of "fair use," while wholesale copying from material that is in the public
domain—material that never was copyrighted, or on which the copyright has
expired—presents no copyright issue at all.

375

Plagiarism of work in the public domain is more common than otherwise. 6 Consider a few examples: *West Side Story* is a thinly veiled copy (with music added) of *Romeo and Juliet*, which in turn plagiarized Arthur Brooke's *The Tragicall Historye of Romeo and Juliet*, published in 1562, which in turn copied from several earlier *Romeo and Juliets*, all of which were copies of Ovid's story of Pyramus and Thisbe.

Paradise Lost plagiarizes the book of Genesis in the Old Testament. 7 Classical musicians plagiarize folk melodies (think only of Dvorak, Bartok, and Copland) and often "quote" (as musicians say) from earlier classical works. Edouard Manet's most famous painting, *Déjeuner sur l'herbe*, copies earlier paintings by Raphael, Titian, and Courbet, and *My Fair Lady* plagiarized Shaw's play *Pygmalion*, while Woody Allen's movie *Play It Again, Sam* "quotes" a famous scene from *Casablanca*. Countless movies are based on books, such as *The Thirty-Nine Steps* on John Buchan's novel of that name or *For Whom the Bell Tolls* on Hemingway's novel.

Many of these "plagiarisms" were authorized, and perhaps none was 8 deceptive; they are what Christopher Ricks in his excellent book *Allusions to the Poets* helpfully terms *allusion* rather than *plagiarism*. But what they show is that copying with variations is an important form of creativity, and this should make us prudent and measured in our condemnations of plagiarism.

Especially when the term is extended from literal copying to the copy- 9 ing of ideas. Another phrase for copying an idea, as distinct from the form in which it is expressed, is dissemination of ideas. If one needs a license to repeat another person's idea, or if one risks ostracism by one's professional community for failing to credit an idea to its originator, who may be forgotten or unknown, the dissemination of ideas is impeded.

I have heard authors of history textbooks criticized for failing to doc- 10 ument their borrowing of ideas from previous historians. This is an absurd criticism. The author of a textbook makes no claim to originality; rather the contrary—the most reliable, if not necessarily the most exciting, textbook is one that confines itself to ideas already well accepted, not at all novel.

It would be better if the term *plagiarism* were confined to literal copying, 11 and moreover literal copying that is not merely unacknowledged but decep- tive. Failing to give credit where credit is due should be regarded as a lesser, indeed usually merely venial, offense.

The concept of plagiarism has expanded, and the sanctions for it, though 12 they remain informal rather than legal, have become more severe, in tandem with the rise of individualism. Journal articles are no longer published anon- ymously, and ghostwriters demand that their contributions be acknowledged.

Replaceable

Individualism and a cult of originality go hand in hand. Each of us 13 supposes that our contribution to society is unique rather than fungible° and so deserves public recognition, which plagiarism clouds.

This is a modern view. We should be aware that the high value placed on 14 originality is a specific cultural, and even field-specific, phenomenon, rather than an aspect of the universal moral law.

Judges, who try to conceal rather than to flaunt their originality, far from 15 crediting their predecessors with original thinking like to pretend that there is no original thinking in law, that judges are just a transmission belt for rules and principles laid down by the framers of statutes or the Constitution.

Resorting to plagiarism to obtain a good grade or a promotion is fraud and 16 should be punished, though it should not be confused with "theft." But I think the zeal to punish plagiarism reflects less a concern with the real injuries that it occasionally inflicts than with a desire on the part of leaders of professional communities, such as journalists and historians, to enhance their profession's reputation.

Journalists (like politicians) have a bad reputation for truthfulness, and 17 historians, in this "postmodernist"° era, are suspected of having embraced an extreme form of relativism and of having lost their regard for facts. Both groups hope by taking a very hard line against plagiarism and fabrication to reassure the public that they are serious diggers after truth whose efforts, a form of "sweat equity," deserve protection against copycats.

Postmodernism is a school of criticism that denies concepts such as scientific certainty and absolute truth.

Their anxieties are understandable; but the rest of us will do well to keep 18 the matter in perspective, realizing that the term *plagiarism* is used loosely and often too broadly; that much plagiarism is harmless and (when the term is defined broadly) that some has social value.

⊖ AT ISSUE: SOURCES FOR UNDERSTANDING PLAGIARISM

1. According to Posner, how do most people define *plagiarism*? How is the definition he proposes different from theirs? Do you think his definition is too broad? Too narrow?

2. Why does Posner believe that the plagiarisms committed by students and professors are the most serious? How would you argue against this position?

3. How do the examples Posner cites in paragraphs 6 and 7 strengthen his argument? Do you agree that the examples he gives here constitute plagiarism? Why or why not?

4. Explain the connection the author makes in paragraph 15 between judges and plagiarism. (Note that Posner himself is a federal judge.)

5. Why, according to Posner, do journalists and historians think plagiarism should be punished severely?

6. According to Posner, "the truth about plagiarism" is that "much plagiarism is harmless and (when the term is defined broadly) that some has social value" (para. 18). Does the evidence he presents in this essay support this conclusion? What connection do you see between this position and his comments about the rise of individualism and the "cult of originality" in paragraphs 12–14?

This article originally appeared in the *Chronicle of Higher Education* on March 30, 2016.

WHEN PLAGIARISM IS A PLEA FOR HELP

HELEN RUBINSTEIN

That summer night, at a dinner table surrounded by writing teachers, the plagiarism stories were hard to stop. There was the freshman who, given the writing prompt "Why Do I Procrastinate?," pasted in Yahoo Answers. I told about the senior who turned in an essay paraphrasing a scholarly article synonym by synonym, word by word. The winning story was the student who asked permission to study a novel written by his professor and then turned in an essay that copied text from the book jacket, including a line from the author bio: "She lives in Chicago with her two sons and their cat."

There was one I didn't tell. It's not a dinner-table story. It might not even be a story about plagiarism. For a while, every time I talked about it, I had to begin by saying, "I'm glad I'm not the kind of person who could feel responsible for something like this." What I meant was that people who believe the death of someone else could be their own fault are usually deluding themselves into a sense of omnipotence. "I'm glad I'm not the kind of person who could feel responsible," I repeated to myself. I needed that to be true.

My student—I'll call her "Susan"—dressed well. Big sweaters she'd tuck a knee into. Long hair, pale face, pretty. Twice that September, she had stayed after class to discuss the recommended reading—she'd actually *done* the recommended reading. When she was sick, she emailed: "Hello Professor! . . . My residence hall is currently experiencing 'the flu' epidemic and just my luck I believe I have it now." She was a freshman, keen to succeed: "Do you think I should soldier through the sickness and come to class anyway? . . . I've never been sick in college before and your class happens to be the only mandatory one I must attend."

It wasn't just the flu that was spreading that semester—so was the plagiarism. One weekend I plowed through 36 first drafts, and Susan's was not the first or the last to be of sketchy origin in that stack. "Why are there so many smokers on campus?," her paper began—innocently enough. Then she turned to the topic of e-cigarettes, citing numbers and statistics without quote marks or attribution. None of it was in answer to the actual assignment. And it didn't take long to find the sources she'd copied.

Susan had already missed several classes because of illness, and sent me countless emails—messages with subject lines that shouted "Hospital" and "Emergency Please Read." "Just focus on getting better," I would respond. "Don't worry about the class." In another email she mentioned she had been "diagnosed with anxiety" recently and was on a "low dose of anxiety medication." She was absent again on the day I handed back the drafts and gave a speech about plagiarism for the benefit of the six or eight students I had caught. *Caught*—the word betrays how I sat hunched over those essays, feeling hunted even as I hunted.

My stern warning surprised students. Some didn't realize the word 6
"plagiarism"—with its trill of alarm—might describe what they'd done.
Some didn't know plagiarism would "count" in a draft. I didn't report
any of those students to the administration, but I did deduct points—
proportionate to the level of plagiarism in each case—that would reduce the
students' final grade. All they had to do to avoid further trouble was not
plagiarize the final paper.

Shortly after, I got an inquiry from the dean's office about Susan, identi- 7
fying her by her student number. She'd apparently been having difficulties in
other classes as well: Had I noticed any problems? I mentioned the plagiarism
incident and noted that she was coming to class again yet performing erratically. The dean's office advised me to "follow protocol"—make sure that she
understood what she had done wrong and that she did not repeat it.

But Susan did repeat it. She had thanked me for being so "tolerant, consid- 8
erate, and kindhearted" after the first incident but when she turned in her final
paper, I was stunned to find that it, too, was plagiarized. I sent Susan a message
expressing my dismay and telling her that I would have to both fail the essay
and submit a report on her plagiarism to the administration.

It's too easy, as a teacher, to let plagiarism propel you toward protocol, 9
that means of moving forward without thinking. It's too easy to feel that you
must turn the tables, prevent the student from *pulling one over* or *getting away
with it*—all of those terrible clichés that hide the reality of how plagiarism, to a
teacher, is the rare instance in which the student seizes power.

After emailing Susan, I met with a col-   10
league to seek his advice. Once the door was
closed, he told me not to bother with proto-   "How can you
col or with reporting the student. It won't be   tell if a student is
worth the trouble, he said—not worth the   just stressed or
onerousness of photocopying, scanning, pro-   out-of-control?"
viding evidence, and navigating the bureau-
cratic near-legalese.

I was still deciding whether to follow his advice when Susan emailed a long, 11
dense reply: "I will not be dragged down because one single professor does not
like me. . . . How can I respect a teacher that has done nothing but bully me and
find any loophole to make me fail? . . . I DO NOT DESERVE THIS PUNISH-
MENT." And: "I will use every ounce of my power to set this straight."

I read it again and again. At dinner with friends that night, I described the 12
email and quoted its subject line: "This Has Gone Far Enough."

"She's crazy," someone said. I had no way of knowing if that was the 13
case. How can you tell if a student is just stressed or out-of-control? But the
truth was: I did feel like I'd been pressuring Susan—with my feverish photocopying, my petty collection of evidence, and now this ha-ha dinnertime
story. "Report the plagiarism," my friends insisted. "Follow protocol. Cover
your ass."

We all want to write about the times we succeed in the classroom. But 14
what about the times we teach poorly? What about the times we fail?

After she died, her essay—with the big green F in my handwriting circled 15 and my comments scrawled across its cover page—sat on a chair in my house for weeks. One day I flipped it over. Eventually I moved it under the chair, then under a table. I'm not supposed to keep student work. Nor am I supposed to throw it away. Nor am I supposed to show it to Susan's parents without her permission. Nor would I ever, ever return this essay to them, with its angry-scrawled F.

A week later, I received the news of her death in an email from the 16 university, with the words "deceased student," followed by her student ID number. (Protocol.) Then came another email from the colleague I had consulted for advice: "Thank God you didn't report her and don't have that now on your conscience."

Except, as far as Susan knew, I *had* reported her. The notice didn't tell 17 me how she died. It explained that she withdrew from college the day after she'd emailed me, and passed away six days after that. Her death seemed to confirm my worst suspicions of myself: that I am heartless, overly bound by some cockeyed ideal of fairness, not in touch enough with my students' human selves. I trembled when I had to tell a room of 18-year-olds that their classmate had died, but I wasn't sure whether that was because I feared I would cry, or because I feared I wouldn't.

Three weeks later, the semester ended. The internet had informed us that 18 Susan died from an overdose of an illegal recreational drug, though I had little idea what to do with that information, what it might mean. The class shared a moment of silence in her memory. And then, after everyone else had left, one student approached my desk. "I can't stop thinking about Susan," he confessed. "I feel so guilty. She asked me where to buy pot and I told her."

I saw then that, in her wake, Susan had left behind a whole universe of 19 people who felt responsible for her death. "It's not your fault," I said with as much conviction as I could muster—hoping to persuade both the young man and myself that it was egotistical to believe any of us have that much power.

But we long for such power. I see the longing in my tendency to experience 20 plagiarism as personal—about me or my class. I see it in my nervousness when faced with a student's power to deceive—even though plagiarism is, more than anything, an expression of a student's powerlessness.

Plagiarism is a gag on the voice, a paper bag over the face. So what if—the 21 next time our students plagiarize—we tried harder to actually see them? What if we could understand plagiarism as an expression of exhaustion, of distress, maybe even a plea for help?

The thing that haunts me, after all, is not Susan's rage in her last message 22 to me, but my own rage in my last message to her. The angrily scrawled F is a guilty conscience I don't want to forget. I didn't kill Susan—I don't have that kind of power. But I did have the power to fail her. And that F is a reminder that the next time a student hides her thinking behind someone else's, what I'd like to do is not fail her, but try to help her *not* fail.

AT ISSUE: SOURCES FOR UNDERSTANDING PLAGIARISM

1. This essay appeared in a publication for college instructors and administrators. Given that this is her audience, do you think Rubinstein's purpose here is to explain or justify her actions? To create awareness of a problem? Or, does she expect her readers to propose—or even to take-some kind of action?

2. What attitude toward plagiarism do the professors discussed in the opening paragraph seem to have? How might you explain that attitude?

3. Why does Rubinstein say that the incident she will discuss "might not even be a story about plagiarism" (para. 2)? If the story isn't about plagiarism, what *is* it about?

4. According to Rubinstein, what exactly did Susan do that constituted plagiarism? What other details does Rubinstein give readers about Susan, and why? For example, why does Rubinstein enumerate the many emails she received from Susan?

5. In paragraph 9, Rubinstein says, "It's too easy, as a teacher, to let plagiarism propel you toward protocol, . . . " What does she mean? Is she questioning her own actions here? Explain.

6. In paragraph 13, Rubinstein asks, "How can you tell if a student is just stressed or out-of-control?" Does she answer this question? How would you answer it?

7. What steps do you think colleges—or individual instructors—could take to avoid a situation like the one Rubinstein describes? How do you suppose Rubinstein might react to your suggestions? Why?

8. Whom (or what) do you blame for the incident's tragic outcome? Why?

9. If Rubinstein were going to write an argumentative essay for the same publication taking a position on how academic plagiarism should be addressed, what would her position be? Suggest a thesis statement for this essay.

This essay originally appeared in the *Los Angeles Times* on June 17, 2012.

ESSAY MILLS: A COARSE LESSON IN CHEATING

DAN ARIELY

Sometimes as I decide what kind of papers to assign to my students, I worry 1
about essay mills, companies whose sole purpose is to generate essays for high
school and college students (in exchange for a fee, of course).

The mills claim that the papers are meant to be used as reference mate- 2
rial to help students write their own, original papers. But with names such as
echeat.com, it's pretty clear what their real purpose is.

Professors in general are concerned about essay mills and their effect on 3
learning, but not knowing exactly what they provide, I wasn't sure how concerned to be. So together with my lab manager Aline Grüneisen, I decided
to check the services out. We ordered a typical college term paper from four
different essay mills. The topic of the paper? Cheating.

Here is the prompt we gave the four essay mills: 4

"When and why do people cheat? Consider the social circumstances 5
involved in dishonesty, and provide a thoughtful response to the topic of cheating. Address various forms of cheating (personal, at work, etc.) and how each
of these can be rationalized by a social culture of cheating."

We requested a term paper for a university-level social psychology class, 6
12 pages long, using 15 sources (cited and referenced in a bibliography). The
paper was to conform to American Psychological Assn. style guidelines and
needed to be completed in the next two weeks. All four of the essay mills
agreed to provide such a paper, charging us in advance, between $150 and
$216 for the paper.

Right on schedule, the essays came, and I 7
have to say that, to some degree, they allayed
my fears that students can rely on the services
to get good grades. What we got back from the
mills can best be described as gibberish. A few
of the papers attempted to mimic APA style, but
none achieved it without glaring errors. Cita-

> "What we got back
> from the mills can
> best be described
> as gibberish."

tions were sloppy. Reference lists contained outdated and unknown sources,
including blog posts. Some of the links to reference material were broken.

And the writing quality? Awful. The authors of all four papers seemed 8
to have a very tenuous grasp of the English language, not to mention how to
format an essay. Paragraphs jumped bluntly from one topic to another, often
simply listing various forms of cheating or providing a long stream of examples
that were never explained or connected to the "thesis" of the paper.

One paper contained this paragraph: "Cheating by healers. Healing is 9 different. There is harmless healing, when healers-cheaters and wizards offer omens, lapels, damage to withdraw, the husband-wife back and stuff. We read in the newspaper and just smile. But these days fewer people believe in wizards."

This comes from another: "If the large allowance of study undertook on 10 scholar betraying is any suggestion of academia and professors' powerful yearn to decrease scholar betraying, it appeared expected these mind-set would component into the creation of their school room guidelines."

And finally, these gems: 11

"By trusting blindfold only in stable love, loyalty, responsibility, and 12 honesty the partners assimilate with the credulous and naive persons of the past."

"Women have a much greater necessity to feel special." 13

"The future generation must learn for historical mistakes and develop the 14 sense of pride and responsibility for its actions."

It's hard to believe that students purchasing such papers would ever do so 15 again.

And the story does not end there. We submitted the four essays to 16 WriteCheck.com, a website that inspects papers for plagiarism, and found that two of the papers were 35 percent to 39 percent copied from existing works. We decided to take action on the two papers with substantial plagiarizing and contacted the essay mills requesting our money back. Despite the solid proof we provided to them, the companies insisted they did not plagiarize. One company even threatened to expose us by calling the dean and saying we had purchased the paper.

It's comforting in a way that the technological revolution has not yet solved 17 students' problems. They still have no other option but to actually work on their papers (or maybe cheat in the old-fashioned way and copy from friends). But I do worry about the existence of essay mills and the signal that they send to our students.

As for our refund, we are still waiting. 18

⊘ AT ISSUE: SOURCES FOR UNDERSTANDING PLAGIARISM

1. Consider the title of this essay. What does the word *coarse* mean? What does it suggest in this context?

2. What is an essay mill? Look up the word *mill*. Which of the definitions provided applies to the word as it is used in the phrase *essay mill*?

3. Why does Ariely decide to investigate the services provided by essay mills? What does he want to find out? Is he successful?

4. What does Ariely conclude about the four companies he surveys? Does he provide enough evidence to support his conclusion? If not, what kind of evidence should he add?

5. In paragraph 15, Ariely says, "It's hard to believe that students purchasing such papers would ever do so again." Given the evidence Ariely presents, how do you explain the continued popularity of essay mills?

6. What information does Ariely provide in his conclusion? Do you think he is departing from his essay's central focus here, or do you think the concluding paragraph is an appropriate and effective summary of his ideas? Explain.

VISUAL ARGUMENT: TERM PAPERS FOR SALE ADVERTISEMENT (WEB PAGE)

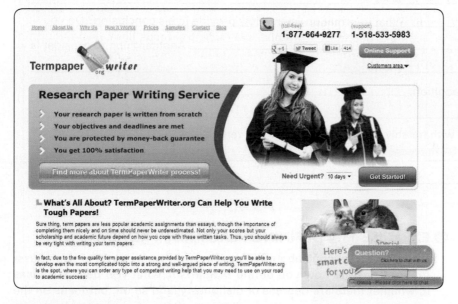

⊘ AT ISSUE: SOURCES FOR UNDERSTANDING PLAGIARISM

1. The web page above is from a site that offers papers for sale to students. What argument does this web page make? What counter-argument could you present?

2. Identify appeals to *logos*, *pathos*, and *ethos* on the TermPaperWriter .org page. Which appeal dominates?

3. Study the images of students on the page. What message do these images convey?

4. Unlike the TermPaperWriter.org page, many other sites that offer papers for sale include errors in grammar, spelling, and punctuation. Search the web for some other sites that offer papers for sale. What errors can you find? Do such errors weaken the message of these ads, or are they irrelevant?

5. A different site offering similar services promises its papers are "100% plagiarism free." Does this promise make sense? Explain.

TEMPLATE FOR WRITING AN ARGUMENT ABOUT PLAGIARISM

Write a one-paragraph argument in which you take a position on where to draw the line with plagiarism. Follow the template below, filling in the blanks to create your argument.

> To many people, plagiarism is theft; to others, however, it is not that simple. For example, some define *plagiarism* as _____
> _____; others see it as _____
> _____. Another thing to consider is
> _____
> _____. In addition, _____
> _____. Despite these differences of opinion,
> plagiarism is often dealt with harshly and can ruin careers and reputations. All things considered,
> _____
> _____.

⊙ EXERCISE 11.4 DEFINING PLAGIARISM: REVIEW

Discuss your feelings about plagiarism with two or three of your class-mates. Consider how you define *plagiarism*, what you believe causes it, whether there are degrees of dishonesty, and so on, but focus on the *effects* of plagiarism—on those who commit it and on those who are its victims. Then, write a paragraph that summarizes the key points of your discussion.

⊙ EXERCISE 11.5 WRITING AN ESSAY

Write an argumentative essay on the topic, "Where Should We Draw the Line with Plagiarism?" Begin by defining what you mean by *plagiarism*, and then narrow your discussion down to a particular group—for exam-ple, high school or college students, historians, scientists, or journalists. Cite the sources on pages 366–85, and be sure to document the sources you use and to include a works-cited page. (See Chapter 10 for informa-tion on documenting sources.)

⊙ EXERCISE 11.6 REVIEWING THE ELEMENTS OF ARGUMENT

Review the four pillars of argument discussed in Chapter 1. Does your essay include all four elements of an effective argument? Add anything that is missing. Then, label the elements of your argument.

⊘ WRITING ASSIGNMENTS: USING SOURCES RESPONSIBLY

1. Write an argument in which you take a position on who (or what) is to blame for plagiarism among college students. Is plagiarism always the student's fault, or are other people (or other factors) at least partly to blame?

2. Write an essay in which you argue that an honor code will (or will not) eliminate (or at least reduce) plagiarism and other kinds of academic dishonesty at your school.

3. Reread the essays by Richard Posner and Jennifer Mott-Smith in this chapter. Then, write an argument in which you argue that only intentional plagiarism should be punished.

4. Do you consider student plagiarism a victimless crime that is best left unpunished? If so, why? If not, how does it affect its victims — for example, the student who plagiarizes, the instructor, the other students in the class, and the school?

Writing Literary Arguments

When you write an essay about literature, you have a number of options. For example, you can write a **response** (expressing your reactions to a poem, play, or story), or you can write an **explication** (focusing on a work's individual elements, such as a poem's imagery, meter, figurative language, and diction). You can also write an **analysis** of a work's theme, a character in a play or a story, or a work's historical or cultural context. Another option, which is discussed in the pages that follow, is to write a literary argument.

What Is a Literary Argument?

When you write a literary argument, you do more than just respond to, explicate, or analyze a work of literature. When you develop a **literary argument**, you take a position about a literary work (or works), support that position with evidence, and refute possible opposing arguments. You might, for example, take the position that a familiar interpretation of a well-known work is limited in some way, that a work's impact today is different from its impact when it was written, or that two apparently very different works have some significant similarities.

It is important to understand that not every essay about literature is a literary argument. For example, you might use a discussion of Tillie Olsen's short story "I Stand Here Ironing," with its sympathetic portrait of a young mother during the Great Depression, to support an argument in favor of President Franklin D. Roosevelt's expansion of social welfare programs. Alternatively, you might use Martín Espada's poem "Why I Went to College" to support your own decision to continue your education. However, writing a literary argument involves much more than discussing a literary work in order to support a particular position or referring to a character to explain a personal choice you made. A literary argument *takes a stand* about a work (or works) of literature.

Stating an Argumentative Thesis

When you develop an argumentative thesis about literature, your goal is to state a thesis that has an edge—one that takes a stand on your topic. Like any effective thesis, the thesis of a literary argument should be clearly worded and specific; it should also be more than a statement of fact.

INEFFECTIVE THESIS (TOO GENERAL)	In "A&P," Sammy faces a difficult decision.
EFFECTIVE THESIS (MORE SPECIFIC)	Sammy's decision to quit his job reveals more about the conformist society in which "A&P" is set than about Sammy himself.
INEFFECTIVE THESIS (STATES A FACT)	The theme of *Hamlet* is often seen as an Oedipal conflict.
EFFECTIVE THESIS (TAKES A STAND)	Although many critics have identified an Oedipal conflict in *Hamlet*, Shakespeare's play is also a story of a young man who is struggling with familiar problems—love, family, and his future.

Here are three possible thesis statements that you could support in a literary argument:

- Charlotte Perkins Gilman's short story "The Yellow Wallpaper," usually seen as a feminist story, is actually a ghost story.

- The two characters in August Strindberg's play *The Stronger* seem to be rivals for the affection of a man, but they are really engaged in a professional rivalry to see who gives the better performance.

- Although many readers might see Wilfred Owen's "Dulce et Decorum Est" as the more powerful poem because of its graphic imagery of war, Carl Sandburg's understated "Grass" is likely to have a greater impact on modern readers, who have been overexposed to violent images.

(For more on developing a thesis statement, see Chapter 7.)

Choosing Evidence

Like any argument, a literary argument relies on evidence. Some of this evidence can be found in the literary work itself. For example, to make a point about a character's antisocial behavior, you would cite specific examples of such behavior from the work. To make a point about a poet's use of biblical allusions, you would present examples of such allusions from the poem.

> **NOTE**
>
> Be careful not to substitute plot summary for evidence. For example, summarizing everything that happens to a character will not convince your readers that the character is motivated by envy. Choose only *relevant* examples—in this case, specific instances of a character's jealous behavior, including relevant quotations from the literary work.

Evidence can also come from **literary criticism**—scholarly articles by experts in the field that analyze and evaluate works of literature. For example, to argue that a particular critical theory is inaccurate, outdated, or oversimplified, you would first quote critics who support that theory and then explain why you disagree with their interpretation. (For more on evaluating potential sources for your essay, see Chapter 8.)

Writing a Literary Argument

The structure of a literary argument is similar to the structure of any other argument: it includes a **thesis statement** in the introduction, supporting **evidence**, **refutation** of opposing arguments, and a strong **concluding statement**. However, unlike other arguments, literary arguments follow specific conventions for writing about literature:

- In your essay's first paragraph, include the author's full name and the title of each work you are discussing.

- Use present tense when discussing events in works of literature. For example, if you are discussing "I Stand Here Ironing," you would say, "The mother *worries* [not *worried*] about her ability to provide for her child." There are two exceptions to this rule. Use past tense when referring to historical events: "The Great Depression *made* things difficult for mothers like the narrator." Also use past tense to refer to events that came before the action described in the work: "The mother is particularly vulnerable because her husband *left* her alone to support her children."

- Italicize titles of plays and novels. Put titles of poems and short stories in quotation marks.

- If you quote more than four lines of prose (or more than three lines of poetry), indent the entire quotation one inch from the left-hand margin. Do not include quotation marks, and add the parenthetical documentation after the end punctuation. Introduce the quotation with a colon, and do not add extra line spaces above or below it.

- When mentioning writers and literary critics in the body of your essay, use their full names ("Emily Dickinson") the first time you mention them and their last names only ("Dickinson," not "Miss Dickinson" or "Emily") after that.

- Use **MLA documentation style** in your essay, and include a works-cited list. (See Chapter 10 for information on MLA documentation.)

- In your in-text citations (set in parentheses), cite page numbers for stories, act and scene numbers for plays, and line numbers for poems. Use the word *line* or *lines* for the first in-text citation of lines from each poem. After the first citation, you may omit the word *line* or *lines*.

The following literary argument, "Confessions of a Misunderstood Poem: An Analysis of 'The Road Not Taken,'" proposes a new way of interpreting a poem that the student writer characterizes as "familiar but frequently misunderstood."

CONFESSIONS OF A MISUNDERSTOOD POEM: AN ANALYSIS OF "THE ROAD NOT TAKEN"

MEGAN MCGOVERN

Introduction (identifies titles and authors of works to be discussed)

In his poem "Introduction to Poetry," Billy Collins suggests that rather than dissecting a poem to find its meaning, students should use their imaginations to experience poetry. According to Collins, they should "drop a mouse into a poem / and watch him probe his way out" (lines 5–6). However, Collins overstates his case when he implies that analyzing a poem to find out what it might mean is a brutal or

1

deadly process, comparable to tying the poem to a chair and "beating
it with a hose" (15). Rather than killing a poem's spirit, a careful and
methodical dissection can often help the reader better appreciate
its subtler meanings. In fact, with patient coaxing, a poem often has
much to "confess." One such poem is Robert Frost's familiar but frequently misunderstood "The Road Not Taken." An examination of Frost's
"The Road Not Taken" reveals a complex and somewhat troubling message about the arbitrariness of our life choices and our need to idealize
those choices.

> The word *lines* is omitted
> from the in-text citation
> after the first reference to
> lines of a poem.
>
> Thesis statement

    On the surface, Frost's poem seems to have a fairly simple
meaning. The poem's speaker talks about coming to a fork in the
road and choosing the "less-traveled" path. Most readers see
the fork in the road as a metaphor: the road represents life, and
the fork represents an individual's choices in life. By following the
less-traveled road, the speaker Is choosing the less conventional—
and supposedly more emotionally rewarding—route. At the end of the
poem, the speaker indicates his satisfaction when he says his choice
"made all the difference" (line 20). However, Frost himself, referring
to "The Road Not Taken," advised readers "'to be careful of that one;
it's a tricky poem—very tricky,'" encouraging readers not to accept
the most appealing or obvious interpretation (qtd. in Savoie 7–8).
Literary critic Bojana Vujin urges readers to look for "poetic booby
traps such as irony or deceit" in this poem and to enjoy the pleasures
and rewards of discovering instances of "deliberate deceit on the
poet's part" (195). In fact, after the speaker's tone and word choice
are carefully examined, the poem's message seems darker and more
complicated than it did initially.

> 2 Refutation of opposing
>   argument

    The speaker's tone in the first three stanzas suggests indecision,
regret, and, ultimately, lack of power. Rather than bravely facing the
choice between one common path and one uncommon path, the
speaker spends most of the poem considering two seemingly equal
roads, "sorry" not to be able to "travel both" (2). Even after choosing
"the other" road in line 6, the speaker continues for two more stanzas to
weigh his options. The problem is that the two roads are, in fact, indis-
tinguishable. As several critics have observed, "the difference between
the two roads, at least when it comes to the amount of treading they

> 3 Evidence: Analysis and
>   explication of Frost poem

Evidence: Literary criticism

have been exposed to, is but an illusion: "'they both that morning equally lay' and neither is particularly travelled by" (Vujin 197). The roads are worn "really about the same" (10). If there is virtually no difference between the two, then why does Frost draw our attention to this fork in the road—this seemingly critical moment of choice? If Frost had wanted to dramatize a meaningful decision, the roads would be different in some significant way.

Evidence: Literary criticism

One critic, Frank Lentricchia, argues that Frost is demonstrating "'that our life-shaping choices are irrational, that we are fundamentally out of control'" (qtd. in Savoie 13). Similarly, another critic contends that Frost wants his readers "to feel his characters' inner conflicts and to feel as conflicted as his characters, who are all too often lost in themselves" (Plunkett). These two critical views help to explain the speaker's indecision in the first three stanzas. The speaker impulsively chooses "the other" road but cannot accept the arbitrariness of his choice; therefore, he cannot stop considering the first road. He exclaims in the third stanza, "Oh, I kept the first for another day!" (13). In the next two lines, when he finally gives up the possibility of following that first road, he predicts, "Yet knowing how way leads on to way, / I doubted if I should ever come back" (14–15). Here, the speaker further demonstrates a lack of control over his own decisions. He describes a future guided not by his own active, meaningful choices but rather by some arbitrary force. In a world where "way leads on to way," he is a passive traveler, not a decisive individualist.

4

Evidence: Analysis and explication of Frost poem

Evidence: Analysis and explication of Frost poem

Given the indecision that characterizes the previous stanzas, the poem's last two lines are surprisingly decisive: "I took the one less traveled by / And that has made all the difference" (19–20). Is the speaker contradicting himself? How has he suddenly become clear about the rightness of his decision? In fact, the last stanza does not make sense unless the reader perceives the irony in the speaker's tone. The speaker is imagining himself in the future, "ages and ages hence," telling the story of his moment at the crossroads (17). He imagines how he will, in hindsight, give his choice meaning and clarity that it did not have at the time. As Vujin argues, the poem's speaker is already "mythologizing his self and his life" (198). The narrator, rather than anticipating

5

the satisfaction that will come from having made the right and braver choice, is anticipating rewriting his own life story to make sense of an ultimately arbitrary chain of events. Vujin explains, "This is not a poem about individuality; this is a poem about self-deceit and the rewriting of one's own history" (198). Reading the last stanza ironically allows readers to make sense of the poem as a whole.

Evidence: Literary criticism

There are many possible interpretations of "The Road Not Taken," most of which can be supported with evidence from the poem itself. However, to understand these interpretations, readers need to take the poem apart, look at how its parts fit together, and reach a thoughtful and logical conclusion. To do so, readers must go against some of Billy Collins's well-meaning advice and be willing to tie the poem—and themselves—to a chair: to read it carefully, ask questions, and stay with it until it confesses.

6   Conclusion

Works Cited

Collins, Billy. "Introduction to Poetry." *Sailing Alone around the Room*. Random House, 1998, p. 16.

Frost, Robert. "The Road Not Taken." *Mountain Interval*. Henry Holt, 1920, *Bartleby.com*, www.bartleby.com/119/1.html.

Plunkett, Adam. "Robert Frost Was Neither Light Nor Dark." *New Republic*, 13 Jun. 2014, newrepublic.com/article/118046 /art-robert-frost-tim-kendall-reviewed-adam-plunkett.

Savoie, John. "A Poet's Quarrel: Jamesian Pragmatism and Frost's 'The Road Not Taken.'" *New England Quarterly*, vol. 77, no. 1, 2004, pp. 5–24. *Academic Search Premier*, www.ebscohost.com/academic /academic-search-premier.

Vujin, Bojana. "'I Took the Road Less Traveled By': Self-Deception in Frost's and Eliot's Early Poetry." *Annual Review of the Faculty of Philosophy*, vol. 36, no. 1, 2011, pp. 195–203.

⏺ The following literary argument, "Not Just a 'Girl,'" argues against the commonly held position that a key character in the 1925 Ernest Hemingway short story "Hills Like White Elephants" is a stereotype.

NOT JUST A "GIRL"

LOREN MARTINEZ

Introduction

In Ernest Hemingway's famous story "Hills Like White Elephants," 1
a couple, "the American and the girl with him," talk and drink while
waiting for a train to Madrid (Hemingway 69). Most readers agree that
the subject of their discussion is whether "the girl," called Jig, should
have an abortion. Most of the story is told through dialogue, and
although the word *abortion* is never mentioned, most readers agree
that the pregnancy is the source of the tension between them. However,
there are other aspects of the story about which readers do not agree.
For example, some critics believe that Hemingway's portrayal of "the
girl" is unfair or sexist. More specifically, some see in her the qualities
of "the typically submissive Hemingway woman" (Nolan 19). However,

Thesis statement

a close reading of the story reveals the opposite to be true: "the girl"
is not a one-dimensional stereotype but a complex, sympathetically
drawn character.

Refutation of
opposing arguments

Most critics who see Hemingway's portrayal of Jig as sexist base 2
their interpretation on Hemingway's reputation and not on the story
itself. For example, feminist critic Katherine M. Rogers points out that
because Hemingway himself "openly expressed fear of and hostility to
women" (263), it "seems fair" to see his male characters "as representative of Hemingway himself" (248). However, although "the American" in
this story may see Jig as just "a pleasant pastime," it would be an oversimplification to confuse the character's opinion of her with the writer's
as Rogers would encourage us to do (251). For example, one could
argue (as many critics have done) that because the name "Jig" has sexual connotations, it reveals the author's sexism (Renner 38). However,
as critic Howard Hannum points out, she is referred to by this name only
twice in the story, both times by the male character himself, not by the
narrator (qtd. in Renner 38). Critic Stanley Renner agrees with Hannum,
rejecting the idea that Hemingway's choice to refer to the character as
"the girl" is equally "belittling" (38). Renner argues that this use of the

word *girl* is necessary to show how the character changes and matures in this story. In fact, he sees "her achievement of mature self-knowledge and assertion [as] the main line of development in the story" (39). All in all, the evidence suggests that "the girl," not "the American," is actually the story's protagonist. Given this central focus on "the girl" and the complexity of her character, the accusations that Hemingway's sexism has led him to create a stereotype do not seem justified.

When students who are not familiar with Hemingway's reputation as a misogynist read "Hills Like White Elephants," they tend to sympathize more often with "the girl" than with "the American" (Bauer 126) and to see the female character's thoughtfulness and depth. Although "the American" refers to the abortion as "'really an awfully simple operation'" (Hemingway 72), downplaying its seriousness, "the girl" has a "more mature understanding" of what her decision might mean (Bauer 130). She recognizes that it is not so "simple," and she is not naive enough to think that having the baby will save the relationship. In fact, she responds to his own naive comments with sarcasm. He claims that they will be "'all right and happy'" if she goes through with the operation; he says he's "'known lots of people who have done it.' 'So have I,' said the girl. 'And afterward they were all so happy'" (Hemingway 73). Despite her sarcasm and her resistance to his suggestions, the man continues to insist that this problem will be easy to fix. Finally, the girl becomes irritated with him and, as readers can see by the dashes that end his lines midsentence, cuts him off, finishing his lines for him as he tries to tell her again how "perfectly simple" the operation is (Hemingway 76). Readers understand her pain and frustration when she finally says, "'Would you please please please please please please please stop talking?'" (Hemingway 76).

3 Evidence: First point in support of thesis

The argument that "the girl" is a flat, stereotypical character portrayed in sexist terms is hard to support. In fact, a stronger argument could be made that it is the man, "the American," who is the stereotype. As critic Charles J. Nolan Jr. points out, "Hemingway highlights Jig's maturity and superiority as he excoriates the selfishness and insensitivity of her companion" (19). Moreover, "the girl" is certainly the central character in this story—the one in conflict, the one who must make the final decision, and the one who grows over the course of the story. At times,

4 Evidence: Second point in support of thesis

she seems willing to listen to the man, even going so far as to say, "'Then I'll do it. Because I don't care about me'" (Hemingway 74). However, soon after, she responds defiantly to his comment, "'You mustn't feel that way'" with "'I don't feel any way'" (Hemingway 75). Thus, as Renner notes, Hemingway's dialogue reveals "the self-centered motives of his male character" while at the same time dramatizing the female character's complex inner struggle (38). By the end of the story, the shallow "American" still expects things to be all right between them. But when the man asks, "'Do you feel better?'" Hemingway shows the girl's quiet power—and her transformation—by giving her the final understated words of the story: "'I feel fine. . . . There's nothing wrong with me. I feel fine'" (Hemingway 77). Although we do not learn what her decision is, we can see that she is now in control: she has decided to shut down the conversation, and what the man has to say no longer matters.

Conclusion

In "Hills Like White Elephants," "the girl" proves herself to be neither "'weak *in* character'" nor "'weak *as* character'" as some have described Hemingway's female characters (Bauer 126). Far from being weak *in* character, she constantly questions and pushes against the male character's suggestions. And far from being weak *as* a character, she acts as the protagonist in this story, winning the reader's sympathies. A stereotypically drawn female character would not be able to carry off **Concluding statement** either of these feats. Although Hemingway may demonstrate sexism in his other stories—and demonstrate it in his own life—readers who evaluate *this* story will discover a complex, conflicted, sympathetic female character.

5

Works Cited

Bauer, Margaret D. "Forget the Legend and Read the Work: Teaching Two Stories by Ernest Hemingway." *College Literature*, vol. 30, no. 3, 2003, pp. 124–37. *Academic Search Premier*, www.ebscohost.com /academic/academic-search-premier.

Hemingway, Ernest. "Hills Like White Elephants." *Men without Women*. Charles Scribner's, 1927, pp. 69–77.

Nolan, Charles J., Jr. "Hemingway's Women's Movement." *Hemingway Review*, vol. 4, no. 1, 1984, pp. 14–22. *Academic Search Premier*, www.ebscohost.com/academic/academic-search-premier.

Renner, Stanley. "Moving to the Girl's Side of 'Hills Like White
    Elephants.'" *Hemingway Review*, vol. 15, no. 1, 1995, pp. 27–41.
    Academic Search Premier, www.ebscohost.com/academic
    /academic-search-premier.

Rogers, Katherine M. *The Troublesome Helpmate: A History of Misogyny
    in Literature*. U of Washington P, 1996.

AP Photo/The Journal and Courier, Tom Leniniger

Documenting Sources: APA

American Psychological Association (APA) documentation style is commonly used in the social sciences. In APA style, parenthetical references refer readers to sources in the list of references at the end of the paper.* Parenthetical citations must be provided for all sources that are not common knowledge, whether you are summarizing, paraphrasing, or quoting.

Using Parenthetical References

In APA style, parenthetical references refer readers to sources in the list of references at the end of the paper. A typical parenthetical reference includes the author's last name (followed by a comma) and the year of publication: (Vang, 2015). Here are some guidelines for specific situations.

- If the author's last name appears in the text, follow it with the year of publication, in parentheses: According to Vang (2015), recent studies suggest . . .

- When quoting from a source, include a page number, if available: (Vang, 2015, p. 33). Once you have cited a source, you can refer to the author a second time without the publication date so long as it is clear you are referring to the same source: Vang also found . . .

- If no author is identified, use a shortened version of the title: ("Mind," 2015).

- If you are citing multiple works by the same author or authors published in the same year, include a lowercase letter with the year: (Peters, 2014a), (Peters, 2014b), and so on.

---

*American Psychological Association, *Publication Manual of the American Psychological Association*, Sixth Edition (2010).

- When a work has two authors, cite both names, separated by an ampersand, and the year: (Tabor & Garza, 2006). For three to five authors, in the first reference, cite all authors, along with the year; for subsequent references, cite just the first author, followed by et al. When a work has six or more authors, cite just the first author, followed by et al. and the year: (McCarthy et al., 2010).

- Omit page numbers or dates if the source does not include them. (Try to find a .pdf version of an online source; it will usually include page numbers.)

- If you quote a source found in another source, cite the original author and the source in which you found it: Psychologist Gary Wells asserted . . . (as cited in Doyle, 2005, p. 122).

- Include in-text references to personal communications and interviews by providing the person's name, the phrase "personal communication," and the date: (J. Smith, personal communication, February 12, 2015). Do not include these sources in your reference list.

If a direct quotation is forty words or less, include it within quotation marks without separating it from the rest of the text. When quoting a passage of more than forty words, indent the entire block of quoted text one-half inch from the left margin, and do not enclose it in quotation marks. It should be double-spaced, like the rest of the paper. Place parenthetical documentation one space after the final punctuation.

Preparing a Reference List

Start your list of references on a separate page at the end of your paper. Center the title References at the top of the page, and follow these guidelines:

- Begin each reference flush with the left margin, and indent subsequent lines one-half inch. Double-space the reference list within and between entries.

- List your references alphabetically by the author's last name (or by the first major word of the title if no author is identified).

- If the list includes references for two sources by the same author, alphabetize them by title.

- Italicize titles of books and periodicals. Do not italicize article titles or enclose them in quotation marks.

- For titles of books and articles, capitalize the first word of the title and subtitle as well as any proper nouns. Capitalize words in a periodical title as they appear in the original.

When you have completed your reference list, go through your paper and make sure that every reference cited is included in the list in the correct order.

Examples of APA Citations

The following are examples of APA citations.

Periodicals

Article in a journal paginated by volume

Shah, N. A. (2006). Women's human rights in the Koran: An interpretive approach. *Human Rights Quarterly, 28*, 868–902.

Article in a journal paginated by issue

Lamb, B., & Keller, H. (2007). Understanding cultural models of parenting: The role of intracultural variation and response style. *Journal of Cross-Cultural Psychology, 38*(1), 50–57.

Magazine article

Von Drehle, D. (2015, April 20). Line of fire. *Time, 185*(14), 24–28.

Newspaper article

DeParle, J. (2009, April 19). Struggling to rise in suburbs where failing means fitting in. *The New York Times,* pp. A1, A20–A21.

Books

Books by one author

Jordan, Jennifer A. (2015). *Edible memory: The lure of heirloom tomatoes and other forgotten foods.* Chicago, IL: University of Chicago Press.

Books by two to seven authors

McFadden, J., & Al-Khalili, J. (2014). *Life on the edge: The coming of age of quantum biology.* New York, NY: Crown.

Books by eight or more authors

Barrett, J. M., Smith, V., Wilson, R. T., Haley, V. A., Clarke, P., Palmer, N. B., . . . Fraser, D. (2012). *How to cite references in APA style.* New York: Cambridge University Press.

Edited book

Brummett, B. (Ed.). (2008). *Uncovering hidden rhetorics: Social issues in disguise*. Los Angeles, CA: Sage.

Essay in an edited book

Alberts, H. C. (2006). The multiple transformations of Miami. In H. Smith & O. J. Furuseth (Eds.), *Latinos in the new south: Transformations of place* (pp. 135–151). Burlington, VT: Ashgate.

Translation

Piketty, T. (2015). *The Economics of inequality* (A. Goldhammer, Trans.). Cambridge, MA: Harvard University Press.

Revised edition

Johnson, B., & Christensen, L. B. (2008). *Educational research: Quantitative, qualitative, and mixed approaches* (3rd ed.). Los Angeles, CA: Sage.

Internet Sources

Entire website

Secretariat of the Convention on Biological Diversity. (2015). *Convention on biological diversity*. Retrieved from https://www.cbd.int/

Web page within a website

The great divide: How Westerners and Muslims view each other. (2006, July 6). In *Pew global attitudes project*. Retrieved from http://pewglobal.org/reports/display.php?ReportID=253

University program website

National security archive. (2009). Retrieved from George Washington University website: http://www.gwu.edu/~nsarchiv/

Journal article found on the web with a DOI

Because websites change and disappear without warning, many publishers have started adding a **Digital Object Identifier (DOI)** to their articles. A DOI is a unique number that can be retrieved no matter where the article ends up on the web.

To locate an article with a known DOI, go to the DOI system website at http://dx.doi.org/ and type in the DOI number. When citing an article that has a DOI (usually found on the first page of the article), you do not need to include a URL in your reference or the name of the database in which you may have found the article.

> Geers, A. L., Wellman, J. A., & Lassiter, G. D. (2009). Dispositional optimism and engagement: The moderating influence of goal prioritization. *Journal of Personality and Social Psychology, 94,* 913–932. doi:10.1037/a0014746

Journal article found on the web without a DOI

> Bendetto, M. M. (2008). Crisis on the immigration bench: An ethical perspective. *Brooklyn Law Review, 73,* 467–523. Retrieved from http://brooklaw.edu/students/journals/blr.php/

Journal article from an electronic database

The name and URL of the database are not required for citations if a DOI is available. If no DOI is available, provide the home page URL of the journal or of the book or report publisher.

> Staub, E., & Pearlman, L. A. (2009). Reducing intergroup prejudice and conflict: A commentary. *Journal of Personality and Social Psychology, 11,* 3–23. Retrieved from http://www.apa.org /journals/psp/

Electronic book

> Katz, R. N. (Ed.). (2008). *The tower and the cloud: Higher education in an era of cloud computing.* Retrieved from http://net .educause.edu/ir/library/pdf/PUB7202.pdf

Video blog post

> Green, J. (2015, July 7). Understanding the financial crisis in Greece [Video file]. Retrieved from https://www.youtube.com /watch?v=tigaryz-1y4

Presentation slides

> Hall, M. E. (2009) *Who moved my job!? A psychology of job-loss "trauma"* [Presentation slides]. Retrieved from http://www.cew .wisc.edu/docs/WMMJ%20PwrPt-Summry2.ppt

Student Essay

The following research paper, "The High Cost of Cheap Counterfeit Goods," follows APA format as outlined in the preceding pages.

APA PAPER GUIDELINES

- An APA paper should have a one-inch margin all around and be double-spaced throughout.

- The first line of every paragraph should be indented, and all pages of the paper, including the first, should be numbered consecutively.

- Every page should have a page header (an abbreviated title in all uppercase letters) typed one-half inch from the top of the page.

- An APA paper has four sections: the *title page*, the *abstract*, the *body of the paper*, and the *reference list*:

  1. The **title page** (page 1) should include a running head (in all uppercase letters) at the top:

     Running Head: COUNTERFEIT GOODS

  2. The title page should also include the title of the paper (upper- and lowercase letters), your name (first name, middle initial, last name), and your school.

  3. The **abstract** (page 2) should be a 150- to 250-word summary of the paper. Type the word **Abstract** (centered); skip one line; and do not indent. After the abstract, skip one line and type *Keywords* (italicized and indented), followed by keywords that will help researchers find your essay in a database.

  4. The **body of the paper** should begin on page 3. After the title page, each page of the paper should include the running head (in all uppercase letters), typed flush left, one-half inch from the top of the page:

     COUNTERFEIT GOODS

  5. The **reference list** should begin on a new page, after the body of the paper. (See pages A-14–A-15 for a discussion of how to format the reference list.)

- Citations should follow APA documentation style.

The High Cost of Cheap Counterfeit Goods

Deniz A. Bilgutay

Humanities 101, Section 1

Professor Fitzgerald

March 4, 2020

Abstract

The global trade in counterfeit products costs manufacturers of luxury goods millions of dollars each year. Although this illegal trade threatens the free market, employs underage labor, and may even fund terrorism, many people consider it a victimless crime. Studies show that some consumers even take pride in buying knock-off products. But a closer look at this illicit trade in counterfeit goods shows that consumers in the United States—and around the world—do not understand the ethical implications of the choices they make. Consumers should stop supporting this illegal business, and law enforcement officials should prosecute it more vigorously than they currently do. In the final analysis, this illegal practice hurts legitimate businesses and in some cases endangers the health and safety of consumers.

Keywords: counterfeiting, terrorism, ethics, crime

The High Cost of Cheap Counterfeit Goods

For those who do not want to pay for genuine designer products, a fake Louis Vuitton bag or knock-off Rolex watch might seem too good to pass up. Such purchases may even be a source of pride. According to one study, two-thirds of British consumers said they would be "proud to tell family and friends" that they bought inexpensive knock-offs (Thomas, 2007). The trade in counterfeit goods, however, is a crime—and not a victimless crime. A growing body of evidence suggests that the makers and distributers of counterfeit goods have ties to child labor, organized crime, and even terrorism. In addition, the global economic cost of counterfeiting is esti- mated at $600 billion a year, according to recent data from the International Chamber of Commerce (Melik, 2011). For these reasons, consumers should stop buying these products and funding the illegal activities that this activity supports.

Much of the responsibility for the trade in counterfeit goods can be placed on the manufacturers and the countries that permit the production and export of such goods. For example, China, which dominates the world counterfeit trade, is doing very little to stop this activity. According to a recent article in *USA Today* by Calum MacLeod (2011), "a major obstacle is China's *shanzhai* culture, whereby some Chinese delight in making cheap imitations, sometimes in parody, of expensive, famous brands." Chinese counterfeiters have gone so far as to create entire fake stores: fake Starbucks stores, fake Abercrombie & Fitch stores, and even fake Apple stores. Although some of these copycats have been prosecuted, there is a high level of tolerance, even admiration, for counterfeiting in China. This attitude toward *shanzhai* is reflected in the country's lax intellectual property protection laws. As one Chinese intellectual property lawyer observed, "The penalties don't

Introduction

Thesis statement

outweigh the benefits" (as cited in MacLeod, 2011). Given this situation, the production of counterfeit goods in China is not likely to slow down any time soon.

Despite such cultural justifications for counterfeiting, there is still an ethical problem associated with the purchase of knock-offs. As Dana Thomas (2007) has written in *The New York Times*, many of these counterfeit products are made by children who are "sold or sent off by their families to work in clandestine factories." To American consumers, the problem of children laboring in Chinese factories may be remote, but it is serious. If it is reasonable to place blame for this flourishing market on the countries that allow it, it is also reasonable to blame the people who buy most of the counterfeit goods—namely, consumers in the United States and Europe. According to a report by U.S. Customs and Border Patrol, 62% of fake goods seized in the United States in 2011 were produced in China (as cited in Coleman, 2012). In Europe, the numbers are even higher. According to *The Wall Street Journal*, 85% of goods seized in the European Union come from China (Nairn, 2011). Consequently, the simple act of buying a counterfeit Coach handbag implicates the consumer in the practice of forced child labor.

Immoral labor practices are not the only reason why the counterfeit market needs to be stopped. Organized crime is behind much of the counterfeit trade, so "every dollar spent on a knockoff Gap polo shirt or a fake Kate Spade handbag may be supporting drug trafficking, . . . and worse" ("Editorial: The True Cost," 2007). Consumer dollars may also be supporting narcotics, weapons, and child prostitution (Thomas, 2007).

This illicit international system also helps to finance groups even more sinister than crime syndicates. American consumers of counterfeit goods should understand that profits from

Evidence: Point 1

Evidence: Point 2

COUNTERFEIT GOODS   5

counterfeit goods support terrorist and extremist groups, including Hezbollah, paramilitary organizations in Northern Ireland, and
FARC, a revolutionary armed faction in Colombia (Thomas, 2007).
According to the International Anti-Counterfeiting Coalition, the   Evidence:
Point 3
sale of knock-off T-shirts may even have funded the 1993 attack
on the World Trade Center. Some observers speculate that terror-
ists annually receive about 2% of the roughly $500 billion trade in
counterfeit goods ("Editorial: The True Cost," 2007). According to
Ronald K. Noble, secretary-general of the international law
enforcement agency Interpol, crime involving counterfeit merchandise "is becoming the preferred method of funding for a
number of terrorist groups" (as cited in Langan, 2003).

Beyond the moral and ethical implications of its links to   Evidence:
Point 4
child labor, crime, and terrorism, counterfeit merchandise also
undermines the mainstay of Western business—respect for
intellectual property. In the context of a vast international market
of counterfeit luxury goods, the issue of intellectual property can
seem insignificant. But the creation of new products requires
time, energy, and money, and "unrestrained copying robs
creators of the means to profit from their works" (Sprigman,
2006). Copyright law exists to make sure that inventors and
producers will be motivated to create original work and be fairly
compensated for it. This principle applies to the designers of
luxury goods and fashion items as well. Christopher Sprigman   Opposing
argument
(2006) disagrees, however, noting that although intellectual
property law does little to protect fashion designs, this is as it
should be. "Trend-driven consumption," says Sprigman, is good
for the fashion industry because the industry's ability to create
trends "is based on designers' relative freedom to copy." But
even this argument—which addresses the influences of legitimate   Refutation
fashion designers and manufacturers—cannot be used to

justify allowing counterfeiters to copy Prada handbags or Hugo Boss suits and pass them off as genuine branded articles. Such illicit activity creates no trends—other than perhaps increasing the market for counterfeit products, which siphons off more profits from original designers.

Evidence: Point 5

The knock-off market is not limited to fashion and luxury goods. For example, fake products such as shoddy brake pads have directly injured many consumers. In addition, each year millions of people in the United States and abroad buy counterfeit drugs that do not work and in many cases are dangerous. Some sources estimate that the majority of drugs used to treat life-threatening diseases in Africa are counterfeit. Not coincidentally, many of the same people who are making and distributing counterfeit luxury goods are also manufacturing these drugs ("Editorial: The True Cost," 2007).

Conclusion

It is time for people to realize the harm that is done by counterfeit merchandise and stop buying it. One way to combat this problem is to educate consumers about the effects of their purchases. As James Melik (2011) of the BBC explains, "People try to save money without realizing that the purchase of counterfeit goods can actually harm themselves, the economy and ultimately, their own pockets." Melik urges consumers to "think twice" before buying "products which promote and fund crime." Another way to confront the problem is for law enforcement to address this issue aggressively. Not only should local authorities do more to stop this illegal trade, but national governments should also impose sanctions on countries that refuse to honor international treaties concerning intellectual property. Only by taking this issue seriously can we ensure that this "victimless" crime does not continue to spread and claim more victims.

COUNTERFEIT GOODS   7

References

Coleman, S. (2012, January 20). China still accounts for majority
      of US counterfeit goods. *Canadian Manufacturers and
      Exporters*. Retrieved from http://www.cme-mec.ca/?lid
      =JCKNC-E742G-1W6JA&comaction=show&cid=DVU6K
      -CVBRZ-C6TZQ

Editorial: The true cost: Illegal knockoffs of name-brand products
      do widespread harm [Editorial]. (2007, December 2). *The
      Columbus* [OH] *Dispatch*, p. 4G.

Langan, M. (2003, July 24). Counterfeit goods make real
      terrorism. *Pittsburgh Post-Gazette*, p. A17.

MacLeod, C. (2011, August 2). China takes knock-offs to a
      new level, copying entire stores. *USA Today*. Retrieved
      from http://www.usatoday.com/money/industries
      /technology/2011-07-31-China-counterfeiting-fake-Western
      -goods-stores_n.htm

Melik, J. (2011, December 18). Fake goods save money but at
      what cost? *BBC News*. Retrieved from http://www.bbc
      .co.uk/news/business-16087793

Nairn, G. (2011, October 18). Countering the counterfeiters. *The
      Wall Street Journal*. Retrieved from http://online.wsj.com
      /article/SB10001424052970204226204576600462442044764
      .html

Sprigman, C. (2006, August 22). The fashion industry's piracy
      paradox [Online forum comment]. Retrieved from http://
      www.publicknowledge.org/node/597

Thomas, D. (2007, August 30). Terror's purse strings. *The New
      York Times*, p. A23.

Accurate evidence: Evidence from reliable sources that is quoted carefully and in context.

***Ad hominem* fallacy:** The logical fallacy of undermining an argument by attacking the person who is making the argument instead of addressing the argument itself.

Allusion: A reference within a work to a person, literary or biblical text, or historical event. This shorthand device reminds the reader of something that enlarges the context of the situation being written about.

Analogy: An extended comparison that explains an unfamiliar item, concept, or situation by comparing it to a more familiar one.

Annotating: Making notes of your questions, reactions, and ideas on the document itself.

Antithesis: An opposing statement that tests whether an argumentative **thesis** is debatable.

Appeal to doubtful authority: The use of nonexperts to support an argument.

Applied ethics: The field of philosophy that applies **ethical principles** to real-life issues (such as abortion, the death penalty, animal rights, or doctor-assisted suicide).

Argument: A logical and persuasive presentation of **evidence** that attempts to convince people to accept (or at least to consider) the writer's position.

Argument by analogy: An argument that claims that its position is valid because it is similar in some ways to a position on another issue that readers are likely to accept.

Backing: In a **Toulmin argument**, the evidence that supports the warrant.

Bandwagon appeal: An attempt to convince people that something is true because it is widely held to be true.

Begging-the-question fallacy: An illogical assumption that a statement is self-evident (or true) when it actually requires proof.

Bias: Preconceived ideas or prejudices, which are often used in an argument instead of factual **evidence**.

Brainstorming: Making quick notes on a topic to generate ideas.

Causal chain: A sequence of events in which one event causes the next, which in turn causes the next, and so on.

Cause-and-effect argument: An argument that explains an event or a situation by considering its likely causes or outcomes.

Circular reasoning: An attempt to support a statement by simply repeating the statement in different terms.

Claim: In a **Toulmin argument**, the main point, usually stated as a **thesis**.

Clustering: Creating a diagram to map out your thoughts.

Common ground: Points of agreement that are shared by those on opposing sides of an argument.

Common knowledge: Factual information (such as a writer's date of birth, a scientific fact, or the location of a famous battle) that can be found in several credible sources. Common knowledge does not require documentation.

Conclusion: The last part of a **syllogism**.

Confirmation bias: The tendency that people have to accept information that supports their own beliefs and to ignore information that does not.

Confrontational argument: A kind of argument that is characterized by conflict and opposition.

Contributory causes: The less important causes in a **causal argument**.

Credibility: Trustworthiness. A credible source is believable.

Criteria for evaluation: Standards by which a subject (or source) is evaluated.

Critical response: A passage in which a writer examines the ideas that are presented in an argument and evaluates them.

Current source: A source containing up-to-date information. Current sources are especially important in discussions of scientific subjects and may be less important in other subjects.

Debatable thesis: A thesis statement that presents a position with which people might disagree.

Deductive reasoning: A form of reasoning that moves from general statements (or **premises**) to specific conclusions. See **inductive reasoning**.

Definition argument: An argument that is based on the idea that something fits or does not fit a particular definition of a key term.

Dictionary definition: A structure for definition that consists of the term to be defined, the general class to which the term belongs, and the qualities that differentiate the term from other items in the same class.

Dilemma: A choice between two or more unfavorable alternatives.

Distortion: An unfair tactic of argument in which the writer misrepresents evidence—for example, by presenting an opponent's view inaccurately or by exaggerating his or her position.

Documentation: Information that identifies the sources used in an argument.

Editing and proofreading: The final steps in the writing process, which check that an essay is well organized, convincing, and clearly written and has no distracting grammatical, spelling, and mechanical errors.

Either/or fallacy: Faulty reasoning that presents only two choices when there are actually three or more choices.

Enthymeme: A **syllogism** with one or two parts of its argument (usually the major premise) missing.

Equivocation: The use of two different meanings for the same key term in an argument.

Ethical argument: An argument that focuses on whether something should be done because it is good or right.

Ethical dilemma: A conflict between two or more possible actions, each of which will potentially have negative outcomes.

Ethical principles: A set of ideas or standards that guides someone to an ethically correct conclusion.

Ethics: The field of philosophy that studies the standards by which an act can be judged right or wrong or good or bad.

Ethos: An appeal to the trustworthiness or credibility of a speaker or writer.

Evaluate: To express an opinion about the quality of something.

Evaluation argument: An argument that presents a positive or negative judgment, asserts that someone else's positive or negative judgment is not accurate or justified, or demonstrates that one thing is or is not superior to another.

Evidence: The facts, observations, expert opinion, examples, and statistics that support a thesis statement. In a **Toulmin argument**, the evidence is called the **grounds**.

Fact: A statement that can be verified (proven to be true).

Fallacy: An error in reasoning that undermines the logic of an argument.

False dilemma: See **either/or fallacy**.

Formal argument: An argument developed according to set rhetorical principles in academic discussion and writing. See **informal argument**.

Formal outline: A presentation of an essay's main and subordinate points that uses a number/letter system to designate the order in which the points will be discussed.

Freewriting: Writing continuously for a set time to generate ideas without worrying about spelling or grammar.

Grounds: In a **Toulmin argument**, the evidence that is used to support the claim.

Hasty generalization: An error in reasoning that occurs when a conclusion is based on too little evidence or when the gap between the evidence and conclusion is too wide.

Highlighting: Using underlining and symbols to identify an essay's most important points.

Identifying tag: A phrase that identifies the source of a **quotation**, **paraphrase**, or **summary**.

Immediate cause: In a **causal argument**, the cause that occurs right before an event.

Inductive leap: In **inductive reasoning**, a stretch of the imagination that enables a writer to draw a reasonable conclusion from the existing information.

Inductive reasoning: A form of reasoning that begins with specific observations (or evidence) and moves to a general conclusion. See **deductive reasoning**.

Inference: A statement that uses what is known to draw a conclusion about what is unknown.

Informal argument: An **argument** that occurs in daily life about politics, sports, social issues, and personal relationships. See **formal argument**.

Informal outline: A list of the ideas that will be discussed in an essay. See **formal outline**.

Jumping to a conclusion: See **hasty generalization**.

Logic: The principles of correct reasoning that enable someone to tell whether a conclusion correctly follows from a set of statements or assumptions.

Logical fallacy: A flawed argument.

Logos: An appeal to logic.

Main cause: In a **causal argument**, the most important cause.

Major premise: See **syllogism**.

Means of persuasion: The appeals—*logos*, *pathos*, and *ethos*—that writers use to persuade their audience.

Metaphor: A comparison in which two dissimilar things are compared without the word *like* or *as*.

Middle term: The term in a **syllogism** that appears in both the major and minor premises but not in the conclusion.

Minor premise: See **syllogism**.

Misuse of statistics fallacy: When data are misrepresented.

Non sequitur **fallacy:** Illogical reasoning that occurs when a conclusion does not follow from the premises or is supported by weak or irrelevant evidence or by no evidence at all.

Objective source: A source that is not unduly influenced by personal opinions or feelings.

Operational definition: A definition of how something acts or works that transforms an abstract concept into something concrete, observable, and possibly measurable.

Opinion: A personal judgment; therefore, an idea that is open to debate.

Parallelism: The use of the same or a similar structure in the repetition of words, phrases, or clauses.

Paraphrase: A passage that presents a source's ideas in detail, including its main idea and key supporting points and perhaps key examples.

Parenthetical references: In MLA and APA **documentation**, citations that identify the source of a paraphrase, quotation, or summary.

Pathos: An appeal to the emotions.

Peer review: The process of having colleagues examine and critique written work. Informally, schoolwork is read by friends or classmates; formally, scholarly work is read by experts in the field to confirm its accuracy.

Persuasion: The act of influencing an audience to adopt a particular belief or to follow a specific course of action.

Plagiarism: The use of the words or ideas of another person without attributing them to their rightful author.

Popular magazine: A periodical that is aimed at general readers. It generally is not an acceptable source for research.

Post hoc **fallacy:** Faulty reasoning that asserts that because two events occur closely in time, one event must have caused the other.

Premises: Statements or assumptions on which an **argument** is based or from which a conclusion is drawn.

Previewing: During active reading, forming a general impression of a writer's position on an issue, the argument's key supporting points, and the context for the writer's remarks.

Propaganda: Biased or misleading information that is spread about a particular viewpoint, person, or cause.

Proposal argument: An argument that attempts to convince people that a problem exists and that a particular solution is both practical and desirable.

Qualifiers: In a **Toulmin argument**, statements that limit the **claim**.

Quotation: Words or sentences taken directly from a source.

Quoting out of context: Removing a quotation from its original setting for the purpose of distorting its meaning.

Reading critically: Questioning or challenging material instead of simply accepting it as true. This often involves assessing the accuracy of facts in sources and considering the evidence that supports them.

Reason: In a **Toulmin argument**, a statement that supports the **claim**.

Rebuttals: In a **Toulmin argument**, refutations of opposing arguments.

Red herring fallacy: An irrelevant side issue that diverts attention from the real issue.

Refutation: The section of an argumentative essay that identifies opposing arguments and presents arguments against them.

Refute: To disprove or call into question.

Relevant evidence: **Evidence** that applies specifically (not just tangentially) to the topic under discussion.

Remote causes: In a **causal argument**, incidents that occurred in the past but may have had a greater impact than more recent events.

Representative evidence: **Evidence** that is drawn from a fair range of sources, not just from sources that support a particular position.

Revision: The careful and critical review of a draft.

Rhetoric: The effect of various elements working together to form a convincing and persuasive **argument**.

Rhetorical analysis: A systematic examination of the strategies that a writer employs to achieve his or her purpose.

Rhetorical question: A question that encourages readers to reflect on an issue but does not call for a reply.

Rhetorical situation: The combination of the writer, the writer's purpose, the writer's audience, the topic, and the context.

Rhetorical strategies: The ways in which argument writers present ideas and opinions, including but not limited to thesis, organization, evidence, and stylistic techniques (**simile, metaphor, allusion, parallelism,** repetition, and **rhetorical questions**).

Rhetorical triangle: A graphic representation of the three kinds of appeals in an argument—*logos* (reason), *ethos* (credibility), and *pathos* (values and beliefs).

Rogerian argument: A model of argument that assumes that people of goodwill can avoid conflict by identifying **common ground** and points of agreement. It is based on the work of Carl Rogers, a twentieth-century psychologist who felt that traditional confrontational arguments could be counterproductive.

Scholarly journal: A periodical that is usually written by experts, documented, and peer reviewed.

Scientific method: A way of using induction to find answers to questions. It involves proposing a hypothesis, making a series of observations to test the hypothesis, and arriving at a conclusion that confirms, modifies, or disproves the hypothesis.

Self-evident: A proposition that requires no proof or explanation.

Simile: A figure of speech that compares two unlike things by using *like* or *as*.

Skeptical: Having an open mind but still needing to be convinced.

Slanting: An unfair tactic that makes an argument appear stronger by presenting only evidence that supports a particular position and ignoring evidence that challenges it.

Slippery-slope fallacy: An illogical argument that holds that one thing will cause a series of events that ends in an inevitable, unpleasant conclusion, usually with no evidence that such a sequence will actually occur.

Sound syllogism: A syllogism that is both true and valid.

Stasis theory: A rhetorical tool that determines the issue explored in a particular argument by slowing down and asking questions designed to isolate that topic.

Straw man fallacy: An intentional oversimplification of an opposing argument to make it easier to refute.

Sufficient evidence: Evidence that includes enough facts, statistics, and expert opinion to support the essay's thesis.

Summary: A concise restatement of the main idea of a passage (or article or book) without the examples, explanations, and stylistic devices of the source.

Sweeping generalization: See **hasty generalization**.

Syllogism: A model for **deductive reasoning** that includes a **major premise**, a **minor premise**, and a **conclusion**.

Synthesis: A combination of **summary**, **paraphrase**, **quotation**, and a writer's own ideas that supports an original conclusion.

Taking a stand: Expressing a position in the form of a **thesis statement**.

Thesis: The position that an argument supports.

Thesis statement: A single sentence in an argumentative essay that states a position on an issue.

Thinking critically: Questioning rather than accepting ideas at face value.

Toulmin argument: An argument that includes the **claim** (the main point), the grounds (the **evidence** a writer uses to support the claim), and the **warrant** (the inference—either stated or implied—that connects the claims to their grounds).

True syllogism: A syllogism in which the **premises** are consistent with the **facts**.

Unfair appeal: An appeal to an audience's fears or prejudices.

Valid syllogism: A system in which a conclusion follows logically from its premises.

Visual: An image—such as a chart, graph, table, photo, drawing, or diagram.

Visual argument: An advertisement, chart, graph, table, diagram, web page, photograph, painting, or other representation that communicates a position through images.

Warrant: In a **Toulmin argument**, the inference or assumption, either stated or implied, that connects a claim to its grounds.

Works-cited list: An alphabetical list of sources that appears at the end of an essay that follows MLA style.

Writing process: The process of planning, drafting, revising, and editing an argument.

You also fallacy (*tu quoque*): An illogical assertion that a statement is false because the speaker has said or done the opposite. It attacks a person for doing the thing that he or she is arguing against.

Text Credits

INDEX OF TITLES AND AUTHORS